phonics lessons

Letters, Words, and How They Work

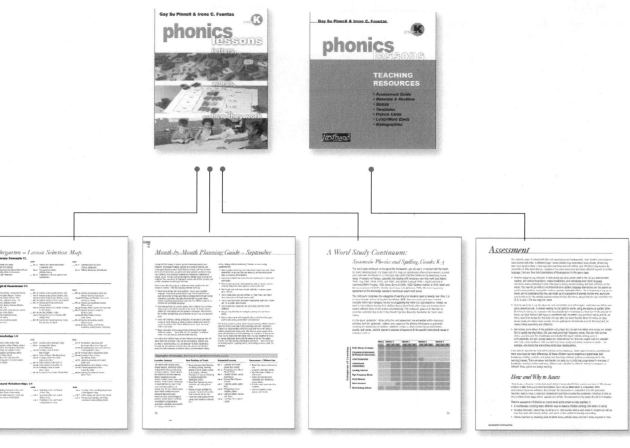

Lesson Selection Map
(page 32)

Month-by-Month Planning Guide
(page 36)

Word Study Continuum
(page 45)

Assessment Guide
(first tab in the *Teaching Resources* binder)

Your Essential Teaching Tools

FirstHand
An imprint of Heinemann
A division of Reed Elsevier Inc.
361 Hanover Street
Portsmouth, NH 03801–3912
www.heinemann.com

Offices and agents throughout the world

The author and publisher wish to thank those who have generously given permission to reprint borrowed material:

"Happy Birthday to You" by Mildred J. Hill and Patty S. Hill. Copyright © 1935 (renewed) Summy-Birchard Music, a division of Summy-Birchard Inc. All rights reserved. Used by permission of Warner Bros. Publications U.S. Inc., Miami, FL 33014.

"Friends Sound March" from *Fall Phonemic Awareness Songs & Rhymes* by Jo Fitzpatrick. Copyright © 1998. Published by Creative Teaching Press, Inc., Huntington Beach, CA. Reprinted by permission of the publisher.

Chant from *First Songs: The Young Child Sings* by Mary Voell Jones. Copyright © 1976 by Mary Voell Jones. Used by permission of Paulist Press. www.paulistpress.com.

"Grade Level ABC Chant" is adapted from *Alphabet* by Gayle Perry. Copyright © 1999. Published by Creative Teaching Press, Inc., Huntington Beach, CA. Adapted by permission of the publisher.

"After a Bath" from *Up the Windy Hill* by Aileen Fisher. Copyright © 1953, 1981 by Aileen Fisher. Used by permission of Marian Reiner for the author.

Library of Congress Cataloging-in-Publication Data

Pinnell, Gay Su.
    Phonics lessons : letters, words, and how they work / by Gay Su Pinnell and Irene C. Fountas.
        p. cm.
    Includes bibliographical references.
    Contents: [1] Grade K — [2] Grade 1 — [3] Grade 2.
    ISBN 0-325-00560-5
    1. Reading — Phonetic method. 2. English language — Phonetics. I. Fountas, Irene C. II. Title.

    LB1573.3 .P54 2003   2002190837
    372.46'5--dc21

Printed in the United States of America on acid-free paper

06 05 04 03   ML   2 3 4 5 6

Phonics Lessons

Letters, Words, and How They Work

Contents

Early Literacy Concepts

Phonological Awareness (Including Phonemic Awareness)

Letter Knowledge

Letter/Sound Relationships

Spelling Patterns

Phonics: Why and How

Welcome to *Phonics Lessons: Letters, Words, and How They Work, Grade K,* a collection of one hundred minilessons. These brief minilessons (so-called to emphasize their targeted focus in both content and delivery) enable you to help children attend to, learn about, and efficiently use information about letters, sounds, and words. While the lessons are most appropriate for kindergartners, they also work for first graders and even second graders who have not yet developed control of related principles. The lessons take into account what children already know and help them acquire the knowledge and concepts they need to learn next. You may connect the lessons to word solving in reading and writing across the language and literacy curriculum or use them as prototypes for other phonics minilessons that you design yourself. Most important, each lesson is organized around a language principle—an essential understanding about language and how it works—thus enabling you to plan and teach efficiently and systematically.

Why Teach Phonics?

The true purpose and promise of phonics instruction is to expand and refine children's reading and writing powers. In the complex processes of reading and writing, letters, sounds, and words are the keys to help children grasp and use language as a tool. Most children acquire this tool and learn how to use it at school under the guidance of a skilled teacher who provides a wide range of learning opportunities. While this volume focuses on children's learning about letters, sounds, and words, *phonics is not a complete reading program, nor is it even the most important component of a reading program.* The lessons here enhance but do not take the place of experiences with texts. Phonics instruction as described here takes only about ten or fifteen minutes of explicit teaching each day, with students spending an additional ten to twenty minutes a day applying and sharing what they have learned.

What's the Best Way to Teach Phonics?

Children learn phonics best as part of a wide range of engaging literacy experiences accompanied by rigorous teaching. As teachers work alongside readers and writers, they demonstrate effective behaviors, draw attention to important information, and prompt children to use their knowledge. The great majority of time in the classroom is devoted to reading and writing continuous text. Children learn to solve words "on the run" while reading for meaning and writing to communicate. The curriculum is content rich and includes a range of instructional approaches, from demonstration and explicit teaching to support for children's independent work.

In the arguments about what constitutes effective instruction, two issues often arise:

- ▶ Should instruction be explicit or *implicit*, that is, embedded in the processes of reading and writing?

- ▶ Should we teach children directly or allow them to discover or generalize essential concepts for themselves?

These two areas of tension make designing instructional programs in literacy quite a challenge.

Children learn much more than we teach them; they often astound us with the creativity of their insights. One goal of our teaching is to help children become active examiners and analyzers of print. We want them always to be searching for connections and patterns, to form categories of knowledge, and to have a store of examples to which they can refer.

In the tug-of-war between direct teaching and discovery, going to extremes can be dangerous. Leaving everything to discovery will almost surely mean that many children will not attend to or acquire the understanding they need. Yet assuming that children learn only through direct teaching may lead us to neglect the power of the learning brain, that is, the excitement that makes learning real.

We believe that well-planned and organized direct teaching of language principles is critical but that our lessons must also contain an element of inquiry. In these minilessons, the principle is stated in simple language appropriate for use in the classroom, but the children are also encouraged to categorize words, notice features of letters and words, and search for examples. In any lesson, you decide whether to state the principle first and then generate examples that will make it clear, always leaving room for children to notice more about letters, sounds, and words, or to show some clear examples first and invite children to make connections and generalizations. The combination of discovery and direct teaching makes learning efficient; teaching prompts discovery.

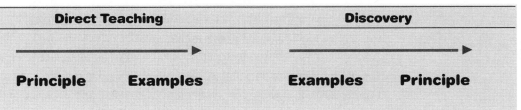

The Word Study Continuum

The Word Study Continuum is the key to the phonics minilessons. You will use it, in concert with the Month-by-Month Planning Guide, the Lesson Selection Map, and continuous informed assessment, to guide your work over the course of a school year. The Continuum comprises nine Categories of Learning. Each category showcases multiple principles your students will develop over time. It is a comprehensive picture of linguistic knowledge. While there are easier and more complex concepts within each category, we are not suggesting that there is a rigid sequence. Instead, we want to help children develop their abilities along a broad front, often using and learning about several different kinds of information simultaneously. The Continuum gives us as teachers an extensive and organized understanding of the body of knowledge that forms the foundation for expert word solving.

As we set out to construct this Continuum, we examined a wide range of research on language and literacy learning over several decades, and we asked both teachers and researchers for feedback. At the heart of literacy is a language process in which children use what they know about the language they speak and connect it to print (Clay 1991). As teachers, we are simultaneously helping children expand their oral language capabilities while we work with them on the understandings needed for literacy. The semantic, syntactic, and phonological systems of language all contribute to literacy learning. Readers must understand the relationships between language and the graphic symbols that represent sounds and words (Moats 2000). Decades of research have shown that when they are meaningfully engaged in using print, children develop awareness of these relationships early (Read 1971; Treiman 1985). It is especially important that children develop awareness of the phonological system, learn about letters, and develop understanding of sound-to-letter relationships and of words and how they work (see Adams 1990; Armbruster, Lehr & Osborn 2001; Clay 1991, 1998, 2001; Juel 1988; Juel, Griffith & Gough 1986; Moats 2000; National Institute of Child Health and Human Development 2001; Pressley 1998; Snow, Burns & Griffin 1989). Our task as teachers is to organize our own knowledge and design systematic ways to present the information to children and help them use it for reading and writing. We found surprising agreement on the knowledge needed to become an expert word solver. It represents an inventory of knowledge that, together, will form a strong foundation for becoming literate.

Let's look at the nine Categories of Learning in more detail.

Nine Categories of Learning

Early Literacy Concepts

Most early literacy concepts are developed through early reading and writing experiences, so we include only a few explicit minilessons in this area. These concepts include distinguishing between print and pictures, understanding the concepts of letters and words, and learning that print has directionality (in other words, in English, we read from top to bottom, left to right). We also provide some basic lessons that will help children use their own names as resources in learning about letters, sounds, and words.

Phonological Awareness (and Phonemic Awareness)

We recommend extensive work in reading aloud and shared reading to develop phonological and phonemic awareness. Songs, rhymes, and poetry give students the background and examples to participate fully in your minilessons in this area. The development of phonemic awareness is basic to other learning about literacy in kindergarten; often you will want to extend these lessons by studying letters as well as sounds.

Letter Knowledge

Children need many different experiences with letters in order to learn "what to look for" when distinguishing one letter from another. They learn that there are many different letters in the set called the alphabet, that each letter has a different name, and that each letter is just a little different from every other letter. Some letters look alike in that they have similar features. Each letter also has an uppercase form and a lowercase form; sometimes these forms look almost alike and sometimes they are different.

Letter/Sound Relationships

Letter/sound learning is also basic in kindergarten and is one of the explicit goals of the curriculum. Your minilessons in this area will help students develop an organized view of the tools of literacy. For kindergarten, we emphasize consonants, but we also explore easy-to-hear vowels.

Spelling Patterns

The patterns in regularly spelled words are especially helpful to kindergartners. As they explore simple phonograms and words that have highly reliable letter/sound correspondence, they learn the first strategies for decoding. Solving larger parts of words helps them read and write more efficiently and also gives them access to many words.

High Frequency Words

High frequency words are also learned in many other components of the language and literacy framework, especially shared/interactive writing and guided reading. Lessons on high frequency words help children develop a useful core of known words that they can use as resources to solve new words, check on their reading, and read and write fluently.

Word Meaning

Children need to know the meaning of the words they are learning to read and write. It is important for them constantly to expand their vocabulary as well as develop a more complex understanding of words they already know. This section of the Continuum describes understandings related to the development of vocabulary—labels and concept words, such as colors, numbers, and days of the week.

Word Structure

Word structure deals with the underlying rules for understanding contractions, compound words, plurals, prefixes, affixes, possessives, and abbreviations. Since most of these concepts are beyond kindergarten, we have not included minilessons that address them. You can, however, incidentally point out such patterns to children during interactive writing and shared reading.

Word-Solving Actions

Readers and writers use a variety of word-solving strategies to decode words when reading or writing continuous text. They also use parts of words and search for patterns they can connect. These strategies are invisible, "in-the-head" actions, although we can sometimes infer them from overt behavior. For example, children will sometimes make several attempts at words, revealing their hypotheses. Or they may work left to right on a word (traditionally called "sounding out"). Or they may make connections with other words. Good readers tend to use these in-the-head word-solving actions to read more smoothly, more sensibly, and more accurately. They orchestrate systems of information, always searching for a "fit." Most kindergartners are only beginning to assemble these sophisticated systems, but they are reaching for them. It is especially important for kindergartners to understand that every bit of information they learn is very useful in literacy processes.

Learning Your Way Around the Minilessons

We have designed these minilessons so that as you use them, you will always consider the particular children you teach. You will decide which lessons to use and whether or not to modify them to meet the needs of your particular students. Certainly, you will note the connections you can make to your own students' discoveries and learning about letters, sounds, and words across the Language and Literacy Framework. Although we present the lessons in a standard format, each one is inherently different because of the conversations you will have with the children you teach. Your students will offer their own examples and make their own connections, and you will enrich their learning as you acknowledge and extend their thinking.

We have included a generous sampling of lessons in each of the nine Categories of Learning. Our goal is to provide clear prototypes from which you can create your own lessons (see *Teaching Resources,* Blank Lesson Template) using the Word Study Continuum that will develop the understanding your students need to experience over time. Within each category, the lessons are numbered for ease of reference, *but we are not implying an unalterable sequence.* Nevertheless, if you are new to teaching or have not taught phonics before, you may want to follow this sequence, because within each learning category we have clustered principles from easier to harder. But easy and hard are relative terms; they refer to students' previous experience, and only you as a teacher know the children's learning background. As you implement these lessons, you will not only learn more about children's development of word-solving strategies but you will also gain invaluable insight into our English linguistic system. Ultimately, feel confident in building your own sequence of explicit lessons that moves your students systematically toward a flexible and powerful range of strategies.

GENERATIVE LESSONS provide a recurring structure you can use with similar items within a knowledge set, for example, to teach beginning consonants. As children acquire knowledge, they build systems for similar learning that accelerate the learning.

All materials needed for TEACH, APPLY, and SHARE sections of the lesson are listed. Specific materials (pictures, word cards, activity templates, etc.) are provided as reproducibles in the accompanying binder, *Teaching Resources*. If children are rotating through a center, you need only enough materials for one small group to work with at a time. If they are working individually, as partners, or in simultaneous small groups, you will need additional materials.

Generative Lesson

early
mid
late

Beginning Consonant Letters and Sounds
Picture Sort

What do your students already know, and what do they need to learn next? Your insights about your own students will guide your choice of lessons and help you plan instruction that targets your students' learning needs.

Typically, it takes several years for young children to learn English as a second language and to learn to read, write, and think consistently in their new language. As you adjust the lesson for English language learners, your instruction becomes clearer and more explicit in ways that help all your students. (See Guidelines: Working with English Language Learners.)

Consider Your Children

This lesson is best used after children can name most letters of the alphabet and have demonstrated that they are able to hear sounds in words, match pictures by sounds, and understand the concept of matching letters and sounds. Learning letters and sounds together will accelerate learning letter/sound relationships and allow children to apply that knowledge to solving words. Children who are very proficient at identifying first letters and sounds will not need this lesson.

Working with English Language Learners

For this lesson, children will need to identify the objects in pictures and associate them with letters representing first letters. It will help your English language learners if you select pictures that they have worked with before and for which they know the names. Be sure that they understand the procedures for the Three-Way Sort Sheet. You may need to do an extra demonstration for a small group to be sure that they can perform the application task independently. Recognize and accept answers that show they are using names in their own language and categorizing them, for example, *luna* (moon) under *L*.

You Need

▸ Pocket charts with a row of letter cards (large and small). Select letters that children know or "nearly know." Start with three or four letters: *Bb, Mm, Pp*, for example.

From *Teaching Resources:*

▸ Picture Cards, Beginning Consonants, whose names have initial sounds that match the letters on the chart: *book, bear, bed; mouse, mask, mitten, moon, motorcycle; pizza, pumpkin, piano, pig, pillow*. Mix in a few that do not match the letters in the chart: *rake, watch, zipper, ladder*.

▸ Letter Cards.

▸ Three-Way Sort Sheets.

Understand the Principle

Connecting an initial letter with its sound helps children begin to decode words in reading.

Once children can identify first letters and generate the sounds associated with them, they can use this information to monitor their reading and to distinguish between words.

Children can check letter/sound information with their sense of meaning and language structure as they read.

Explain the Principle

" You can hear the sound at the beginning of a word. "

" You can match letters and sounds at the beginning of a word. "

CONTINUUM: LETTER/SOUND RELATIONSHIPS — RECOGNIZING AND USING BEGINNING CONSONANT SOUNDS AND THE LETTERS THAT REPRESENT THEM

(317)

We help you understand the language principle underlying each minilesson so you can teach with clarity and a well-defined purpose.

Each lesson highlights a key principle from the Word Study Continuum.

Concise, clear language "rings inside students' heads." Avoid jargon and technical labels; use a common language that enables you to reach your readers and writers simply and easily. Sometimes you will show children examples and invite them to think of the principle; other times, you will state the principle, give a few examples, and invite the children to add examples. You determine which approach will be more effective.

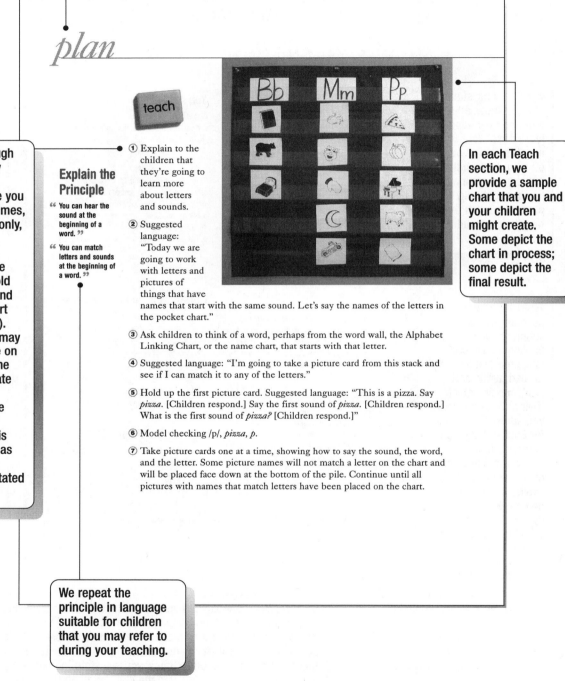

Modify the steps for implementing the lesson to fit your own group of children. Much will depend on your children's experience and how well you have taught routines.

plan

teach

We take you through the lesson step by step, suggesting effective language you might use. Sometimes, the lesson is oral only, without written examples. Make frequent use of the pocket chart to hold pictures, letters, and words (or use chart paper on an easel). Occasionally, you may write the principle on the chart before the lesson and generate examples with children during the lesson, but in kindergarten this is done infrequently as the concepts are simple and best stated verbally.

Explain the Principle

❝ You can hear the sound at the beginning of a word. ❞

❝ You can match letters and sounds at the beginning of a word. ❞

① Explain to the children that they're going to learn more about letters and sounds.

② Suggested language: "Today we are going to work with letters and pictures of things that have names that start with the same sound. Let's say the names of the letters in the pocket chart."

③ Ask children to think of a word, perhaps from the word wall, the Alphabet Linking Chart, or the name chart, that starts with that letter.

④ Suggested language: "I'm going to take a picture card from this stack and see if I can match it to any of the letters."

⑤ Hold up the first picture card. Suggested language: "This is a pizza. Say *pizza*. [Children respond.] Say the first sound of *pizza*. [Children respond.] What is the first sound of *pizza?* [Children respond.]"

⑥ Model checking /p/, *pizza*, *p*.

⑦ Take picture cards one at a time, showing how to say the sound, the word, and the letter. Some picture names will not match a letter on the chart and will be placed face down at the bottom of the pile. Continue until all pictures with names that match letters have been placed on the chart.

In each Teach section, we provide a sample chart that you and your children might create. Some depict the chart in process; some depict the final result.

We repeat the principle in language suitable for children that you may refer to during your teaching.

Children work independently (individually, with partners, in small groups) to apply and practice what they've learned in the lesson.

Each lesson suggests the approximate time of year to teach the lesson. (See Lesson Selection Map.)

early
mid
late

apply

▶ Give the children a Three-Way Sort Sheet with key letters in the top spots. They will also need selected picture cards, including some with names that match the key letters and some that don't. One child takes the cards, sorts them, and then reads them while her partner watches and checks the completed sort. Then they mix the cards up and switch roles.

Bb Mm Pp

share

Ask children what pictures they have matched with letters. Invite them to give one more word for each letter in the chart.

The lesson routines are identified in concise words on tags that you can post in the word study center to remind children of what to do. If you are not using centers, you can post the tags where everyone can refer to them as they work. Tags help your children become independent learners.

LS 3
Letter/Sound Relationships

Easy-to-use tabbing organization (referenced to the Lesson Selection Map as well as the Month-by-Month Planning Guide) helps you to find and select appropriate lessons for your children.

Use the guidelines to reinforce the principles and help children share their learning. In many lessons, we suggest behaviors to notice and support.

In each Apply section, we provide a photo showing an example of the product or process children will engage in as they practice and apply what they've learned.

Connect learning across the Language and Literacy Framework through interactive read-aloud, shared reading, guided reading, interactive writing, and independent writing. (You will use the guided reading connections when your kindergartners begin to work in smaller guided reading groups.) Your observations across learning contexts will help you think of specific connections you can bring to your children's attention; add your own notes to enhance the lesson.

We provide a variety of useful bibliographies in Teaching Resources.

For each lesson, we provide two suggested read-aloud titles chosen specifically to support the principle and work of each lesson.

Assess the impact of the minilesson and application in ways that are informal and integral to the work children are doing. For some lessons, we suggest using the more formal and systematic procedures in the Assessment Guide (in *Teaching Resources*) to help you determine children's needs for further lessons.

Link

Interactive Read-Aloud: Read aloud stories that emphasize beginning sounds. (See the Alliteration Bibliography in *Teaching Resources* for suggestions.) Examples are:

▸ *The Accidental Zucchini: An Unexpected Alphabet* by Max Grover

▸ *The Wacky Wedding* by Pamela Duncan Edwards

Shared Reading: When rereading familiar texts, such as "This Is the Way We Wash Our Face (see *Sing a Song of Poetry*), cover the first letter of a word. Ask children to read up to the word and predict the first letter by thinking about the sound.

Guided Reading: Encourage children to try unfamiliar words by reading up to the new word and saying the sound of the first letter: "I like to eat /p/ancakes."

Interactive Writing: When thinking how to write a word, have children say it slowly and decide what the first letter is likely to be.

Independent Writing: Encourage children to say words slowly when they are writing and to write the first letter.

assess

▸ Notice whether the children are able to write the first letters of words.

▸ Observe whether the children say the first sound of a word while reading.

▸ Notice whether the children use the first letter/sound of a word to monitor and check on their reading.

▸ Place letter cards in the pocket chart and ask individual children to match a limited set of pictures quickly.

Expand the Learning

Extend the activity by increasing the number and variety of letters.

Mix children's names and high frequency word cards (*Teaching Resources,* High Frequency Words) into the picture card set so that they are matching both pictures and words with the letters.

Connect with Home

Reproduce picture cards and letters (*Teaching Resources,* Picture Cards, Beginning Consonants, and Letter Cards) that children can take home, cut apart, and match.

Have family members make letter posters with the children. They write a letter at the top of a sheet and draw (or cut out from a magazine) pictures of objects whose names start with that letter. Have them check the beginning sound of the name with the first letter.

If children need more experience, you can repeat the lesson format using these suggestions for variations, different examples, or more challenging activities.

These are not homework assignments; rather, they are ways you can help family members and caregivers make connections between home and school.

Available separately: *Sing a Song of Poetry K* provides reproducibles of hundreds of your favorite rhymes, songs, and poems that will help kindergarten children use and enjoy oral and written language.

Gay Su Pinnell & Irene C. Fountas

grade K

sing a song of poetry

A Teaching Resource for Phonemic Awareness, Phonics, and Fluency

firsthand

Hey didd
The cat and
the cow jum

Teaching Resources is your comprehensive professional resource for everything from diagnostic assessment to an Alphabet Linking Chart.

Gay Su Pinnell & Irene C. Fountas
grade K
phonics lessons
TEACHING RESOURCES
• Assessment Guide
• Materials & Routines
• Games
• Templates
• Picture Cards
• Letter/Word Cards
• Bibliographies
firsthand
Assessment
Picture Cards
Materials & Routines
Letter/Word Cards
Games
Bibliographies
Templates

The Assessment Guide includes more formal, performance-based Assessment Tasks across the nine Categories of Learning.

We've provided a variety of bibliographies listing hundreds of books categorized for ease of use. They include Language Play, Rhymes, Poetry, Songs, and Read-Alouds.

You will find descriptions of and directions for the materials and daily routines most important for your classroom. These are comprehensive lists of the hands-on materials and activities that undergird effective teaching.

Additionally, look for picture, word, and alphabet cards, templates, and reproducibles to make an array of your own cards and ready-to-use booklets. We include game materials and directions for Lotto, Concentration, and Follow the Path. We also provide numerous reproducibles for student activities.

Essential Literacy Concepts Every Kindergartner Should Know

The most effective teaching is responsive teaching—sensitive instruction that addresses the needs of children. Every lesson in *Phonics Lessons* begins with a consideration of your children. What do they know, and what do they need to know? Your guiding question as you use the phonics minilessons is: What are the essential literacy concepts my students need to understand to become accomplished readers and writers?

There is little disagreement about the complex understandings that children must acquire as they become literate. Kindergartners are learning about written language in a broad exploratory way, acquiring knowledge on several fronts at once. At first, this knowledge may appear as separate items, but as children read and write, they discover the intricate connections among bodies of information. In the following pages we explore four different kinds of information, each of which is essential for developing an efficient early reading process.

More extensive discussions of kindergarten learners may be found in McCarrier, Pinnell & Fountas (2000), Pinnell & Fountas (1998, Chapter 9), and Fountas & Pinnell (1996, Chapter 2). The expectations inherent in these descriptions are consistent with recommended literacy standards for kindergarten through third grade (New Standards Primary Literacy Committee, National Center on Education and the Economy and the University of Pittsburgh, 1999). These expectations assume whole-day kindergarten. Most children who attend half-day kindergarten will take longer to acquire this knowledge. For the shorter day, you will need to adjust experiences, schedules, and expectations.

Essential Literacy Concepts Every Kindergartner Should Know

Phonemic Awareness—kindergarten children are learning to:

- ► Recognize pairs of rhyming words.
- ► Produce rhyming words.
- ► Identify initial consonant sounds in single-syllable words.
- ► Identify onsets and rimes in single-syllable words.
- ► Blend onsets and rimes to form words.
- ► Identify separate phonemes in words.

Letters and Sounds—kindergarten children are learning to:

- ► Recognize and name most letters.
- ► Recognize and say the common sounds that are connected to most letters.
- ► Write many letters to match spoken sounds.
- ► Use their knowledge of sounds and letters to produce early approximated writing.

Reading Words—kindergarten children are learning to:

- ► Read a small core of high frequency words quickly and automatically.
- ► Use letters and sounds to figure out a few simple, regularly spelled single-syllable words.
- ► Recognize easy spelling patterns in words (we, me).

Early Reading Concepts—kindergarten children are learning to:

- ► Use information from pictures to help them learn about the print.
- ► Move left to right across print (within a word and across the lines of a text).
- ► Return to the left margin to read the next line.
- ► Match one spoken word to one word in print, as defined by space.
- ► Notice and isolate words within a text.
- ► Read simple one- to three-line texts using high frequency words and letter/sound relationships to monitor their reading and solve new words.
- ► Have high expectations of print—that it will make sense and sound like the language.
- ► Use their own background experience to make sense of a text.
- ► Build vocabulary by noticing new words, discussing word meaning and visual structure, and collecting the words they encounter in books.

Phonological Awareness and Phonemic Awareness

We communicate by putting sounds together into words, phrases, and sentences having special meaning for other speakers. Children learn oral language easily and interactively within their homes and communities. To take on written language, children must realize that the visible signs represent words and then realize that words are made up of separate sounds, or *phonemes.* A *phoneme* is the smallest unit of sound that makes a difference in meaning (for example, *it* as opposed to *in*). Called *phonemic awareness,* this critical knowledge opens the door to the alphabetic principle—that is, children discover the relationship between letters and sounds.

Phoneme Chart

We examine forty-four phonemes. The actual sounds in the language can vary as dialect, articulation, and other factors in speech vary. The following are common sounds for the letters listed.

Consonant Sounds

b /b/ box	n /n/ nest	ch /ch/ chair
d /d/ dog	p /p/ pail	sh /sh/ ship
f /f/ fan	r /r/ rose	wh /hw/ what
g /g/ gate	s /s/ sun	th /th/ think
h /h/ house	t /t/ top	th /TH/ the
j /j/ jug	v /v/ vase	ng /ng/ sing
k /k/ kite	w /w/ was	zh /zh/ measure
l /l/ leaf	y /y/ yell	
m /m/ mop	z /z/ zoo	

Vowel Sounds

/ă/ hat	/ā/ gate	/ōō/ moon	/û/ bird
/ĕ/ bed	/ē/ feet	/ŏŏ/ book	/ə/ about
/ĭ/ fish	/ī/ bike	/ou/ house	/ä/ car
/ŏ/ mop	/ō/ boat	/oi/ boy	/â/ chair
/ŭ/ nut	/ū/ mule	/ô/ tall	

Phonological awareness is a broader concept that includes the child's developing ability to notice and connect sounds, recognize sounds, recognize rhyme, and hear the syllables in words. This extra sensitivity to the sounds of language is the basis for the more specific development of phonemic awareness. As children enjoy the rhyme and rhythm of songs and poetry, they become conscious or "aware" of sounds.

The narrower *phonemic awareness* involves noticing and thinking about the *individual sounds* in words. It includes children's knowledge that words are made up of sequences of sounds and that there are relationships between those sounds and the letters of the alphabet. *Phonemic awareness* includes the conscious recognition of sounds as well as the ability to identify and manipulate sounds.

The extent of a child's *phonemic awareness* when he or she enters kindergarten is one of the best predictors of how well he or she will learn to read. It is important to teach sounds and letters together. Children become aware of the sounds in words by hearing and enjoying rhymes. They learn to recognize pairs of rhyming words and to produce them. As they say words slowly (while attempting to write words, for example), they become aware of easy-to-hear consonants in both the initial and final position. Note: *s* = letter; /s/ = sound; /TH/ = voiced. Most English consonants come in pairs that occur in the same part of the mouth and differ only in whether they are voiced (i.e., are produced with vocal chords vibrating) or unvoiced. We have included the r-controlled vowel sounds that primary children need to distinguish.

Letters and Sounds

At the same time they are learning about sounds (the phonological system) in words, children are becoming familiar with the *orthographic* system, or the symbols. Through many experiences with the letters of the alphabet, they learn the distinctive features that make each letter different from every other letter, and they learn the names of letters. They learn the movements necessary to form letters. When a child can identify a letter by its features, he can attach a sound to it. By the end of the year, we expect kindergartners to be able to recognize and articulate the common sounds attached to most letters. And we expect that they will be able to write letters to match spoken sounds. Their own names are a powerful source of information as they learn to recognize them and connect them (by sound, letter, or word part) to other words.

Sometimes, *phonemic awareness* instruction focuses only on oral activities that help children learn about sounds. For example, children might sort pictures by the beginning sounds they hear in the names of the things the pictures represent. When instruction in phonemic awareness is connected to letters, *it becomes phonics instruction. Phonics instruction* focuses on the complex relationships *between* letters and sounds.

In a sense, children are building two bodies of knowledge that come together as they grasp the alphabetic principle. They begin to predict letters in words by connecting them with the sounds they hear, and they also learn to predict a word by noticing the letters and connecting them with sounds. This basic ability grows as children practice working with sounds and create categories.

Reading Words

Through a wide range of reading and writing activities, kindergartners soon acquire a small core of words that they know "by sight," that is, they recognize them as whole entities quickly and automatically. The first word a child recognizes is probably his or her name, but words such as *the, it, I, an,* and *to* follow quickly because they are ubiquitous in the language. Kindergartners also begin to use letters and sounds to solve a few simple, regularly spelled single-syllable words and in doing so become familiar with easy spelling patterns (*cat* and *mat,* for example). What's more, they can then use beginning and ending sounds to monitor and check on their reading of longer words.

As they experience print and work with words, kindergartners notice patterns. For example, they:

- ► Connect words that start alike.
- ► Notice that some letters appear together frequently.
- ► Notice that some words begin or end with clusters of letters.
- ► Notice that some letters are doubled.

After they understand that patterns exist and are useful in figuring out words, children begin to search for them.

Children rapidly expand their oral vocabularies in kindergarten, especially if they have many conversations with adults and hear a great deal of written language read aloud. Vocabulary acquisition is important in word learning because it is very difficult to decode a word that you do not know, have never heard, and cannot say. To solve new words efficiently, children need to know how to use the letter/sound information inherent in the high frequency words they automatically recognize.

Many kindergartners are simultaneously learning concepts, labels for the concepts (colors, number words, days of the week, for example), and the printed symbols that represent the labels. This is even more true for children whose first language is not the language of instruction. We need to recognize the complexity of this learning in order to provide support. Kindergartners who are encountering English for the first time will require a great deal of oral language experience along with their work with print. It is especially important that they continually expand their speaking and listening vocabularies.

Early Reading Concepts

Although phonemic awareness, letter/sound knowledge, and word knowledge are important, we would not want to wait until children had "mastered" this body of information before having them read. Through shared reading and then by reading very simple texts themselves, kindergartners learn the left-to-right directional movement that is basic to reading, as well as the return sweep to the left. They learn that there is a relationship between spoken words and the clusters of letters on a page that are defined by white space. They learn to recognize and locate words that are embedded in continuous text.

Combining the knowledge they have of language, words, letters, sounds, and the way print works, kindergartners begin to read very simple texts of one or two lines. This active processing of text enables children to simultaneously put into action all of the information they have been gathering about letters, sounds, and words and to learn more about them. They begin, as Clay (2001) has said, to "assemble working systems" for constructing meaning from print. These beginners, often called "emergent readers," have high expectations of print. They expect it to make sense, sound like language, and be enjoyable; they show these expectations by their consistent search for meaning even as they get better at decoding words. All the time, they are expanding their vocabularies through the words they hear in read-alouds as well as through the books they explore on their own.

What to Do If Children Are Learning to Speak English

You are likely to have many children in your class who not only can speak one language but are learning a second or even a third language. If English is an additional language, then it will be important that you understand and value the child's expansion of both home and school language. Usually, it takes several years for young children to learn English as a second language and to read, write, and think consistently in their new language.

You will want to adjust your teaching to make sure that English language learners have access to your teaching about letters, sounds, and words. Often, these adjustments are minor and easy to implement, but they are necessary to promote essential understandings on the part of these learners. In addition, many of these adjustments will help all of the children in your classroom because they help to make instruction more explicit and clear.

For each lesson in this book, look for a section labeled "Working with English Language Learners." In this section, you will see one or two suggestions specifically related to the implementation of that lesson. On the following pages, we have placed some general suggestions for each of four areas—Oral Language, Reading, Writing, and Phonics and Word Study. It is obvious that these four areas overlap and are interconnected. Work in one area will tend to support learning in all other areas as well.

Oral Language

① Show children what you mean when you give directions. You may need to act out certain sequences of action and have children do it while you coach them. Have them repeat directions to each other or say them aloud as they engage in the activity. Support them during their first attempts rather than expecting independence immediately.

② Give English language learners more "wait and think" time. You could say, "Let's think about that for a minute" before calling for an answer. Demonstrate to students how you think about what you are going to say.

③ Paraphrase and summarize for students. Repeat the directions or instructions several different ways, watching for feedback that they understand you. Paraphrase until you can see that they understand.

④ Use pictures and objects that children understand and that connect to their homes and neighborhoods. At the same time, avoid examples that may be completely strange to children and to which they have difficulty bringing meaning.

⑤ Use short simple sentences in shared reading, interactive writing, and oral conversations. Avoid complex, embedded sentences that children will find hard to follow if they are just learning English. When a complex sentence is used (for example, in read-aloud or shared reading), watch for evidence of confusion on the part of students and paraphrase with simpler sentences when necessary.

⑥ Bring children's familiar world into the classroom through family photos, holiday souvenirs, and objects from home. Expand children's world by bringing in other objects that will give them new experiences.

⑦ Demonstrate using language structures while talking about familiar topics. Involve children in games that require repeating these simple language structures, for example: "My name is _____." "_____ has two brothers." "I like to eat _____." "Josiah likes to (verb)."

⑧ Make instruction highly interactive, with a great deal of oral language surrounding everything children are learning.

⑨ Expand the activities using children's names. Be sure that you are pronouncing all children's names correctly and clearly as you draw their attention to the particular word that is a child's name. Help children learn the names of other children in the class by using them in sentences and placing them on charts.

⑩ Engage English language learners in repeating and enjoying songs, rhymes, and repetitive chants. Incorporate body movements to enhance children's enjoyment of songs, rhymes, and chants and help them remember and understand the language better.

Reading

① Provide an extensive collection of simple alphabet books so that children can encounter the same letters, in the same sequence, with picture examples in different texts.

② Read aloud often to students; in general, it is wise to increase the amount of time that you read aloud and discuss books with students. Be sure that the material you are reading to students is comprehensible, that is, within their power to understand with your support.

③ Stick to simple and understandable texts when you read aloud to students. Watch for signs of enjoyment and reread favorites. Rereading books to children will help them acquire and make use of language that goes beyond their current understandings.

④ Be sure that children's own cultures are reflected in the material that you read aloud to them and that they read for themselves. They should see illustrations with people like themselves in books. They should see their own culture reflected in food, celebrations, dress, holidays, everyday events, and so on.

⑤ Understand that shared reading involves children in a great deal of repetition of language, often language that is different from or more complex than they can currently use in speech. This experience gives children a chance to practice language, learn the meaning of the words, and use the sentence structure of English.

⑥ Use a shared reading text over and over, inserting different names or different words to vary it. Rhythmic and repetitive texts are beneficial to English language learners. This repetition will give children maximum experience with the syntax of English and will help them to develop an implicit understanding of noun-verb agreement, plurals, and other concepts. Once a text is well known in shared reading, it can serve as a resource to children. Revisit shared reading texts for examples of language structure and for specific words and their meaning.

⑦ As soon as English language learners can join in easily in shared reading, know some high frequency words, and independently read shared reading texts with high accuracy, consider including them in guided reading groups. Guided reading is a very valuable context for working with English language learners because you can scaffold their reading and their language through an introduction that clears up confusion and you can observe them closely to gain information as to the accuracy and ease of their reading. Through observation and discussion, you can find what is confusing to them and respond to their questions.

⑧ Be sure to use oral language, pictures, concrete objects, and demonstration when you introduce stories to help children untangle any tricky vocabulary or concepts they are reading in texts for themselves in guided and independent reading. They may encounter words that they can "read" but do not understand.

⑨ Help them in guided reading relate new words to words they already know. During and after reading, check with children to be sure they understand vocabulary and concepts; build into lessons a time when they can bring up any words they did not know.

⑩ Include word work on a regular basis in the guided reading lessons for English language learners. Make strong connections to what they have been learning in phonics and word study.

Writing

① Value and encourage children's drawing as it represents thinking and connects their ideas to early writing.

② Have children repeat several times the sentence they are going to write so that they will be able to remember it. If the sentence is difficult for children to remember, that may be a sign that it is too complex for their present level of language knowledge; consider simplifying the structure or rephrasing the sentence so that it is easier for students.

③ Focus on familiar topics and everyday experiences in interactive writing so that children can generate meaningful sentences and longer texts. Reread the piece of interactive writing many times, encouraging fluency as children gain control over the language.

④ Guide children to produce some repetitive texts that use the same sentence structure and phrases over and over again, so that children can internalize them.

⑤ Know that once a text has been successfully produced in interactive writing and children can easily read it, this text is a resource for talking about language—locating specific words, noticing beginning and ending sounds, noticing rhymes, and so on.

⑥ Encourage English language learners to write for themselves. Demonstrate how to think of something to write and repeat it so that you remember it. Demonstrate how to say words slowly, providing more individual help and demonstration if needed.

⑦ Surround children's independent writing with a great deal of oral language. Talk with them and help them put their ideas into words before they write. Encourage them to tell their stories and share their writing with others and extend their meanings through talk.

⑧ Provide a great many models of writing for English language learners—interactive writing, shared reading, charts about people in the room or experiences. Encourage them to reread and revisit these models to help them in their writing. In the beginning, they may use phrases or sentences from charts around the room, varying their own sentences slightly. Gradually, they will go beyond these resources, but models will be a helpful support for a time.

⑨ Learn something about the sound system of the children's first language. That knowledge will give you valuable insights into the way they "invent" or "approximate" their first spellings. For example, notice whether they are using letter/sound associations from the first language or whether they are actually thinking of a word in the first language and attempting to spell it.

⑩ Accept spellings that reflect the child's own pronunciation of words, even if it varies from standard pronunciation. Notice the strengths in the child's attempts to relate letters and sounds. Show that you value attempts rather than correcting everything the child writes.

Phonics and Word Study

① Use many hands-on activities so that children have the chance to manipulate magnetic letters and tiles, move pictures around, and work with word and name cards.

② Be sure that the print for all charts (ABC charts, name charts, shared writing, picture and word charts, etc.) is clear and consistent so that children who are working in another language do not have to deal with varying forms of letters.

③ Make sure your English language learners are not sitting in an area that is peripheral to the instruction (for example, in the back or to the side). It is especially important for these learners to be able to clearly see and hear all instruction.

④ Provide a "rehearsal" by working with your English language learners in a small group before you provide the minilesson to the entire group. Sometimes they may find it more difficult than other children to come up with words as examples; however, only a few minutes (for example, thinking of *s* words) will help these learners come up with responses in whole-group settings. It will not hurt them to think about the concepts twice because that will provide greater support.

⑤ Use real objects to represent pictures and build concepts in children's minds. For example, bring in a real lemon that children can touch and smell rather than just a picture of a lemon. When it is not possible to use real objects to build concepts, use clear pictures that will have meaning for children. Picture support should be included whenever possible.

⑥ Be sure to enunciate clearly yourself and accept children's approximations. If they are feeling their own mouths say the sounds (or approximate), they will be able to make the connections. Sounds and letters are abstract concepts and the relationships are arbitrary. It will be especially complex for children whose sound systems do not exactly match that of English. They may have trouble saying the sounds that are related to letters and letter clusters.

⑦ Accept alternative pronunciations of words with the hard-to-say sounds and present the written form to help learners distinguish between them. Minimal pairs (sounds that are like each other, have similar tongue positions, and are easily confused, such as *s* and *sh, r* and *l, sh* and *ch, f* and *v*) are often quite difficult for English language learners to differentiate. English language learners often have difficulty with inflected endings *(s, ed)*.

⑧ Speak clearly and slowly when working with children on distinguishing phonemes and hearing sounds in words, but do not distort the word so much that it is unrecognizable. Distortion may confuse English language learners in that it may sound like another word that they do not know.

⑨ Use the pocket chart often so that children have the experience of working with pictures and words in a hands-on way. They can match pictures with words so that the meaning of words becomes clearer.

⑩ Work with a small group of English language learners to help them in the application activity and make your instruction more explicit. Notice concepts that they find particularly difficult and make note to revisit them during word work.

Get Ready to Teach

Inside the Classroom: Organizing to Teach

As the schedules demonstrate, your explicit phonics lessons are ideally embedded in a rich language and literacy framework that offers an organized combination of experiences, each of which contributes uniquely to children's literacy development. We describe a Language and Literacy Framework that features three blocks for learning: Language and Word Study, Reading Workshop, and Writing Workshop.

Language and Literacy Framework		
Language and Word Study	**Whole Group**	**Community Meeting/Calendar** **Interactive Read-Aloud** **Language and Word Play** **Modeled/Shared Reading** **Modeled/Shared/Interactive Writing** **Phonics and Word Study Minilesson** ► **Active Exploration/Application** ► **Sharing and Evaluation** ► **Connection to Reading and Writing**
Reading Workshop	**Small Group and Individual Work**	**Guided Reading** **Independent Work in Centers** **Sharing and Evaluation**
Writing Workshop	**Whole Group, Small Group, and Individual Work**	**Writing Minilesson** **Writing and Individual Conferences** **Guided Writing** **Sharing and Evaluation**

Language and Word Study

Language and Word Study includes a variety of activities designed to immerse young children in language and help them learn about it. For half-day kindergarten we suggest about forty minutes for reading aloud, interactive writing, shared reading, and word study. For whole-day kindergarten, we recommend about forty-five minutes for the language and word study block and another fifteen minutes at day's end for interactive read-aloud and more opportunities for oral expression such as singing songs, reading poetry, storytelling, or shared reading.

Community Meeting/Calendar The block begins with a community meeting involving group activities such as calendar. You will want to make use of selections from *Sing a Song of Poetry* (Pinnell and Fountas 2004) for many of the experiences to link letter, sound, and word learning to texts.

Interactive Read-Aloud By hearing written language read aloud, children learn about the structure, or syntax, of written language, which is different in many ways from oral language. Being read to is especially important for kindergartners because the patterns and specialized vocabulary children encounter are the foundation for their learning to read for themselves. You should select texts with language that will delight children because of the way the author plays with rhymes and sounds.

Language and Word Play Language is not only a useful tool for children; it is a source of delight. Children enjoy hearing language read aloud. They enjoy repetition and rhyme; they love to chant, sing, or say poems together. They enjoy the expressive action of oral storytelling. Listening to poems and rhymes provides a foundation for learning about letters, sounds, and words because it invites children to explore all aspects of written language (Pinnell and Fountas 2004).

Modeled/Shared Reading When teachers model the reading of a text, children learn from demonstration how a reader processes text. When kindergartners read in unison with the teacher from an enlarged text, they observe and participate in a powerful demonstration of reading. Functioning as readers, with the support of the group, they develop important early reading behaviors, begin to recognize high frequency words, and learn to use letters and sounds as critical and important information (see Holdaway 1987; Hundley & Powell 1999).

Modeled/Shared/Interactive Writing In modeled writing, the teacher demonstrates by writing for the children; the children learn that talk can be written down and reread. In shared writing, a group of children compose a common text; together, the teacher and children develop a meaningful text, and then, with input from the children, the teacher writes the text, which is reread many times. In interactive writing, the teacher and children "share the pen"; the teacher writes some of the text and invites children to make contributions by coming up to the easel and writing selected words and letters (for a detailed description, see McCarrier, Pinnell & Fountas 2000).

Modeled, shared, and interactive writing are especially powerful tools in kindergarten because they expose the writing process in a very explicit way. Children are helped to remember the next word in the message, say it slowly, and think of the letters and sounds. They are also able to use high frequency words that they know and to make connections between words that start or end alike and have similar parts. Teachers make special use of the name chart as a tool in this process.

Phonics and Word Study Minilesson Phonics instruction is another part of the language and word study block. Here, you present a brief, lively minilesson on a principle related to the use of letters, sounds, or words. Minilessons are quick and efficient; they usually take only ten to fifteen minutes and are followed by an application activity that students can complete independently after they have learned the essential routines. The application activity usually takes another ten or fifteen minutes and may be accomplished in different ways: individuals working at their seat; small groups rotating through the word study center; whole-class independent, partner, or small-group work. The application is followed by a sharing session in which the work is summarized and the principle is reexamined.

Reading Workshop

We recommend about sixty minutes for the reading block for whole-day kindergarten. For half-day kindergarten, we recommend forty-five minutes for guided reading groups and independent literacy work.

Guided Reading As kindergartners participate in shared reading, they begin to notice letters and words, read left to right, and match word by word. They also learn to monitor their reading, making sure they are saying one spoken word for each written word. They learn to look at the right place as they read. When they know and can use a few high frequency words as anchors and can use some letter and sound knowledge in shared reading, you will want to begin asking them to read very easy texts in guided reading. In general, you will want to phase the children into working with little books in guided reading partway through the school year, with a goal of all children reading simple text by year's end.

Guided reading is small-group instruction (for two, three, or four children) in which teachers provide specific instruction on effective strategies (word solving, for example) that support the comprehension of emergent readers (Fountas & Pinnell 1996). You will begin guided reading at different points for different children as you observe their behavior. Groups are homogeneous in terms of students' development of a reading process at a particular time. Using a gradient of texts organized by level of difficulty (Fountas & Pinnell 2000), you select a book that is within the learners' control but offers a small challenge. You introduce the book, and then each member of the group reads the whole text softly to himself.

While children are reading, you can look for effective behaviors (including, but not limited to, the application of phonics principles) and interact briefly with children, helping them apply the principles you are teaching them in word study. Following the reading, you discuss the meaning of the story and teach processing strategies. Often, you will do some quick work with letters or words at the end of the lesson, using magnetic letters, the chalkboard, or a white dry-erase board. This is another opportunity to reinforce principles that you have explored with the children in word study.

The minilessons provided here include specific guidance on how to connect principles in the phonics lesson with your work in guided reading.

Independent Work in Centers While you are working with a small group of children in guided reading, the other children pursue a variety of independent literacy activities. Children can rotate through a number of "centers" or work at their desk or table alone or with a partner.

A center is a specific location in the classroom that has supplies and materials and space to work. Children learn routines for the centers and complete different activities in them over time. If you are using centers, typically you would begin the year by teaching children the routines for independent work at one center or activity at a time and helping them do the work.

Suggestions for Managing and Using Centers for Word Study

▶ Clearly organize supplies so that only one kind of material is in a single container.

▶ Label supplies with both words and pictures.

▶ Using words and pictures, label the place on the shelf where the container is stored.

▶ Have all supplies that children will need for a given activity organized and available.

▶ Teach children routines for getting and returning materials.

▶ Establish and explicitly teach the routines that will be needed for a learning activity.

▶ Post simple directions in the center using both words and pictures.

▶ Limit the number of routines children are expected to follow—a few essential activities can be varied to explore different principles (for example, sorting).

▶ Stick to a consistent schedule.

▶ Introduce only one new application activity each day—typically, children will engage in one activity related to a principle over a period of three to five days.

▶ Place needed resources (charts, word wall) on the wall near the center so that they will be available.

▶ "Walk through" the activity so that you can accurately estimate the time it will take.

▶ Allocate an appropriate amount of time for selected activities and teach children the routines so that they can perform them at a good rate.

▶ Teach children to speak softly while working independently and model this behavior by speaking softly yourself.

▶ Have regular meetings with children to self-evaluate the productivity of work in the word study center.

Examples of Productive Literacy Activities

▶ Independent reading from "browsing boxes" filled with little books that are very easy for children because they have been read in shared or guided reading.

▶ Listening to books on tape.

▶ Exploring letters, sounds, and words connected to the minilesson.

▶ Writing.

▶ Painting and drawing.

▶ Reading and exploring books and looking at illustrations.

▶ Building familiar poems in pocket charts.

▶ Drama and role playing.

▶ Hands-on activities using sand, blocks, or water.

Sharing and Evaluation At the end of the reading period, you will want to have a brief whole-group gathering so children can share some of the things they've learned about or written using the word study principle you've taught. This period of sharing will, of course, encompass more than word study, but you will want to take two or three minutes to remind children of the specific principle and elicit their thinking and discoveries. Involve the children in evaluating the work session.

Writing Workshop

The writing workshop includes a minilesson on some aspect of writing, independent writing, conferences with individual children, and a time for reinforcing and extending the learning. We recommend between forty and sixty minutes for both whole-day and half-day kindergarten.

Writing Minilesson In a writing minilesson you demonstrate principles related to the conventions and craft of writing. The first minilessons may be procedural—showing children how to use the paper and other writing materials, for example. For kindergartners, these minilessons will focus on simple topics, such as how to choose a topic for drawing or writing, how to tell stories, where to start writing on a page, how to say words slowly, how to use spaces, how to create illustrations that match your story, or how to write words to tell about your illustrations.

Writing and Individual Conferences Children write independently while you interact with individuals and/or small groups, helping them clarify and expand their messages. Individual conferences are a good time to remind a child of what he has learned in the word study minilesson. You will also gather very valuable information that will help you design effective and timely word study minilessons. Writing is important for kindergartners because they are examining the details of written language and using the word, letter, and sound knowledge they have accumulated.

Guided Writing You may want to pull together a small group of children who have similar writing or drawing needs to "guide" their writing. You can work with them closely to support shifts in their learning.

Sharing and Evaluation In a brief session at the end of the period, children can share their writing and get feedback. In addition to discussing the meaning and voice of the stories children write, you can reinforce the learning you introduced in the minilesson. Involve the children in evaluating the work time.

Phonics Minilessons That Really Work

Materials Make a Difference

When you teach a minilesson, it is very important to do so in a clearly defined space in which all children can see and hear easily. They should be able to sit comfortably on the floor without touching other children. You will want an easel, a small white dry-erase board, markers, magnetic letters, and a vertical magnetic board. You will also need a pocket chart on which you can post letters or words on cards large enough for the whole group to see. The name chart and Alphabet Linking Chart are useful tools to have nearby, close enough for you to point to. Children should be able to see the word wall from where they sit.

Basic Principles: Designing/Implementing Effective Minilessons

Designing Effective Minilessons

▶ Focus on one principle that is appropriate and useful for your students at a particular point in time.

▶ State the principle in simple, clear terms.

▶ Think of a few good examples in advance so that you have them ready to show the students.

▶ Have in mind why you selected the minilesson, which probably will help you connect it to children's work in other components of the language/literacy framework; make connections explicit.

▶ Have in mind how you can connect your minilesson principle to the children's names (on the name chart).

▶ Design an application activity that students can do independently (after being taught routines), and that will be productive in their learning.

▶ Design multilevel activities that permit advanced students to go beyond the given activity and make more discoveries and allow children who are less experienced to complete the minilessons.

Implementing Effective Minilessons

▶ Have all materials organized and quickly available.

▶ Be sure that all children can see and hear as you demonstrate the principle or write examples on a chart.

▶ Make a clear statement of the principle as you begin the lesson, or clearly state the principle at the end as children come to their own conclusions from examples.

▶ Use a conversational rather than a lecture style. Promote interaction so children can be active, engaged learners.

▶ Invite interaction so that children bring their own knowledge to bear on the application of the principle.

▶ Invite children to connect the principle and examples to their names; use names as examples when possible.

▶ Share examples and add examples from children (if children are unable to provide some examples, then either the principle is not clearly stated or it is too difficult).

▶ Keep minilessons brief; a few examples are enough.

▶ Make connections to previous word study minilessons or understandings and discoveries made in any other component of the Language and Literacy Framework.

▶ Check for understanding by asking children to locate and talk about examples.

▶ Summarize the minilesson by returning to the principle and stating it again.

▶ Place an example on the word wall for the children's response when teaching minilessons on words.

▶ Demonstrate the application activity explicitly so that you know children can perform it independently.

▶ Provide all necessary materials for the application activity in one place—for example, the word study center or a clearly defined and organized materials center.

▶ Convene children for a brief sharing period so that they can comment on what they have learned and you can reinforce the principle again.

We recommend using black or dark-colored markers on white or cream-colored chart paper. You may want to use colored transparent highlighter tape to emphasize certain words or letters, but, in general, it is better not to clutter up the examples with color-coding, which is usually a distraction for kindergartners. Also, it may confuse them; we want them to look at the distinctive features of letters—not the color! If you have set up centers in your classroom, be sure that all the necessary materials are readily available in the word study center where students will use the application. If students work at their own tables, arrange materials in a central area or on each table. If the activity is new or difficult, place a model in clear view so that children can check their results. For additional information about the materials, read the Material Description List in *Teaching Resources*.

Classroom Routines for Smart Teaching

Routines refers both to the basic routines of how to live and learn in the classroom (where to store materials or how to participate in a class meeting, for example) and to a series of instructional routines like making words, sorting pictures, and creating name puzzles that children will use again and again as they learn a range of concepts. Teach the routines carefully when you first begin using word study minilessons. First demonstrate the activity precisely, and then have everyone do it at once. If you run into a logistical problem (not having enough magnetic letters, for example), ask children to take turns with a partner or in a small group and check each other. When you know that children can perform the routine on their own, then they can work individually, as partners, or in groups. (You will need to demonstrate the activity again in relation to the particular principle you are exploring in the minilesson.) For a comprehensive overview of routines, see the descriptions and directions in *Teaching Resources;* additionally, you will find many references to routines in the Month-by-Month Planning Guide.

Consider Your Language and Delivery

Minilessons should be conversational. You will want to state the principle clearly at the beginning of the lesson (or at the end, if you think it is appropriate for students to derive it through inquiry and example). Your tone should be that of *I'm going to show you something interesting about how words work* or *What do you notice about these words?* Invite children to make connections to their names and anything else they know. Invite them to contribute further examples and recognize and praise their thinking even if the examples don't quite fit. Always try to understand their thinking and build on a partially correct response. Help them clarify their suggestions as necessary.

Remember that a minilesson is *brief.* Don't let it go on too long. Depending on the particular principle, you'll need only a few examples to make an understanding clear. Your goal is for students to integrate some of these examples into their own thinking so they can connect them to new learning when they are working on their own.

At the end of the minilesson, summarize the understanding you are trying to instill and take another moment to restate the principle. If appropriate, place an example on the word wall. Then explain and demonstrate the application activity.

Options for Application Activities

① Present the minilesson to the entire class and then involve all children simultaneously in the application activity. They can work individually or with partners as you circulate around the room. Immediately follow the activity with sharing.

② Present the minilesson to the entire class, but involve children in application activities in small groups that you supervise. Have the rest of the children involved in independent reading/writing activities. Follow the activity with sharing as soon as all groups have completed it.

③ Present the minilesson to the entire class and explain the application activity. Have children complete it first (simultaneously for the whole group) and then move to another independent activity. Work with small groups in guided reading or writing while children work independently.

④ Present the minilesson to the entire class and explain the application activity. On the same day, have children rotate to a word study center to complete the activity. Have a brief sharing at the end of the period.

⑤ Present the minilesson to the entire class and explain the application activity. Over several days, have children rotate to a word study center to complete the activity. Have a brief sharing at the end of each day. Ask the children who participated to talk about what they learned.

So What Did We Learn? Sharing and Evaluation

After independent work, convene a brief sharing period in which children can discuss the principle and share their examples. This community meeting is a good way to ask children to evaluate themselves. You can ask how many completed the activity and ask them to evaluate their work. Recognizing their independent work gives it value and emphasis. If you have made a chart, refer to it again and restate the principle. You may want to add some of their examples. Recognize children's thinking as they share their ideas. Make further connections with reading and writing in other components of the Language and Literacy Framework.

Your Essential Tools for Teaching

Phonics Lessons and *Teaching Resources* comprise multiple tools that work together to support your teaching. The tools are:

- ▶ The Lesson Selection Map
- ▶ The Assessment Guide (in *Teaching Resources*)
- ▶ The Month-by-Month Planning Guide
- ▶ The Word Study Continuum: Systematic Phonics and Spelling

You will also want to use selections from *Sing a Song of Poetry: A Teaching Resource for Phonemic Awareness, Phonics, and Fluency* (Pinnell and Fountas 2004).

The Lesson Selection Map

The Lesson Selection Map catalogs all kindergarten lessons by Continuum category and suggested time of year (early, middle, or late). In creating this Map, we considered how children's experience is likely to build throughout the year as a result not only of the direct teaching of principles related to letters, sounds, and words but also of their daily experiences hearing written language read aloud and participating in shared, independent, and guided reading and interactive and independent writing.

Again, this Map is not a rigid sequence; it is a continuum of easier to harder principles. It will help you think in broad strokes about the program you are designing for the children in your classroom, which must always be considered in light of your observations and assessments of what your students know and can do at any given point. If children are very knowledgeable and experienced, you may decide that some lessons can be abbreviated or omitted. If children are very inexperienced in a given area, lessons may need to be repeated using different examples.

A whole year of lessons may seem overwhelming; however, keep in mind that:

- ▶ Any one lesson takes ten minutes or less.
- ▶ Some lessons can be skipped or shortened.
- ▶ Some lessons will go very quickly because children have acquired most of the requisite knowledge already through reading and writing in the classroom.

Even if you do not use all the lessons, reflecting on the Map will help you be aware of the entire body of knowledge that is important for kindergarten children to acquire as a foundation for literacy learning.

The Map contains two kinds of information:

▶ Using the rows, you can take one category of the Continuum and follow children's development of a principle from easier to harder throughout the year. For example, lessons on phonological awareness begin with songs, rhymes, and chants. You'll help your students become more sensitive to the sounds of language by having them match rhyming pictures and listen for the parts in words. Later in the year you will give closer attention to individual sounds in words and help your students develop insights into the structure of words by identifying and manipulating these sounds. Each category of the Continuum offers room for growth throughout the year.

▶ You can look down the columns to get a sense of the understanding children are building across the entire continuum. Working across categories, you ensure that children not only develop phonological awareness but also learn to look at print—distinguish letters and learn their names—as well as think about word meanings and become familiar with some high frequency words that will help accelerate their learning.

Look at the Map both ways. Your students might be more advanced in one area than another. It is obvious that planning a program is not always neat and tidy; however, the concept of easier to harder, in combination with assessment, should allow you to design an efficient program that:

▶ Makes the most of what children know by allowing them to work at the edge of their knowledge.

▶ Ensures clear, explicit teaching and meaningful practice to deepen conceptual knowledge.

▶ Ensures that principles do not have to be taught again and again.

▶ Does not blindly demand that you spend time on exercises teaching what children already know.

Here are some easy directions for using the Map as a practical tool in lesson planning:

▶ Reproduce a copy of the Map to keep in the front of your lesson-planning book. (Another copy of the Map is included in *Teaching Resources.*)

▶ When you have used a lesson, highlight it on the Map or place a check on the line next to it.

▶ Write additional lessons that you design and implement in the empty spaces in each section.

▶ Make notes about adaptations that are helpful to your children because of their native language, background, or culture.

▶ If you determine that children do not need a particular lesson because they have learned the principle in some other context, cross out the line or highlight it in another color.

Used in this way, the Map becomes a record as well as a planning tool, because you will know at a glance what you have taught (or determined not to be necessary) and what you need to consider teaching next.

Kindergarten – Lesson Selection Map

Early Literacy Concepts ELC

early

___ **ELC 1** Recognizing Names (Name Chart)
___ **ELC 2** Learning Your Name
(Songs and Chants)
___ **ELC 3** Hearing Words in Sentences
(Cut-Up Sentences)

mid

___ **ELC 4** Sorting and Connecting Names
(Three-Way Sort)
___ **ELC 5** Recognizing First and Last Letters
(Making Names)
___ **ELC 6** Locating *First* and *Last* in Print
(Little Books)

late

___ **ELC 7** Matching Word by Word
(Cut-Up Sentences)
___ **ELC 8** Making Sentences (Little Books)

Phonological Awareness PA

early

___ **PA 1** Hearing Rhymes (Songs and Poems)
___ **PA 2** Hearing More Rhymes (Poems)
___ **PA 3** Hearing Rhymes (Picture Sort)
___ **PA 4** Hearing Syllables (Picture Sort)
___ **PA 5** Hearing Syllables (Chant)
___ **PA 6** Hearing, Saying, and Clapping Syllables
(Picture Sort)
___ **PA 7** Saying Words Slowly to Hear Sounds
(Picture-Word Match)
___ **PA 8** Hearing Beginning Sounds
(Picture Match)
___ **PA 9** Hearing Beginning Sounds
(Picture Sort)

mid

___ **PA 10** Hearing Ending Sounds (Picture Sort)
___ **PA 11** Hearing Ending Sounds (Picture Lotto)
___ **PA 12** Hearing Ending Sounds (Picture Cards)
___ **PA 13** Making Rhymes (Picture Concentration)
___ **PA 14** Hearing and Producing Rhymes
(Rhyming Lotto)
___ **PA 15** Hearing Long Vowel Sounds in the
Middle of Words (Picture Match)
___ **PA 16** Blending Syllables (Syllable Lotto)
___ **PA 17** Hearing First and Last Sounds (Writing
Words)
___ **PA 18** Hearing and Saying Beginning Sounds
(Trip and Line-Up Games)

late

___ **PA 19** Hearing and Blending Onsets and
Rimes (Follow the Path)
___ **PA 20** Identifying and Blending Onsets and
Rimes (Go Fish)
___ **PA 21** Hearing and Substituting Sounds
(Picture Cards)
___ **PA 22** Hearing Middle Sounds (Two-Way Sort)
___ **PA 23** Hearing Sounds in Sequence
(Picture Cards)
___ **PA 24** Blending Sounds in Words
(Lotto Game)
___ **PA 25** Hearing, Saying, and Deleting
Beginning Sounds (Picture Cards)
___ **PA 26** Hearing and Deleting Sounds
(Picture Cards)

Letter Knowledge LK

early

___ **LK 1** Exploring Letters (Letter Play)
___ **LK 2** Recognizing Letters (Magnetic Letters)
___ **LK 3** Learning Letters (Names with Stars)
___ **LK 4** Learning Letters (Name Puzzle)
___ **LK 5** Recognizing and Naming Letters
(Alphabet Linking Chart)
___ **LK 6** Making Letters (Art Materials)
___ **LK 7** Learning Letter Forms and Names
(Letter Match)

mid

___ **LK 8** Learning Letters (Alphabet Soup Game)
___ **LK 9** Learning Letter Names
(Letter Minibooks)
___ **LK 10** Learning Letters in Names
(Name Graph)
___ **LK 11** Learning Letters in Names (Marching
Game)
___ **LK 12** Learning to Write Your Name
(Name Card Trace)
___ **LK 13** Learning to Look at Letter Features 1
(Letter Sort)
___ **LK 14** Learning to Look at Letter Features 2
(Letter Sort)
___ **LK 15** Identifying Letters in Words
("Bingo" Song)
___ **LK 16** Learning to Form Letters (Verbal Path)

late

___ **LK 17** Recognizing Uppercase and Lowercase
Letters (Two-Way Sort)
___ **LK 18** Recognizing Uppercase and Lowercase
Letters (Alphabet Lotto)
___ **LK 19** Forming Letters (Handwriting Books)
___ **LK 20** Learning to Form Letters (Handwriting
Books)
___ **LK 21** Labeling Consonants and Vowels
(Letter Sort)
___ **LK 22** Understanding Alphabetical Order
(Magnetic Letters)
___ **LK 23** Learning Alphabetical Order (Follow the
Path)
___ **LK 24** Learning the Initials for Names (Name
Chart)

Letter/Sound Relationships LS

early

mid

___ **LS 1** Beginning Consonant Letters and
Sounds (Pocket Chart Match)
___ **LS 2** Connecting Beginning Sounds and
Letters (Picture-Word Match)
___ **LS 3** Beginning Consonant Letters and
Sounds (Picture Sort)
___ **LS 4** Beginning Consonant Letters and
Sounds (Picture Lotto)
___ **LS 5** Beginning Consonant Letters and
Sounds (Finding Words in Print)

late

___ **LS 6** Learning Letters and Beginning Sounds
(Class Alphabet Book)
___ **LS 7** Learning Letter Names and Sounds
(ABC Board)
___ **LS 8** Recognizing Beginning and Ending
Consonant Sounds (Making Words)

Spelling Patterns SP

early	mid	late
	___ **SP 1** Noticing Word Features (Two-Way Sort)	___ **SP 5** Making Words with -*and* (Magnetic Letters)
	___ **SP 2** Making Words with -*at* (Magnetic Letters)	___ **SP 6** Making Words with -*ake* (Magnetic Letters)
	___ **SP 3** Making Words with -*an* (Magnetic Letters)	___ **SP 7** Making Words with -*ike* (Magnetic Letters)
	___ **SP 4** Making Words with -*ay* (Magnetic Letters)	

High Frequency Words HF

early	mid	late
	___ **HF 1** Building and Writing High Frequency Words 1 (Making Words)	___ **HF 5** Building and Writing High Frequency Words 4 (Making Words)
	___ **HF 2** Building and Writing High Frequency Words 2 (Making Words)	___ **HF 6** Building and Writing High Frequency Words 5 (Making Words)
	___ **HF 3** Recognizing High Frequency Words (Word Lotto)	___ **HF 7** Locating High Frequency Words in Text (Poems and Songs)
	___ **HF 4** Building and Writing High Frequency Words 3 (Making Words)	

Word Meaning WM

early	mid	late
	___ **WM 1** Learning Color Words (Matching Words)	___ **WM 5** Connecting Words That Go Together (Family Pictures)
	___ **WM 2** Locating Color Words in Text (Words in Poems)	___ **WM 6** Learning the Days of the Week (Matching Words)
	___ **WM 3** Learning Number Words (Matching Words)	___ **WM 7** Locating Days of the Week in Text (Making Sentences)
	___ **WM 4** Locating Numerals and Number Words in Text (Making Words)	

Word Structure WS

early	mid	late
		___ **WS 1** Learning Words: Simple Plurals (Plural Concentration)
		___ **WS 2** Adding *s* to Change Word Meanings (Making Words)
		___ **WS 3** Learning about Compound Words (Highlighting Words)
		___ **WS 4** Recognizing Syllables (Syllable Sort)

Word-Solving Actions WSA

early	mid	late
___ **WSA 1** Making Connections Between Names and Other Words (Name Lotto)	___ **WSA 3** Making New Words by Changing the First Letter 1 (Magnetic Letters)	___ **WSA 6** Using Parts of Words to Solve New Words (Highlighting Word Parts)
___ **WSA 2** Using Letter/Sound Analysis (Writing Words)	___ **WSA 4** Making New Words by Changing the First Letter 2 (Magnetic Letters)	___ **WSA 7** Changing Last Letters to Make New Words (Magnetic Letters)
	___ **WSA 5** Using Known Words in Simple Texts (Cut-Up Sentences)	___ **WSA 8** Changing First and Last Letters to Make New Words (Magnetic Letters)
		___ **WSA 9** Using Known Words to Solve New Words (Cut-Up Sentences)

The Assessment Guide

There is a time to use systematic, planned tasks that are designed to gather information about particular aspects of children's growing word knowledge. Performance-based assessment may involve observation, but it also represents more formal structured experiences in which the tasks are standardized. Standardization of the procedure creates a reliable assessment situation that is more objective than daily ongoing observation. The goal is to get a picture of what each student can do independently. Usually, you do not actively teach during a performance-based assessment, but you may make teaching points after the neutral observation.

The Assessment Guide includes more formal, performance-based Assessment Tasks across the nine Categories of Learning. You can use these tasks in multiple ways: as diagnostic tools to determine what your students know and need to know; as monitoring tools to help you keep track of your teaching and your students' learning; and as documentation of the teaching and learning you and your students have accomplished. You and your colleagues may even decide to place some of the summary sheets in your children's permanent cumulative folders as a way to create a schoolwide record of the phonics and word study program.

As noted, the opportunities for informal assessment are embedded in each lesson in the Assess feature. Look for more formal assessment opportunities across the nine Categories of Learning in the Assessment Guide inside *Teaching Resources*.

The Month-by-Month Planning Guide

The Month-by-Month Planning Guide outlines and describes a year of instructional contexts and ways to organize that instruction—whole-group, independent, and small-group work. It also lists the instructional routines (which include everything from where to store supplies to how to play Alphabet Lotto) you will need to teach so that children will be able to complete the application activities. Although you'll teach only a few new routines each month, children's knowledge accumulates. Once a routine (sorting, for example) has been learned, children can use it again and again in different ways. Finally, our yearly plan suggests specific lessons by month, from easier to harder, and lists specific competencies that you can determine through observation and assessment. These simple assessments of what children can do will help you identify children who are having more difficulty and may need repetition or additional word study work in a small group.

This yearly plan is a ladder of support as you work with children over time. Don't worry if your group does not progress in precisely the same way this plan implies. They may learn more rapidly in one area than another, but referring to the plan will help you reflect on areas where you need to invest more instruction.

If you are new to teaching (or new to teaching in this area), you may want to follow this month-by-month plan closely. You will learn from the experience and over the year will begin to see how you can adapt the plan for greater effectiveness with your own students and also how you can teach more efficiently.

Here's a more detailed look at how the year is broken up and the progression of activities.

Early Kindergarten

The beginning of kindergarten is an exciting time for both you and your new students. For many children, kindergarten is their first experience with large-group instruction. The first three months of kindergarten are critical for turning this group of twenty or more individuals into a community that works together cooperatively and productively. You want children to share with and support one another and to treat you, their materials, and one another with respect. Your work with them on classroom routines is very important and time well spent. You will want to have a very predictable schedule and a highly organized classroom and to teach children gradually and explicitly how to move about the room, use materials, and follow directions. The first two months of school are when you "set the scene" for learning.

Middle Kindergarten

By December most children will have settled into the routines of kindergarten and be able to perform them automatically. They can sustain independent work for longer periods of time and be responsible for themselves and for materials. You will still need to be explicit and clear in your demonstrations and to reteach routines if things are falling apart for some children.

Late Kindergarten

During the last three months of the year, children will be integrating their knowledge of reading, writing, and how words work. Learning accelerates as you connect word study with children's work in reading and writing. Your children will have established a strong foundation as emergent readers and writers to continue their learning.

Month-by-Month Planning Guide—September

During this first month of school, you will continually assess your students' knowledge of letters, sounds, and words so that you can make informed decisions about which lessons to teach and how to teach them. At the same time, you will teach valuable routines to help your students work and learn together. Additionally, you will introduce a repertoire of stories, songs, rhymes, and chants that the children will enjoy and that will heighten their awareness of language's sounds and written symbols and provide teaching examples on which you can draw for instruction.

Work mainly with the group as a whole and move quickly from one activity to another. Plan the following activities each day:

▶ Read aloud stories several times a day that have repetition, rhyme, and enjoyable language. Select books that are easy to follow and that will engage children through humor, interesting characters, and easy-to-remember language. Reread favorites and invite the children to join in on refrains and predictable language.

▶ Use enlarged texts for shared reading. Teach children how to follow along as you read aloud and point to the words. To begin, choose simple two-line poems and one-sentence messages. Read them aloud to the children several times and invite them to join in.

▶ Work with children's names. Prepare a name chart and create name cards to use in the pocket chart. Teach children how to "read" the name chart as you point.

▶ Begin interactive writing using simple sentences that include children's names—"Jason likes red," for example. Invite children to come up to the easel to write any letter they can.

It is critical that children begin to learn behavior and language that will serve them well at school. They will be using pencils, crayons, and markers to explore writing. It is not necessary to teach handwriting formally, but you will want to teach them the correct way to hold a pencil and draw attention to motions when you demonstrate writing

letters, helping children individually. Additionally, teach the routines that enable an effective, harmonious learning environment. Teach your children how to:

▶ Gather on the rug or in some other central area and "check themselves" to be sure they are sitting up, not touching anyone else, and looking at the teacher.

▶ Sit at tables and move from the central area to tables and back again.

▶ Come up to the chart quickly (to write or insert a card or sentence strip) and return again to a spot on the floor.

▶ Get, use, and return simple materials—crayons, paper, glue, scissors.

▶ Take books out, look at them or "read" them, and return them, face out, to the book rack or shelf.

▶ Use color codes for books if appropriate (such as a "yellow dot" for a certain type of book).

▶ Enter the classroom, line up to leave, and take home materials.

▶ Follow step-by-step directions for using the name puzzle and name charts.

▶ Make words with magnetic letters and other letter types such as link letters, foam letters, and letter tiles.

▶ Work together in centers.

For the first month of school, select lessons that help children attend to print and at the same time build a sense of community. If children already know how to read and write their names, then lessons using names will be quick; if they do not, then it is very important to focus on names intensively. Also select lessons that help develop phonological and print awareness. You will want to create many opportunities for authentic reading and writing in the drama (housekeeping), art, blocks, and sand/water centers so children can learn more about literacy in their world.

Organization of Instruction: *Whole group; some independent work with teacher circulating to observe, interact, and provide support.*

Learning Contexts	New Routines to Teach	Suggested Lessons	Assessment—Children Can:
Get started with reading aloud, shared reading, interactive writing, independent writing and drawing and play activities. Show children the classroom and the materials. Build a repertoire of songs, chants, familiar stories, poems, and rhymes. Build a sense of community by teaching them to care for the room and use routines in an orderly way. Be sure children know each other's names and yours. Use early lessons to build resources (such as knowledge of names), explore letters, and build a foundation of phonological awareness. Establish responsibility for taking materials home.	▶ Basic classroom routines for sitting, moving, listening, getting a turn to speak, joining in for singing, chanting, listening to a story, participating in shared reading and interactive writing. ▶ Basic routines for using materials and putting them away. ▶ Names of class activities (for example, "circle time") and the typical daily schedule. ▶ Using the name puzzle and the name chart (locating, matching, etc.). ▶ Working together in structured play centers.	**ELC 1** Recognizing Names (Name Chart) **ELC 2** Learning Your Name (Songs and Chants) **PA 1** Hearing Rhymes (Songs and Poems) **PA 2** Hearing More Rhymes (Poems) **LK 1** Exploring Letters (Letter Play) **LK 2** Recognizing Letters (Magnetic Letters) **LK 3** Learning Letters (Names with Stars) **LK 4** Learning Letters (Name Puzzle)	▶ Read their names and locate in text. ▶ Build and write their names. ▶ Say the names of letters in their names. ▶ Notice and talk about the similarities and differences among letters. ▶ Perform basic classroom routines. ▶ Join in on poems, songs, rhymes, and chants.

October

By October, you want your students to understand the schedule and to have internalized basic classroom routines. If they still have difficulty, reteach routines, emphasizing consistency, because you will now introduce more complex routines that will allow them to work independently. Continue to build children's knowledge of familiar stories, chants, songs, and rhymes so that they attend to print and acquire a repertoire of examples. Complete initial assessments so that you have a good understanding of the early literacy concepts they understand, the letters and sounds they know, and words they can read and/or write.

Continue read-alouds, shared reading, interactive writing, independent writing and drawing, and role-playing activities. Use mainly whole-group activities, but schedule time every day when children work independently as you circulate and guide them. Introduce centers slowly, one at a time, judging (based on observation) when children are ready to learn another independent activity. Continue monitoring and encouraging children's attempts at drawing and writing; help them hold pencils correctly and emphasize directional movements in writing.

Establish the routine of a focused phonics lesson followed by an application activity and then sharing. First teach the routines for the application activity and have the whole group work at the same time while you observe and assist them. Follow the application activity with a sharing period. Teach children to sit in a circle on the floor so that everyone can see and hear what is being shared. If your group is too large for a circle, try a square in which each child has space without touching anyone else. Sharing should be quick; not every child can share something every day. It is very important to establish sharing as a routine, however, because it:

▶ Builds accountability for the application activity as children want to report their discoveries.

▶ Sharpens their thinking *during* the application because they are mentally preparing to share.

▶ Sets up a routine that encourages discoveries beyond the precise lesson you have taught.

▶ Gives you valuable information about what children have learned from the lesson and application activity.

In October, continue teaching and reinforcing basic classroom routines, including those related to any centers you have set up. Add several new routines, including using the word wall: (1) labeling the word wall; (2) placing words on the word wall; (3) reading the word wall; and (4) locating words on the word wall. Also teach children how to match picture cards by placing them side by side, saying words slowly, and clapping syllables. Demonstrate putting together a cut-up sentence on the pocket chart and also teach routines for using the pocket chart: (1) placing picture cards in it and taking them out; (2) putting in sentence strips; (3) highlighting words or letters using clear plastic; and (4) sorting picture, letter, or word cards. Select lessons that help children recognize that there are separate words in sentences and that help them hear rhymes, beginning consonant sounds, and syllables. Seek continued opportunities to integrate reading and writing in structured play centers such as blocks, sand/water, art, and drama (housekeeping or role play). Introduce some literacy-based centers such as a listening center or poem book.

Organization of Instruction: *Whole group; some independent work with teacher circulating to observe, interact, and provide support.*

Learning Contexts	New Routines to Teach	Suggested Lessons	Assessment—Children Can:
Continue reading aloud, shared reading, interactive writing, independent writing and drawing, and play activities. Establish the routine of a phonics lesson with application activity. Set up the word wall and add to it as children become familiar with words in lessons, shared reading, and interactive writing. Introduce the word wall using children's names and one or two easy high frequency words they have seen in shared reading and interactive writing.	▶ Basic classroom routines (reinforce so they are automatic). ▶ Using the word wall. ▶ Matching picture cards. ▶ Using the pocket chart: (1) placing picture cards in it and taking them out; (2) putting in sentence strips and taking them out; (3) highlighting words or letters using plastic. ▶ Putting together cut-up sentences (demonstration). ▶ Saying words and clapping syllables. ▶ Saying words slowly. ▶ Word-by-word matching (demonstrations).	**ELC 3** Hearing Words in Sentences (Cut-Up Sentences) **PA 3** Hearing Rhymes (Picture Sort) **PA 4** Hearing Syllables (Picture Sort) **PA 5** Hearing Syllables (Chant) **PA 6** Hearing, Saying, and Clapping Syllables (Picture Sort) **PA 7** Saying Words Slowly to Hear Sounds (Picture-Word Match) **LK 5** Recognizing and Naming Letters (Alphabet Linking Chart)	▶ Hear and identify rhyming words. ▶ Match rhyming pictures. ▶ Match pictures of words that begin the same. ▶ Say words to hear and clap syllables. ▶ Identify the number of syllables in a word. ▶ Say words slowly to hear one sound. ▶ Hear words in a sentence. ▶ Hear and identify beginning sounds in words.

Month-by-Month Planning Guide—November

By November, children will be ready for more centers. You will still rely on whole-group instruction and continue to build the children's repertoire of stories, songs, and poems. Shared reading and interactive writing are important learning contexts because they allow children to behave like readers and writers in a highly supported way. Intensive work in reading aloud, shared reading, and shared writing exposes children in an authentic way to all of the concepts that they will be using more explicitly in word study throughout the year. Continue to support children in writing; they should be producing more accurately formed letters.

Continue to reinforce basic routines if children do not have them under full control. If they do not yet know how to use materials independently, you may need to rethink the way you have organized your materials. You will still be working with the whole group much of the time, but you will want to encourage independence and increase independent work.

Help children sustain interest and concentration through two or even three activities at centers or at their tables. You should find that they need your help less and less. Work with individuals and small groups to help them engage productively in independent activities.

Some new routines to teach in relation to word study applications include sorting picture cards and matching words by looking at the letters. Lotto is another new routine you will want to teach. Select lessons that help children hear beginning sounds of words, learn letter forms, distinguish letters from one another by their features, and connect beginning sounds and letters.

Think about the kinds of literacy props that can be added to the block, sand/water, art, and drama (role play) centers so that children can see how what they are learning about letters, sounds, and words can be applied to their world.

Organization of Instruction: *Whole group; increased independent work with teacher circulating to observe, interact, and provide support.*

Learning Contexts	New Routines to Teach	Suggested Lessons	Assessment—Children Can:
Continue developing elements of the Language and Literacy Framework, giving increased time for independent work including writing and drawing. Add one or two independent activities, for example, "listening center," puzzles, looking at books. Add one independent phonics/word study application activity after the routine has been learned. Establish responsibility for taking home materials and using them as directed. (Work with family members as well.)	► Working independently in centers: listening, puzzles, games, looking at books, drawing, writing, and others as appropriate, introducing one at a time. ► Sorting picture cards. ► Lotto using pictures to match.	**PA 8** Hearing Beginning Sounds (Picture Match) **PA 9** Hearing Beginning Sounds (Picture Match) **LK 6** Making Letters (Art Materials) **LK 7** Learning Letter Forms and Names (Letter Match) **WSA 1** Making Connections Between Names and Other Words (Name Lotto) **WSA 2** Using Letter/Sound Analysis (Writing Words)	► Match more pictures of words with the same sound at the beginning. ► Match letters by looking at their features. ► Say words slowly to hear more than one sound. ► Say most letter names. ► Construct words in writing using known letter/sound relationships.

December

By now you will have fully established the phonics lesson/application activity/sharing routine. As you make more connections across the Language and Literacy Framework, you will find that children are beginning to make their own connections. They will notice known words, letters, and parts of words during read-alouds, shared reading, and interactive writing; they will also actively use letter/sound knowledge to write more complete words independently. Increase the time children spend rereading the texts you've used in shared reading. Many of the children will be pointing, reading simple texts accurately, and monitoring their reading using some knowledge of letters and sounds.

While children are working independently, you may want to bring together small guided reading groups (two or three children at a time) who can read simple texts at level A or B (see Fountas and Pinnell 1996). In guided reading, you can help your students take on new texts that have not been read to them. These first guided reading groups will be quite short, five or ten minutes, so you will still have time to assist individuals while they are working independently on word study applications and other activities at centers. Add some literacy centers such as poetry, pocket chart, or listening centers.

Establish "sorting" as a generic activity that children can apply to many different concepts (letters, pictures, words, objects, etc.). Also be sure that children understand the routine of "reading" a book: moving from the front cover onward, one page at a time, pointing to each word and saying it, and looking at the pictures. Practicing this routine will help children realize that reading is not simply flipping through a book. Also work with children to strengthen handwriting, beginning with their names. The routine of writing their names in letter order in the best handwriting they can manage will help them realize that letters are written in a particular way.

Also begin developing a small core of high frequency words that children can read, build, and write. You'll work all year to establish the twenty-five high frequency words for kindergarten, and these words will be important in helping children begin to read simple texts. Children use these known words as "anchors" to help them check on their reading.

In December, select lessons that help children use their names as resources, develop the concepts of "first" and "last" as they relate to print, hear ending sounds of words, internalize more high frequency words, notice letter features, learn more letter names, and explore letter/sound relationships for consonants. Encourage children to write and help them learn to hold pencils or markers correctly.

Assess your use of literacy props such as fiction and nonfiction books, pencils, pens, markers, notepads, telephone books, menus, empty food containers, magnetic letters, cookbooks, catalogs, recipe cards, or a telephone in structured play centers.

Organization of Instruction: *Whole group; independent work—some without teacher circulating; one or two small groups.*

Learning Contexts	New Routines to Teach	Suggested Lessons	Assessment—Children Can:
Continue using elements of the Language and Literacy Framework, including phonics lesson and application. Assess children's knowledge of letters, sounds, and early literacy concepts and convene at least one guided reading group (if appropriate). Increase children's experience in reading and rereading very simple books. Use the name chart, Alphabet Linking Chart, and word wall as tools. Increase time in independent activities.	▸ "Sorting" as a routine that can be used in many ways (letters, pictures, names, other words). ▸ "Independent reading" as a routine—go through the whole book, pointing, etc. ▸ "Independent writing" as making letters using specific directions in order and checking them. ▸ Using a model to build and write words. ▸ Using the Making Words Sheet to record words. ▸ Matching words by looking at letters.	**ELC 4** Sorting and Connecting Names (Three-Way Sort) **ELC 5** Recognizing First and Last Letters (Making Names) **ELC 6** Locating *First* and *Last* in Print (Little Books) **PA 10** Hearing Ending Sounds (Picture Sort) **PA 11** Hearing Ending Sounds (Picture Lotto) **LK 8** Learning Letters (Alphabet Soup Game) **LK 9** Learning Letter Names (Letter Minibooks) **LK 10** Learning Letters in Names (Name Graph) **LK 11** Learning Letters in Names (Marching Game) **LK 12** Learning to Write Your Name (Name Card Trace) **LS 1** Beginning Consonant Letters and Sounds (Pocket Chart Match) **LS 2** Connecting Beginning Sounds and Letters (Picture-Word Match) **HF 1** Building and Writing High Frequency Words 1 (Making Words) **WM 1** Learning Color Words (Matching Words)	▸ Recognize and match color words. ▸ Identify first and last in sentences. ▸ Identify first and last letters in words. ▸ Hear and identify the last sound of words. ▸ Make connections between names by letters, sounds, and letter patterns. ▸ Write their names accurately and legibly. ▸ Write some known high frequency words.

Month-by-Month Planning Guide—January

In January, you may want to add one or two more guided reading groups as appropriate for the children in your class. Establish specific "browsing boxes" that contain books children have read previously in shared reading or in guided reading groups or that you know will be easy enough for them to read independently. Many teachers demonstrate the routine of taking out three books, reading each from front to back, and replacing them in the box before going on to the next activity. Oral rereading helps children build fluency and remember words and features of words visually.

Continue to add words to the word wall as a regular feature of your word study lesson. For example, when working with phonograms to build words, select one or two examples and place them on the word wall; also continue to introduce more high frequency words. Introduce new routines to teach word study applications: Concentration, matching pictures whose labels have the same middle sound, locating words in

print, building words using phonograms, and substituting a different first letter to make a new word. As children learn these routines, they will become more flexible in working with words and will make many discoveries beyond your teaching. Encourage them to talk about their discoveries during sharing time. Select lessons that help children consolidate letter knowledge, learn to hear sounds in the middle of words, generate rhyming words, internalize more high frequency words, build words using the easy phonogram -at, and make new words by changing letters. Work for full control of the names of letters and the common sounds associated with consonants.

Kindergarten children will continue to learn more about environmental print and other functional uses of print in the structured play opportunities you plan for the block, sand/water, drama, and art centers. Children will need many other literacy opportunities in listening, reading, and writing centers.

Organization of Instruction: *Whole group; independent work—some without teacher circulating; one or two small groups.*

Learning Contexts	New Routines to Teach	Suggested Lessons	Assessment—Children Can:
Continue using all elements of the Language and Literacy Framework; add guided reading groups as appropriate. Establish "browsing boxes" and the new routines associated with them. As children acquire more high frequency words and as you use phonograms in the minilessons, add exemplar words to the word wall. Increase the time children spend on reading and rereading simple texts and on writing.	► "Concentration." ► Matching pictures of words with the same middle sound. ► Sorting letters. ► Locating words in print. ► Building words using phonograms. ► Substituting the first letter to make a new word.	**PA 12** Hearing Ending Sounds (Picture Cards) **PA 13** Making Rhymes (Picture Concentration) **PA 14** Hearing and Producing Rhymes (Rhyming Lotto) **PA 15** Hearing Long Vowel Sounds in the Middle of Words (Picture Match) **LK 13** Learning to Look at Letter Features 1 (Letter Sort) **LK 14** Learning to Look at Letter Features 2 (Letter Sort) **LS 3** Beginning Consonant Letters and Sounds (Picture Sort) **LS 4** Beginning Consonant Letters and Sounds (Picture Lotto) **LS 5** Beginning Consonant Letters and Sounds (Finding Words in Print) **SP 1** Noticing Word Features (Two-Way Sort) **SP 2** Making Words with -at (Magnetic Letters) **HF 2** Building and Writing High Frequency Words 2 (Making Words) **WM 2** Locating Color Words in Text (Words in Poems) **WSA 3** Making New Words by Changing the First Letter 1 (Magnetic Letters)	► Hear and generate rhymes. ► Build words using the known phonogram -at. ► Notice several features of letters and sort letters by feature. ► Reading and write one- to three-letter high frequency words. ► Make a new word by changing the first letter. ► Write more known high frequency words. ► Construct words in writing using known letter/sound relationships.

February

The word wall will become an increasingly important tool as children add words to it and use it as a resource in writing and word study. Also work to establish the Alphabet Linking Chart as a tool for making connections. Increase the amount of reading and writing children do independently, and add reading groups as appropriate. Children will have learned to hold and use a pencil or marker for drawing and writing and, with your support, can increase their control over this manual task. You will have been describing letter formation verbally; now undertake more formal handwriting instruction by teaching children to recount the verbal path themselves and be more conscious of the way they write letters.

Teach the Trip and Line-Up games as an ongoing quick way for children to practice the knowledge they've developed so far. (For example, to line up, each child says a word that starts with /p/ or a word that contains *-at*.) Once the children have learned these games, you can fill transitional moments with opportunities to learn in an enjoyable way.

You will have been working for some time on matching word by word in reading, but now you will want to use explicit instruction to bring this early skill under full control for texts that have just a few lines.

In February, select lessons that help children blend syllables, hear and use the first and last sounds of words, develop efficient ways of writing letters and words, make words with a wider range of phonograms, make new words using their current knowledge, internalize more high frequency words, and use what they know about letters, sounds, and words to help them read unfamiliar texts.

Continue to guide small groups of two or three children who would benefit from reading little books with your support. With all the children, continue shared and interactive writing and a writing workshop. Freshen up the centers with new literacy props.

Organization of Instruction: *Whole group; independent work with teacher circulating on new routines; one or two small groups.*

Learning Contexts	**New Routines to Teach**	**Suggested Lessons**	**Assessment—Children Can:**
Continue to add words to the word wall and use it as a tool. Help children notice word parts in their names as you work with phonograms. Use Line-Up games to do quick practice of principles that they know (such as first and last sounds of words). Increase the time children spend on reading and rereading texts as well as on writing.	▶ Line-Up games using various kinds of knowledge ▶ "Trip" game. ▶ Using a verbal path (saying directions while writing a letter). ▶ Naming letters in words (spelling). ▶ Pointing to words while reading.	**PA 16** Blending Syllables (Syllable Lotto) **PA 17** Hearing First and Last Sounds (Writing Words) **PA 18** Hearing and Saying Beginning Sounds (Trip and Line-Up Games) **LK 15** Identifying Letters in Words ("Bingo" Song) **LK 16** Learning to Form Letters (Verbal Path) **SP 3** Making Words with *-an* (Magnetic Letters) **SP 4** Making Words with *-ay* (Magnetic Letters) **HF 3** Recognizing High Frequency Words (Word Lotto) **HF 4** Building and Writing High Frequency Words 3 (Making Words) **WM 3** Learning Number Words (Matching Words) **WSA 4** Making New Words by Changing the First Letter (Magnetic Letters) **WSA 5** Using Known Words in Simple Texts (Cut-Up Sentences)	▶ Identify and blend syllables to say a word. ▶ Use the Alphabet Linking Chart to make connections to words. ▶ Identify and name letters in words. ▶ Use a verbal path to help in making letters efficiently. ▶ Build words using known phonograms *-an* and *-ay*. ▶ Use known words to check on their reading. ▶ Write more known high frequency words. ▶ Construct words in writing using known letter/sound relationships.

Month-by-Month Planning Guide—March

By the end of March, provide small-group instruction in guided reading for most children and, by late spring, aim to include all children in guided reading. You'll determine your course of instruction based on your assessments of individual students. A short period of small-group instruction each day is beneficial to all children, especially those who have difficulty with shared reading and independent work. Guided reading groups enable you to establish early reading behaviors and help children give more attention to the details of print. You will also want to continue writing workshops—minilesson, independent work with conferring, and sharing. Children will be writing and drawing as before but beginning to produce longer pieces with more accurately spelled words and more complete approximations. Remember that saying words slowly and representing sounds with letters and letter clusters are the best ways to help children learn letter/sound relationships.

You will teach new word study applications such as Follow the Path and Go Fish. You'll also want to be sure children understand sorting in a very flexible way; that is, they need to be able to look for and select several different patterns and features, in relation to both letters and words. Also, introduce the handwriting book and begin direct handwriting instruction. Children should now be using appropriate and efficient directional movements to make letters. Select lessons that help children build handwriting proficiency, hear and blend onsets and rimes, hear and substitute sounds to make new words in oral language, solidify learning of letter names and sounds, internalize more high frequency words, expand their knowledge of phonograms, and make words using a variety of information.

Work with children at a variety of centers where they can learn from each other as they participate in literacy experiences and other structured play opportunities.

Organization of Instruction: *Whole group; independent work with teacher circulating on new routines; individual conferring; small groups to involve all children in a group.*

Learning Contexts	New Routines to Teach	Suggested Lessons	Assessment—Children Can:
Continue building children's knowledge of language and principles as you read stories and nonfiction texts aloud. Implement all elements of the Language and Literacy Framework, including participation of all children in guided reading. Increase time on writing and introduce minilessons. Help children write, confer, and share following the framework for writing workshop.	▶ Follow the Path. ▶ Go Fish. ▶ Sorting letters many ways. ▶ Using the handwriting book.	**PA 19** Hearing and Blending Onsets and Rimes (Follow the Path) **PA 20** Identifying and Blending Onsets and Rimes (Go Fish) **PA 21** Hearing and Substituting Sounds (Picture Cards) **LK 17** Recognizing Uppercase and Lowercase Letters (Two-Way Sort) **LK 18** Recognizing Uppercase and Lowercase Letters (Alphabet Lotto) **LK 19** Forming Letters (Handwriting Books) **LS 6** Learning Letters and Beginning Sounds (Class Alphabet Book) **LS 7** Learning Letter Names and Sounds (ABC Board) **SP 5** Making Words with *-and* (Magnetic Letters) **HF 5** Building and Writing High Frequency Words 4 (Making Words) **WM 4** Locating Numerals and Number Words in Text (Making Words)	▶ Say first and last parts of words (onsets and rimes). ▶ Blend onsets and rimes. ▶ Read the Alphabet Linking Chart and other alphabet charts. ▶ Build and write about half of the twenty-five high frequency words. ▶ Make words with the known phonogram *–and*. ▶ Recognize beginning and ending sounds in words. ▶ Identify letters by name and related sound. ▶ Add continually to writing vocabulary. ▶ Read simple texts (level A) independently with introduction and support.

April

Continue implementing all elements of the Language and Literacy Framework, especially reading aloud and shared reading. Continue to work for five to ten minutes with two or three children at a time in guided reading of little books. Provide continued opportunities for writing in a writing workshop, in a writing center, and in structured play centers. When your students enter first grade, they will encounter more complex texts containing concepts, language structure, and vocabulary that may go beyond their experiences. Hearing many kinds of stories and nonfiction texts will build a valuable foundation for later reading. Continue to use the word wall and Alphabet Linking Chart as tools and work to ensure that all children gain control of word-by-word matching in reading. Some children will now be able to follow along visually, so don't insist on pointing after it is clear their eyes are doing the work.

You will have worked across the Language and Literacy Framework components to help children expand their vocabulary. Direct attention to words helps children form categories by connecting word meanings as well as noticing how words look or sound.

In April, select lessons that help children make words through a variety of means (phonograms, for example), internalize more high frequency words, understand concept words, categorize words by meaning, and form letters efficiently and fluently while writing. Also work to help children use their knowledge of letters, sounds, and words to solve new words in reading. Teach a new routine: assemble a cut-up sentence and read it to check whether it makes sense.

Organization of Instruction: *Whole group; independent work with teacher circulating on new routines; individual conferring; small groups to involve all children in a group.*

Learning Contexts	New Routines to Teach	Suggested Lessons	Assessment—Children Can:
Continue implementing all elements of the Language and Literacy Framework; emphasize reading aloud to children to build principles and language knowledge. Continue guided reading, independent work, and writing workshop. Continue to add words to the word wall.	▶ Building cut-up sentences using a model to match.	**ELC 7** Matching Word by Word (Cut-Up Sentences) **PA 22** Hearing Middle Sounds (Two-Way Sort) **PA 23** Hearing Sounds in Sequence (Picture Cards) **LK 20** Learning to Form Letters (Handwriting Books) **LS 8** Recognizing Beginning and Ending Consonant Sounds (Making Words). **SP 6** Making Words with *-ake* (Magnetic Letters) **HF 6** Building and Writing High Frequency Words 5 (Making Words) **WM 5** Connecting Words That Go Together (Family Pictures) **WM 6** Learning the Days of the Week (Matching Words) **WM 7** Locating Days of the Week in Text (Making Sentences) **WS 1** Learning Words: Simple Plurals (Plural Concentration) **WSA 6** Using Parts of Words to Solve New Words (Highlighting Word Parts) **WSA 7** Changing Last Letters to Make New Words (Magnetic Letters) **WSA 8** Changing First and Last Letters to Make New Words (Magnetic Letters)	▶ Say and read the days of the week. ▶ Build most of the twenty-five high frequency words. ▶ Read and write most of the twenty-five high frequency words. ▶ Make words with known phonogram *-ake.* ▶ Make new words by changing first and last letters. ▶ Use known parts of words to solve unknown words in reading. ▶ Use known parts of words to spell (or attempt to spell) new words in writing. ▶ Continually add to writing vocabulary. ▶ Read simple texts (level A) independently. ▶ Read level B texts with support.

Month-by-Month Planning Guide—May/June

In many communities, the end of May and the first part of June mark the end of a year of learning. Remember that if your school year begins and ends at a different time, you'll need to adjust plans and expectations to whenever your year ends. Many children enter kindergarten knowing something about literacy; for others, print is a new world. But all children can leave kindergarten with a large and rich store of knowledge about stories, poems, rhymes, letters, sounds, and words. They know how to make words using patterns they recognize and/or by connecting individual letters with sounds. They can read very simple texts, and some will be able to read longer stories. Most important, they know how to use their knowledge of letters, sounds, and words within the context of reading and writing.

By the end of the kindergarten year, the children will feel like readers and writers as they have enjoyed extensive opportunities to participate in reading and writing texts and received explicit instruction with letters, sounds, and words. As emergent readers and writers, they will be well prepared to continue the literacy journey in the next school year.

In May and June, select lessons that help children become more skilled at hearing, identifying, and manipulating the individual sounds in words and in making and recognizing words with a range of easy phonograms or word patterns. Recognizing syllable breaks will help them begin to take apart longer words, and they will also become familiar with easy compound words. Children will enjoy consolidating their knowledge of the alphabet by using alphabetical order and learning to use their own initials and those of their friends.

Organization of Instruction: *Whole group; independent work with teacher circulating on new routines; individual conferring; small groups to involve all children in a group.*

Learning Contexts	New Routines to Teach	Suggested Lessons	Assessment — Children Can:
Continue implementing all elements of the Language and Literacy Framework; emphasize reading aloud to children to build principles and language knowledge. Continue guided reading, independent work, and writing workshop. Continue to add words to the word wall.	▶ Using alphabetical order. ▶ Recognizing components of words by noticing and using parts.	**ELC 8** Making Sentences (Little Books) **PA 24** Blending Sounds in Words (Lotto Game) **PA 25** Hearing, Saying, and Deleting Beginning Sounds (Picture Cards) **PA 26** Hearing and Deleting Sounds (Picture Cards) **LK 21** Labeling Consonants and Vowels (Letter Sort) **LK 22** Understanding Alphabetical Order (Magnetic Letters) **LK 23** Learning Alphabetical Order (Follow the Path) **LK 24** Learning the Initials for Names (Name Chart) **SP 7** Making Words with *-ike* (Magnetic Letters) **HF 7** Locating High Frequency Words in Text (Poems and Songs) **WS 2** Adding *s* to Change Word Meanings (Making Words) **WS 3** Learning about Compound Words (Highlighting Words) **WS 4** Recognizing Syllables (Syllable Sort) **WSA 9** Using Known Words to Solve New Words (Cut-Up Sentences)	▶ Make words using known phonograms *-at, -an, -ay, -and, -ake,* and *-ike.* ▶ Add *s* to words to achieve agreement in language structure. ▶ Take words apart to say syllables. ▶ Put letters in alphabetical order. ▶ Identify words within simple compound words. ▶ Use a known word or part of a word to read and write new words. ▶ Use known words or parts of words to check on their reading. ▶ Read level B texts independently. ▶ Read level C texts with support.

The Word Study Continuum

Systematic Phonics and Spelling, Grades K–3

The Word Study Continuum is the key to the minilessons. Over the course of the school year, you will use it, in concert with the Month-by-Month Planning Guide, the Lesson Selection Map, and continuous assessment, to inform your work. The Continuum comprises nine Categories of Learning your students need to develop over time; it is a comprehensive picture of linguistic knowledge. Although there are easier and more complex concepts within each category, we are not suggesting that there is a rigid sequence. Instead, we want to help children develop their abilities along a broad front, often using and learning about several different kinds of information simultaneously.

While instruction and assessment are embedded within classroom activities, both are systematic. Indeed, every aspect of the phonics minilessons is systematic, including the observation of children, collection of data on what children know about letters, sounds, and words; and the teacher's selection of lessons to fit the specific instructional needs of individual children. Teaching is efficient and systematic when lessons are carefully selected and sequenced to provide what children need to learn next.

The shaded area of the Continuum performs two important functions. First, it serves as a guide for introducing principles to children; second, it helps you understand what principles you can expect your students to fully control and when. You'll notice that the shaded areas cross grade levels. These shaded areas provide broad indicators of expected achievement; however, learning rate and time will vary with individual children as well as for different groups. In general, at grade level (the earliest period of time indicated by shading), you can begin to assess children's knowledge of a specific principle and refer to the principle during reading and writing activities. Additionally, you will select specific lessons that help them expand their knowledge of the chosen principle. At the latest time indicated by shading, take steps to ensure that children fully understand and can use the principle. You may need to increase time spent on lessons related to the principle or work with small groups of children who are still having difficulty.

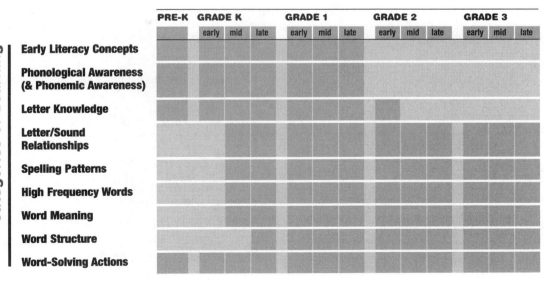

Early Literacy Concepts

Learning about literacy begins long before children enter school. Many children hear stories read aloud and try out writing for themselves; through such experiences, they learn some basic concepts about written language. Nearly all children begin to notice print in the environment and develop ideas about the purposes of print. The child's name, for example, is a very important word. Kindergartners and first graders are still acquiring some of these basic concepts, and they need to generalize and systematize their knowledge. In the classroom, they learn a great deal through experiences like shared and modeled reading and shared and interactive writing. Explicit teaching can help children learn much more about these early concepts, understand their importance, and develop ways of using them in reading and writing.

Early Literacy Concepts

PRINCIPLE	EXPLANATION OF PRINCIPLE
Distinguishing between print and pictures	" We read the print to find out what the words say. "
Understanding the purpose of print in reading	" We look at the print to read the words in stories and other messages. "
Understanding the purpose of print in writing	" We write letters and words so readers will understand what we mean. "
Recognizing one's name	" Your name has letters in it. " " Your name starts with a letter that is always the same. " " Your name starts with a capital letter. The other letters are lowercase. " " Your name is always written the same way. " " You can find your name by looking for the first letter. "
Using letters in one's own name to represent it or "write" a message	" You can write the letters in your name. " " You can use the letters in your name along with other letters to write messages. "
Understanding the concept of "letter"	" A letter has a name and a shape. "
Understanding the concept of "word"	" A word is a group of sounds that means something. " " A word in writing is a group of letters with space on either side. "
Using left-to-right directionality of print	" We read and write from left to right. "
Understanding the concepts of "first" and "last" in written language	" The first word in a sentence is on the left. " " The last word in a sentence is before the period or question mark. " " The first letter in a word is on the left. " " The last letter in a word is before the space. " " The first part of a page is at the top. " " The last part of a page is at the bottom. "
Understanding that one spoken word matches one group of letters	" We say one word for each word we see in writing. "
Using one's name to learn about words and make connections to words	" Your name is a word. " " You can connect your name with other words. "

Column headers (spanning across the Explanation of Principle section):
PRE-K | GRADE K (early, mid, late) | GRADE 1 (early, mid, late) | GRADE 2 (early, mid, late) | GRADE 3 (early, mid, late)

Early Literacy Concepts, continued

PRINCIPLE	EXPLANATION OF PRINCIPLE

	PRE-K	GRADE K			GRADE 1			GRADE 2			GRADE 3		
		early	mid	late	early	mid	late	early	mid	late	early	mid	late

Locating the first and last letters of words in continuous text

" You can find a word by noticing how it looks. "
" You can find a word by looking for the first letter. "
" You can check a word by looking at the first and last letters. "

Understanding the concept of a sentence

" A sentence is a group of words that makes sense. "

	early	mid	late	early	mid	late	early	mid	late	early	mid	late
	PRE-K	GRADE K			GRADE 1			GRADE 2			GRADE 3		

ELC
EARLY LITERACY CONCEPTS

Phonological Awareness

Phonological awareness is a broad term that refers to both explicit and implicit knowledge of the sounds in language. It includes the ability to hear and identify words (word awareness), rhymes (rhyme awareness), syllables (syllable awareness), onsets and rimes (onset and rime awareness), and individual sounds (sound awareness).

Phonemic awareness is one kind of phonological awareness. Phonemic awareness refers to the ability to identify, isolate, and manipulate the individual sounds *(phonemes)* in words. Principles categorized as phonemic awareness are labeled Phonemes [PA] in this Continuum.

Phonological awareness (and phonemic awareness) is taught orally or in connection with letters, when it is called *phonics.* Phonics instruction refers to teaching children to connect letters and sounds in words. While very early experiences focus on hearing and saying sounds in the absence of letters, most of the time you will want to teach children to hear sounds in connection with letters. Many of the lessons related to this section begin with oral activity but move toward connecting the sounds to letters. You will not want to teach all of the PA principles in this Continuum. It is more effective to teach children only two or three ways to manipulate phonemes in words so that they learn how words work.

Principles related to letter/sound relationships, or phonics, are included in the letter/sound relationships category of this Continuum.

Phonological Awareness

PRINCIPLE	EXPLANATION OF PRINCIPLE
Words	
Hearing and recognizing word boundaries	" You say words when you talk. " " You can hear words in a sentence if you stop after each one. [*I - have - a - dog.*] "
Segmenting sentences into words	" You can say each word in a sentence. [*I - like -to - go - shopping.*] "
Rhyming Words	
Hearing and saying rhyming words	" Some words have end parts that sound alike. They *rhyme* [*new, blue*]. " " You can hear the rhymes in poems and songs. " " You can say words and hear how they rhyme. "
Hearing and connecting rhyming words	" You can hear and connect words that rhyme [*fly, high, buy, sky*]. "
Hearing and generating rhyming words	" You can make rhymes by thinking of words that end the same. [*I can fly in the ____.*] "

Grade bands (both top and bottom of chart): PRE-K | GRADE K (early, mid, late) | GRADE 1 (early, mid, late) | GRADE 2 (early, mid, late) | GRADE 3 (early, mid, late)

Phonological Awareness, continued

PRINCIPLE	EXPLANATION OF PRINCIPLE

Syllables

Hearing and saying syllables
" You can hear and say the syllables in a word [*to-ma-to, tomato*]. "
" Some words have one syllable [*cat*]. "
" Some words have two syllables [*can-dy, candy*]. "
" Some words have three or more syllables [*um-brel-la, umbrella*]. "

Blending syllables
" You can blend syllables together [*pen-cil, pencil*]. "

Onsets and Rimes

Hearing and segmenting onsets and rimes
" You can hear and say the first and last parts of a word [*c-ar, car; pl-ay, play*]. "

Blending onsets with rimes
" You can blend word parts together [*d-og, dog*]. "

Phonemes [PA]

Hearing and saying individual phonemes (sounds) in words
" You can say a word slowly. "
" You can hear the sounds in a word [*m-a-k, make*]. "

Segmenting words into phonemes
" You can say each sound in a word [*b-a-t*]. "

Hearing and saying two or three phonemes in a word
" You can say a word slowly to hear all the sounds [*r-u-n*]. "

Hearing and saying beginning phonemes in words
" You can hear the first sound in a word [*s-u-n*]. "
" You can say a word to hear the first sound. "

Hearing and saying ending phonemes in words
" You can hear the last sound in a word [*r-u-n*]. "
" You can say a word to hear the last sound. "

Hearing similar beginning phonemes in words
" Some words sound the same at the beginning [*run, race*]. "
" You can connect words that sound the same at the beginning [*mother, mom, make*]. "

Hearing similar ending phonemes in words
" Some words sound the same at the end [*win, fun*]. "
" You can connect words that sound the same at the end [*get, sit, Matt*]. "

Blending two or three phonemes in words
" You can blend sounds together to say a word [*d-o-g = dog*]. "

Adding phonemes to the beginning of words
" You can add sounds to a word [*it + s = sit*]. "
" You can add sounds to the beginning of a word [*rate + c = crate*]. "

Manipulating phonemes at the beginning of words
" You can change the first sound in a word to make a new word [*not, hot*]. "

Manipulating phonemes at the ending of words
" You can change the last sound in a word to make a new word [*his, him*]. "

Hearing and saying middle phonemes in words
" You can hear and say the sound in the middle of a word [*s-u-n*]. "

Hearing similar middle phonemes in words
" Some words sound the same in the middle [*cat, ran*]. "
" You can match words that sound the same in the middle [*stop, hot, John*]. "

Hearing four or more phonemes in a word
" You can say a word slowly to hear all the sounds [*s-p-e-n-d*]. "

Grade columns header: PRE-K | GRADE K (early mid late) | GRADE 1 (early mid late) | GRADE 2 (early mid late) | GRADE 3 (early mid late)

PA
PHONOLOGICAL AWARENESS

Phonological Awareness, continued

Phonemes [PA]

Principle	Explanation of Principle
	EXPLANATION OF PRINCIPLE

	PRE-K	GRADE K			GRADE 1			GRADE 2			GRADE 3		
		early	mid	late	early	mid	late	early	mid	late	early	mid	late

Hearing and identifying phonemes in a word in sequence
" You can say a word slowly to hear all the sounds, from first to last [/r/ *(first)*, /u/ *(next)*, /n/ *(last)* = *run*]. "
" You can write the letter or letters for each sound. "

Blending three or four phonemes in words
" You can blend sounds together to say a word [*n-e-s-t = nest*]. "

Deleting phonemes in words
" You can say words without some of the sounds [*can – c = an; sand – s = and*]. "
" You can say a word without the first sound [*ch – air = air*]. "
" You can say a word without the last sound [*ant – t = an*]. "

Adding phonemes to the end of words
" You can add sounds to the end of a word [*an + d = and; and + y = Andy*]. "

Manipulating phonemes in the middle of words
" You can change the sounds in the middle of a word to make a new word [*hit, hot*]. "

		early	mid	late	early	mid	late	early	mid	late	early	mid	late
	PRE-K	GRADE K			GRADE 1			GRADE 2			GRADE 3		

Letter Knowledge

Letter knowledge refers to what children need to learn about the graphic characters that correspond with the sounds of language. A finite set of twenty-six letters, two forms of each, is related to all of the sounds of the English language (approximately forty-four phonemes). The sounds in the language change as dialect, articulation, and other speech factors vary. Children will also encounter alternative forms of some letters—for example, g, g; a, a; y, y—and will eventually learn to recognize letters in cursive writing. Children need to learn the names and purposes of letters, as well as the particular features of each. When children can identify letters by noticing the very small differences that make them unique, they can then associate letters and letter clusters with phonemes and parts of words. Knowing the letter names is useful information that helps children talk about letters and understand what others say about them. As writers, children need to be able to use efficient directional movements when making letters.

Letter Knowledge

Identifying Letters

PRINCIPLE	EXPLANATION OF PRINCIPLE
	PRE-K / GRADE K (early, mid, late) / GRADE 1 (early, mid, late) / GRADE 2 (early, mid, late) / GRADE 3 (early, mid, late)
Understanding the concept of a letter	" The alphabet has twenty-six letters. " " A letter has a name and a shape. "
Distinguishing letter forms	" Letters are different from each other. " " You can notice the parts of letters. " " Some letters have long sticks. Some letters have short sticks. " " Some letters have curves, circles, tunnels, tails, crosses, dots, slants. "
Producing letter names	" You can look at the shape of a letter and say its name. "
Categorizing letters by features	" You can find parts of letters that look the same. " " You can find the letters that have long sticks [short sticks, curves, circles, tunnels, tails, crosses, dots, slants]. "
Understanding alphabetical order	" The letters in the alphabet are in a special order. "
Recognizing uppercase and lowercase letters	" A letter has two forms. One form is uppercase (or capital) and the other is lowercase (or small) [B, b]. " " Your name starts with an uppercase letter. " " The other letters in your name are lowercase letters. " " Some lowercase forms look like the uppercase forms [W, w] and some look different [R, r]. "
Recognizing letters that represent consonant and vowel sounds	" Some letters are consonants [b, c, d, f, g, h, j, k, l, m, n, p, q, r, s, t, v, w, x, y, z]. " " Some letters are vowels [a, e, i, o, u, and sometimes y and w]. " " Every word has a vowel. "
Understanding special uses of letters	" Your initials are the first letters of your first name and your last name. " " You use capital letters to write your initials. "

(table footer scale:) PRE-K / GRADE K (early, mid, late) / GRADE 1 (early, mid, late) / GRADE 2 (early, mid, late) / GRADE 3 (early, mid, late)

Letter Knowledge, continued

PRE-K | GRADE K (early, mid, late) | GRADE 1 (early, mid, late) | GRADE 2 (early, mid, late) | GRADE 3 (early, mid, late)

	Principle	Explanation of Principle
Recognizing Letters in Words and Sentences	Understanding that words are made up of letters	"Words have letters in them." "Your name has letters in it." "You can say the first letter of your name."
	Making connections between words by recognizing letters	"You can find words that have the same letters in them."
	Recognizing the sequence of letters in words	"Letters in a word are always in the same order." "The first letter is on the left." "You can find the first letter in a word."
	Recognizing letters in words	"You can find letters in words." "You can say the names of letters in words."
	Recognizing letters in continuous text	"You can find letters in sentences and stories."
	Making connections between words by recognizing letter placement	"You can find words that begin with the same letter." "You can find words that end with the same letter." "You can find words that have the same letter in the middle."
Forming Letters	Using efficient and consistent motions to form letters	"You can make the shape of a letter." "You can say words that help you learn how to make a letter." "You can check to see if your letter looks right."

PRE-K | GRADE K (early, mid, late) | GRADE 1 (early, mid, late) | GRADE 2 (early, mid, late) | GRADE 3 (early, mid, late)

Letter/Sound Relationships

The sounds of oral language are related in both simple and complex ways to the twenty-six letters of the alphabet. Learning the connections between letters and sounds is basic to understanding written language. Children first learn simple relationships that are regular in that one phoneme is connected to one grapheme, or letter. But sounds are also connected to letter clusters, which are groups of letters that appear often together (for example, *cr, str, st, bl, fr*), in which you hear each of the associated sounds of the letters; and consonant digraphs *(sh, ch)*, in which you hear only one sound. Vowels may also appear in combinations *(ea, oa)* in which you usually hear the first vowel *(ai)* or you hear a completely different sound *(ou)*. Children learn to look for and recognize these letter combinations as units, which makes their word solving more efficient. It is important to remember that children will be able to hear and connect the easy-to-identify consonants and vowels early and progress to the harder-to-hear and more difficult letter/sound relationships—for example, letter clusters with two and three letters and those that have more than one sound. You will want to connect initial letter sounds to the Alphabet Linking Chart (see *Teaching Resources*). It is not necessary to teach every letter as a separate lesson. When using the children's names to teach about words, substitute *name* for *word* when explaining the principle.

Letter/Sound Relationships

PRINCIPLE	EXPLANATION OF PRINCIPLE

		PRE-K	GRADE K			GRADE 1			GRADE 2			GRADE 3		
			early	mid	late	early	mid	late	early	mid	late	early	mid	late

Consonants

Recognizing that letters represent consonant sounds
" You can match letters and sounds in words. For example: *b* is the letter that stands for the first sound in *bear*. "

Recognizing and using beginning consonant sounds and the letters that represent them:
s, m, t, b, f, r, n,
p, d, h, c, g, j, l,
k, v, w, z, qu, y, x
" You can hear the sound at the beginning of a word. "
" You can match letters and sounds at the beginning of a word. "
" When you see a letter at the beginning of a word, you can make its sound. "
" When you know the sound, you can find the letter. "
" You can find a word by saying it and thinking about the first sound. "

Recognizing similar beginning consonant sounds and the letters that represent them
" Words can start with the same sound and letter [*box, big*]. "

Recognizing and using ending consonant sounds and the letters that represent them:
b, m, t, d g, n,
p, f, l, r, s, z, x,
ss, ll, tt, ck
" You can hear the sounds at the end of a word. "
" You can match letters and sounds at the end of a word. "
" When you see a letter at the end of a word, you can make its sound. "
" When you know the sound, you can find the letter. "
" You can find a word by saying it and thinking about the ending sound. "

Recognizing similar ending consonant sounds and the letters that represent them
" Words can end with the same sound and letter [*duck, book*]. "

Recognizing and using middle consonant sounds sometimes represented by double letters:
bb, dd, ll, mm,
nn, pp, rr, tt, zz
" You can hear consonant sounds in the middle of a word. "
" You can match letters and sounds in the middle of a word. "
" When you see letters in the middle of a word, you can make their sound. "
" When you know the sound in the middle of a word, you can find the letter. "
" Sometimes two consonant letters stand for the consonant sound in the middle of a word. "
" You can find words by saying the word and thinking about the sound in the middle. "

	early	mid	late	early	mid	late	early	mid	late	early	mid	late
PRE-K	GRADE K			GRADE 1			GRADE 2			GRADE 3		

PRINCIPLE

Consonants

Recognizing and using consonant sounds represented by consonant digraphs: *sh, ch, th, ph* (at the beginning or end of a word), and *wh*

Recognizing and using letters that represent two or more consonant sounds at the beginning of a word: *c, g, th, ch*

Recognizing and using consonant clusters that blend two or three consonant sounds (onsets): *bl, cl, fl, pl, pr, br, dr, gr, tr, cr, fr, gl, sl, sn, sp, st, sw, sc, sk, sm, scr, squ, str, thr, spr, spl, shr, sch, tw*

Recognizing and using consonant letters that represent no sound: *lamb, light*

Recognizing and using letters that represent consonant clusters at the end of a word: *ct, ft, ld, lp, lt, mp, nd, nk, nt, pt, rd, rk, sk, sp, st*

Recognizing and using letters that represent consonant digraph sounds at the end of a word (making one sound): *sh, th, ch, ck, tch, dge, ng, ph, gh*

Recognizing and using letters that represent less frequent consonant digraph sounds at the beginning of a word (making one sound): *gh, gn, kn, ph, wr*

Vowels

Understanding letters that represent consonant sounds or vowel sounds

Hearing and identifying short vowel sounds in words and the letters that represent them

Recognizing and using short vowel sounds at the beginning of words: *at, apple*

EXPLANATION OF PRINCIPLE

	PRE-K	GRADE K			GRADE 1			GRADE 2			GRADE 3		
		early	mid	late	early	mid	late	early	mid	late	early	mid	late

Recognizing and using consonant sounds represented by consonant digraphs:
- " Some clusters of consonants stand for one sound that is different from either of the letters. They are called consonant digraphs. "
- " You can hear the sound of a consonant digraph at the beginning or end of a word. "
- " You can match a consonant digraph at the beginning or end of a word with its sound. "
- " You can find words by saying the word and thinking about the sound of the consonant digraph. "

Recognizing and using letters that represent two or more consonant sounds:
- " Some consonants make two or more different sounds [*car, city; get, gym; think, they; chair, chorus, chateau*]. "

Recognizing and using consonant clusters that blend:
- " Some consonants go together in clusters. "
- " A group of two or three consonants is a consonant cluster. "
- " You can hear each sound in a consonant cluster. "
- " You can hear and connect consonant clusters at the beginning of words. "
- " You can hear and connect consonant clusters at the end of words. "
- " You can find a word by saying the word and thinking about the first (or ending) sounds. "
- " Knowing a consonant cluster helps you read and write words. "

Recognizing and using consonant letters that represent no sound:
- " Some words have consonant letters that are silent. "

Recognizing and using letters that represent consonant clusters at the end of a word:
- " You can hear each sound in a consonant cluster at the end of a word. "
- " You can hear and connect consonant clusters at the end of words. "
- " You can find a word by saying it and thinking about the ending sounds. "
- " Knowing an ending consonant cluster helps you read and write words. "

Recognizing and using letters that represent consonant digraph sounds at the end of a word:
- " You can hear the sound in a consonant digraph at the end of a word. "
- " You can connect a consonant digraph at the end of a word with its sound. "
- " You can find a word by saying it and thinking about the last sound (consonant digraph). "

Recognizing and using letters that represent less frequent consonant digraph sounds at the beginning of a word:
- " You can hear the sound of a consonant digraph at the beginning of a word. "
- " You can connect a consonant digraph at the beginning of a word with its sound. "
- " You can find a word by saying it and thinking about the first sound (consonant digraph). "

Understanding letters that represent consonant sounds or vowel sounds:
- " Some letters are consonants and some letters are vowels. "
- " Every word has a vowel sound. "
- " A, e i, o, and u are vowels (and sometimes y and w). "

Hearing and identifying short vowel sounds:
- " In some words, a sounds like the a in *apple* and *can*. "
- " In some words, e sounds like the e in *egg* and *net*. "
- " In some words, i sounds like the i in *igloo* and *sit*. "
- " In some words, o sounds like the o in *octopus* and *hot*. "
- " In some words, u sounds like the u in *umbrella* and *up*. "

Recognizing and using short vowel sounds at the beginning of words:
- " Some words have one vowel at the beginning [*apple, at, Andrew*]. "
- " The sound of the vowel is *short*. "

	PRE-K	GRADE K			GRADE 1			GRADE 2			GRADE 3		
		early	mid	late	early	mid	late	early	mid	late	early	mid	late

PRINCIPLE	EXPLANATION OF PRINCIPLE

Vowels

Recognizing and using short vowel sounds in the middle of words (CVC): *hat, bed*
> " Some words have one vowel between two consonants [*hat, bed*] and the sound of the vowel is *short*. "

Hearing and identifying long vowel sounds in words and the letters that represent them
> " In some words, a sounds like the *a* in *name* and *came*. "
> " In some words, e sounds like the *e* in *eat* and *seat*. "
> " In some words, i sounds like the *i* in *ice* and *kite*. "
> " In some words, o sounds like the *o* in *go* and *boat*. "
> " In some words, u sounds like the *u* in *use* and *cute*. "

Recognizing and using long vowel sounds in words
> " You can hear and say the vowel in words like *make, pail, day*. "
> " You can hear and say the vowel in words like *eat, meat, see*. "
> " You can hear and say the vowel in words like *I, ice, ride*. "
> " You can hear and say the vowel in words like *go, grow, boat*. "
> " You can hear and say the vowel in words like *use, cute, huge*. "

Recognizing and using vowels in words with silent *e* (CVC*e*): *make, take, home*
A: *make, ate, take, came, same, base*
[Exceptions: *are, dance*]
E: *Pete, breeze* [Exception: *edge*]
I: *bite, bike, five, ice, slime, shine*
[Exceptions: *mince, fringe*]
O: *rode, hole, joke* [Exceptions: *come, some, goose*]
U: *use, cube, cute, fume*
[Exceptions: *judge, nurse*]
> " Some words end in an *e* that is silent and the vowel usually has the long sound (sounds like its name). "

Contrasting long and short vowel sounds in words
> " A vowel can have a sound like its name [*a* as in *make*], and this is called a long vowel sound. "
> " A vowel can have a sound that is different from its name [*a* as in *apple*], and this is called a short vowel sound. "

Recognizing and using *y* as a vowel sound: *happy, family, my, sky*
> " *Y* is a letter that sometimes makes a vowel sound. "
> " *Y* sounds like *e* on the end of words like *happy, funny, family*. "
> " *Y* sounds like *i* in words like *my, sky, by*. "

Recognizing and using other vowel sounds: *oo* as in *moon, look*; *oi* as in *oil*; *oy* as in *boy*; *ou* as in *house*; *ow* as in *cow*; *aw* as in *paw*
> " Some letters go together and make other vowel sounds [*moon, look, oil, boy, house, cow, paw*]. "

Recognizing and using letter combinations that represent long vowel sounds: *ai, ay, ee, ea, oa, ow, ie, ei*
> " Some vowels go together in words and make one sound. "
> " When there are two vowels [*ai, ay, ee, ea, oa, ow*], they usually make the sound of the name of the first vowel [*rain, day, meat, seat, snow*]. "

Recognizing and using vowel sounds in open syllables: (CV): *ho-tel*
> " Some syllables have a consonant followed by a vowel. "
> " The sound of the vowel is long [*ho-tel, Pe-ter, lo-cal*]. "

Recognizing and using vowel sounds in closed syllables: (CVC): *lem-on*
> " Some syllables have a vowel that is surrounded by two consonants. "
> " The sound of the vowel is short [*lem-on; cab-in*]. "

Recognizing and using vowel sounds with *r*: *car, first, hurt, her, corn*
> " When vowels are with *r* in words, you blend the vowel sound with *r* [*car, her, fir, corn, hurt*]. "

	PRE-K	GRADE K			GRADE 1			GRADE 2			GRADE 3		
		early	mid	late	early	mid	late	early	mid	late	early	mid	late

LS LETTER/SOUND RELATIONSHIPS

Spelling Patterns

Phonograms are spelling patterns that represent the sounds of *rimes* (last parts of words). They are sometimes called *word families.* You will not need to teach children the technical word *phonogram,* although you may want to use *pattern* or *word part.* A phonogram is the same as a rime, or ending of a word or syllable. We have included a large list of phonograms that will be useful to primary-age children in reading or writing, but you will not need to teach every phonogram separately. Once children understand that there are patterns and learn how to look for patterns, they will quickly discover more for themselves.

Another way to look at phonograms is to examine the way simple words and syllables are put together. Here we include the consonant-vowel-consonant (CVC) pattern in which the vowel often has a short, or terse, sound; the consonant-vowel-consonant-silent *e* (CVC*e*) pattern in which the vowel usually has a long, or lax, sound; and the consonant-vowel-vowel-consonant (CVVC) pattern in which the vowel combination may have either one or two sounds.

Knowing spelling patterns helps children notice and use larger parts of words, thus making word solving faster and more efficient. Patterns are also helpful to children in writing words because they will quickly write down the patterns rather than laboriously work with individual sounds and letters. Finally, knowing to look for patterns and remembering them help children make the connections between words that make word solving easier. The thirty-seven most common phonograms are marked with an asterisk.

Spelling Patterns

PRINCIPLE	EXPLANATION OF PRINCIPLE	PRE-K	GRADE K early	mid	late	GRADE 1 early	mid	late	GRADE 2 early	mid	late	GRADE 3 early	mid	late
Recognizing that words have letter patterns that are connected to sounds (phonograms are spelling patterns)	" Some words have patterns (parts) that are the same. " " You can find patterns (parts) that are the same in many words. "													
Recognizing and using the consonant-vowel-consonant (CVC) pattern	" Some words have a consonant, a vowel, and then another consonant. The vowel sounds like the *a* in *apple* [*i* in *igloo, o* in *octopus, e* in *egg, u* in *umbrella*]. "													
Recognizing and using simple phonograms with a VC pattern (easiest): -ad, -ag, -am, -an*, -at*, -ed, -en, -et, -ig, -in*, -it*, -og, -op*, -ot*, -ut	" You can look at the pattern (part) you know to help you read a word. " " You can use the pattern (part) you know to help you write a word. " " You can make new words by putting a letter or letter cluster before the word part or pattern. "													
Recognizing and using more difficult phonograms with a VC pattern: -ab, -ap*, - ar, -aw*, -ay*, -eg, -em, -ib, -ip*, -ix, -ob, -od, -ow (blow), -ow (cow), -ug*,-um, -un	" You can look at the pattern (part) you know to help you read a word. " " You can use the pattern (part) you know to help you write a word. " " You can make new words by putting a letter or letter cluster before the word part or pattern. "													
Recognizing and using phonograms with a vowel-consonant-silent *e* (VC*e*) pattern: -ace, -ade, -age, -ake*, -ale*, -ame*, -ane, -ape, -ate*, -ice*, -ide*, ike, -ile, -ime, -ine*, -ite, -ive, -obe, -oke*, -ope, -ore*	" Some words have a vowel, a consonant, and a silent *e*. The vowel sound is usually the name of the vowel [*a* in *make, e in Pete, i* in *ride, o* in *rode, u* in *cute*]. "													
		PRE-K	GRADE K early	mid	late	GRADE 1 early	mid	late	GRADE 2 early	mid	late	GRADE 3 early	mid	late

* Indicates most common phonograms.

Spelling Patterns, continued

Recognizing and using phonograms that end with double letters (VCC): -all, -ell*, -ill*, oll, -uff

Recognizing and using phonograms with double vowels (VVC): -eek, -eel, -eem, -een, -eep, -eer, -eet, -ood, -ook, -ool, -oom, -oon

Recognizing and using phonograms with ending consonant clusters (VCC): -ack*, -act, -alk; -amp, -and, -ank*, -ant, -ard, -ark, -arm, -art, -ash*, -ask, -ath, -aw*, -eck, -elp, -elt, -end, -ent, -esh, -est*, -ick*, -ift, -igh, -ing*, -ink*, -ish, -ock*, -old, -ong, -uck*, -ump*, -ung, -unk*, -ush

Recognizing and using phonograms with vowel combinations (VVC): -aid, -ail*, -ain*, air, -ait, -ay*, -aw, -ea, -ead, -eak, -eam, -ean, -eap, -ear, -eat*, -oad, -oak

Recognizing and using more difficult phonograms (VVCC, VVCe, VCCe, VCCC, VVCCC): -aint, -aise, -ance, -anch, -arge, -aste, -atch, -each, -ealth, -east, -eath, -eave, -edge, -eech, -eeze, -eight, -ench, -ight*, -itch, -ooth, -ouch, -ound, -udge, -unch

EXPLANATION OF PRINCIPLE

	PRE-K	GRADE K			GRADE 1			GRADE 2			GRADE 3		
		early	mid	late	early	mid	late	early	mid	late	early	mid	late

" Some words have double consonants at the end. The sound of the vowel is short. "

" Some words have double vowels followed by a consonant. "
" Sometimes the vowel sounds like its name (long sound). "
" Sometimes the vowel stands for other sounds. "

" Some words have patterns that end with consonant clusters. "

" Some words have two vowels together (vowel combinations). "
" The vowel sound in the middle is usually the name of the first vowel. "

" Some words have patterns (parts) that are the same. "
" You can find patterns (parts) that are the same in many words. "
" You can use the pattern you know to help you read (or write) a word. "

	PRE-K	GRADE K			GRADE 1			GRADE 2			GRADE 3		
		early	mid	late	early	mid	late	early	mid	late	early	mid	late

High Frequency Words

A core of known high frequency words is a valuable resource as children build their reading and writing processes. Young children notice words that appear frequently in the simple texts they read; eventually, their recognition of these words becomes automatic. In this way, their reading becomes more efficient, enabling them to decode words using phonics as well as attend to comprehension. These words are powerful examples that help them grasp that a word is always written the same way. They can use known high frequency words to check on the accuracy of their reading and as resources for solving other words (for example, *this* starts like *the*). In general, children learn the simpler words earlier and in the process develop efficient systems for learning words. They continuously add to the core of high frequency words they know. Lessons on high frequency words help them look more carefully at words and develop more efficient systems for word recognition.

High Frequency Words

PRINCIPLE	EXPLANATION OF PRINCIPLE
Recognizing and using high frequency words with one or two letters	" You see some words many times when you read: *I, is, in, at, my, we, to, me, am, an.* " " Some have only one letter: *I* and *a.* " " Some have two letters: *am, an, as, at, be, by, do, go, he, in, is, it, me, my, of, on, or, so, to, up, us, we.* " " Words you see a lot are important because they help you read and write. "
Locating and reading high frequency words in continuous text	" When you know a word, you can read it every time you see it. " " You can find a word by knowing how it looks. "
Recognizing and using high frequency words with three or four letters	" You see some words many times when you read. " " Some have three or four letters: *the, and, but, she, like, come, this.* " " Words you see a lot are important because they help you read and write. "
Recognizing and using high frequency words with five or more letters	" You see some words many times when you read. " " Some have five or more letters: *would, could, where, there, which.* " " Words you see a lot are important because they help you read and write. "

Grade range headers (top and bottom): PRE-K, GRADE K (early, mid, late), GRADE 1 (early, mid, late), GRADE 2 (early, mid, late), GRADE 3 (early, mid, late)

Word Meaning

Children need to know the meaning of the words they are learning to read and write. It is important for them constantly to expand their vocabulary as well as develop a more complex understanding of words they already know. Word meaning is related to the development of vocabulary—labels, concept words, synonyms, antonyms, and homonyms. Concept words such as numbers and days of the week are often used in the texts they read, and they will want to use these words in their own writing. When children learn concept words (color words are another example), they can form categories that help in retrieving them when needed. In our complex language, meaning and spelling are intricately connected.

Often you must know the meaning of the word you want to spell or read before you can spell it accurately. In addition to lists of common concept words that children are often expected to know how to read and spell, we include synonyms, antonyms, and homonyms, which may be homographs (same spelling, different meaning and sometimes different pronunciation) or homophones (same sound, different spelling). Knowing synonyms and antonyms will help children build more powerful systems for connecting and categorizing words; it will also help them comprehend texts better and write in a more interesting way. Being able to distinguish between homographs and homophones assists in comprehension and helps spellers to avoid mistakes.

Word Meaning

PRINCIPLE	EXPLANATION OF PRINCIPLE

PRINCIPLE	EXPLANATION OF PRINCIPLE	PRE-K	GRADE K			GRADE 1			GRADE 2			GRADE 3		
			early	mid	late	early	mid	late	early	mid	late	early	mid	late
Recognizing and learning concept words: color names, number words, days of the week, months of the year	" A color (number, day, month) has a name. " " Days of the week have names and are always in the same order. " " Months of the year have names and are always in the same order. " " You can read and write the names of colors (numbers, days, months). " " You can find the names of colors (numbers, days, months). "													
Recognizing and using words that are related	" Some words go together because of what they mean: *mother–father; sister–brother;* clothing; animals; food. "													
Recognizing and using synonyms (words that mean about the same)	" Some words mean about the same and are called synonyms: *begin/start, close/shut, fix/mend, earth/world, happy/glad, high/tall, jump/leap, keep/save, large/big.* "													
Recognizing and using antonyms (words that mean the opposite)	" Some words mean about the opposite and are called antonyms: *hot/cold, all/none, break/fix, little/big, long/short, sad/glad, stop/start.* "													
Recognizing and using homophones (same sound, different spelling and meaning). (It is not necessary to teach children the technical term *homophone.*)	" Some words sound the same but look different and have different meanings: *to/too/two; there/their/they're; hare/hair; blue/blew.* "													
Recognizing and using homographs (same spelling, different meaning and may have different pronunciation—heteronym). (It is not necessary to teach children thetechnical term *homograph or heteronym.*)	" Some words look the same, have a different meaning, and may sound different: *bat/bat, well/well; read/read; wind/wind.* "													
Recognizing and using words with multiple meanings (a form of homograph)	" Some words are spelled the same but have more than one meaning: *beat, run, play.* "													
		PRE-K	GRADE K			GRADE 1			GRADE 2			GRADE 3		
			early	mid	late	early	mid	late	early	mid	late	early	mid	late

WM
WORD MEANING

Word Structure

Looking at the structure of words will help children learn how words are related to each other and how they can be changed by adding letters, letter clusters, and larger word parts. Being able to recognize syllables, for example, helps children break down words into smaller units that are easier to analyze. In phonological awareness lessons, children learn to recognize word breaks and to identify the number of syllables in a word. They can build on this useful information in reading and writing.

Words often have affixes, parts added before or after a word to change its meaning. An affix can be a prefix or a suffix. The word to which affixes are added can be a *base* word or a *root* word. A base word is a complete word; a root word is a part with Greek or Latin origins (such as *phon* in *telephone*). It will not be necessary for young children to make this distinction when they are beginning to learn about simple affixes, but working with suffixes and prefixes will help children read and understand words that use them as well as use affixes accurately in writing.

Endings or word parts that are added to base words signal meaning. For example, they may signal relationships *(prettier, prettiest)* or time *(running, planted)*. Principles related to word structure include understanding the meaning and structure of compound words, contractions, plurals, and possessives as well as knowing how to make and use them accurately. We have also included the simple abbreviations that children often see in the books they read and want to use in their writing.

Word Structure

Syllables

PRINCIPLE	EXPLANATION OF PRINCIPLE
	PRE-K · GRADE K (early/mid/late) · GRADE 1 (early/mid/late) · GRADE 2 (early/mid/late) · GRADE 3 (early/mid/late)
Understanding the concept of syllable	" You can hear the syllables in words. " " You can look at the syllables to read a word. "
Recognizing and using one or two syllables in words	" You can look at the syllables in a word to read it [*horse, a-way, farm-er, morn-ing*]. "
Understanding how vowels appear in syllables	" Every syllable of a word has a vowel. "
Recognizing and using three or more syllables in words	" You can look at the syllables in a word to read it [*bi-cy-cle, to-geth-er, ev-er-y, won-der-ful, li-brar-y, com-put-er, au-to-mo-bile, a-quar-i-um, un-der-wat-er*]. "
Recognizing and using syllables in words with double consonants	" Divide the syllables between the consonants when a word has two consonants in the middle [*run-ning, bet-ter*]. "
Recognizing and using syllables ending in a vowel (open syllable)	" When a syllable ends with a vowel, the vowel sound is usually long [*ho-tel*]. "
Recognizing and using syllables ending in a vowel and at least one consonant (closed syllable)	" When a syllable ends with a vowel and at least one consonant, the vowel sound is usually short [*lem-on*]. "
Recognizing and using syllables with a vowel and silent *e*	" When a vowel and silent *e* are in a word, the pattern makes one syllable with a long vowel sound [*hope-ful*]. "

PRE-K · GRADE K (early/mid/late) · GRADE 1 (early/mid/late) · GRADE 2 (early/mid/late) · GRADE 3 (early/mid/late)

	PRINCIPLE	EXPLANATION OF PRINCIPLE	PRE-K	GRADE K			GRADE 1			GRADE 2			GRADE 3		
				early	mid	late	early	mid	late	early	mid	late	early	mid	late
Syllables	Recognizing and using syllables with vowel combinations	" When vowel combinations are in words, they usually go together in the same syllable [poi-son, cray-on, ex-plain]. "													
	Recognizing and using syllables with a vowel and *r*	" When a vowel is followed by *r*, the *r* and the vowel form a syllable [corn-er, cir-cus]. "													
	Recognizing and using syllables made of a consonant and *le*	" When *le* is at the end of a word and preceded by a consonant, the consonant and *le* form a syllable [ta-ble]. "													
Compound Words	Recognizing and understanding simple compound words: *into, itself, myself, cannot, inside, maybe, nobody, outside, sunshine, today, together, upset, yourself, without, sometimes, something*	" Some words are made up of two words put together and are called compound words. " " You can read compound words by looking at the two words in them. "													
	Recognizing and understanding more complex compound words: *airplane, airport, another, anyone, anybody, anything, everyone, homesick, indoor, jellyfish, skyscraper, toothbrush, underground, whenever*	" Some words are made up of two words put together and are called compound words. " " You can read compound words by looking at the two words in them. "													
Contractions	Understanding the concept of contractions	" A contraction is one word made from two words [can + not = can't]. A letter or letters are left out and an apostrophe is put in. " " A contraction is a short form of the two words. "													
	Recognizing and understanding contractions with am: *I'm*	" To make a contraction, put two words together and leave out a letter or letters. Write an apostrophe where letter(s) are left out. Here is a contraction made with *I + am: I'm.* "													
	Recognizing and understanding contractions with is: *here's, he's, it's, she's, that's, there's, what's, where's, who's*	" To make a contraction, put two words together and leave out a letter or letters. Write an apostrophe where the letter(s) are left out. " " Many contractions are made with is: *here + is = here's.* "													
	Recognizing and understanding contractions using will: *I'll, it'll, he'll, she'll, that'll, they'll, we'll, you'll*	" To make a contraction, put two words together and leave out a letter or letters. Write an apostrophe where the letter(s) are left out. " " Many contractions are made with will: *I + will = I'll.* "													
	Recognizing and understanding contractions with not: *aren't, can't, couldn't, didn't, doesn't, don't, hadn't, hasn't, haven't, isn't, mustn't, needn't, shouldn't, wouldn't*	" To make a contraction, put two words together and leave out a letter or letters. Write an apostrophe where the letter(s) are left out. " " Many contractions are made with not: *can + not = can't.* "													
	Recognizing and understanding contractions with are: *they're, we're, you're*	" To make a contraction, put two words together and leave out a letter or letters. Write an apostrophe where the letter(s) are left out. " " Many contractions are made with are: *they + are = they're.* "													
	Recognizing and understanding contractions with have: *could've, I've, might've, should've, they've, we've, would've, you've*	" To make a contraction, put two words together and leave out a letter or letters. Write an apostrophe where the letter(s) are left out. " " Many contractions are made with have: *should + have = should've.* "													
				early	mid	late	early	mid	late	early	mid	late	early	mid	late
			PRE-K	GRADE K			GRADE 1			GRADE 2			GRADE 3		

WS
WORD STRUCTURE

Word Structure, continued

PRE-K	GRADE K			GRADE 1			GRADE 2			GRADE 3		
	early	mid	late	early	mid	late	early	mid	late	early	mid	late

Contractions

Recognizing and understanding contractions with is or has: *he's, it's, she's, that's, there's, what's, where's, who's*

" To make a contraction, put two words together and leave out a letter or letters. Write an apostrophe where the letter(s) are left out. "
" Many contractions are made with is and/or has: *he + is = he's* [*He's going to the zoo*]; *he + has = he's* [*He's finished his work*]. "

Recognizing and understanding contractions with would or had: *I'd, it'd, she'd, there'd, they'd, we'd, you'd*

" To make a contraction, put two words together and leave out a letter or letters. Write an apostrophe where the letter(s) are left out. "
" Many contractions are made with would or had: *she + would = she'd; they + would = they'd*. "

Recognizing and understanding contractions with us: *let's*

" To make a contraction, put two words together and leave out a letter or letters. Write an apostrophe where the letter(s) are left out. "
" Many contractions are made with us: *let + us = let's* [*Let's go*]. "

Plurals

Understanding the concept of plural

" Plural means more than one. "

Recognizing and using plurals that add *s: dogs, cats, apples, cans, desks, faces, trees, monkeys*

" Add *s* to some words to show you mean more than one (make them plural). "
" You can hear the *s* at the end. "

Recognizing and using plurals that add *es* when words end with *x, ch, sh, s, ss, tch, zz: buzzes, branches, buses, boxes, dishes, kisses, patches, peaches, quizzes*

" Add *es* to words that end with *x, ch, sh, s, ss, tch,* or *zz* to make them plural. "
" The *s* at the end sounds like /z/. "

Recognizing and using plurals that change the spelling of the word: *child/children, foot/feet, goose/geese, man/men, mouse/mice, ox/oxen, woman/women*

" Change the spelling of some words to make them plural. "

Recognizing and using plurals that add *s* to words that end in a vowel and *y: boys, days, keys, plays, valleys*

" Add *s* to words that end in a vowel and *y* to make them plural. "

Recognizing and using plurals that add *ies* to words that end in a consonant and *y: babies, candies, cities, countries, families, flies, ladies, ponies, skies, stories*

" Change the *y* to *i* and add *es* to words that end in a consonant and *y* to make them plural. "

Recognizing and using plurals that change *f* to *v* and add *es* for words that end with *f, fe,* or *lf: hooves, lives, scarves, selves, shelves, wives, wolves*

" Change *f* to *v* and add *es* to words that end with *f, fe,* or *lf* to make them plural. "

Recognizing and using plurals for words that end in a consonant and *o* by adding *es: heroes, potatoes, volcanoes, zeroes*

" Add *es* to words that end in a consonant and *o* to make them plural. "

Recognizing and using plurals for words that end in a vowel and *o* by adding *s: kangaroos, radios, rodeos*

" Add *s* to words that end in a vowel and *o* to make them plural. "

Recognizing and using plurals that are the same word for singular and plural: *deer, lamb, moose, sheep*

" Some words are spelled the same in both the singular and plural forms. "

PRE-K	GRADE K			GRADE 1			GRADE 2			GRADE 3		
	early	mid	late	early	mid	late	early	mid	late	early	mid	late

Word Structure, continued

Verb Endings

PRINCIPLE	EXPLANATION OF PRINCIPLE
	PRE-K GRADE K (early, mid, late) · **GRADE 1** (early, mid, late) · **GRADE 2** (early, mid, late) · **GRADE 3** (early, mid, late)
Recognizing and using endings that add *s* to a verb to make it agree with the subject: *skate/skates; run/runs*	" **Add *s* to the end of a word to make it sound right in a sentence.** " " She can *run*. " " She *runs*. " " She can *skate*. " " She *skates*. "
Recognizing and using endings that add *ing* to a verb to denote the present participle: *play/playing; send/sending*	" **Add *ing* to a base word to show you are doing something now.** " " I can *read*. " " I am *reading*. " " She can *jump*. " " She is *jumping*. "
Recognizing and using endings that add *ed* to a verb to make it past tense: *walk/walked; play/played; want/wanted*	" **Add *ed* to the end of a word to show that you did something in the past.** " " I can *play* a game today. " " I *played* a game yesterday. " " I *want* to play. " " I *wanted* to play. "
Recognizing and using endings that add a *d* to a verb ending in silent *e* to make it past tense: *like/liked*	" **Add *d* to words ending in silent *e* to make the *ed* ending and show it was in the past.** " " I *like* vanilla ice cream. " " I *liked* vanilla ice cream, but I don't anymore. "
Recognizing and using endings that add *ing* to words that end in a single vowel and consonant to denote the present participle: *run/running; bat/batting; sit/sitting*	" **Double the consonant and add *ing* to words ending in a single vowel and consonant.** " " I can *run*. " " I am *running*. "
Recognizing and using endings that add *ing* to words ending in silent *e* to denote the present participle: *come/coming; write/writing; bite/biting*	" **Drop the *e* and add *ing* to most words that end with silent *e*.** " " Will she *come*? " " She is *coming*. " " I can *write*. " " I am *writing*. "
Recognizing and using endings that add *ing* to words that end in *y* to denote the present participle: *carry/carrying; marry/marrying*	" **Add *ing* to words that end in *y*.** " " I can *carry* the flag. " " I am *carrying* the flag. "
Recognizing that *ed* added to a word to make it past tense can sound several different ways	" **When you add *ed* to a word, sometimes it sounds like /d/:** *grabbed, played, yelled.* " " **When you add *ed* to a word, sometimes it sounds like /ed/ (short *e* plus the /d/ sound):** *added, landed, melted.* " " **When you add *ed* to a word, sometimes it sounds like /t/:** *dressed, liked, talked, laughed, walked.* " " **Sometimes you change the *y* to *i* and add *ed* and the ending sounds like *d*:** *cried, fried, carried.* "
	PRE-K GRADE K (early, mid, late) · **GRADE 1** (early, mid, late) · **GRADE 2** (early, mid, late) · **GRADE 3** (early, mid, late)

Verb Endings

PRINCIPLE	EXPLANATION OF PRINCIPLE

		PRE-K	GRADE K			GRADE 1			GRADE 2			GRADE 3		
			early	mid	late	early	mid	late	early	mid	late	early	mid	late

Recognizing and using endings that add *es* to a verb: *cry/cries; try/tries; carry/carries*

" You can add endings to a word to make it sound right in a sentence. "
" Change the *y* to *i* and add *es* to words that end in a consonant and *y*. "
" I can *carry* the flag. "
" She *carries* the flag. "

Recognizing and using endings that add *es* or *ed* to verbs ending in a consonant and *y* to form present or past tense: *cry/cries/cried; try/tries/tried*

" You can add word parts to the end of a word to show you did something in the present or in the past. "
" Change the *y* to *i* and add *es* or *ed* to words that end in a consonant and *y*. "
" I can *try* to run fast. "
" He *tries* to run fast. "
" We *tried* to run fast in the race yesterday. "

Recognizing and using endings that add *ed* to verbs ending in a single short vowel and consonant or a vowel and double consonant to make it past tense: *grab/grabbed; grill/grilled; yell/yelled*

" You add word parts to the endings of words to show you did something in the past. "
" Double the consonant before adding *ed* to words ending in a short vowel and one consonant. Add *ed* if the word ends with a vowel and a double consonant. "
" She can *yell* loud. "
" She *yelled*, 'Run!' "
" Mom can *grill* the hot dogs. "
" Mom *grilled* the hot dogs. "
" *Grab* the end of the rope. "
" She *grabbed* the end of the rope. "

Recognizing and using endings that add *er* to a verb to make it a noun: *read/reader; play/player; jump/jumper*

" Add *er* to a word to talk about a person who can do something. "
" John can *read*. "
" John is a *reader*. "

Recognizing and using endings that add *er* to a verb that ends with a short vowel and a consonant: *dig/digger; run/runner*

" Double the consonant and add *er* to words ending in a short vowel and one consonant. "
" Sarah can *run*. "
" Sarah is a *runner*. "

Recognizing and using endings that add *r* to a verb that ends in silent *e: bake/baker; hike/hiker*

" Add *r* to words that end in silent *e* to make the *er* ending. "
" I like to hike. "
" I am a *hiker*. "

Recognizing and using endings that add *er* to a verb that ends in *y: carry/carrier*

" Change the *y* to *i* and add *er* to words that end in *y*. "
" He can *carry* the mail. "
" He is a mail *carrier*. "

	early	mid	late	early	mid	late	early	mid	late	early	mid	late
PRE-K	GRADE K			GRADE 1			GRADE 2			GRADE 3		

Word Structure, continued

PRINCIPLE	EXPLANATION OF PRINCIPLE

PRE-K | GRADE K (early mid late) | GRADE 1 (early mid late) | GRADE 2 (early mid late) | GRADE 3 (early mid late)

Adjectives—Comparatives and Superlatives

Recognizing and using endings that show comparison (er, est): cold/colder; hard/harder; dark/darker; fast/faster; tall/taller; rich/richest; thin/thinner/thinnest

  " Add *er* or *est* to show how one thing compares with another. "
" John can run *fast*, but Monica can run *faster*. "
" Carrie is the *fastest* runner in the class. "

Recognizing and using endings that show comparison for words ending in e: pale/paler/palest; ripe/riper/ripest; cute/cuter/cutest

  " Add *r* or *st* to words that end in silent *e* to make the *er* or *est* ending. "
" Jolisa has a *cute* puppy. "
" Matthew has a *cuter* puppy. "
" Jaqual has the *cutest* puppy. "

Recognizing and using endings that show comparison for words ending in a short vowel and a consonant

  " Double the consonant and add *er* or *est* to words that end in a short vowel and one consonant. "
" The red box is big. "
" The blue box is bigger. "
" The green box is biggest. "

Recognizing and using endings that show comparison for words ending in y: scary/scarier/scariest; funny/funnier/funniest

  " Change *y* to *i* and add *er* or *est* to words that end in *y*. "
" Ciera told a *funny* story. "
" Kyle's story was *funnier* than Ciera's. "
" Amanda told the *funniest* story of all. "

Prefixes

Recognizing and using common prefixes (re meaning again): make/remake; tie/retie

  " Add a word part or prefix to the beginning of a word to change its meaning. "
" Add *re* to mean *do again*. "
" I *made* the bed and took a nap. I had to *remake* the bed. "

Recognizing and using common prefixes (un meaning not or the opposite of): do/undo; tie/untie; known/unknown; believable/unbelievable

  " Add a word part or prefix to the beginning of a word to change its meaning. "
" Add *un* to the beginning of a word to mean *not* or *the opposite of*. "
" I don't *believe* it. That is *unbelievable*. "
" I *tied* my shoes and then they came *untied*. "

Recognizing and using more complex prefixes (im, in, il, dis [meaning not]): possible/impossible; valid/invalid; like/dislike

  " Add a word part or prefix to the beginning of a word to change its meaning. "
" Add *im, in, il*, or *dis* to the beginning of words to mean *not*. "
" That is not *possible*. It is *impossible*. "
" We cannot *cure* the disease. It is *incurable*. "
" It is not *legal*. It is *illegal*. "
" I do not *like* broccoli. I *dislike* broccoli. "

Possessives

Recognizing and using possessives that add an apostrophe and an s to a singular noun: dog/dog's; woman/woman's, girl/girl's, boy/boy's

  " A person, animal, place, or thing can own something. To show ownership, you add *'s* to a word. "
" The collar belongs to the *dog*. It is the *dog's* collar. "
" The ball belongs to the *girl*. It is the *girl's* ball. "
" The *book* has a cover. It is the *book's* cover. "

Recognizing and using possessives for words that end in s: dogs' dishes, pigs' houses, Marcus' papers, Charles' lunch box

  " If a word already ends in s, just add an apostrophe to show ownership. "
" Those balls belong to the *boys*. They are the *boys'* balls. "
" Here is *Marcus'* lunch box. It belongs to *Marcus*. "
" The *girls* are getting the jump ropes. The ropes belong to the *girls*. They are the *girls'* jump ropes. "

Abbreviations

Recognizing and using common abbreviations: Mrs., Ms., Mr., Dr., St., Ave., Rd., months of the year, days of the week

  " Some words are made shorter by using some of the letters and a period. "
" They are called abbreviations. "

early mid late | early mid late | early mid late | early mid late
PRE-K GRADE K | GRADE 1 | GRADE 2 | GRADE 3

WS WORD STRUCTURE

Word-Solving Actions

Word-solving actions are the strategic moves readers and writers make when they use their knowledge of the language system to solve words. These strategies are "in-the-head" actions that are invisible, although we can infer them from some overt behavior. The principles listed in this section represent children's ability to *use* the principles in all previous sections of the Continuum.

All lessons related to the Continuum provide opportunities for children to apply principles in active ways; for example, through sorting, building, locating, reading, or writing. Lessons related to word-solving actions demonstrate to children how they can problem-solve by working on words in isolation or while reading or writing continuous text. The more children can integrate these strategies into their reading and writing systems, the more flexible they will become in solving words. The reader/writer may use knowledge of letter/sound relationships, for example, either to solve an unfamiliar word or to check that the reading is accurate. Rapid, automatic word solving is a basic component of fluency and important for comprehension because it frees children's attention to focus on the meaning and language of the text.

Word-Solving Actions

PRINCIPLE	EXPLANATION OF PRINCIPLE
Recognizing and locating words (names)	" You can find your name by looking for the letters in it. "
Making connections between names and other words	" You can find the letters that are in your name in other words. " " You can connect your name with other names [*Mark, Maria*]. " " You can connect your name with other words [*Mark, make*]. "
Using the letters in names to read and write words: *Chuck, chair*	" You can connect your name with the words you want to spell or read. "
Using known words to monitor reading and spelling	" You can use words you know to check on your reading. "
Using first and last names to read and write words	" You can think of the first and last names you know to help you read and spell words [*Angela, Andy*]. "
Recognizing and spelling known words quickly	" You can read or write a word quickly when you know how it looks [*the*]. " " When you know how to read some words quickly, it helps you read fast. " " When you know how to write some words quickly, it helps you write fast. "
Using letter/sound knowledge to monitor reading and spelling accuracy	" You can use what you know about letters and sounds to check on your reading (and writing). "
Using parts of known words that are like other words: *my/sky; tree/try; she/shut*	" You can use parts of words you know to read or write new words. "
Using what you know about a word to solve an unknown word: *her, mother*	" You can use what you know about words to read new words. "

Grade headings: PRE-K | GRADE K (early, mid, late) | GRADE 1 (early, mid, late) | GRADE 2 (early, mid, late) | GRADE 3 (early, mid, late)

Using What Is Known to Solve Words

PRINCIPLE

Taking Words Apart to Solve Them

PRE-K	GRADE K			GRADE 1			GRADE 2			GRADE 3		
	early	mid	late	early	mid	late	early	mid	late	early	mid	late

Saying words slowly to hear sounds in sequence

" You can say words slowly to hear the sounds. "
" You can hear the sounds at the beginning, middle, or end of a word. "
" You can write the letters for the sounds you can hear. "
" You can say words slowly to hear the sounds from left to right. "

Changing beginning letters to make new words: *sit/hit; day/play*

" You can change the first letter or letters of a word to make a new word. "

Listening for sounds to write letters in words

" You can say words slowly to hear the sounds. "
" Hearing and saying the sounds help you write words. "

Changing ending letters to make new words: *car/can/cat*

" You can change the last letter or letters of a word to make a new word. "

Changing middle letters to make new words: *hit/hot; sheet/shirt*

" You can change the middle letter or letters of a word to make a new word. "

Using letter/sound analysis from left to right to read a word

" You can read words by looking at the letters and thinking about the sounds from left to right. "

Learning to notice the letter sequence to spell a word accurately

" You can make a word several times to learn the sequence of letters. "

Studying features of words to remember the spelling

" You can look at a word, say it, cover it, write it, and check it to help you learn to spell it correctly. "

Noticing and correcting spelling errors

" You can write a word, look at it, and try again to make it 'look right.' "
" You can notice and think about the parts of words that are tricky for you. "
" You can write words to see if you know them. "

Noticing and using word parts (onsets and rimes) to read a word: *br-ing*

" You can use word parts to solve a word. "
" You can look at the first and last parts of a word to read it. "

Changing the onset or rime to make a new word: *bring/thing; bring/brown*

" You can change the first part or the last part to make a new word. "

Adding letters to the beginning or end of a word to make a new word: *in/win; bat/bats; the/then*

" You can add letters to the beginning of a word to make a new word. "
" You can add letters to the end of a word to make a new word. "

Adding letter clusters to the beginning or end of a word to make a new word: *an/plan; cat/catch*

" You can add letter clusters to the beginning or end of a word to make a new word. "

Removing letters or letter clusters from the beginning of words: *sit/it; stand/and; his/is*

" You can take away letters from the beginning of a word to make a new word. "

Removing letters from the end of a word to make a new word: *and/an; Andy/and; kite/kit*

" You can take away letters from the end of a word to make a new word. "

PRE-K	GRADE K			GRADE 1			GRADE 2			GRADE 3		
	early	mid	late	early	mid	late	early	mid	late	early	mid	late

WSA
WORD SOLVING ACTIONS

Word-Solving Actions, continued

EXPLANATION OF PRINCIPLE

	PRE-K	GRADE K			GRADE 1			GRADE 2			GRADE 3		
		early	mid	late	early	mid	late	early	mid	late	early	mid	late

Taking Words Apart to Solve Them

Recognizing and using word parts (onsets, rimes) to read a word: *br-ing, cl-ap*
- " You can notice and use word parts to read (or write) a new word. "
- " You can look at the first part and last part to read a word. "

Taking apart compound words or joining words to make compound words: *into, sidewalk, sideways*
- " You can read compound words by finding the two smaller words. "
- " You can write compound words by joining two smaller words. "

Removing letter clusters from the end of a word to make a new word: *catch/cat*
- " You can take away letter clusters from the end of a word to make a new word. "

Removing the ending from a base word to make a new word: *sit/sits/sitting; big/bigger/biggest*
- " You can take off the ending to help you read a word. "

Breaking down a longer word into syllables in order to decode manageable units: *for-got-ten*
- " You can divide a word into syllables to read it. "

Making Connections Between and Among Words to Solve Them

Connecting words that mean the same or almost the same: *wet/damp*
- " You think about the words that mean almost the same. "

Connecting words that start the same: *tree/tray*
- " You can connect the beginning of a word with a word you know. "

Connecting words that end the same: *candy/happy*
- " You can connect the ending of the word with a word you know. "

Connecting words that have the same pattern: *light/night; running/sitting*
- " You can connect words that have the same letter patterns. "

Connecting words that sound the same but look different and have different meanings: *blew/blue*
- " You can read words by noticing that they sound the same but look different and have different meanings. "

Connecting words that rhyme: *fair/chair*
- " You can think about words that rhyme. "

Connecting words that look the same but sometimes sound different and have different meanings: *read/read*
- " You can read words by remembering that some words look the same but sometimes sound different and have different meanings. "

Connecting and comparing word patterns that look the same but sound different: *dear/bear*
- " You can read words by remembering that some words have parts or patterns that look the same but sound different. "

Connecting and comparing word patterns that sound the same but look different: *said/bed*
- " You can read words by remembering that some words have parts or patterns that sound the same but look different. "

		early	mid	late	early	mid	late	early	mid	late	early	mid	late
	PRE-K	GRADE K			GRADE 1			GRADE 2			GRADE 3		

Early Literacy Concepts

Learning about literacy begins long before children enter school. Many children hear stories read aloud and try out writing for themselves; through such experiences, they learn some basic concepts about written language. Nearly all children begin to notice print in the environment and develop ideas about the purposes of print. The child's name, for example, is a very important word. Kindergartners and first graders are still acquiring some of these basic concepts, and they need to generalize and systematize their knowledge. In the classroom, they learn a great deal through experiences like shared and modeled reading and shared and interactive writing. Explicit teaching can help children learn much more about these early concepts, understand their importance, and develop ways of using them in reading and writing.

Connect to Assessment

See related ELC Assessment Tasks in the Assessment Guide in *Teaching Resources:*

- ▶ Name Writing

- ▶ Locating Name (1) in a List and (2) in a Text

- ▶ Locating Words

- ▶ Locating Letters

- ▶ Matching Word by Word

- ▶ Finding First and Last Letters

Develop Your Professional Understanding

See *Word Matters: Teaching Phonics and Spelling in the Reading/Writing Classroom* by G.S. Pinnell and I.C. Fountas. 1998. Portsmouth, New Hampshire: Heinemann.

Related pages: 5, 8–10, 47–48, 67–69, 76–77, 88–89, 123, 141–142, 252, 254.

Recognizing Names
Name Chart

Consider Your Children

This lesson is appropriate for children who are just beginning to learn about print. It will familiarize them with the letters that make up their names and will help them attend to sequence and orientation. This early lesson involves children in learning the details of their own names and also draws their attention to others' names. This lesson is also appropriate for children who already recognize or can write their names because they will be learning the names of their friends. You will use a pocket chart to involve the children with the names. Following this lesson, copy the names of the children, grouped by first letter, onto a permanent chart for daily reference in reading, writing, and word study activities. You can involve the children in circling the group of names that start with the same letter.

Working with English Language Learners

For English language learners, recognizing their own names in print will provide a first entry into written English. It will be important that you pronounce their names accurately and explicitly emphasize the first letter and point it out. As you say the child's name, run your finger along the letters so that she can begin to notice the connections between letters and sounds. Give the children many opportunities to locate their names quickly on the name chart, which will be an important resource in reading and writing.

You Need

► Pocket chart or blank chart paper.
► Glue sticks.
► Individual boxes such as empty milk cartons.
► Magnetic letters (or Letter Cards, if needed).

From *Teaching Resources:*

► Large name cards, two for each child (Pocket Chart Card Template).
► Small name cards (Word Card Template).

Understand the Principle

Beginning with their own names, children come to realize that words are made up of distinct letters and that words are always spelled with the same letters in the same order.

This principle sets the scene for noticing spelling patterns in words.

Explain the Principle

" Your name starts with a letter that is always the same. "

" You can find your name by looking for the first letter. "

CONTINUUM: EARLY LITERACY CONCEPTS — RECOGNIZING ONE'S NAME

plan

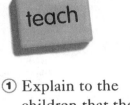
teach

Explain the Principle

❝ **Your name starts with a letter that is always the same.** ❞

❝ **You can find your name by looking for the first letter.** ❞

① Explain to the children that they are going to be working with their names.

② Prepare cards for the pocket chart with children's first names on them. Print should be large enough for all children to see while seated on the rug. In alphabetical order, hold up each child's name, say it, and ask the children to repeat it. Then have each child put his or her name on the chart as you point to the place.

③ Suggested language: "This is Avery's name. Avery starts with an *A*. Say *Avery*. [Children respond.] Say *A for Avery*. [Children respond.] Avery, put your name on the chart."

④ Repeat with each child in the class.

⑤ Read the complete name chart with the children.

⑥ Following this lesson, you will want to create a permanent name chart. Write the children's names on chart paper and involve the children in circling groups of names that start with the same letter.

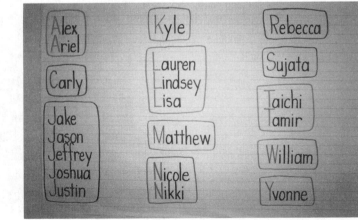

glue
write
draw

▶ Ask the children to take the small card with their name on it, glue it onto a piece of paper, write the name underneath, and then draw a self-portrait. These pieces of paper can be stapled into a class book of names or placed in alphabetical order on a bulletin board. (You might also take a photograph of each child and make a class book with photographs or another name chart with photographs.)

▶ Prepare a box for each child that contains his name on a card and the magnetic letters to make his name. Children make their own names with magnetic letters using the card as a model. Then have them work with a partner to switch names, make them with magnetic letters, and check them.

share

Ask the children to show their pictures and read their names. Then ask them to exchange names with a partner and show and read the name they have.

Remove the names from the chart and mix them up. Go quickly through the names again and have each child put his name in the chart. Then read the chart several different ways: backward, skip around, etc.

Link

Interactive Read-Aloud: Read aloud alphabet books (see *Teaching Resources, Alphabet Books Bibliography*). Examples are:

- ► *What's Your Name? (From Ariel to Zoe)* by Eve Sanders and Marilyn Sanders
- ► *A Book of Letters* by Ken Wilson-Max

Shared Reading: Read the class name chart quickly each morning for a week so children develop fluency with the variety of names.

Guided Reading: During word work, have children make their names with magnetic letters, and also have them make some very easy high frequency words.

Interactive Writing: Refer to the class name chart to show children how to make letters ("a *b* like the *b* in *Rebecca*").

Independent Writing: Have children write their names on their drawings and other writing. Remind children they can use the letters they know from their names while writing stories.

assess

- ► Notice how many of the letters children can produce when they write their names.
- ► Observe whether the children use their names as a resource for interactive writing and independent writing.

Expand the Learning

Repeat the lesson having children work with names of others in the class.

Read the chart together. Then have individual children locate their names by first thinking about the beginning letter.

Play a game: "I'm thinking of a boy whose name starts with *A*. He has a red shirt." Let children respond by going up and pointing to the name and reading it.

After children can identify names by their first letter, ask them to locate names by the next letter or the last letter: "I'm thinking of a girl whose name starts with *C*. The next letter is *a*."

Make a class name chart on paper to display next to your easel so that it will be there for handy reference.

Connect with Home

Have the children take home their name cards and find and glue on the paper a picture of something that starts with the same beginning letter.

Invite caregivers to create a mini–name chart with names of family or friends. Give them a copy of the class name chart as a model and a blank grid (Word Card Template) to make a family name chart. Encourage them to read the chart several times a day.

Learning Your Name
Songs and Chants

Consider Your Children

Use this lesson as one of children's first school experiences with print. A child's name is a very important word because it has personal meaning. By learning to recognize their names, children learn the concept of word and begin to notice visual aspects of print. Young children will enjoy the chants. It will be important for those who do not recognize their names to locate them within continuous text. Children who already recognize their names will find them quickly and will notice other words within familiar texts.

Working with English Language Learners

Some English language learners will not initially understand what is being said in the classroom; English in print will be extremely difficult for them. They can begin to enter the world of English language and literacy by seeing and hearing their names. Be sure that you learn how to pronounce children's names accurately in their own languages and say those names often. Help children find their names as a way of orienting them to print. Help them say and find the names of other children in the class. Be sure that you repeat the chants and songs in this lesson a sufficient number of times so that they can join in easily and use their own names within them. Showing that you value all children's names helps create a sense of community and welcomes English language learners to that community.

You Need

▶ "Name" songs or chants on charts or sentence strips (e.g., "Happy Birthday" or "Good Morning").

▶ Class name chart (see example in Lesson ELC 1).

From *Teaching Resources:*

▶ Cards (Pocket Chart Card Template) with each child's name printed clearly (the backs of the cards can have a strip of Velcro® if you wish).

Understand the Principle

Starting with their names, children learn to recognize words by noticing the visual features of letters. They also begin to connect visual features of letters to sounds in words.

Once the name is learned, it is a resource to which other words can be connected. Children can also use the letters in their names to produce beginning writing.

Explain the Principle

❝ Your name has letters in it.❞

❝ Your name is always written the same way.❞

❝ You can find your name by looking for the first letter.❞

plan

Explain the Principle

" Your name has letters in it. "

" Your name is always written the same way. "

" You can find your name by looking for the first letter. "

① Tell children they'll be learning to read their names as they sing and chant.

② First teach a song or chant (one that incorporates children's names) orally.

③ After children know the song or chant, introduce the enlarged written form on a chart or on sentence strips. Read it in a shared way.

④ Select a name card and ask children to look at it carefully but not to say the name. Put it in the appropriate place on the song or chant. Pointing to each word, read up to the name; then drop out and let children read the name. Afterward, ask children to talk about how they "read" the name.

⑤ Repeat this process with several name cards. Afterward, ask children to talk about how they "read" the name.

⑥ Explain to the children that today they are going to have a copy of two different songs. They will read the songs, write their names on the blank line, and illustrate them.

Happy Birthday to you.

Happy Birthday to you.

Happy Birthday dear Lisa

Happy Birthday to you.

Happy Birthday to you.

Happy Birthday to you.

Happy Birthday dear ⸺ EMILY.

Happy Birthday to you.

write
draw
read

▶ Distribute photocopies of the songs or chants. Have children write their names in the blanks and add an illustration. They can read the songs and chants to a partner and take them home to read to family members.

share

Ask the children what they have noticed about names. Responses like the following will let you in on their thinking:

"A name starts with a capital letter."

"Some of our names start the same."

"You look at the letters to know it's your name."

Link

Interactive Read-Aloud: Read aloud books that feature names. Examples are:

- ▶ *Who Took the Cookies from the Cookie Jar?* by Bonnie Lass and Philemon Sturges
- ▶ *My Son John* by Jim Aylesworth

Shared Reading: Make a big book of name songs and chants so that children can read them. See the variety of examples in *Sing a Song of Poetry* such as "Charlie Over the Ocean" or "Elsie Marley." Also, poems such as "Who Is Wearing Red?" and "Come, Butler, Come" allow children to insert their names.

Guided Reading: Have the children locate familiar words by first predicting the letter at the beginning. During word work, have them use magnetic letters to make their names.

Interactive Writing: Use the name songs and chants as resources for words.

Independent Writing: Encourage children to put their names on their writing papers. You can also give them copies of songs they know well and have them put their names in the blanks and draw pictures.

Expand the Learning

Create a new name chart with storybook characters. Take the names of the children's favorite storybook characters (for example, Goldilocks, Clifford, Chrysanthemum, Peter Rabbit, or Frances) and place them in the song or chant for shared reading.

Place the first letter of a name on the chart and ask children to put in a name starting with that letter. Teach them how to check against the class name chart.

Repeat the lesson using chants such as "Pat-a-Cake" and "Jack Be Nimble" (see *Sing a Song of Poetry*). In "Pat-a-Cake," children insert an initial letter as well as a name; in "Jack Be Nimble," they insert the name three times.

Connect with Home

Send home copies of "name" songs and chants with the child's name inserted. Also send home blank versions, and encourage parents or caregivers to put other family members' names in the blanks and read the songs and chants with their child.

assess

- ▶ Check the children's progress in recognizing their own and others' names.

- ▶ Notice evidence of children's growing ability to make connections among names and between names and other words (beginning sounds, ending sounds, patterns such as double letters).

- ▶ Observe the children's progress in writing their names accurately and with fluency.

Generative Lesson

early
mid
late

ELC 3
EARLY LITERACY CONCEPTS

3 *Hearing Words in Sentences*
Cut-Up Sentences

Consider Your Children

Early understanding about sentences is best developed through shared reading and shared and interactive writing. When students have the "feel" for what sentences are, focus a few very explicit lessons on these principles. Early in the year, work with just one sentence at a time. These same teaching guidelines can be used in combination with interactive writing and with simple poems from shared reading.

Working with English Language Learners

This lesson will give English language learners more opportunities to compose and write sentences. Stick with very simple sentences and topics that all children easily understand. Start with shorter sentences and move to longer ones. Using repetitive language will scaffold English language learners in their composition of sentences. Allow them to use structures you provide, varying only one or two words. Provide many opportunities to repeat sentences and reread them.

You Need

► Blank chart paper.

► Pocket chart.

► Message on sentence strips for pocket chart (for day 2).

► Copies of message to distribute to children (for day 2).

► Sheets for gluing sentences.

► Glue sticks.

Understand the Principle

Children need to understand that sentences are made up of words that, put together, communicate meaning. They also need to understand that when they read, they match one spoken word to one cluster of printed letters.

This information will be valuable as children read sentences in books, monitor their reading, and compose and write sentences.

Explain the Principle

❝ We say one word for each word we see in writing. ❞

plan

Explain the Principle

" **We say one word for each word we see in writing.** "

① Tell your children they are going to learn about writing and reading sentences.

② Ask the children to generate some ideas that you will write for them. Choose a simple topic that will allow you to shape the language. Suggested language: "Do you think it would be a good idea to think of things that we like to do in kindergarten? Then, if people visit our room, they can read about what we like to do."

③ Have a discussion that will generate written sentences. Model language by saying some of the ideas in sentences suitable for the chart, but be sure that children generate the language you finally use.

④ Reach consensus on the first sentence. Write it word by word on the chart. Reread the sentence a couple of times, telling children to watch how you are pointing to each word. Point out that you start reading on the left. Count the words. Point out the period at the end.

⑤ Use the first sentence as a model for one or two more. Write them yourself, but have the children come up to point out the spaces and show where to start reading. Reread the sentences word by word. *This will probably be enough work for one day.*

⑥ *On the second day,* have the lines of the message written on sentence strips in the pocket chart and read them.

⑦ Take out all but the first sentence strip. Cut the first sentence up into individual words. Place the words randomly at the bottom of the pocket chart.

8 Have the children help you put the sentence together one word at a time. Suggested language: "The first word is *we*. I'll put it in the pocket chart. What is the next word?" Children will have just reread the message, so most will probably remember the next word.

9 Model looking for the next word, *read*. Place the word in the pocket chart and reread the first two words. Continue putting together the simple sentence; then reread it. Move along at a good pace; don't let the lesson drag.

10 Replace the words randomly at the bottom of the pocket chart; then put the sentence together again quickly with the children's participation.

make
read

▶ Provide cut-up versions of the sentences for the children to put together, glue on a sheet, and illustrate. In pairs, they take turns pointing to the words and reading the sentences they make.

Ask the children to share what they learned about how spaces help you when you read. Have them go up to the chart to locate the spaces.

Link

Interactive Read-Aloud: Read aloud books with large print (see *Teaching Resources, Large Print Books Bibliography*). When children look at these books independently, they can clearly see words and spaces. For example:

- ▶ *Barnyard Banter* by Denise Fleming
- ▶ *Dinosaurs, Dinosaurs* by Byron Barton

Shared Reading: Point out the spaces in familiar poems and songs such as "Good Morning" or "Apples, Peaches" (see *Sing a Song of Poetry*) and show children how to read word by word with a pointer.

Guided Reading: Prompt children to point crisply under the words, using the same finger each time. Ask them, "Did it match?" or "Did you have enough words?" They will be reading very simple, predictable texts. Your goal is to help them monitor their reading by pointing to and matching the words.

Interactive Writing: Explicitly point out spaces; reread messages word by word. Invite a child to use the pointer while others read.

Independent Writing: Ask children to write their own stories about what they like to do in kindergarten and to draw a picture. Encourage them to leave spaces between words.

assess

- ▶ Observe children in shared reading and notice whether they can read left to right and match word by word.

- ▶ Look at children's writing and notice whether they are using spaces.

- ▶ Conduct a quick test by asking individuals to point to the words as you read a couple of sentences.

Expand the Learning

Apply these teaching guidelines to texts from shared reading and interactive writing. Using simple sentences, make sentence strips for children to cut up and put back together.

Connect with Home

Send home copies of your series of sentences for children to read to their family members.

Let children take their cut-up sentences home. Inform parents that children are not expected to read the words in isolation (as in word cards) but are to put them back together into a sentence, glue them on paper, illustrate the sentence, and read it with pointing.

Generative Lesson

early
mid
late

ELC 4
EARLY LITERACY CONCEPTS

Sorting and Connecting Names
Three-Way Sort

Consider Your Children

This lesson is best used after children can read most of the names of class members. In this lesson, you show children how to notice different aspects of words by asking them to sort names in a variety of ways. Depending on the group, you may want to show only one way of sorting on a given day. Children will also learn the routine of sorting.

Working with English Language Learners

It will be especially important for English language learners to make connections among names and use them as resources for learning more about print. At the same time, in a multilingual classroom, many names may be different from those children have encountered in their homes and communities. Give children many opportunities to pronounce the names as you draw attention to the print. Emphasize the importance of saying individuals' names exactly as *they* say them (as much as you possibly can). There may be letter/sound relationships with names that do not fit regular English phonology; point out that these differences make people's names interesting and unique and that we can all learn different ways of saying names.

You Need

▸ Pocket chart.

From *Teaching Resources:*

▸ Children's names on cards, arranged by first letter (Pocket Chart Card Template).
▸ Three-Way Sort Cards or Sheets.
▸ Sets of small name cards (Word Card Template).

Understand the Principle

By closely examining their own and their classmates' names, children learn that words are made up of letters and that the order of letters is always the same. These concepts are important in recognizing words by sight (by letter patterns), beginning to recognize spelling patterns, and noticing relationships between letters and sounds.

Sorting names helps children attend more closely to the specific features of names and make spelling to sound corrections.

Explain the Principle

" You can connect your name with other words. "

plan

Explain the Principle

" You can connect your name with other words. "

① Explain to the children that today they will be learning more about their names.

② Ask children to read the names in the pocket chart as you point.

③ Take all the names away except for one group (for example, the names that begin with *M*). Suggested language: "These names go together because they are alike in some way. How are they alike? [Children respond.] Yes, they have the same first letter. They all have an *M*."

④ "Here is another name, *Donna*. [Put the name in the pocket chart.] Say *Donna*. Look at the first letter. Now look at this name, *Darien*. Does it have the same first letter as *Donna?* [Children respond.] Let's say them: *Donna, Darien*. Do they sound alike at the beginning? Do they look alike at the beginning? They both have a *D*." Put Darien's name card below Donna in the chart.

⑤ Continue showing names and deciding whether they go with *Donna*. Place names that start with other letters in a third row that has a question mark at the top.

⑥ Demonstrate the three-way sorting process again using two more names that start with other letters. Place a question mark in the third column for names that don't start with these letters. Suggested language: "We have sorted our names by putting together the ones that have the same first letter. I'm going to put two names at the top of the chart, *Sunny* and *Robin*. [Read them.] As we look at the rest of the names, we'll decide whether they belong with *Sunny* or with *Robin*. The names that don't go with either one, we'll just put to the side as an 'other' category under the question mark."

⑦ If you feel the children are ready, repeat the three-way sorting process focusing on the last letter in the names. Suggested language: "Now let's sort the names by the last letter." Place two or three children's names in the pocket chart and match names by last letter.

sort
read
mix
sort
read

▸ Have children, working with partners, use the Three-Way Sort Cards to sort the small name cards by the first letter on the left. They can complete several sorts, using different pairs of names each time. As they finish each sort, have them take turns reading the list of names to each other.

▸ Ask them to mix up the cards and say and sort them by the last letter on the right. Again, they read the list of names to each other.

Name:		Three-Way Sort
Alex	Nadia	?
Amy	Nick	Barbara
	Nora	Zack
	Naveen	

THREE-WAY SORT SHEET

Ask children to say their names and find someone in the room who has a name that starts the same. They can refer to the name chart. (Have some picture cards of familiar objects in the pocket chart for children whose names won't have a match.)

Link

Interactive Read-Aloud: Read aloud books that have characters' names in the title, such as:

- ► *Leo the Late Bloomer* by Robert Kraus
- ► *Bill and Pete* by Tomie dePaola

Shared Reading: Read poems that have character names, such as "Mary Wore Her Red Dress" or "Sally Go 'Round" and substitute children's names. See *Sing a Song of Poetry* for this poem and more examples.

Guided Reading: After reading and discussing a text, have children quickly locate words that begin with a particular letter.

Interactive Writing: Write stories with children's names in them: "Emily likes red. Justin likes blue." "Emily wore her blue sweater."

Independent Writing: Encourage children to write their names on their papers.

assess

- ► Notice the children's ability to sort names by first and last letters.
- ► Notice the children's ability to write the first letter of their names.
- ► Observe whether the children use first or last letters of names as resources in interactive and independent writing.

Expand the Learning

When the children can sort names easily by the first and last letters, ask them to think of other ways of sorting names. For example:

By number of letters in the name.

By names that have double letters and those that don't.

By names that have the letter *a* (or any other vowel) and those that don't.

By girl and boy.

Place names in the pocket chart and invite children to sort them in a certain way. Ask other children to guess how they are sorted.

Connect with Home

Make copies of the class name chart. Have children take the chart home, cut it apart into individual names, and sort them by first letter. Have them glue four names into a four-page folded book (see *Teaching Resources,* Four-Page Fold Book Template) and write a sentence about those classmates.

Recognizing First and Last Letters

Making Names

Consider Your Children

Be sure children have had experience with the class name chart and can read some of the names. Also, it would be good to have them put together their names as puzzles (Lesson LK 4) before this minilesson. If children are very inexperienced, focus only on the concept of "first"; save the concept of "last" for another lesson.

Working with English Language Learners

English language learners' names will be known words and will provide an ideal way to learn the concept of "first letters" and "last letters" in words. Be sure to be explicit in demonstrating the meaning of the words *first, last,* and *letter.* If you know these words in the children's own languages, you may want to use them to draw attention to the items. Also, help children pronounce the names of their friends as they glue them on their alphabet squares. Have them "read" their charts of friends' names several times. If necessary, work in a small group to help them highlight first and last letters.

You Need

► Name chart (in a pocket chart or written on chart paper; see ELC 1).

► Transparent plastic or highlighter tape or highlighter marker.

► Glue sticks.

► Highlighter pens.

► Sheets of blank paper.

From *Teaching Resources:*

► Letter cards.

Understand the Principle

A key concept in beginning reading is that *first* and *last* have particular meanings when applied to print. The first letter of a word is the first graphic symbol on the left; the last letter is the symbol farthest to the right.

To solve words, children need to learn to connect the temporal sequence of sounds with the symbols arranged spatially in print from left to right.

Explain the Principle

" The first letter in a word is on the left. "

" The last letter in a word is before the space. "

plan

Explain the Principle

" The first letter in a word is on the left. "

" The last letter in a word is before the space. "

① Tell your children they are going to use their names to learn about first and last letters.

② Suggested language: "This is Elizabeth's name. What is the *first* letter of Elizabeth's name? [Children respond.] That's right, it's an *E*. The first letter is on the left. It is at the beginning of the word. It's a capital letter because all of our names begin with a capital letter." Use the acceptable language in your school: capital and small letters; uppercase and lowercase letters.

③ "What is the *last* letter of Elizabeth's name? [Children respond.] That's right, it's an *h*. The last letter is at the end of the word, right before the space." *Remember that children may not understand the terms* left *and* right. *It will be necessary to point to the letters as you say them.*

④ Suggested language: "I'm going to make the first letter of Elizabeth's name yellow. [Do so.] I'm going to make the last letter of Elizabeth's name orange." Use highlighter tape, transparent plastic, or highlighter marker. Or you can underline letters. Circling the letters often obscures the features of the letter.

⑤ Repeat the process with several other names, each time asking children to identify the first and last letters.

say
glue
color

▸ Have the children use letter cards to glue classmates' names on a sheet of paper, letter by letter, saying each one. Then ask them to take a highlighter pen and highlight or color the first letter in each name.

Play a game: "I'm thinking of someone whose name begins with *T.*" Children search the name chart for the answer. After your demonstration, children can pose the questions and call on someone to answer.

Vary the game by asking for a name with a last letter.

Make the game more challenging: "I'm thinking of someone whose name begins with *T* and ends with *y.*" After your demonstration, children can pose the questions and call on someone to answer.

Link

Interactive Read-Aloud: Read aloud alphabet books (see *Teaching Resources,* Alphabet Books Bibliography). Point out the first and last letters of the characters' names. Examples are:

- ▸ *The Letters Are Lost* by Lisa Campbell Ernst
- ▸ *Alphabears* by Kathleen Hague

Shared Reading: Have children locate known words in poems by first predicting the beginning letter. Frame with a masking card or otherwise highlight high frequency words with a highlighter marker and point out first and last letters.

Guided Reading: After reading and discussing a text, have children locate easy high frequency words and tell the first and last letters of the word.

Interactive Writing: When showing children how to write a word or having a child come to the easel to write, use the terms *first* and *last* to talk about letters.

Independent Writing: Have children write their names on their drawings and other writing. Remind children they can use the letters in their names while writing. When you confer with them, use the terms *first* and *last* to talk about letters in words.

assess

- ▸ Notice how many of the letters the children can produce when they write their own and their classmates' names.
- ▸ Observe whether the children use their names as resources for interactive writing and independent writing.

Expand the Learning

Have children make five names of boys and girls in their class, using the magnetic letters and the class name chart as a reference. Use additional sets of words, such as color words, number words, or days of the week. With days of the week, children will notice that they start with different letters but all end in *y*.

Connect with Home

Have the children cut up their names into letters; then ask them to take the letters home, reassemble them into their names, and then find the last and first letters.

Caregivers can make and cut up names of family members for children to put together and glue on a sheet of paper.

Have children collect a list of family members, friends, and storybook characters whose names have the same first or last letters.

6 Locating First *and* Last *in Print*

Little Books

Consider Your Children

For this early lesson, provide only sentences that begin on the left side of the page. Avoid compound sentences that require commas. Most books for very young readers have this kind of "friendlier" layout. After children have had a great deal more experience in shared reading, you can repeat this lesson to help them understand that a sentence may start in the middle of a line, after a period. In this lesson, it is important to generate and write sentences as quickly as possible, so you will not be using interactive writing. The goal is to firmly establish the concepts of *first* and *last* as they apply to written text. If you find that all the children understand the concepts and can demonstrate them, you will not need to return to this lesson.

Working with English Language Learners

English language learners often seem as though they do not know the answer to a question when they do not understand the vocabulary you are using for instruction. For example, they may know the concept of "first word" but not understand the direction in English. Be sure that you demonstrate by pointing and make your directions very explicit. If you know comparable words in the children's languages, use them. This lesson involves children in composing and writing sentences. Be appreciative of their approximations and realize that they may not yet have full control of English language syntax.

You Need

► Chart paper and markers.

From *Teaching Resources:*

► Blank four-page books (Blank Book Page Template).

Understand the Principle

Children need to know what you mean by *first* and *last* when you are teaching them about letters, sounds, and words. *First* and *last* in oral language refer to time of production. The first word in a printed sentence is the one on the left of the page or the one after a period or other ending punctuation. The first line of print on a page is usually the top line, and the last line of print on a page is usually the bottom line.

To solve words, children need to connect the temporal sequence of spoken sounds with the corresponding print symbols arranged spatially from left to right.

Explain the Principle

❝ The first word in a sentence is on the left. ❞

❝ The last word in a sentence is before the period or question mark. ❞

plan

What color do you like?

Miss Yardley likes red.

Chamique likes blue.

Parker likes brown.

Tanya likes yellow.

Michael likes red.

Denine likes blue.

Explain the Principle

" The first word in a sentence is on the left. "

" The last word in a sentence is before the period or question mark. "

① Explain to the children that they are going to write sentences with color words. (You can generate other kinds of sentences than those using color words—in other words, any topic matching your curriculum and children's interests.)

② Suggested language: "Let's write something today about the children in our room and let's use the color words we have been learning. Let's write about ourselves and what colors we like. I wrote a sentence about myself and the color I like. Let's read it together." Read the sentence, using shared reading and pointing.

③ "The first word of my sentence is. . . . [Point to the word; children respond.] That's right. In this story the first word of the sentence is on the left. It begins with a capital letter, doesn't it? This first word also begins with a capital letter because it is my name, but remember that the first letter of a sentence always begins with a capital letter."

④ "Now let's find the last word of the sentence." From their experience in shared reading, many children will know how to find the last word. Confirm their choices. "The last word is right before the period, isn't it?"

⑤ "Now let's make a sentence about Chamique. Chamique, what color do you like? [Chamique responds.] Can we say, *Chamique likes blue*?" Write the sentence quickly. Ask children to point to the first word in the sentence and the last word in the sentence. Consider drawing a patch of the color at the end of the sentence to provide a support for reading.

⑥ Repeat the process for other names. (It is not always necessary to write a sentence for every child in the room because you will write other stories using other names.) You will end up with a chart something like the one pictured.

⑦ When the text is finished for the day, point out the first *line* and the last *line* of the text. Help children understand that you can point to the first word or the first line when you look at a message in print.

write
draw
read

▸ Place the text on the wall. Ask the children to write something about themselves and three friends or family members—what they like or what they are wearing—in four sentences, one on each page of a four-page blank book. Have them draw a picture to illustrate each sentence. They should make their own attempts at spelling but can use the group text as a resource if they want. When the children are finished, they read their writing to a partner.

Have the children read their stories and show their pictures. For some of the writing that is shared, ask the group to identify the first word and the last word.

Read the group story again together.

Link

Interactive Read-Aloud: Read aloud books that combine color words and animal words, one sentence on each page. After you have read the text several times, children can approximate reading for themselves and locate color words. Examples are:

- ▶ *I Like Me* by Nancy Carlson
- ▶ *Tough Boris* by Mem Fox

Shared Reading: Read the group story several times and have the children locate particular color words with a masking card (see *Teaching Resources*) or highlighter tape.

Guided Reading: In the simple texts they are reading, have children point to the first word, the last word, the first line, and the last line.

Interactive Writing: Use the terms *first* and *last* when referring to a text while constructing the message.

Independent Writing: Use the terms *first* and *last* when talking with children about the texts they are writing.

assess

- ▶ Notice whether the children know what you mean when you refer to the first and last words in a sentence.
- ▶ Ask individual children to point to the first and last words in a line of print.

Expand the Learning

Write a sentence about every child in the room on separate sheets of paper for children to illustrate; then staple the sheets together to make a class book.

Cut the class text for this lesson into sentence strips and glue the sentences onto separate pages to make an illustrated book.

Connect with Home

Have children take home the stapled book they created and read it to their family members.

Generative Lesson

early
mid
late

ELC 7
EARLY LITERACY CONCEPTS

Matching Word by Word
Cut-Up Sentences

Consider Your Children

Children need to learn to match one spoken word with one cluster of letters (defined by space) in lines of print. This is best developed through shared reading and shared and interactive writing, but when students have the "feel" of it, focus a few very explicit lessons on word-by-word matching. These same teaching guidelines can be used in combination with interactive writing and with simple poems from shared reading.

Working with English Language Learners

Matching one spoken word with one word in print is a challenge to all young children, especially those who may not fully understand word boundaries in English. Before you expect children to work on matching, be sure that they can say and understand the meaning of the sentences they are working on. Using children's names will give them words they know so they can check on themselves as they point and read. Provide many opportunities for repetition of the task.

You Need

► Pocket chart.

► Photocopied sentence strips of sentences with names of children from the class.

► Glue sticks.

From *Teaching Resources:*

► Large word cards (Pocket Chart Card Template).

► Small word cards (Word Card Template).

► Four-page blank books (Blank Book Page Template).

Understand the Principle

Children need to understand that sentences are made up of words and that written words are defined by space.

This concept is a foundation for learning to match word by word in reading and for learning to identify and solve individual words while reading and writing.

Explain the Principle

" We say one word for each word we see in writing. "

Explain the Principle

" We say one word for each word we see in writing. "

① Explain to the children that they are going to write sentences and read the words.

② Display a pocket chart that contains several children's names and some blank word cards.

③ Ask the children to look at the names on the pocket chart as you read them together. Suggested language: "Today we are going to write something about Caroline, Sara, and Jamal. We're going to write the words on these cards and make a sentence about each one."

④ Generate ideas for the name *Caroline*, such as "Caroline likes to read" or "Caroline has a yellow shirt." Guide the language so that the sentence is short enough to write on cards to be inserted into the pocket chart, but be sure that the language is the children's own and that they can repeat the sentence chosen.

⑤ After the sentence about Caroline is decided, put Caroline's name in a pocket on the left. "*Caroline* is the first word of our sentence. Caroline. . . . [Children respond with the second word, for example, *likes*.]"

⑥ Write the second word on a card and place it right after Caroline (or invite a student to do it). Point out that you are leaving space between the words and invite the children to read it together as you point. Suggested language: "Caroline likes. . . . [Children respond with the third word.]"

⑦ Write the third word on a card and repeat the process of rereading. Continue until the sentence is written on cards. Place a period after the last word. Read it all together and ask children to check to see whether they have left spaces between words.

⑧ Repeat the process using one or two more children's names. Emphasize individual words and spacing. Reread each time you add a word. Help children see that each word stands alone and that some sentences are shorter or longer than others. Point out how the period means to come to a full stop. For multisyllable words, clap the word and show how it is one word with space on either side. Finally, read all the sentences together as a unit.

cut
glue
draw

▶ Distribute photocopied sentence strips for children to cut apart and then glue back together into sentences that they illustrate.

▶ As an alternative, give each child a four-page blank book stapled along the 8½-inch side. Ask children to draw a friend or family member on each page and write a short sentence about this person, one word at a time, on small word cards (e.g., *Ben likes football*). Have them glue the cards in order at the bottom of the page to make a sentence about the picture. (Their spelling will be approximated.)

Ask children to share the sentences they have put together or written.

Link

Interactive Read-Aloud: Read aloud books with large type in which children can clearly see the words and spaces. As you and the children explore these books, help them notice the words and spacing. Examples are:

- ▶ *I Went Walking* by Sue Williams
- ▶ *Willy the Dreamer* by Anthony Browne

Shared Reading: Point out spaces and show children how to read word by word in short poems, songs, and chants, such as "Jerry Hall" or "Go to Bed" (see *Sing a Song of Poetry*).

Guided Reading: Prompt children to point crisply under words, using the same finger each time, while reading very simple, predictable texts. Ask them, "Did it match?" Your goal is to help them monitor their reading by pointing to and matching the words.

Interactive Writing: Explicitly point out spaces; reread messages word by word.

Independent Writing: Ask children to check their independent writing to be sure they are leaving spaces.

Expand the Learning

Prepare a pocket chart and cards with the names of children in the class and other words to combine for sentences. Ask children to put together sentences using a name card and other word cards. As they become more familiar with the messages (or more are added), they can vary the sentences they compose.

Using shared or interactive writing, create sentences about every child in the class and make a class big book with a page and drawing or photo for each child.

Connect with Home

Send the four-page books home for children to read to family members.

Create sentence puzzles (three cut-up words) in envelopes for children to take home and glue on a sheet of paper. They can illustrate the sentence and read it to a family member.

assess

- ▶ Observe the children's writing and notice whether they are using spaces.
- ▶ Observe the children reading independently to see whether they are noticing individual words and pointing word by word.

Generative Lesson

early
mid
late

ELC 8
EARLY LITERACY CONCEPTS

8 *Making Sentences*

Little Books

Consider Your Children

This lesson is best used after children have taken part in a great deal of shared reading. Be sure that children have already engaged in talking with each other, that they are somewhat familiar with the name chart, and that they recognize their own names and some of the names of their friends. It is also helpful for them to know what you mean by the first letter of a word and the first word in a sentence. You may want to incorporate those understandings into this lesson. They should also have heard many stories read aloud and participated in shared reading so that they have gained an internal sense of what a sentence "sounds like."

Working with English Language Learners

Many children have difficulty with the sentence structure of English because their own languages have different syntactic rules. Allow English language learners to approximate sentences without correcting them. Model correct syntax in your responses and expand their sentences in a conversational way. They will gradually acquire knowledge of English syntax if they have many opportunities to hear the language read aloud and to participate in lessons where it is easy for them to use their knowledge. Give English language learners more opportunities to practice saying sentences.

You Need

► Chart with sentences.
► Drawing supplies.

From *Teaching Resources:*
► Blank Book Page Template.

Understand the Principle

Children need to understand that sentences are made up of words that are put together to communicate meaning.

This information will be valuable to children as they read sentences in books and as they compose and write sentences.

Explain the Principle

" A sentence is a group of words that makes sense. "

Dan is wearing a blue shirt

Jason has new blue sneakers

Explain the Principle

" A sentence is a group of words that makes sense. "

① Explain to your children that words can be put together to tell something that can be understood or that makes sense.

② Using children's names, give examples of simple complete and incomplete sentences:

Cindy has a new red sweatshirt.
Jarrod is wearing new shoes.
Diana has new.
Craig does not like.
Synda is going to a birthday party.

③ Ask children to evaluate each sentence to decide whether it makes sense.

④ Using the class name chart (Lesson ELC 1), invite the children to say sentences about one another until all the names have been used.

⑤ Read several simple sentences, some complete and some incomplete, inviting the children to give a quiet signal (such as touching the nose) each time a sentence is complete:

Dan is wearing.
Shara wants to go to the gym.
Jason has.
Shana is wearing a new dress.
Rashon has a new jacket.
Mary has a red.

When a sentence is not complete, ask a child to add to it to make it complete.

6 Conduct the same activity using sentences in a story you have read to them, sentences about a picture from a big book, or sentences about an experience everyone has shared.

► Give children a stapled four-page 8½" × 11" blank book and invite them to write statements about a friend, one sentence on each page. They will approximate the spelling of words except for the names that they copy. They can also illustrate their books.

Say a portion of a sentence and call on children to finish it.

Ask children to share the sentences they wrote in their books.

Link

Interactive Read-Aloud: Read aloud books to help children internalize various types of sentence structure. Examples are:

- *Jasper's Beanstalk* by J. Nick Butterworth
- *Circle Dogs* by Kevin Henkes

Shared Reading: Pull out sentences from texts that are very familiar and read them in partial form, masking the rest of the sentence. Ask children to make the sentences complete.

Guided Reading: As children are reading, ask them to think about whether what they read makes sense.

Interactive Writing: During composition, guide children to create complete sentences.

Independent Writing: Encourage children to make complete sentences by reading back to them what they wrote and asking, "Does that make sense? Do you need to add anything?"

assess

- Observe children's reading behavior. Are they checking to see whether what they read makes sense? Do they reread or repeat to figure out what is meant?
- Notice whether children are making complete sentences in their independent writing.
- Check whether children are composing complete sentences in interactive writing.

Expand the Learning

Repeat the lesson using sentences from shared reading pieces, leaving out some parts of some sentences. Ask children to evaluate whether sentences are complete.

Prepare cut-up versions of some of the sentences you have created and read them with the children. Have them put words in the pocket chart to re-create sentences and then read them.

Connect with Home

Have children take their sentence books home to read to family members.

Give them a stapled four-page blank book (*Teaching Resources,* Blank Book Page Template) to take home; on each page, have them write a sentence about a family member or friend and illustrate it.

Phonological Awareness

Phonological awareness is a broad term that refers to both explicit and implicit knowledge of the sounds in language. It includes the ability to identify and make rhymes, hear syllables in words, hear the parts of words (onsets and rimes), and hear individual sounds in words.

Phonemic awareness is one kind of phonological awareness. Phonemic awareness refers to the ability to identify, isolate, and manipulate the individual sounds *(phonemes)* in words. Concepts categorized as phonemic awareness are labeled PA in this Continuum.

Phonological awareness (and phonemic awareness) is taught orally or in connection with letters, when it is called *phonics.* Phonics instruction refers to teaching children to connect letters and sounds in words. While very early experiences focus on hearing and saying sounds in the absence of letters, most of the time you will want to teach children to hear sounds in connection with letters. Many of the lessons related to this section begin with oral activity but move toward connecting the sounds to letters. You will not want to teach all of the PA principles in this Continuum. It is more effective to teach children only two or three ways to manipulate phonemes in words so that they learn how words work.

Principles related to letter/sound relationships, or phonics, are included in the letter/sound relationships category of this Continuum.

Connect to Assessment

See related PA Assessment Tasks in the Assessment Guide in *Teaching Resources:*

- ▸ Identifying Word Boundaries
- ▸ Hearing Syllables
- ▸ Hearing Rhymes
- ▸ Identifying Beginning Consonant Sounds
- ▸ Identifying Ending Consonant Sounds
- ▸ Identifying Sounds in Words

- ▸ Blending Word Parts
- ▸ Segmenting Word Parts
- ▸ Blending Sounds to Make Words
- ▸ Segmenting a Word into Sounds
- ▸ Adding Sounds to Words
- ▸ Deleting Sounds from Words

Develop Your Professional Understanding

See *Word Matters: Teaching Phonics and Spelling in the Reading/Writing Classroom* by G.S. Pinnell and I.C. Fountas. 1998. Portsmouth, New Hampshire: Heinemann.

Related pages: 5, 63–64, 76–77, 82, 90–91, 95, 98–99, 137.

Hearing Rhymes
Songs and Poems

Consider Your Children

Start with just one song. Teach it to the children by singing it. This lesson will be more successful if children first learn the song or chant as an oral activity. They can feel the rhythm of it and enjoy it; then the print will be more meaningful. Having strong familiarity with the rhyme will enable them to focus on the rhyming words and they will enjoy the variations.

Working with English Language Learners

Some children may be hearing these rhymes for the first time and/or may not implicitly understand the concept of "rhyme." Illustrate the rhyming objects (for example, *sheep, jeep* or *frog, log*) by pictures and by pointing as you say them. Have children say the rhymes so that they can feel the pronunciation in their own mouth. Be sure to repeat the chant with children, using rhythm in an enjoyable way, so that they can remember it.

You Need

▶ Chart or pocket chart containing the words of "Did You Ever See" or another song.

▶ Pointer.

▶ Highlighter tape (or marker).

From *Teaching Resources:*

▶ Large word cards (three sets) for *sheep, jeep* (Pocket Chart Card Template).

▶ Various word/picture cards to insert to vary the rhyme: *star* on a *car; mouse* in a *house; duck* in a *truck; dog* on a *log; fly* in the *sky; bug* on a *rug; cat* on a *mat.* (Using the Pocket Chart Card Template, make simple drawings yourself or have the children do them.)

▶ Blank Book Page Template.

Understand the Principle

Enjoying rhymes and songs helps children become more sensitive to the sounds of language, particularly rhyming words.

Internalized rhymes and songs are powerful exemplars that help children connect words and learn how they "work."

Explain the Principle

❝ Some words have end parts that sound alike. They rhyme. ❞

❝ You can hear the rhymes in poems and songs. ❞

Explain the Principle

" Some words have end parts that sound alike. They rhyme. "

" You can hear the rhymes in poems and songs. "

① Tell your children they will be learning a song that will help them know about rhyming words.

② Children may have previously learned to sing "If You're Happy and You Know It, Clap Your Hands." (See *Sing a Song of Poetry*.) If so, they will know the tune; if not, teach them this new rhyme to go with the tune. Introduce the song by singing it with the children, emphasizing enjoyment.

③ Invite the children to think about the two words *sheep* and *jeep*. Point out that they rhyme. Say each word and help children recognize that these two words sound alike at the end. The last part is the same.

④ After children have learned the basic song and sung it several times, using one or two more pairs of rhyming words, invite them to suggest their own rhyming words to put in the blanks. The idea is to enjoy rhymes, so you can allow some "nonsense" words while they catch on to the idea.

⑤ Vary how the children enjoy this song:

▸ Have half the group sing the question and the other half sing the answer.

▸ Sing the song and clap when you come to the rhyming words (demonstrate first) to reinforce the rhyme pattern.

▸ Say the verse and snap your fingers when you come to the rhyming words to draw more attention to the sound patterns.

▸ Point to the written text as you and the children sing. Drop out on the second rhyming word and let the children sing it by themselves. Talk about how they can check themselves by saying the two words and listening to the sounds.

6 Place the chart on the wall or set up a pocket chart version and invite children to point and read. Provide colored transparent plastic to highlight rhymes.

write
draw
read

▶ Create four-page books with "Did You Ever See" on the front cover. On each page have the phrase "a _____ in a _____" on the bottom. Ask children to fill in the blanks with their own words in approximated spelling and to illustrate each page. Then have them read their books to a partner.

Have children sing the song together again and identify the rhyming words. Invite children to share one page from their books.

Link

Interactive Read-Aloud: Read aloud books with rhyming words, such as:

- ▸ *Down by the Bay* by Raffi
- ▸ *There's a Spider on the Floor* by Raffi

Shared Reading: Reread familiar rhymes and songs from charts. Have children locate the rhyming words. Any familiar songs, such as "A-hunting We Will Go" or "Mary Had a Little Lamb," are good material. Refer to *Sing a Song of Poetry* for these and other suggestions.

Guided Reading: Help children notice any words that rhyme.

Interactive Writing: If the writing has rhyming words, point them out and ask children to say them.

Independent Writing: Encourage children to connect the words they are writing with words that rhyme.

assess

- ▸ Observe how easily the children can identify words that rhyme.
- ▸ Notice if the children are able to match pictures of things that have labels that rhyme.

Expand the Learning

Have children select rhyming pictures (perhaps with word labels underneath) to create variations of the song in the pocket chart. (See *Teaching Resources,* Picture Cards, Short Vowels.)

Change the answer in the chart to

Yes, I saw a ____ in a ____.
Yes, I saw a ____ in a ____.
Yes, I saw a ____ that was sitting in a [standing on a, or whatever is required] ____.
Yes, I saw a ____ in a ____.

Once children have learned alternate "yes" and "no" versions, they can think about whether you could *really* see a frog on a log or not and select either the "yes" or the "no" version.

Connect with Home

After children have learned the song, let them take home a copy to read to their family members. Communicate to family members that "reading" poems like this helps children learn phonics but that they are not yet ready to read the words in isolation. Family members and caregivers can have fun making up new variations of the song.

Send home a blank four-page "Did You Ever See" book for the children to make with family members.

Generative
Lesson

early
mid
late

PA 2
PHONOLOGICAL AWARENESS

Hearing More Rhymes
Poems

Consider Your Children

Use these teaching guidelines and variations with appropriate poems and chants (*Sing a Song of Poetry* includes many examples). This early lesson will help to build children's knowledge of traditional rhymes. You will want to engage children in a great deal of shared reading of rhymes and poems before moving to identify or work with the rhyming words. If they know the chant and have enjoyed it many times, they will have an internal sense of the rhythm and rhyme that will make this explicit lesson easier and more meaningful.

Working with English Language Learners

Be aware that many English language learners will be hearing traditional English nursery rhymes for the first time. They can enjoy them but will need many more lively repetitions to become fluent. Ask children if they know any rhymes like these that they say at home and appreciate their contributions even if you cannot understand them. There may be some translations that will be helpful to you. Use illustrations to help children understand the rhyming words you are using (for example, "quick" and "candlestick"). Look at *Sing a Song of Poetry* or a similar anthology to select rhymes that you think English language learners will have the best chance of understanding.

You Need

► Chart or pocket chart on which you have written a short poem or song.
► Pointer.
► Highlighter tape (or a marker suitable for underlining).
► Glue sticks.
► Drawing supplies.
► Photocopies of the selected poem or song.

Understand the Principle

Enjoying rhymes leads children to pay close attention to how language sounds. They learn to hear similarities and differences. Eventually, they hear individual speech sounds and are able to connect them to letter symbols.

Explain the Principle

" Some words have end parts that sound alike. They rhyme. "

" You can say words and hear how they rhyme. "

① Tell your children they will be learning more nursery rhymes.

Explain the Principle

" Some words have end parts that sound alike. They rhyme. "

" You can say words and hear how they rhyme. "

② Introduce the poem or chant by reading it aloud to the children without showing the print. Emphasize enjoyment of the language, the rhythm, and the rhyme. Don't read and point to the words yet—save the chart for later. (For beginners, avoid having too many lines on one page.)

> Jack be nimble,
>
> Jack be quick,
>
> Jack jump over
>
> The candlestick.
>
> Jack be nimble,
>
> Quick as a fox.
>
> Jack jump over
>
> This little box.

③ Say the rhyme, one line at a time, having children repeat after you. After doing this several times, invite children to say the verse with you. Reread it a few times so the children become very familiar with it.

④ After children have learned the verse, vary what you do:

- Have half the group say the first line, the other half say the second line, and so on throughout the poem.
- Divide the children into the appropriate number of groups and have each group say one line of the poem.
- Whisper the whole verse.
- Say the verse and clap when you come to the rhyming words. (Demonstrate first.)
- Say the verse and snap your fingers when you come to the rhyming words.
- Say the verse in a normal voice, but whisper when you come to the rhyming words.
- Start saying the poem loud and get softer as you get to the end. End in a whisper.

▶ Say the poem together, but designate one child to say the rhyming words. Have everyone else stop while this child reads the rhyming words alone.

▶ Read the poem while quickly pointing to the written words on the chart.

▶ Have children locate the words that rhyme and put highlighter tape over them or underline them.

glue
draw
read

▶ Give the children a copy of the poem to glue on a piece of paper and illustrate. Ask the children to glue the copy of the poem into their individual poetry book and read it to a partner. Have them add poems to this book all through the year.

Jack be nimble,
Jack be quick,
Jack jump over
This candlestick.

Jack be nimble.
Quick as a fox.
Jack jump over
This little box.

Have the children say the poem together again and clap on the rhyming words.

Link

Interactive Read-Aloud: Read aloud books that emphasize rhyme and rhythm, such as:

- ▶ *Over on the Farm* by Christopher Gunson
- ▶ *Bam Bam Bam* by Eve Merriam

Shared Reading: Reread familiar rhymes such as "Little Fishes in a Brook" or "Jack, Jack" from charts and give children copies to glue in their poetry book. (See *Sing a Song of Poetry.*) Have them use highlighter tape to mark the rhyming words.

Guided Reading: Point out pairs of words that rhyme. In word work, make one or two words with magnetic letters and have the children tell a rhyming word.

Interactive Writing: If the writing has rhyming words, point them out and ask children to say them.

Independent Writing: Encourage children to write some of the simple rhymes that include their own names. Do not be concerned if they copy some of the rhyme, but help them say words slowly to write some of the rhyme for themselves.

assess

- ▶ Notice how easily children identify words that rhyme.
- ▶ As a general assessment, say two or three words and have the children give rhyming words.

Expand the Learning

Repeat the lesson and variations with other nursery rhymes, poems, and chants, such as "Jack and Jill" or "Hickory, Dickory, Dock." (See *Sing a Song of Poetry.*)

Print a copy of the poem in an 18-point font and glue it on a large piece of cardboard (about 16" × 22"). Put this "poem card," along with similar ones, in a box labeled *Poetry.* Have children choose and read these poems they have previously learned. Provide colored highlighter tape for them to place on rhyming words.

Connect with Home

After children have learned a poem (or a verse of a poem), have them take home a copy to read to family members. Communicate to caregivers that reading poems helps children learn more about phonics. Explain that the language supports the learning of letters and sounds but that the children are not yet ready to read the words in isolation.

Encourage caregivers to read poems and books that have rhymes and to sing songs with rhymes. Tell them to stop before the second word in the rhymed pair to invite prediction.

3 Hearing Rhymes

Picture Sort

Consider Your Children

This activity is best used after children have participated in a great deal of shared reading of poems. (See *Sing a Song of Poetry*.) If rhyming is a very new concept for children, begin with only two or three pairs of rhymes. Do not use printed words with the pictures: this is an oral activity. (Later, you can repeat the lesson with pictures and words and then with just words.)

Working with English Language Learners

Children who are not accustomed to English phonology will need many experiences to be able to hear rhymes and understand the concept. Be sure that children can say and understand the meaning of the picture cards that you use; discard those that are too far from their experience or that you cannot explain. To identify rhymes, use poems that they already know through shared reading and have practiced many times.

You Need

▶ Pocket chart.

▶ Glue sticks.

▶ Scissors.

From *Teaching Resources:*

▶ Rhyming picture sets to use in the pocket chart (Picture Cards, Rhymes). (Enlarge the pictures and glue them on cards.)

▶ Two-Way Sort Sheets.

Understand the Principle

Hearing and identifying words that rhyme, or sound alike, helps children realize that words are made up of sounds and also helps them distinguish individual sounds so that they understand that letters and sounds are related.

This knowledge will help them break words apart to solve them.

Explain the Principle

" You can hear and connect words that rhyme. "

plan

Explain the Principle

" You can hear and connect words that rhyme. "

① Tell children that today they are going to work again with rhyming words.

② Using picture cards, line up two easy rhyming words at the top of a pocket chart. Have children say the labels of

these pictures. Suggested language: "Some words sound alike at the end. Listen to these two words, *bee, tree.* [Point to the pictures as you say the words.] Now say those words with me. [Children respond.] They sound alike, don't they? When they sound alike at the end, they *rhyme.*"

③ Guide children to talk about how the words sound alike at the end. Then demonstrate matching another pair of pictures, having children say the labels with you: *cat, bat.*

④ Line up pictures of the car, fish, fan, and snake in a column on the left of the pocket chart. Then ask one child to find the picture that rhymes with *car* and say both words to check it, asking the class to judge whether the words rhyme.

⑤ Proceed through the rest of the pictures, matching rhyming pairs and saying the words aloud each time. Have children match rhyming pictures for *car, star; fish, dish; fan, van; snake, rake.*

say
cut
match
glue

▶ Have sheets of rhyming pictures for children to say, cut, match, and glue on a Two-Way Sort Sheet.

Have children share their pairs of
rhyming pictures by saying the pairs aloud. Afterward you may want to read
a poem together and identify two words that rhyme.

Link

Interactive Read-Aloud: Read aloud books and poems that have fun with rhymes, such as:

- ► *The Hungry Thing* by Jan Slepian and Ann Seidler
- ► *Is Your Mama a Llama?* by Deborah Guarino

Shared Reading: Read rhyming poems together such as "Jack Sprat" or "High and Low" (see *Sing a Song of Poetry*). After children know them, identify easy rhyming words.

Guided Reading: Point out words that rhyme, reminding children that the last parts sound the same.

Interactive Writing: When what you are writing together includes rhyming words, point them out to children.

Independent Writing: When children are saying words slowly to hear sounds, encourage them to make connections to words that rhyme.

assess

- ► Observe the children's ability to recognize rhymes and put rhyming pairs together.
- ► Notice the children's spontaneous recognition of rhymes in shared reading.

Expand the Learning

Repeat this lesson adding more pictures—*hat, mat; bar, jar.* Include some words that do not rhyme with any others in the set.

Repeat this lesson with the following pairs: *bear, chair; pen, hen; mouse, house; dog, log; shell, bell; bib, crib; pen, hen; shirt, skirt; crown, clown; socks, box; moon, spoon.*

Have children sort the entire set of rhyming words, saying them out loud to check their work.

After children have read simple poems many times in shared reading, have them glue copies of the poems in their personal poetry books and illustrate them. On some poems, they can identify and highlight rhyming words.

Connect with Home

Give children another sheet of rhyming pictures to cut apart and match at home.

Invite family members to play rhyming games. The adult says two words and the child repeats them. The child claps if the words rhyme and doesn't clap if they don't rhyme. Another game is to have the family member say three words and the child stands if they all rhyme and sits if one does not. A variation: say a series of rhyming words: *dog, frog, log, fog.* The child sits when she hears one in the series that does not rhyme: *dog, frog, log, fog, hot.*

4 Hearing Syllables
Picture Sort

Consider Your Children

In this minilesson, children learn a valuable routine they will use in word sorting over the next few years. Do not use print with the pictures at first; initially this exercise is only for hearing syllables. Later you may use the pictures and the words or only the words. You may want to start with one- and two-syllable words in this lesson and add three-syllable words to the next lesson.

Working with English Language Learners

English language learners will need to know the labels for pictures before they can hear syllables. Go over the pictures several times so that you are sure that they know them and can say them. For these students, eliminate pictures that are beyond their present understanding and experience. Observe and/or work with them the first time they do the application activity so that you are sure they understand the task.

You Need

▶ Pocket chart divided into three sections: one-, two-, and three-syllable words. Head each section with a picture that has a red line under or around it or that has been drawn on a different-color card stock. These are the key words.

From *Teaching Resources:*

▶ Selected picture cards representing one-, two-, and three-syllable words (Picture Cards, Syllables).

▶ Three-Way Sort Sheets.

Understand the Principle

Hearing the syllables in words helps children learn how to break them down into parts that can be represented with letters and letter clusters. It helps children relate the oral language they know to the written language.

Explain the Principle

" You can hear and say the syllables in a word. "

" Some words have one syllable. "

" Some words have two syllables. "

" Some words have three or more syllables. "

plan

Explain the Principle

" You can hear and say the syllables in a word. "

" Some words have one syllable. "

" Some words have two syllables. "

" Some words have three or more syllables. "

① Explain to the class that today they are going to learn about the parts they can hear in words. These parts are called syllables.

② Have the children say the name of each of the three key pictures (*bird*, *monkey*, and *elephant*) and clap when they hear each syllable. Each time ask, "How many syllables can you hear?" Demonstrate several times if necessary.

③ Place each of the key pictures along the top of the pocket chart. You may want to use a red line (or different-color stock) to mark off the top row and mention that these are the key pictures.

④ Go through the rest of the pictures, each time asking children to say and clap the syllables for the word the picture represents and then decide whether the word belongs with *bird, monkey,* or *elephant.* When finished, you will have sorted all the pictures.

⑤ Quickly demonstrate the task of sorting smaller pictures on a tabletop using Three-Way Sort Sheets. Children place the key pictures at the top of the sheet. Then they say the word associated with each picture and place the picture under the appropriate key picture.

say
sort
read

▸ Have the children, in pairs, place the key pictures at the top of each column of a Three-Way Sort Sheet. Then have them say and sort the pictures. First, one partner says the name of each item pictured, sorts the pictures according to the number of syllables in the name, and reads the completed list. Then they mix up the set of cards, and the other partner repeats the activity.

▸ You might have several sets of picture cards copied on different-color paper so that the children can practice with a partner using different sets.

Have the children demonstrate saying and clapping a few one-, two-, and three-syllable words of their choice.

Link

Interactive Read-Aloud: When you find an interesting two- or three-syllable word in a book you are reading aloud, ask children to say and clap it.

- ▸ *To Market, To Market* by Anne Miranda
- ▸ *I Love You, Little One* by Nancy Tafuri

Shared Reading: When reading poetry together, point out two- and three-syllable words and have children say and clap them. Invite children to cover or flag (see *Teaching Resources, Materials/Routines*) words with a certain number of syllables in familiar poems or songs such as "Bouncing Ball" or "Dormy, Dormy, Dormouse" (see *Sing a Song of Poetry*).

Guided Reading: Highlight syllables by clapping when children have trouble matching longer words one to one; build the concept that a single word can have one or more parts.

Interactive Writing: Say and clap words before writing them. Write the word one part at a time (for example, *kang-a-roo*). Show children how they can use their knowledge to represent a part of a longer word (*sneak-er*).

Independent Writing: Encourage children to clap words they want to write and listen for the parts in words they can represent with letters.

assess

- ▸ Observe the children's ability to say and clap the syllables in words.
- ▸ Notice whether children recognize and use syllables when writing.

Expand the Learning

Repeat the lesson with other pictures: *book, dog, bus; turtle, balloon, carrot, toothbrush, football, hammer, pencil, pumpkin; bicycle, umbrella.*

You may want to clap some four-syllable words: *caterpillar, motorcycle, watermelon, pepperoni.*

Connect with Home

Explain to parents or caregivers, in a newsletter or at a meeting, how to highlight syllables by saying words and clapping on each part. Then they can practice, with their children, listening for and clapping word parts as they prepare dinner, clean the house, or walk in the neighborhood.

At home, have children cut out magazine pictures representing words with one, two, and three syllables. Have them glue these pictures on pieces of paper, divided into three columns, one for each category.

5 *Hearing Syllables*
Chant

Consider Your Children

This lesson is appropriate early in kindergarten. It will help to build a foundation for children's attention to the sounds in words and parts of words. Be sure that children understand the routines of shared reading and readily join in when you invite them.

We have used the technical term *syllable* here. A syllable indicates a "break" in a word. Use your own judgment about the appropriateness of the technical term for your students. "Syllable" may be included as one type of word part.

Working with English Language Learners

This lesson requires children to remember a repetitive chant. For English language learners, go over the chant many times so that they can say it quickly. Have pictures of the foods that you are using and be sure that they understand the meaning of the English word. To enrich the lesson with a variety of foods, ask English language learners what foods they would put in the blank. If you do not have pictures of the foods they suggest, they may be able to provide drawings.

You Need

► Pocket chart or chart displaying chant about food.

► Drawing supplies.

From *Teaching Resources:*

► Pairs of word cards (Pocket Chart Card Template) with food names, two of each word, to substitute in the blanks (for example, *hamburgers, soup, cereal, chicken, tacos, potatoes, cake, cookies*). You might want to draw simple pictures of the food next to the word.

► Four-page book (Blank Book Page Template) of the "I love . . ." rhyme.

Understand the Principle

Hearing the syllables in words helps children learn how to break them down into parts that can be represented with letters and letter clusters.

Hearing syllables in words contributes to children's understanding of word-by-word matching when reading continuous text: even though a word has more than one part, you point to it only once when reading.

Explain the Principle

" You can hear and say the syllables in a word. "

" Some words have one syllable. "

" Some words have two syllables. "

" Some words have three or more syllables. "

plan

Explain the Principle

66 **You can hear and say the syllables in a word.** 99

66 **Some words have one syllable.** 99

66 **Some words have two syllables.** 99

66 **Some words have three or more syllables.** 99

① Explain to the class that today they are going to learn a new chant that will help them think about the parts in words.

② Suggested language: "You have been learning to clap words to hear the number of syllables."

③ Introduce the chant orally and say it enough times that children can join in comfortably.

④ When the children say the chant, have them clap the food word while saying it. Suggested language: "When we clap *pizza*, we hear two parts." Demonstrate.

⑤ Demonstrate clapping with several other food words until clapping becomes an integral part of the chant. "Let's clap 'I love *hamburgers*' together." Or: "I love *potatoes*" [*clap, clap, clap* quickly while saying the word].

⑥ Once the chant is learned, ask children to vary the chant using other foods. Display the rhyme on sentence strips in a pocket chart, or prewrite it on chart paper and use tape or large stick-on notes for words. Have some food words with simple drawings already written on cards and/or quickly write children's suggestions on cards.

⑦ Point to the words while children read the chant in a shared way. Suggested language: "When you read, you point to each word. Look at the word *hamburgers*. How many syllables or parts does it have? [Demonstrate clapping—children respond.] A word can have three parts, so when you read, you keep your finger [or pointer] under it while you say all three parts."

⑧ Demonstrate and repeat this process with different food words. Continue shared reading of the chant, as the children clap on the food word syllables and you point to the words. Discuss how you keep your pointer or finger under the word while you say it.

apply

draw
read
clap

▶ Give each child a four-page stapled book of the "I love . . ." rhyme (leaving blanks for the food words), with one line on each page. Ask children to write or draw their own food in the blanks and then read the book to a partner, clapping the food words when they come to them. If they write the word, accept approximated spelling. The point is to choose words and listen for the parts.

share

Read through the chant again and have children talk about what they learned about words. You may hear comments like:

"*Tacos* has two syllables." (Children may say "parts.")

"*Hamburgers* has three syllables."

"*Cookies* has two syllables."

If terms like *ice cream* or *hot dogs* come up, explain that they are made up of two separate words that go together. Have children clap each word. "*Ice cream* is really two words, isn't it? How can you tell? [Children may respond that there is a space between them. If they don't, point it out.] Let's say and clap the first word, *ice.* [Demonstrate.] Let's say and clap the next word, *cream.* [Demonstrate.] You point to each word when you read, like this. [Demonstrate.]"

Link

Interactive Read-Aloud: Read aloud books that have rhythms that children will enjoy. Clap some of the longer words after the first read.

- ▸ *Tick Tock* by Lena Anderson
- ▸ *Wheels on the Bus* by Raffi

Shared Reading: Read other poems, songs, and chants such as "Ladybug! Ladybug!" or "I'm Dusty Bill" (see *Sing a Song of Poetry* for suggestions), pointing under each word as you go along. Clap words to help children hear the syllables.

Guided Reading: Prompt children to point crisply *under* each word while reading. At the end of the lesson, have children find one or two words with one or two syllables.

Interactive Writing: Clap words you want to write to break them down into parts for writing.

Independent Writing: Prompt children to clap words to break them down into parts for writing.

assess

- ▸ Perform a quick individual assessment by asking children to clap a series of words: *horse, pony, butterfly,* and *caterpillar,* for example.

- ▸ Notice the extent to which children are representing syllables in their writing. Notice their use of vowels, which indicates increasing sophistication.

Expand the Learning

Repeat the activity with more word choices. You might want to use pictures of food from the collection of syllable pictures *(Teaching Resources)* or pictures of food from magazines. If children have trouble recognizing the words, you can place the picture on the front or back of a word card. The point here is not to learn the words but to hear the syllables.

You might want to display the chant on several pocket charts around the room. Place food words along the bottom of the chart, and have children choose three different food words and read the chant three times, pointing under each word as they say it. Children will need to distinguish between words by noticing the first letter or some other visual feature, as well as match word by word while reading continuous text.

Connect with Home

Give each child a one-page sheet containing the chant. Leave a blank space where the food word goes. Have family members help the child draw a small picture and attempt to write the word.

Have children read their "I love . . ." books to family members.

Explain to parents or caregivers, at a meeting or in a newsletter, how to help their children listen to and clap the parts they hear in words. Then give each child a sheet containing five or six animal, clothing, or food pictures (you can select some from Picture Cards, Syllables, in *Teaching Resources*) to take home and use to practice saying and clapping. Encourage family members to play the syllable clapping game with names of objects they see while in the car on the way to school or at the shopping mall.

Hearing, Saying, and Clapping Syllables

Picture Sort

Consider Your Children

If clapping syllables is new to children, begin with one- and two-syllable words only, and add three-syllable words in the next lesson. Clapping syllables will be a new technique for many of the children early in the year. This technique will be very useful as they learn to take words apart, but it may take some practice to coordinate saying and clapping the words. Be sure that they can listen to you say the word and then repeat it after you. The contrast of words with one part and two parts will help them understand the concept you are demonstrating. Before moving to three-syllable words, work with one- and two-syllable words until children can coordinate the action.

Working with English Language Learners

For this activity, select words that English language learners can say, including all the syllables of the word. Articulate the words slowly and carefully, and provide many opportunities for them to repeat the words and clap them. Clearly demonstrate the application task. Invite children to say and clap their first and last names as well as some words in their own languages. For example, *cat* is *gato* in Spanish and could be placed in the two-syllable column. Be sure to use English words the children can understand or learn easily from the pictures.

You Need

▶ Pocket chart.

▶ Glue sticks.

From *Teaching Resources:*

▶ Pictures representing one-, two-, and three-syllable words (select from Picture Cards, Syllables).

▶ Two-Way Sort Cards or Sheets.

Understand the Principle

Hearing the syllables in words helps children learn how to break them down into parts that can be represented with letters and letter clusters. It also helps them learn how to match their oral language to the written language as they begin to read.

Explain the Principle

" You can hear and say the syllables in a word. "

" Some words have one syllable. "

" Some words have two syllables. "

" Some words have three or more syllables. "

plan

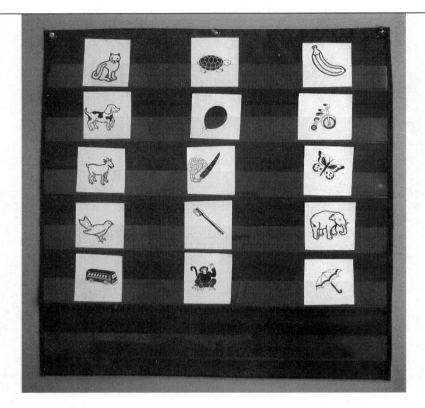

Explain the Principle

❝ You can hear and say the syllables in a word. ❞

❝ Some words have one syllable. ❞

❝ Some words have two syllables. ❞

❝ Some words have three or more syllables. ❞

① Tell your children they are going to clap the parts of words.

② Begin by showing the picture representing the first one-syllable word. Ask children to say and clap the word. Suggested language: "When we say words, we can clap the parts we hear. They are called syllables. [Demonstrate with *cat*.] How many syllables do you hear in *cat?* We hear one syllable and we clap once."

③ Say and clap the rest of the one-syllable words.

④ Suggested language: "Some words have two syllables that we can hear and clap. [Demonstrate with *turtle*.] We hear two syllables and we clap two times."

⑤ Continue through the rest of the two- and three-syllable words.

⑥ Saying and clapping the words may be enough for one minilesson. If you feel the children can continue, move to the next part of the lesson.

⑦ Display a pocket chart with three columns.

⑧ Go through the pictures again. This time, have children tell you where to place the picture—under 1, 2, or 3, according to the number of syllables. Say and clap words as many times as needed for children to hear the syllables.

say
sort
glue
read

▶ Have the children use Two-Way
Sort Cards to say and sort pictures
representing two- and three-syllable
words. Alternatively, give them a
Two-Way Sort Sheet and pictures to
say, sort, and glue. They should
read their final lists to a partner.

As a review, have children choose a word of their own and clap the syllables.
You may want to give them a category (e.g., food, clothes, animals).

Link

Interactive Read-Aloud: When you find an interesting two- or three-syllable word in a book you are reading aloud, ask children to say and clap it.

- ▶ *The Wizard* by Bill Martin, Jr.
- ▶ *A Honey of a Day* by Janet Marshall

Shared Reading: When reading poetry together such as "Little Jack Horner" or "Open, Shut Them" (see *Sing a Song of Poetry*), point out two- and three-syllable words and have children say and clap them.

Guided Reading: When children are reading simple texts, have them clap two- and three-syllable words (for example, *monkey* or *banana*) to illustrate how a single word can have parts that you can hear, but you point to the word only once.

Interactive Writing: Say and clap some words when writing them, or revisit the text to clap words.

Independent Writing: Encourage children to say and clap words to identify the parts so that they can hear the sounds and connect them to letters.

Expand the Learning

Repeat the lesson with other words: *book, goat, bus, top, house, grapes; lemon, wagon, football, flower, hammer, pencil, pumpkin, water; dinosaur, icicle, kangaroo, tornado, strawberry.*

You may want to clap four-syllable words (*alligator, caterpillar, escalator, motorcycle, pepperoni, watermelon*) as an oral activity.

Connect with Home

Show family members how to say and clap syllables with children. The caregiver might say a word and have the child beat a pan with a wooden spoon or clap the number of syllables he or she can hear in each. They can clap words in the supermarket or in the kitchen while cooking. Suggest starting with the names of family and friends.

assess

- ▶ Observe the children's ability to say and clap the syllables in words.
- ▶ Notice whether children recognize and use syllables when writing.

Saying Words Slowly to Hear Sounds

Picture-Word Match

Generative Lesson

early
mid
late

PA7
PHONOLOGICAL AWARENESS
(PHONEMIC AWARENESS)

Consider Your Children

The skill of saying words slowly is most powerfully developed through daily interactive writing. This lesson is most successful if children have previously participated in a great deal of interactive writing, during which saying words slowly has been modeled and elicited. This lesson provides explicit demonstrations to help children systematize the technique. When children attempt to write or tell letters for sounds they hear, confirm any letter that can represent the sound they hear (e.g., *bar*).

Working with English Language Learners

Saying words slowly will make the phonology of English words more available to English language learners and will help them considerably in their writing. Be sure that you enunciate clearly and provide many demonstrations. Accept children's approximations as they pronounce words. Some sounds may be very difficult for them, and eventually they will simply need to remember the graphic sign even if they cannot say all parts of the word. Internally, they will probably be making their own connections with idiosyncratic pronunciations of words.

You Need

► Pocket chart.

From *Teaching Resources:*

► Word cards (Pocket Chart Card Template).

► Picture Cards, Consonant-Vowel-Consonant (enlarged).

► Blank cards (Pocket Chart Card Template).

► Two-Column or Two-Way Sort Sheets.

Understand the Principle

Children need to understand that words are a sequence of sounds. They need to isolate and identify a large number of these sounds in order to understand the alphabetic principle—that there is a relationship between letters and sounds in words.

The goal is to get children to say words slowly to hear each of the sounds clearly.

Explain the Principle

“ You can say a word slowly. ”

“ You can hear the sounds in a word. ”

plan

Explain the Principle

❝ **You can say a word slowly.** ❞

❝ **You can hear the sounds in a word.** ❞

① Tell the children they will be learning how to say words slowly and write the letters.

② Place pictures of a dog, a moon, a cat, a bear, and a sun on the pocket chart. Be sure the things you select do not represent words that most of the children already know how to write.

③ Have clearly written cards displaying the label for each picture. Have blank cards ready on which to demonstrate writing the words.

④ Suggested language: "If you say a word slowly, you can hear the sounds in it."

⑤ Show the picture of a dog, saying the word slowly, not segmenting the sounds but exaggerating slightly so that it is easier to hear them. The sounds should be smoothly blended.

⑥ Suggested language: "Now, you say the word with me. [Children respond.] Can you hear some of the sounds? [Children make the isolated sound they hear or identify letters.]"

⑦ Show the word card, *dog*. "Could this be *dog?* [Children respond.] How do you know? [Children may suggest there is a *d*, *o*, or *g*.] Yes, you can hear the [letter]." Try to elicit several sounds. Then place the word card in the second column opposite the picture card.

⑧ Repeat with each of the five words. Have children say the word slowly and generate letters, which you write on a card. (Fill in the letters they do not come up with so that the spelling is standard.)

say
write
(find)

apply

▶ On a Two-Column or Two-Way Sort
Sheet, have children place a picture
on the left side and try to write
some letters for the sounds they
hear in each word (or find the
magnetic letters) on the right side.
Include some pictures for simple
words that will be new to children.

share

Have children play a game in which one child says a word slowly and the
others try to come up with one sound from the word.

PA 7
PHONOLOGICAL AWARENESS (PHONEMIC AWARENESS)

Link

Interactive Read-Aloud: Read aloud books that draw the children's attention to the sounds of words, such as:

► *Boo to a Goose* by Mem Fox

► *Chugga-Chugga Choo-Choo* by Kevin Lewis

Shared Reading: Using stick-on notes, cover some words in a text that children have read several times. When you approach the covered word, have children say it and predict what the first letter will be. Then remove the cover to check their prediction letter by letter.

Guided Reading: When a child meets an unknown word, instead of telling what it is, ask, "Could it be [word]?" Ask the child to say it slowly and check each of the letters.

Interactive Writing: When solving a word, ask children to say it slowly and think about the letters. They can suggest many of the letters while you fill in the rest to achieve standard spelling.

Independent Writing: Encourage children to say slowly the new words they are attempting to spell (e.g., *can, two, my*), representing as many letters as they can.

Expand the Learning

Repeat the lesson with more words and picture cards to practice saying words slowly, listening for and recording sounds in letter form.

Connect with Home

Give children copies of some picture and word cards that represent clear sounds *(cat, pan)* so that they can match them at home. Explain to caregivers that the children should say each word very slowly in order to hear each sound. As children say the word, caregivers should have them raise one finger for each sound they hear and then have them match the picture with the word. Be sure to explain to family members that this is a matching task related to phonics rather than a drill on words in isolation.

assess

► Notice the extent to which children are able to represent letters in words accurately in their writing.

► Observe whether the children are using letter/ sound cues to check on their reading and to solve new words in reading.

► Notice which children are representing all easy-to-hear sounds in their writing.

► Note which sounds are hard to hear for certain children.

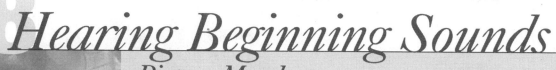

8 Hearing Beginning Sounds
Picture Match

Consider Your Children

This lesson works best after the children have worked with their names and have done some interactive writing. In this lesson, they learn an important routine for matching beginning sounds. Children will be using matching and sorting in many different ways.

Working with English Language Learners

Matching pictures and saying the words to hear beginning sounds will help children take on the phonology of English. Saying these words slowly with emphasis on the beginning letter will make words more available to children than when they are following them within the rapid pattern of normal speech. Be sure that they know, understand, and can say the word for items in the pictures before they are expected to match them. Work with a small group to play the matching game so that they understand the task. Provide for several repetitions of the task.

You Need

► Pocket chart.

From *Teaching Resources:*

► Picture Cards, Beginning Consonants (enlarged).

► Two-Way Sort Cards or Sheets.

Understand the Principle

Children need to be able to identify beginning sounds in words so that they make connections between words and also make sound-to-letter connections. It is important for them to say words slowly and listen for sounds in particular locations.

Explain the Principle

❝ Some words sound the same at the beginning. ❞

❝ You can connect words that sound the same at the beginning. ❞

plan

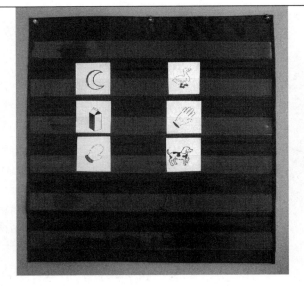

Explain the Principle

" Some words sound the same at the beginning. "

" You can connect words that sound the same at the beginning. "

① Explain to the children that they are going to learn about the beginning sounds in words.

② Place a picture card of something beginning with the /m/ sound at the top of the pocket chart. Have other picture cards ready, some that begin with *m* and others that have contrasting beginning sounds: *milk, moon, mitten, mouse, motorcycle, monkey, cow, camera, cat, duck, dog, goat, glove, gum, house.*

③ Have children say the word *moon* slowly and think about the sound at the beginning of the word. Suggested language: "Look at my mouth and listen as I say a word. [Say *moon* slowly.] What do you hear at the beginning of the word? [Children respond.] That's right, it's /m/. When we say the word, we can hear the sound at the beginning. Say this word, *milk*. [Children respond.] Does it have the same sound at the beginning as *moon*? [Children respond.] Say *moon, milk*. [Children respond.] You can hear the same sound at the beginning. Place the picture of the milk under the moon." Go through two or three more *m* words *(mitten, mouse)*, each time having children say the word and think about how it is like *moon* at the beginning. Each time, place the picture under the moon. Show the picture of the duck and have the children say it. Suggested language: "Does *duck* begin like *moon?*" [Children respond.] Place the picture of the duck on the other side of the pocket chart.

④ "We are going to play a game to decide which pictures begin like *moon* and which do not begin like *moon*. First say *moon*, listen to the first sound, and then say the name of the picture, like this. [Demonstrate.] If they have the same beginning sound, put the picture under the moon. If not, put them in the other column. [Demonstrate with the stack of pictures, inviting children to join in.] Say both words to tell whether they are the same at the beginning."

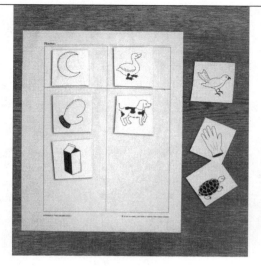

apply

say
match
put

▶ Have children repeat the routine with individual Two-Way Sort Cards or sheets. They mix up all the pictures and match the picture to *moon* by first saying *moon* and then the name of each picture. They place the pictures that begin like *moon* under the picture and those that do not begin like *moon* in the other column of the Two-Way Sort Card. If children use Two-Way Sort Sheets, they can glue the pictures and have a product.

▶ It doesn't matter that children may have varied labels in mind for some pictures *(rat, mouse)*. The point is for them to say the words and think about the sounds. Over time, they will accumulate labels for all of the pictures in *Teaching Resources* and be able to use those labels to think about letters, sounds, and words in different ways.

share

Have children bring their papers to a circle discussion and say the names of the pictures they've sorted or the name of what they drew to go along with *moon*.

Show the pocket chart with pictures accurately matched under *moon* and others to the side, and ask children to talk about what they notice. Statements like these reveal what children are noticing as they hear sounds in words:

> "*Gum* ends like *moon*."
>
> "*Hat* starts with *h*, or like *house*."
>
> "There's an *m* in *camera*."

Link

Interactive Read-Aloud: Read aloud books that draw children's attention to the beginning sounds in words, such as:

▸ *A You're Adorable* by Buddy Kaye

▸ *An Alphabet Book of Cats and Dogs* by Sheila Moxley

▸ *Ten Terrible Dinosaurs* by Paul Strickland

Shared Reading: Bring children's attention to two successive words in the text that begin with the same sound (like *brown bear*). Have them say both words and think about the beginning sound. Check the sound with the initial letters in the words. "Five Fat Peas" and "Grandpa Grig" are two examples (see *Sing a Song of Poetry*).

Guided Reading: When a child approaches an unfamiliar word, instead of telling what it is, say, "Could it be [word]?" Ask the child to say the word and check the first letter to be sure that it matches the sound.

Interactive Writing: Have children say a word slowly and think how to start it. Connect the word to picture cards you have used or to the name chart to decide whether it starts like another word.

Independent Writing: Encourage children to say the words they want to write and think how to start them.

assess

▸ Observe whether the children can match picture card labels by their beginning sound.

▸ Notice whether the children can come up with examples of words that begin like the one they want to write in interactive writing.

Expand the Learning

Repeat the lesson with key words that have the other consonants as the beginning sound.

Repeat the lesson matching ending consonant sounds (*Teaching Resources,* Picture Cards, Ending Consonants).

Connect with Home

Reproduce and cut apart a collection of small pictures (*Teaching Resources,* Picture Cards, Beginning Consonants). Send home with each child a piece of paper with a key picture (for example, *bear*) at the top above a large circle. Have children select pictures of things whose names begin like the name of the key picture and glue them in the circle. Show them how to say the name of the key picture along with the name of each picture in the circle.

Encourage family members to play silly sentence games like *Mary makes many muffins* and *Peter packs pickles.*

Generative Lesson

early
mid
late

PA 9

PHONOLOGICAL AWARENESS (PHONEMIC AWARENESS)

Hearing Beginning Sounds
Picture Sort

Consider Your Children

This lesson works best after children have worked with their names and have participated in interactive writing. Before using this lesson you will want to be sure that children can recognize their names and also know the concepts of "first" and "last" as they apply to letters in words. It will also be helpful to involve children in shared reading and interactive writing so that they begin to understand the usefulness of beginning letters in locating words and writing and reading words.

Working with English Language Learners

Be sure that your English language learners know the labels of all items in the picture cards that you use and give them many opportunities to say the names. Remember that they may only approximate English pronunciation, so be alert to situations in which they are using phonology from their own languages. You may want to work with them in a small group to be sure that they understand how to sort picture cards under the three key pictures.

You Need

▶ Pocket chart.

From *Teaching Resources:*

▶ Picture cards for *bear, hat,* and *moon* (Picture Cards, Beginning Consonants).

▶ Other picture cards of objects starting with the same letters: *banana, bat, box, bird; horse, helicopter, heart, hook; mouse, mitten, motorcycle, monkey.* (See Picture Cards, Beginning Consonants, for more examples.)

▶ Three-Way Sort Sheets.

▶ Three-Way Sort Extension.

Understand the Principle

Children need to be able to identify beginning sounds in words so that they can connect them to letters. They need to learn how to listen for, say, and recognize the consonant sounds so they will be able to attach the sounds to letters.

Explain the Principle

❝ Some words sound the same at the beginning. ❞

❝ You can connect words that sound the same at the beginning. ❞

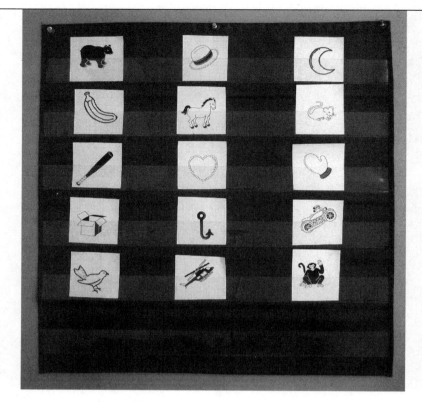

Explain the Principle

" **Some words sound the same at the beginning.** "

" **You can connect words that sound the same at the beginning.** "

① Explain to the children that they are going to learn more about the sounds they can hear in words.

② Have the children say the word *bear* slowly and think about the sound at the beginning of the word. Suggested language: "What do you hear at the beginning of the word? [Children respond.] That's right, it's a *b* [or isolate the /b/ sound]. When we say the word, we can hear the sound at the beginning. Say this word, *banana*. [Children respond.] Does it have the same sound at the beginning as *bear?* [Children respond.] Say *bear, banana.* [Children respond.] You can hear the same sound at the beginning." Ask a child to place the picture of the banana under the key picture of the bear.

③ Go through one or two more *b* words, each time having children say the two words and think about how they are alike at the beginning.

④ Repeat with *h* and *m* words.

⑤ Remove the pictures the children have put on the chart, mix up the pile, and pick up one card at a time. Invite children to say the word and then decide whether the picture goes under the bear, the hat, or the moon. Encourage children to check their categories by saying the words: *bear, bird.*

⑥ Categorize all the picture cards. Check the columns by having children say the name of the key picture and move down the entire column, saying all the words that have the same beginning sounds.

say
put
read

▶ Give the children a pile of selected picture cards. Instruct children to place three key pictures (e.g., *bear*, *hat*, *moon*) at the top of a Three-Way Sort Sheet. Then have them take each remaining picture card, say the word, and place the picture in the correct column. They can use the Three-Way Sort Extension if they have more pictures than will fit in the columns on the first sheet. Ask them to read their completed list of pictures to a partner.

Show the categorized words in the pocket chart at circle time. Ask children to discuss what they noticed about the beginning sounds of words. Demonstrate by making some comments yourself. Comments such as these reveal children's thinking about sounds in words:

"*Bear* and *bird* start the same."

"*Hat* and *mitten* have different sounds at the beginning."

"*Hat* has an /h/ at the beginning and a /t/ at the end."

"If it's *mouse*, it starts like *moon*, but if it's *rat*, it doesn't."

Link

Interactive Read-Aloud: Read aloud books that emphasize beginning sounds, such as:

▶ *What Pete Ate from A–Z* by Maira Kalman

▶ *Alligators All Around: An Alphabet* by Maurice Sendak

Shared Reading: Cover a word in the text with a stick-on note. Have children say the word and predict the beginning sound; then remove the cover to check it.

Guided Reading: When a child approaches an unfamiliar word, instead of telling what it is, say, "Could it be [word]?" Ask the child to say the word and check the first letter to be sure that they match.

Interactive Writing: Ask children to say a word before writing it and predict the first letter. Then start to write the word, and ask, "Were you right?"

Independent Writing: Encourage children to say a word and think about the beginning sound before writing it.

assess

▶ Check whether the children are noticing first letters of words and verifying that the letters match the sounds.

▶ Notice whether the children can match words that begin alike.

Expand the Learning

Repeat the lesson matching other beginning consonant and vowel sounds. Use key words beginning with consonants and vowels from the Alphabet Linking Chart (*Teaching Resources*, Materials & Routines): *apple, bear, cat, dog, egg, fish, gate, hat, igloo, jack-in-the-box, kite, leaf, moon, nest, octopus, pig, queen, ring, sun, turtle, umbrella, vacuum, window, x-ray, yo-yo, zipper.* Use different pictures for sorting, gradually increasing the range of sounds children can work with at a time.

After children become very proficient, show the key pictures and give directions without going through the entire set. That will leave some challenges for them to work out independently and discuss during sharing time.

Connect with Home

Give each child a paper with a key picture on it. Ask them to find pictures of things (or the objects themselves) at home that match the beginning sound. Alternatively, give each child an envelope with the key picture glued on the outside. In the envelope, they can place pictures of things (or actual small objects) that begin with the key sound.

Invite family members to play a game like this one. The caregiver says, "I'm going on a trip and I'm taking bananas." The child repeats the sentence and adds another word that starts the same: "I'm going on a trip and I'm taking bananas and a basket." The caregiver then says, "I'm going on a trip and I'm taking a basket and bread."

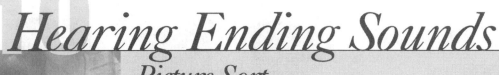

Hearing Ending Sounds
Picture Sort

Consider Your Children

If children have been accustomed to listening for beginning sounds, you can then provide clear demonstrations to help them attend to last sounds. Use a variety of words rather than phonograms or rhyming words only. Also, use some two-syllable words. You want children to become flexible in listening for the last sound. Because of dialect and individual differences, some children may not say the last sounds in exactly the same way you do. For this exercise, demonstrate standard articulation and have children practice it. Finally, remember that children are listening for the last sound they hear, independent of letters. It doesn't matter here that *kite* has an *e* at the end.

Working with English Language Learners

For English language learners, you may need to work in a small group to have them clearly articulate the words and say and hear the last sound. Students will be expected to use picture cards to categorize words by last sound, so they will need to hear the similarities in the final phoneme. Provide more examples and be sure that children are saying the words themselves rather than just listening to you say them. Start with a limited set of picture cards; have them say and place the picture cards. Be sure they know and can say the names of the words they will be using and that they understand the words *first* and *last* in English.

You Need

▶ Pocket chart.

From *Teaching Resources:*

▶ Selected picture cards (Picture Cards, Ending Consonants): *cat, moon, basket, kite, coat, bat, net, hat, spoon, fan, sun, bone, lion, ten, nine.* (Enlarge cards for demonstration purposes.)

▶ Two-Way Sort Cards or Sheets.

Understand the Principle

Children need to be aware of more than the beginning sounds of words. They also need to develop the concepts of "first" and "last" with reference to the sounds in words.

Hearing ending sounds helps children represent more of a word in writing and to notice more details when solving words in reading.

It also helps them distinguish between words that begin in a similar way but end differently.

Explain the Principle

" Some words sound the same at the end. "

" You can connect words that sound the same at the end. "

plan

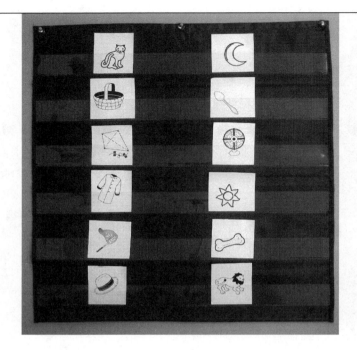

Explain the Principle

" Some words sound the same at the end. "

" You can connect words that sound the same at the end. "

① Explain to your children that they are going to learn how to listen for the last sound in a word.

② Suggested language: "Say the word *cat* slowly. What do you hear at the end of the word? [Children respond.] That's right, it's a *t* [or isolate the /t/ sound]. When we say the word, we can hear the sound at the end. Say this word, *basket*. [Emphasize the last sound when you pronounce it. Children respond.] Does it have the same sound at the end as *cat?* [Children respond.] Say *cat, basket*. [Children respond.] You can hear the same sound at the end." Place the picture of the basket under the cat.

③ Go through one or two more /t/-ending words, each time having the children say the key word and the second word and think about whether they sound alike at the end *(kite, coat, bat, net, hat)*.

④ Then repeat the process for words ending with /n/ *(spoon, fan, sun, bone, lion, ten, nine)*. You may want to use *moon* as the key picture.

⑤ Mix up the pile of pictures and go through them, one at a time. Invite the children to say the word and then to decide whether the picture goes under the cat or the moon.

⑥ Encourage them to check their categories by saying *cat, basket* and so on, accentuating the last sound.

⑦ When finished, you will have categorized all of the picture cards into two columns.

⑧ Check the columns by having children say the name of the key picture and move down the entire column, saying all the words that have the same last sounds.

take
say
put

▶ Have children complete a two-way sort using a pile of picture cards. The children place two key pictures at the top of the card. They take a picture card, say the word, and place the card in the correct column. They take turns with a partner. Each partner places all the cards in the column, saying the words. Each reads the completed columns of pictures as a final check and then mixes up the cards for his or her partner to take a turn.

Display the categorized words in the pocket chart. Ask children to discuss what they noticed about the ending sounds of words. Demonstrate by making some comments yourself. You may hear comments like these, which reveal children's thinking about sounds in words:

"*Cat* and *net* end the same."

"*Nine* sounds like *moon* at the end but like *net* at the beginning."

"*Nine* sounds like /n/ at the end, but there's an *e.*"

Link

Interactive Read-Aloud: Read aloud books that emphasize ending sounds, such as:

▸ *The Grumpy Morning* by Darcia Labrosse

▸ *Ten Little Bears* by Kathleen Hague

Shared Reading: Cover the last letter of some words in the text with a stick-on note. Have children say the word and predict the ending sound; then remove the cover to check it.

Guided Reading: Notice when children must distinguish between words that end alike (for example, *get* and *want*). Show them how looking at the last letter can help.

Interactive Writing: Ask children to say the word before writing and predict the first letter. Write the word up to the last letter and ask them to say it again and predict the last letter.

Independent Writing: Encourage children to say the word and think about the ending sound before writing it.

assess

▸ Observe whether the children are noticing and using ending letters of words while reading and representing ending sounds while writing.

▸ Notice whether the children can match words that end alike.

▸ When you have worked with ending sounds for a while, you can ask all the children to try to write three to five words. Check their approximations to see if they are representing ending sounds.

Expand the Learning

Repeat the lesson, matching other ending sounds (*Teaching Resources,* Picture Cards, Ending Consonants). Use different pictures for sorting, gradually increasing the range of sounds children can work with at a time.

After children become very proficient, you can show the key pictures and give directions without going through the entire set. That will leave some challenges for them to work out independently and discuss during sharing time.

Connect with Home

Give each child a paper with a key picture on it. Ask children to find pictures of objects in magazines at home that represent words that match the ending sound. Alternatively, give each child an envelope with the key picture glued on the outside. In envelopes, they can place three pictures or small objects representing words that end with the key sound and bring them to school to share.

11 Hearing Ending Sounds

Picture Lotto

Consider Your Children

This lesson is best used after children have had some experience matching pictures for ending sounds. Lotto is similar to Bingo except that players cover every square, so there is more work to do. In this game, children match the last sounds of the words represented by the pictures. They say both words to show that they match. Remember that a picture may have more than one label (for example, *mouse* or *rat, hat* or *cap*). The important thing is to match ending sounds.

Working with English Language Learners

You will be using this lesson after English language learners have already learned the labels for quite a few picture cards. You may be expanding their repertoire in this lesson, so be sure that you go over the labels and have them say the words several times. Also, act out the directions for a clear demonstration of the game of Lotto. The first time English language learners play the game, either observe and coach them or play with them so that you are sure they understand the basic directions.

You Need

► Pocket chart.

From *Teaching Resources:*

► Enlarged picture cards: *bed, train, bell, sun, cat, star, cake, bus, soap* (Picture Cards, Ending Consonants).

► Lotto Game Cards.

► Directions for Lotto .

► Selected additional picture cards (Picture Cards, Ending Consonants).

Understand the Principle

Being able to hear the sounds in words and connect words with the same ending sound helps children become more aware of the sequence of sounds in words, connect words by sound, connect letters and sounds, and distinguish between words that start the same.

Explain the Principle

" Some words sound the same at the end. "

" You can connect words that sound the same at the end. "

plan

Explain the Principle

" Some words sound the same at the end. "

" You can connect words that sound the same at the end. "

① Tell your children that today they are going to learn to play a game using sounds.

② Using the pocket chart, place the picture cards in three rows.

③ Suggested language: "Some words sound the same at the end, like *sit* and *get* or *mom* and *dream*. Today we are going to learn to play a game to practice ending sounds. It is called Picture Lotto. In this game you get to match things that sound alike at the end. Let's try it with the pictures I have in the pocket chart. Let's say the names of these pictures and listen for the last sound of the word." Have children say the names. Some of them may identify the last sound by letter or say it in an isolated way.

④ Suggested language: "I'm going to take a picture card from this stack and see if I can match it to the pictures on my square."

⑤ Hold up the first picture card. Suggested language: "I can see that this is a *cup*. Now I'm going to see if there is a picture that sounds like *cup* at the end. Can anyone see something that ends like *cup?*" Children respond.

⑥ Model checking *cup* and *soap* by saying both words. Have children say both words and check whether they sound alike at the end. Place the picture card of the cup over the picture card of the soap.

⑦ Draw cards one at a time, showing how to check for a match by saying both words. Some words will not match anything on the chart and are placed face down again.

⑧ Continue until all the pictures on the chart have been matched. Suggested language: "I've covered all the spaces on my chart. That's what you do to win the Picture Lotto game. Remember to say both words to check your matches."

⑨ Ask children to discuss what you have to do to fill your Lotto card. Then demonstrate the game with three or four children in a circle on the floor. Be sure each child has a different-color card (e.g., purple, pink, blue, yellow). Show them how to take turns taking cards and matching them to the pictures on their squares. The first to cover all the boxes on the card wins the game.

take
say
cover

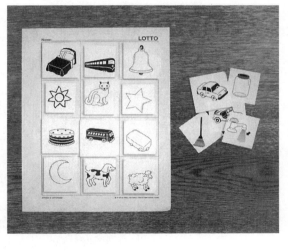

▶ Children play the ending-sounds Picture Lotto game in groups of three or four. If you have enough cards and squares, several games can be going on at once (see the Lotto directions).

Ask the children to remember and share some of the matching words they found while they played the Picture Lotto game.

You may get comments such as, "If it's a rat, it ends like cat, but if it's a mouse, it ends like bus."

Welcome these comments because they are evidence that children are becoming more flexible with phoneme awareness.

Link

Interactive Read-Aloud: Read aloud stories that include words that end alike. Talk about the way rhyming words—*duck* and *stuck,* for example—have the same sound at the end but not all words that have the same ending sound rhyme—*rake* and *bike,* for example. All four words end with /k/, but *duck* and *stuck* rhyme because the entire ending sounds the same. Examples are:

▸ *One Duck Stuck* by Phyllis Root

▸ *The Itsy Bitsy Spider* by Lorainne Siomades

Shared Reading: When reading poems and stories, draw children's attention to words that sound alike at the end: "Can someone find a word in our story that ends like *bed?*" Invite them to use a masking card, flag, or highlighter tape to point out similarly ending words in the text.

Guided Reading: After reading a story, have children find a particular word on a page. Have them say it and articulate the sound they hear at the end.

Interactive Writing: When children are thinking about how to write a word, have them say it slowly and connect it to a name or other word that ends the same.

Independent Writing: Encourage children to say words slowly when they are writing. They may be representing the beginning sound already, but by saying the word again they can represent more sounds, including the ending sound.

assess

▸ Notice whether the children are able to hear ending sounds of words during interactive and independent writing.

▸ Place a few picture cards in the pocket chart and then, holding up other picture cards one at a time, ask individual children to say the names of these picture cards and match them to a card in the pocket chart. This will give you an idea which ending consonant sounds children are hearing and connecting.

Expand the Learning

Vary the sounds and expand the repertoire of sounds when playing the Picture Lotto game. Gradually increase the complexity of the game and/or take away the easy-to-match sounds. You can include ending vowel sounds such as *tree, bee; two, zoo; fly, pie.*

Connect with Home

Give each child a photocopy of three or four Picture Lotto game sheets and an envelope of picture cards to use to play Lotto with family members. The sheets and cards can be the same as those used in this lesson, or you can create new ones.

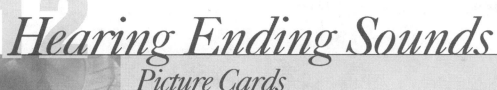

Hearing Ending Sounds
Picture Cards

Consider Your Children

This activity will be effective for children who have had a great deal of experience saying and hearing sounds in words, matching words for ending sounds, and associating letters and sounds in their names. Be sure that children know the meaning of "last" in a word. This lesson sets up a routine for word play that can be used at any time during the school day. For example, if you have a minute or two of "down-time" between activities, you can make a game of one or two quick problems.

Working with English Language Learners

In this lesson English language learners will be using picture cards to prompt them to say the word slowly and notice the last sound. Articulation will be important and some words may be difficult for these learners. First, be sure that all children know the English labels for the picture cards that they will be using. Check their articulation, especially noticing their ability to make the last sound of the word clearly. Eliminate picture cards that are too difficult at this time. The important thing here is the *concept* of attending to the last sound. You will also want to be sure they understand what you mean by the words *first* and *last*.

You Need

From *Teaching Resources:*
► Selected Picture Cards, Ending Consonants.

Understand the Principle

As children become more aware of the sounds in words, they learn to isolate and identify the last sound heard. This ability is the foundation for connecting sounds and letters beyond the first letter, knowledge that helps readers begin to decode words and also monitor their reading of continuous text.

Explain the Principle

" You can hear the last sound in a word. "

" You can say a word to hear the last sound. "

plan

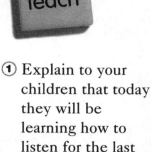

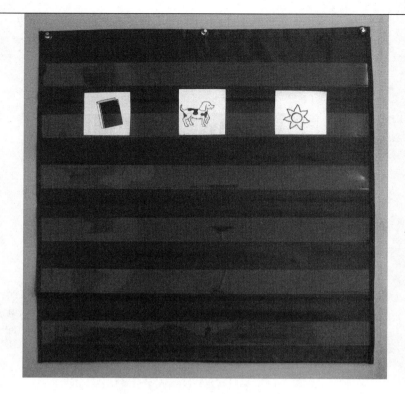

① Explain to your children that today they will be learning how to listen for the last sound in words they can say.

② Suggested language: "When you say a word, you can hear the first sound, can't you? Say *dog*. [Say the word slowly, but don't distort it, emphasizing the first letter. Children respond.] You can hear the first sound of *dog*, can't you?"

③ "We've learned to say just the first sound of *dog* [demonstrate]. You try it. [Children demonstrate.] Now I'm going to say just the last sound of *dog*—/g/ [demonstrate]. That's the last sound you hear at the end of the word. You say it like this: "Dog, /g/.""

④ "Let's try another one. Say *sun*. [Children respond.] The first sound is . . . [children respond]. The last sound is . . . [children respond]. Let's try one more, just thinking about the last sound. Say *book*. [Children respond.] Say the last sound of *book*. [Children respond.]"

⑤ Continue to demonstrate with two or three more examples, focusing on just the last sound, and invite children to offer examples.

⑥ For a variation, take some of the names of children in your class and say them, isolating the ending sound.

⑦ When children in the group can easily say the last sound of a word, this exercise will no longer be necessary.

take card
say word
say last sound

▶ Children have a pile of about twenty picture cards to use with a partner.

▶ They take turns drawing a card, saying the name of the picture, and then saying the last sound.

Encourage the children to come up with a variety of words in a category, such as school or home, and then to say the words and tell their last sounds.

Link

Interactive Read-Aloud: Read aloud books that offer examples of the repetition of final sounds, such as:

- ► *I See the Moon and the Moon Sees Me* by Jonathan London

- ► *What's That Sound, Woolly Bear?* by Philemon Sturges

Shared Reading: Conduct shared readings of poems and nursery rhymes such as "Pussycat, Pussycat" or "Polly Put the Kettle On" that offer flexible play with letter sounds and words (see *Sing a Song of Poetry*).

Guided Reading: After reading a simple book, invite the children to name something in a picture and tell the last sound.

Interactive Writing: Have children say a word slowly and think how to start it. After representing the sound, write the rest of the word up to the final sound. Ask children to say the word again and think about the last sound. When they articulate the sound, you can say, "We use this letter [write and name it] for that sound."

Independent Writing: Encourage children to say the words they want to write and think how to start them. Encourage them to say the word again and try to represent more sounds. Show them how to listen for the last sound in some words and write the letter.

assess

- ► Notice whether the children can hear and identify final sounds in words. A quick check of just two or three examples will tell you whether they understand the concept.

Expand the Learning

When children can easily come up with the last sound of a word, starting with simple examples, show them how to connect the picture with the last letter.

You may not need to do more on this principle, but if you do, repeat the lesson with other picture cards.

Connect with Home

At a meeting or in a newsletter, teach family members to play several kinds of word games, including listening for the last sound with their children. Give them examples or categories to use, such as colors, animals, or food: *red*—/d/, *mouse*—/s/, *bread*—/d/.

Emphasize that the activity should be quick and fun and that the idea is to make children curious about words and enjoy manipulating sounds.

*Generative
Lesson*

early
mid
late

PA 13
PHONOLOGICAL AWARENESS

13 *Making Rhymes*
Picture Concentration

Consider Your Children

This activity will be effective after your children have listened to many rhyming books and poems just for the enjoyment of the story. Once they have listened to many rhyming texts, you can draw their attention to the concept and help them recognize and understand it. The routine of Concentration will be useful in practicing the application of many other concepts.

Working with English Language Learners

For games like this one, you will be using the same picture cards over and over. English language learners will be developing a repertoire of labels that they know and can say and use in different ways. Be sure that they understand the procedures of the game; you may want to work with a small group, playing the game for a short time with each child in turn. When you read books aloud, stop and call attention to rhymes that children know so that they begin to understand that they will meet the same words and labels in other contexts.

You Need

From *Teaching Resources:*

► Books with stories that rhyme (Rhyme Books Bibliography).

► Picture Cards, Rhymes.

► Directions for Concentration.

Understand the Principle

When children recognize words that rhyme (for our purposes here, words that have identically sounded and spelled endings), they can make connections between words.

This information helps them take words apart to solve them and helps them understand letter/sound relationships.

Explain the Principle

❝ Some words have end parts that sound alike. They rhyme. ❞

❝ You can make rhymes by thinking of words that end the same. ❞

plan

Explain the Principle

❝ Some words have end parts that sound alike. They rhyme. ❞

❝ You can make rhymes by thinking of words that end the same. ❞

① Tell your children that they are going to learn about rhymes.

② Read a variety of rhyming stories. Some examples are *Better Not Get Wet, Jesse Bear*, by Nancy White Carlstrom; *"Fire! Fire!" Said Mrs. McGuire*, by Bill Martin; *Brown Bear, Brown Bear, What Do You See?* by Bill Martin; and the classic *The Cat in the Hat*, by Dr. Seuss.

③ As you read, emphasize the rhythm and rhyme so the children will anticipate words and listen actively. Invite them to join in on the rhyming parts as they become more familiar with the story.

④ As you reread the story, stop after a pair of rhyming words and ask the children to identify the words that sound alike, or rhyme.

⑤ Reread the story and invite the children to elaborate on the text. They can think of another word that would rhyme ("Change the tire," said Mrs. McGuire) or think of two different rhyming words ("Come here quick," said Mrs. Flick). They can also search for words that rhyme with names of children in the class ("Up the hill," said Bill). Or they can put classmates' names into the existing rhyme ("Elizabeth, Elizabeth, what do you see? I see Javon looking at me").

⑥ Write the variations that children create on charts and place them on the walls so that children can "read around the room."

say
match

► Have the children
play Rhyming
Concentration with a
partner using the
selected picture
cards.

As they hear familiar rhyming stories, have children clap on the rhyming
word and/or identify it afterward.

Ask the children to share rhyming parts they have discovered.

Link

Interactive Read-Aloud: Read aloud books with rhyming stories to build up a large repertoire of rhymes that children can predict. Examples are:

- ▸ *Hush! A Thai Lullaby* by Minfong Ho
- ▸ *Barnyard Song* by Rhonda Gowler Greene

Shared Reading: Read poems such as "Red, White and Blue" or "Six Little Ducks" together. (See *Sing a Song of Poetry*.) After children are familiar with the poems, identify easy rhyming words.

Guided Reading: Emphasize words that rhyme in the oral reading of simple, predictable texts.

Interactive Writing: Point out rhyming words in writing you are doing with the class.

Independent Writing: Help the children say words slowly to hear the sounds in words and encourage them to make connections to words that rhyme.

assess

- ▸ Notice the children's ability to recognize rhymes in texts.
- ▸ As a quick assessment, say three to five words and have the children tell a rhyming word.

Expand the Learning

Read other rhyming texts aloud and bring rhymes to children's attention. On a subsequent rereading, stop briefly before the second in a pair of rhyming words and ask the children to predict the word.

Have children play the game several times with other rhyming pictures.

Connect with Home

Create a rhyming book using the names of the children in the class. Model the text on books such as *Brown Bear, Brown Bear, What Do You See?* or "*Fire! Fire!" Said Mrs. McGuire* or any other simple rhyming text. (See *Sing a Song of Poetry*.) Send a photocopy home with children to read to family members.

Invite family members to play rhyming games in the car or in the kitchen. The caregiver names an object, like *tree,* and the child gives a rhyme, like *knee.*

14

Hearing and Producing Rhymes

Rhyming Lotto

Consider Your Children

This activity is best used after the children have participated in shared reading of poems, which helps them learn to "string" rhymes together. They will have internalized the concept of rhyme and are ready to expand their knowledge. Generating rhymes represents an application of the concept of rhyme, and children's ability to generate rhymes represents rhyme awareness.

Working with English Language Learners

Be sure that your English language learners know and can repeat some rhymes that are meaningful and enjoyable to them. These rhymes will provide resources to them in thinking of rhymes. Go over some rhymes with these children just before you play this game (tossing a beanbag) so that they have some responses ready. Give a little more "wait and think" time to children who are just learning English rhymes. Accept responses that repeat those just made by other children or quickly make suggestions—for example, "Would *cake* be a good thing to take on the trip?" As children grow in understanding rhyme and build a repertoire, you can challenge them more.

You Need

▸ Drawing and writing materials.

From *Teaching Resources:*

▸ Pairs of Picture Cards, Rhymes.

▸ Lotto Game Cards.

▸ Directions for Lotto.

Understand the Principle

When children recognize words that rhyme (have ending parts that are alike), they can make connections between words that have the same ending sounds.

This information helps them understand letter/sound relationships and break words apart to solve them. It is important for children to develop sensitivity to the sounds of the oral language so they can connect sounds to letter patterns.

Explain the Principle

" You can make rhymes by thinking of words that end the same. "

plan

Explain the Principle

" You can make rhymes by thinking of words that end the same. "

① Tell the children they are going to learn to make rhymes.

② Suggested language: "We're going to play a game about rhymes. I'll start the story, and then you can help me by thinking of rhymes. There once was a group of magic bunnies who decided to pack their spaceship with lots of good things to take with them to a new planet. They packed some *hats, mats,* and *cats.* What do you notice about the things they packed?" Children respond that they rhyme.

③ Suggested language: "That's right. They think of the first thing and then everything else they pack has to have a rhyme. Let's try another one. This time I'll start with something and I'll throw this beanbag [or ball] to someone to think of the next thing." Repeat the introduction. "They packed some *cats.* . . ."

④ Throw the beanbag to a child, who thinks of an object that rhymes. Then tell that child to throw the beanbag to another child, who tries to think of another rhyme.

⑤ When the child with the beanbag can no longer think of a rhyme, he or she throws it back to you; you start another rhyme. Some examples are *cakes, rakes, flakes; bears, chairs, pears; goats, boats, coats; fishes, dishes, wishes; dogs, logs, hogs; trees, bees, keys; cans, vans, fans; jars, bars, cars; clowns, crowns, gowns.*

⑥ Children will learn to play this game quickly and will enjoy the rhymes. Keep it easy at first so things move along quickly.

early
mid
late

say
match

▸ Have the children play Rhyming Lotto with pictures.

▸ Introduce one or two free cards showing a bunny in a spaceship to add some fun to the game. This card matches any picture—when children draw a free card, they can place it on any space on the Lotto card.

Invite each child to share a rhymed pair from the game they played.

Link

Interactive Read-Aloud: Read aloud books that draw attention to rhymes, such as:

- ▶ *"Fire! Fire!" Said Mrs. McGuire* by Bill Martin, Jr.
- ▶ *Monkey Do!* by Allan Ahlberg

Shared Reading: Read poems such as "Stop, Look, and Listen" or "Stretching Fun" together (see *Sing a Song of Poetry*). After children know them, have the children identify easy rhyming words by going up to the chart and pointing out two rhyming words using highlighter tape or a masking card.

Guided Reading: Point out rhyming words in stories the children read.

Interactive Writing: When the writing you are doing has rhyming words, point them out.

Independent Writing: Encourage children to write some of the rhyming words they have found.

assess

- ▶ Notice the children's ability to recognize and generate rhymes.
- ▶ Observe the children's spontaneous recognition of rhymes in interactive read-alouds or shared reading.

Expand the Learning

Repeat the lesson with a variety of other rhymes. Use other themes like packing for a trip to the beach or the park.

Connect with Home

In a meeting or a newsletter, share this rhyming game with family members so that they can play it with their children.

Invite caregivers to have children cut pictures that represent rhyming pairs of words—*house* and *mouse, pan* and *man*—from magazines and glue them on a sheet.

Suggest that family members play Let's Go Shopping using magazine and newspaper pictures of food and other objects. The caregiver cuts out the pictures and spreads them on the table face down. The child turns over a picture and says its name and a rhyming word—*meat* and *feet* or *fish* and *dish,* for example. Then the child can put the picture in the bag. At the end the child takes out all the objects and names them and the caregiver says a rhyming word for each.

Hearing Long Vowel Sounds in the Middle of Words

Picture Match

Consider Your Children

This lesson is best presented after children have worked with their names and taken part in interactive writing using a variety of words. They should understand the concept of "word" and be able to hear consonants at the beginning and end of words. In this lesson, children will learn an important routine for matching vowel sounds in the middle of words. Use one-syllable words. If children are very inexperienced in hearing sounds in the middle of words, you will want to practice for several days. In this lesson, they listen for middle sounds that represent the names of the vowels, or the long vowel sounds.

Working with English Language Learners

English language learners will be successful in this exercise if they know, understand, and can say the labels of the pictures on the cards and have had previous experience identifying the first and last sounds of words. They will need to learn to listen for the middle vowel sound, which sounds like the name of the letter, so they may need many demonstrations. Play the matching game with them the first time so that you will be sure they are saying the word slowly and matching by middle sound.

You Need

► Pocket chart.

From *Teaching Resources:*

► Selected Picture Cards, Long Vowels.

► Three-Way Sort Sheets.

Understand the Principle

Children need to say and hear medial sounds in words to develop a beginning understanding of the structure of words. The long vowel sounds, which sound like their letter names *(a,e,i,o,u)*, are the easiest to hear.

First listening to the sounds without looking at the letters will lead children to attend more carefully to all parts of words, so that later they will begin to compare words and connect sounds with letters and letter clusters. Quickly move on to introduce the letters along with the sounds.

Explain the Principle

" You can hear and say the sound in the middle of a word. "

plan

Explain the Principle

66 **You can hear and say the sound in the middle of a word.** 99

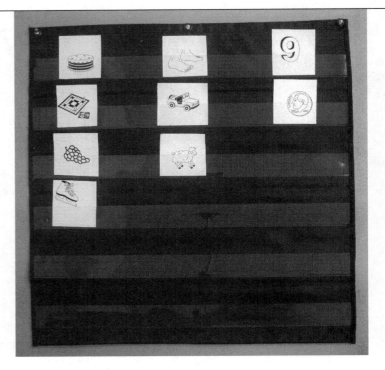

① Tell your children that they are going to listen for the sounds in the middle of words.

② Suggested language: "You have been thinking hard about the beginning sounds in words and also about the ending sounds. Today we are going to think about the sound in the middle of words. Say *cake*. [Children respond.] What do you hear at the beginning? [Children respond.] What do you hear at the end of *cake?* [Children respond.]"

③ Suggested language: "Now say the word *cake* and think about the sound in the middle." After children give the long /a/ sound, place the picture card for *cake* in the pocket chart.

④ Suggested language: "*Game* has an /a/ in the middle just like *cake* did. Say those words. [Children respond.] It's easy to hear, isn't it, because it sounds like the letter *a*. I've got some pictures here. Let's say the names of the things in these pictures and see if they sound like *cake* in the middle. *Grapes, skate*—they sound the same in the middle. Say them with me." Say the words along with the children, *slightly* exaggerating the middle sound without segmenting the word.

⑤ Repeat the process using *feet* and *nine* as key words, matching one or two pictures for each.

⑥ Suggested language: "Today you are going to sort picture cards by thinking about the middle sound. By saying both words, you can tell whether the sound is the same in the middle."

say
sort

▶ Children place the key picture cards—*game*, *feet*, and *nine*—at the top of a Three-Way Sort Sheet. Using a pile of selected picture cards, children sort the pictures into the three columns according to the vowel sound they hear in the middle of each picture name.

Using the class name chart (see Lesson ELC 1), have children find pairs of names that have the same sound in the middle (for example, *Steve, Pete; Mike, Lila*).

Link

Interactive Read-Aloud: Read aloud books such as the following that include many words with long vowel sounds:

- ▸ *Edwina the Emu* by Sheena Knowles
- ▸ *Jake Baked the Cake* by B.G. Hennessy

Shared Reading: Point out words in the shared reading text that have the same sound in the middle—*green, queen*, for example.

Guided Reading: Show children how to check beyond the first letter of an unfamiliar word to be sure the word they read is right.

Interactive Writing: Have children say a word slowly and think about how to write all the letters.

Independent Writing: Encourage children to say the words they want to write and think about how to write the vowel sound they hear in the middle. Do not expect conventional spelling of vowels, but encourage the children to make an attempt.

assess

- ▸ Observe whether the children can identify the cards whose names have /ā/, /ē/, or /ī/ in the middle (long vowel sounds).

- ▸ Notice whether the children make good attempts at writing vowels during interactive writing.

Expand the Learning

Repeat the lesson adding the long vowels *o* and *u* (*Teaching Resources,* Picture Cards, Long Vowels).

Repeat the lesson using the Picture Cards for Short Vowels or Consonant-Vowel-Consonant.

Have children make an 8 ½" × 11" book with five stapled pages (one for each long vowel) on which they glue pictures of objects whose labels contain the appropriate middle sound. They can "read" their books by saying the names of the pictures on each page.

Connect with Home

Have children take home their vowel books (or pages of vowels with pictures) and read them to a family member.

16

Blending Syllables
Syllable Lotto

Consider Your Children

This lesson is most successful after the children have learned how to write their names and have participated in interactive writing. They should know how to count the parts in words by clapping syllables. In this lesson, they take a more analytic look at syllables by identifying and blending them. You will be saying syllables in words, pausing very briefly after each, which requires children to think about the whole word and its parts. If children find this task confusing, say the word more smoothly, emphasizing syllables rather than segmenting them. The important thing is for them to grasp the concept of breaks within words.

Working with English Language Learners

Saying words and clapping syllables will help English language learners give more attention to the parts of words and set the scene for taking words apart. Be sure that they can say the words with some accuracy. Eliminate words that they have great difficulty pronouncing and do not understand. If you can, include some words in their own language (for example, *gato* or *paloma*); the principle of clapping syllables is the same. Demonstrate the game of Syllable Lotto until you are sure that they understand what to attend to (number of syllables) in placing the picture cards. Be sure that the children know the names of pictures on the cards.

You Need

From *Teaching Resources:*

▶ Lotto Game Cards.

▶ Directions for Lotto.

▶ Selected Picture Cards, Syllables.

Understand the Principle

Blending individual sounds to form a word requires children to put together discrete elements. Identifying and blending syllables is easy and natural for children, so it is a good place to start.

Separating the parts of words (syllables) is consistent with the natural breaks that children can hear and helps them think more about the parts of words.

Explain the Principle

" You can hear and say the syllables in a word. "

" You can blend syllables together. "

plan

Explain the Principle

66 **You can hear and say the syllables in a word.** 99

66 **You can blend syllables together.** 99

① Explain to your children that today they will be thinking about the syllables in words.

② Suggested language: "You are really good at clapping the syllables in words. Let's try some." Demonstrate with words such as *apple, jumping, bicycle, caterpillar, sandwich, not, go, cat, tree, water,* and *waterfall.* Let children think of some words to clap.

③ Suggested language: "Today, we are going to play a game with the syllables or parts in words. I'm going to say a word slowly. I'll stop between each syllable. You try to think what the word is that I'm saying, but don't say it out loud. *Mon–key*—are you thinking of the word?" Children respond.

④ Try several more words, separating the syllables and then asking children to say the whole word. Some examples are *happy, louder, monster, paper, pencil, planet, pretzel, sandbox, kangaroo, underneath, vacation, watery, wonderful, adventure, butterfly, crocodile, elephant, bicycle, alligator, pepperoni, motorcycle,* and *watermelon.* Children respond with the whole word. If they find segmenting confusing, say the word with only *very* brief pauses—just a suggestion of segmentation.

⑤ Suggested language: "Now I'm going to say a word and I want you to say the syllables separately like I did." Use some of the same words you used earlier; have children practice separating the syllables.

⑥ Suggested language: "Today you are going to play Syllable Lotto. In this game you have cards with numbers on them—1, 2, and 3. [Show the game board.] You draw a picture card and say the name of the picture. You think how many syllables the word has. I'll draw this card—*cat*. [Say it.] How many syllables does it have? [Children respond.] That's right—one, so I'll put this card (or marker, such as a penny or plastic cup) on a square that has a 1 and the next person takes a turn. [Demonstrate again with a two-syllable and a three-syllable word.] When you have filled all the squares, you have won the game."

take
say parts
cover

▸ Have children play Syllable Lotto.

Ask the children to clap the syllables in a few words they used in the game.

Link

Interactive Read-Aloud: Read aloud books such as the following:

- ▸ *I Love You, Little One* by Nancy Tafuri
- ▸ *Rush Hour* by Christine Loomis

Shared Reading: Using a masking card or flag, call attention to words in the shared reading text that have two or more syllables.

Guided Reading: As children are learning to match the sounds they say with the words they see on a page, teach them to hold a finger under a word longer when it has more than one syllable. You can clap the longer words to help them understand.

Interactive Writing: Have children clap the syllables in words in order to think about how to write the first syllable and the remaining syllables.

Independent Writing: Encourage children to say the word and break it down into syllables by clapping when they say each syllable. They can then write the syllables.

assess

- ▸ Give the children five words to clap, and notice whether they are able to hear one, two, or three syllables.

- ▸ Notice whether children use the idea of syllables when they attempt to write multisyllable words.

Expand the Learning

Repeat the Syllable Lotto game with different words, or add four-syllable words to increase the challenge.

Connect with Home

Give children blank four-page books (*Teaching Resources,* Blank Book Page Template) to take home in which they can glue picture cards (Picture Cards, Syllables) representing two-syllable words. Have them glue a picture on each page and then "read" the book by saying the name of the picture and saying the syllables in the word.

Give children photocopies of Lotto Cards and Picture Cards, Syllables *(Teaching Resources)* so that they can play the game at home with family members.

Hearing First and Last Sounds
Writing Words

Consider Your Children

This activity is best used after the children have had a great deal of experience saying and hearing sounds in words, matching the initial sounds of words, and associating letters and sounds. Be sure that the children know what "first" and "last" mean in relation to a word. Slightly emphasizing and/or isolating beginning or ending sounds will help children more easily identify them, but do not let children become dependent on your pronunciation. Move quickly to simply saying the whole word clearly. As you work with students in guided and independent reading, they will learn a great deal more about the sequence of sounds in words. It is not necessary for the children to be completely successful in this activity before they begin to read and write stories.

Working with English Language Learners

The Alphabet Linking Chart will be an especially important resource for English language learners because it contains the key words that they will use for connecting sounds and letters. You will be working on hearing first and last sounds but will also be teaching children to "read" the chart and associate the key words there with other words that start with the same sound. Be sure that English language learners know and can say the key words on the Alphabet Linking Chart. If needed, work with them in a small group to read the chart in a shared way several times.

You Need

From *Teaching Resources:*

▶ Four-Box Sheet.

▶ Selected Picture Cards, Consonant-Vowel-Consonant.

▶ Large picture cards for pocket chart (enlarge the Consonant-Vowel-Consonant Picture Cards).

▶ Alphabet Linking Chart.

Understand the Principle

As children become more aware of the sounds in words, they learn to isolate and identify the sounds in sequence.

The better children can hear sounds, the easier it will be for them to connect sounds and letters within words.

Explain the Principle

" You can say a word slowly to hear all the sounds. "

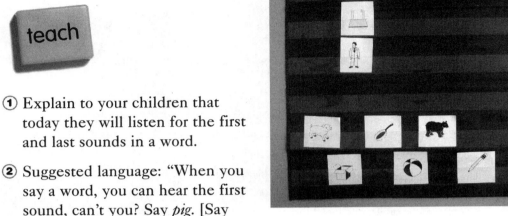

Explain the Principle

❝ **You can say a word slowly to hear all the sounds.** ❞

① Explain to your children that today they will listen for the first and last sounds in a word.

② Suggested language: "When you say a word, you can hear the first sound, can't you? Say *pig*. [Say the word slowly, without distorting it, emphasizing the first letter. Children respond.]"

③ "Now I'm going to say just the first sound of *pig* [demonstrate]. Look at my mouth. Can you hear the first sound of *pig?* You try it. [Children demonstrate.]"

④ "I'll say *pig* again. I can hear a *g* at the end of *pig*. Say the sound at the end. [Children demonstrate.]"

⑤ "Let's try another one. Say *box*. [Children respond.] The first sound is . . . [children respond]. Now say it again. What can you hear at the end? [Children respond.]"

⑥ Present two or three more examples, or hold up picture cards and invite children to sound out the words they represent: *man, pan, map*. Some children may come up with the name of the letter; accept either the letter name or the sound in isolation.

⑦ For a variation, use some of the names of children in your class. Say them and have the children isolate the first sound and the last sound.

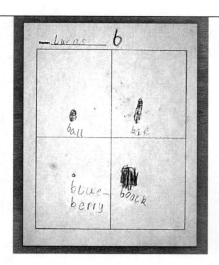

apply

write
draw
label

▸ Using the Alphabet Linking Chart, children read each box and say the beginning and ending sounds to a partner: *A, a, apple, /a/, B, b, bear, /b/.* For each word, they tell another word that starts the same way.

▸ Children choose one letter, write it at the top of a Four-Box Sheet, and draw and label four items that begin with this letter.

share

Children share their beginning-sound sheets with a partner by reading each box.

Keeping the same picture cards in the pocket chart, ask children to quickly locate a word that begins and ends the same.

For example, you can have them find a word that starts like *man* or find a word that ends like *pig.* You may want to expand beyond the cards you have.

Link

Interactive Read-Aloud: Read aloud books containing words that sound alike at the beginning and/or the end. (See *Teaching Resources,* Alliteration Bibliography, for suggestions.) Examples are:

- ▸ *My Crayons Talk* by G. Brian Karas
- ▸ *Grandma's Cat* by Helen Ketteman

Shared Reading: Use shared reading of poems and nursery rhymes that include flexible play with words. (See *Sing a Song of Poetry*.)

Guided Reading: During word work, make a few simple words with magnetic letters, and have the children read them and tell the first or last sound.

Interactive Writing: Have children say a word slowly and think how to start it. Then write the first letter. Repeat for the last letter.

Independent Writing: Encourage children to say the words they want to write and think how to start them. Encourage them to connect words that have the same first letter.

assess

- ▸ Notice whether the children can hear and say first and last letters. A quick check of just two or three examples will tell you whether they understand the concept.
- ▸ Check whether the children can generate appropriate examples.

Expand the Learning

Have the children use a Two-Column Sheet (*Teaching Resources* Template) for first and last sounds. They pick a letter and draw or glue on pictures in the first column that begin with the letter. In the second column, they draw pictures or glue on pictures that end with that letter.

Connect with Home

At a meeting or in a newsletter, teach caregivers to play several kinds of word games with their children in the home or in the car. Suggest that they name objects they see and have children tell the first or last sound and perhaps the names of three or four objects that start or end with the same sound. Emphasize that the activity should be quick and fun and that the idea is to make children curious about words and get them to enjoy manipulating sounds.

Hearing and Saying Beginning Sounds

Trip and Line-Up Games

Consider Your Children

This lesson sets up routines for quick games that can be played anytime during the school day. When children have to line up for some activity, for example, you can have them do so by playing a game that calls their attention to sounds in words. These games are also a good way to help children realize that the print on the walls is a resource for reading and writing. To successfully play the game, children need to hear and say the word, mentally identifying and isolating the beginning sound and then connecting that sound to other words—a complex task.

Working with English Language Learners

This lesson helps you build language play into classroom routines. As you implement these games, be sure that you have prepared English language learners so that they have some key examples as a resource and can respond to the games (for example, coming up with *coat* to take to *California*). Allow more "wait and think" time for children who are working in English as their second language. Accept responses even if they repeat the answer of children before them. This repetition will help these learners expand their repertoires.

You Need

► Print on the walls: ABC charts, the word wall, charts for shared reading.
► Drawing supplies.
► Glue sticks.

Understand the Principle

Children need to learn that words are made up of sounds in sequence. Being able to identify the first sound in a word and connect that word to other words with the same beginning sound is an essential step in connecting sounds with the letters that represent them.

Once children have learned that there is a relationship between the first letter and sound of a word, they can use this information to monitor reading continuous text and for writing words.

Explain the Principle

" Some words sound the same at the beginning. "

" You can connect words that sound the same at the beginning. "

plan

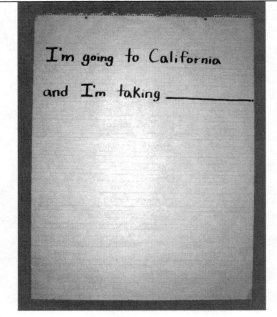

I'm going to California
and I'm taking _____.

Explain the Principle

66 **Some words sound the same at the beginning.** 99

66 **You can connect words that sound the same at the beginning.** 99

① Tell your children that they are going to learn a word game.

② Suggested language: "We're going to play a game today. Let's pretend we're going on a trip. You know, when you go on a trip, you have to pack. You have to take something with you. On this trip, we're going to California. Say *California*. [Children respond.] What is the first sound? [Children respond.] Yes, it's a /k/ sound, so everyone needs to take something that starts with the /k/ sound. Like this: I'm going to California and I'm taking a *coat*. Say those words, *California, coat*. [The isolated phoneme here is /k/. For this hearing and seeing game, it's not important that children distinguish between the letters *c* and *k*, only that they hear this sound or phoneme at the beginning of a word.] What else could I take? [Children make suggestions.]"

③ Have children say the phrase, "I'm going to California and I'm taking _____," filling in more examples. Some possibilities are a *car*, a *computer*, a *candy*, a *can*, a *cap*, a *cat*, a *kite*, a *camera*, a *key*, a *clock*, *cranberries*, a *cake*, *cookies*, *crumbs*.

④ Use the name chart for some examples: "I'm going to California and I'm taking Carlos."

⑤ Prompt children to look around the room for ideas (on the ABC chart or word wall, for example). Tell them that not *every* word will work. If a child says, for example, "I'm going to California and I'm taking *climb*," explain that he did good thinking about the sound and help him come up with a word that will also make sense.

⑥ Line up chairs as if they were seats on a bus, and have children, one at a time, say, "I'm going to California and I'm taking _____." After successfully generating a /k/ example, the child can get on the "bus."

⑦ At first, accept any /k/ word children generate. After children know the game, make it more challenging by requiring a *different* word from the one before or from any words that have been used so far. *If a child cannot generate an appropriate word, you can also say, "Would you like to take a [word]?" The child can say yes and use it in the sentence.*

⑧ Have children practice finding /k/ words somewhere in the room. They can point to or go to the word or object while saying, "I'm going to California and I'm taking *a coat*." This variation will help children become more aware of how to use print resources.

⑨ Repeat using other locations and sounds *(I'm going to the store and I'm going to get a sweater/a sandwich/soup; I'm going to the beach and I'm taking a ball/Bob/a basket/a banana).*

say
draw
read

▶ Have children choose a place they are going from a limited selection (store, market, beach). Prepare a piece of paper with the destination word and one picture clue (for example, *market* and a picture of *mustard*).

▶ Have children say and draw four other items (or cut out pictures of items from magazines) and then read them to a partner.

Have children bring their pictures to a circle discussion and say the names of what they drew. Their pictures can be glued on a chart, labeled, and displayed in the room.

Link

Interactive Read-Aloud: Read aloud books that draw attention to sounds in words, such as:

- ▸ *I Unpacked My Grandmother's Trunk* by Susan Ramsey Hoguet
- ▸ *Alphabet Atlas* by Arthur Yorinks

Shared Reading: Bring children's attention to two successive words in the text that begin with the same sound such as *Miss* and *Muffet* in "Little Miss Muffet" or in the title words of "Windshield Wiper" (see *Sing a Song of Poetry*). Have them say both words and think about the beginning sound. Check the sound with the initial letters in the words.

Guided Reading: When a child approaches an unfamiliar word, instead of telling what it is, say, "Could it be [word]?" Ask the child to say the word and check the first letter to be sure that it matches the sound.

Interactive Writing: Have children say a word slowly and think how to start it. Connect the word to picture cards you have used or to the name chart (see Lesson ELC 1) to decide whether it starts like another word.

Independent Writing: Encourage children to say the words they want to write and think how to start them.

Expand the Learning

Play the game with other beginning sounds. Select towns or places that are familiar to children and that will engage their attention. Generic place-names you can use are the desert, the zoo, the subway, the seashore, the mountains, a train, a bus, a plane.

Have children play the game as they line up to go to the gym or get a snack.

Connect with Home

At a meeting or in a newsletter, encourage family members to play the "similar sounds" game with their children. Suggest several clear examples as starters: "I'm going to the beach" or "I'm going to the park." Families can play these games in the supermarket or on other family trips.

assess

- ▸ Observe whether the children can generate appropriate examples for the "I'm going to . . ." game.
- ▸ Check whether the children can come up with examples of words that begin like the one they want to write in interactive writing.

Hearing and Blending Onsets and Rimes

Follow the Path

Consider Your Children

Blending onsets and rimes is an oral task in which you say the parts of a word and ask the children to put them together smoothly as a whole word. This activity is best used after children have had experience clapping the syllables they hear in words and have participated in shared reading of rhymes and songs. You will want to work with only one-syllable words. Ultimately, you want children to hear and say a word and automatically identify parts. This segmentation will demonstrate the operation, making it easy at first, but move quickly back to saying the whole word slowly and smoothly after children understand how to identify the parts. It is not necessary for children to know the technical words *onset* and *rime* to understand the concept.

Working with English Language Learners

The task in this Follow the Path game is to say the word, then say the word in a divided way (*onset* plus *rime*), and then say the word in whole form again. To perform this task, your English language learners will need to know the labels on the pictures and understand the articulation process. Provide as many examples as necessary when you are teaching children to divide words into onsets and rimes.

You Need

From *Teaching Resources:*
▶ Directions for Follow the Path.
▶ Picture cards representing single-syllable words (Consonant-Vowel-Consonant and Onsets and Rimes). (Enlarge some to use for demonstration purposes.)

Understand the Principle

Onsets and rimes are parts within a single syllable. Syllables are easy for children to identify because they can hear the breaks in words and clap them. Syllabic structure helps them analyze the sounds in words. Most syllables have an *onset*, which consists of whatever is before the vowel, and a *rime*, which is the vowel and whatever comes after it (in that syllable). A syllable can be a single word *(cat)*, or a word can have several syllables *(caterpillar)*.

If children can hear the first and last parts of words as syllables within words and blend them together, they have taken the first step toward word analysis by letter and sound.

Explain the Principle

❝ You can hear and say the first and last parts of words. ❞

❝ You can blend word parts together. ❞

plan

Explain the Principle

" You can hear and say the first and last parts of words. "

" You can blend word parts together. "

① Tell the children they are going to learn about parts in words.

② Suggested language: "When we say a word, we can think about the first and last parts. Say *make*. [Children respond.] Now I'll say the first part by itself and then I'll say the last part: *m-ake, make*. You say that. [Children respond.]"

③ Suggested language: "Let's try another one. Say *t-ake*. [Children respond.] When I say those two parts smoothly, the word is *take*. I'll say the parts of a word and you say the whole word smoothly. Try *br-own*. [Children respond.]"

④ Have the children try several other examples: *gr-een, r-ed, n-est, st-ick, r-ing*.

⑤ Now present a series of pictures and have children take turns saying the onset and rime (first part and last part) and then the whole word.

⑥ Introduce the Follow the Path game. Children throw a die to determine the number of spaces to move forward, say the word that represents the picture in the space they land on, then say the first and last parts of the word separately, and finally say the word again. An alternative is to use a blank Follow the Path trail and have players draw picture cards, say the word parts, and throw a die to determine how many spaces to move.

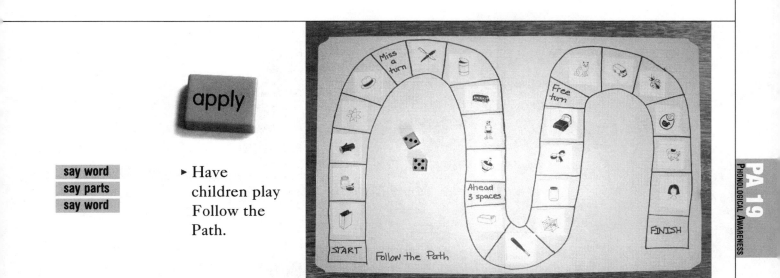

say word
say parts
say word

▶ Have
children play
Follow the
Path.

share

Encourage children to discuss their thinking about the first and last parts of words by sharing some words they dealt with during the game. Demonstrate and encourage comments like these:

"The first part of *bear* and *bat* sounds the same."

"*Bat* and *cat* sound the same at the end."

Link

Interactive Read-Aloud: Read aloud books that have many one-syllable words. After reading, choose two or three words to take apart and put back together. Examples are:

- *Mouse Mess* by Linnea Riley
- *What Will the Weather Be Like Today?* by Paul Rogers

Shared Reading: Use poems and nursery rhymes, such as "Hickory Dickory Dock," that play with words (see *Sing a Song of Poetry*). After enjoying a poem together, invite the children to say the first and last parts of two or three words. Using a stick-on note, cover the last part of a word prior to another reading. Invite children to read the first part of the word and predict the last part. Uncover the word to confirm children's predictions.

Guided Reading: When the children come to an unfamiliar word, show them how to start the first part and then look at the last part (for example, *m-an*). During word work, use magnetic letters to make the first and last parts of some simple words. Show children how to put the two parts together.

Interactive Writing: Have the children say a word and think about the first and last parts as they write the word. If children understand vowels, point out that the last part contains the vowel and the letters after it.

Independent Writing: Encourage the children to say the words they want to write and think about the letters they need for the first part and the last part.

assess

- Say four or five words, one at a time. Ask children to say the parts of each word.

- Notice whether the children are using the first part of words in their reading and writing to figure out new words.

Expand the Learning

Play Follow the Path with other pictures/labels (or cards) on the path.

Blend onsets and rimes using names of objects in the classroom.

Connect with Home

At a family meeting or in a newsletter, teach parents to play a word game with their children in which they identify the first and last parts of the word. Demonstrate with several examples, like *tr-unk, c-ar,* and *d-oor.* Emphasize that the activity should be quick and fun and that the idea is to make children curious about words and get them to enjoy manipulating sounds.

Send a Follow the Path game and directions home with children to play with family members.

Identifying and Blending Onsets and Rimes

Go Fish

Consider Your Children

This activity is effective for children who have learned to hear and clap syllables in words and have participated in shared reading of rhymes and songs. Be sure that children know the meaning of *first* and *last* in relation to oral and written language. It is not necessary for children to know the technical words *onset* and *rime;* refer to the *first part* and the *last part.* It will be important to select one-syllable picture words for this lesson. Overtly segmenting first and last parts of words will accelerate children's understanding of component parts, but be sure they maintain a sense of the whole word.

Working with English Language Learners

The phonology of English may be difficult for children who are just beginning to speak it; however, they are fast learners who are very flexible in learning new sounds. Repeat the names of the objects in pictures and have children say them. Discard those that children cannot understand because they are not within their experience. Use real objects, or act out the meaning of other items. Give learners many opportunities to say the names of the items in pictures before expecting them to play the game. The first time they play Go Fish, play it yourself with a small group to show them the routines.

You Need

▶ Pocket chart.

From *Teaching Resources:*

▶ Picture Cards (Beginning Consonants, Beginning Consonant Clusters and Digraphs).

▶ Go Fish Cards (Deck Card Template).

▶ Directions for Go Fish.

Understand the Principle

Taking the word or syllable apart (often called segmenting) helps children give close attention to the parts of words. Blending involves putting the parts together.

Teaching children to hear, segment, and blend onsets and rimes will give them a foundation for thinking analytically about words and is a natural way for them to break up words in preparation for thinking about individual phonemes.

Explain the Principle

❝ You can blend word parts together. ❞

plan

Explain the Principle

" **You can blend word parts together.** "

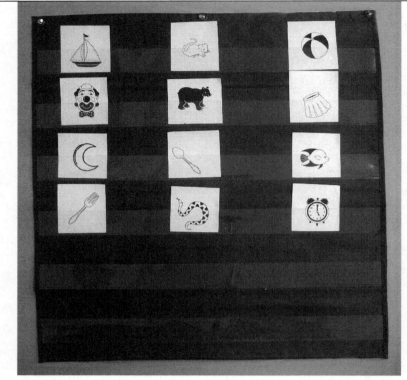

① Tell the children they will be playing a word game.

② Suggested language: "I'm going to say the first part of a word and then I'll say the last part. *D-ay.* I can put those parts together to make a word, *d-ay, day.* Now I'll say another word, but I'll just say the two parts, and you say the whole word. *St-ay.*" Children respond with *stay*.

③ Repeat using several more words, each time saying the two parts and then having children say the whole word: *w-ay, way; b-ay, bay; p-ay, pay; pl-ay, play*. Give children feedback on their responses. You may need to say the parts more than once.

④ Take a collection of picture cards (Beginning Consonant Sounds and Beginning Consonant Cluster Sounds) and place them on the easel or in the pocket chart. Examples include *boat, mouse, ball, clown, bear, skirt, moon, spoon, fish, fork, snake, clock;* use a good variety. Suggested language: "I'm going to say the first part and last part of a word. It will be one of the pictures. Tell me which one it is."

⑤ Have children say the first and last parts of words for others to guess. This action requires both segmenting and blending onsets and rimes.

⑥ Model how to play Go Fish by bringing two children to the front of the group. Create a deck of between forty and forty-eight cards (or simply use picture cards as is) that includes twenty to twenty-four pairs of pictures.

Deal each child five cards. Alternating turns, each asks the other for a particular picture by saying the word in segmented form: "Do you have *c-at?*" If the other child has a picture of a cat, he responds by saying *cat* and giving it to the first player. That player has a match and puts the two cards down on the table. If the responding player does not have the card requested, he says, "Go fish," and the first player takes a card from the deck placed in the middle. The winner is the first one to run out of cards.

ask
match
take

▸ Have children play Go Fish with a partner or in groups of three or four.

Ask children what they learned from playing the game.

Briefly play the oral onset and rime game (see steps 2 and 3 under "Teach") again with a few new words.

Link

Interactive Read-Aloud: After reading aloud books like those mentioned below, reread the books and segment the onset and rime in the last word of each line, inviting the children to put it together.

- ▶ *In the Tall Tall Grass* by Denise Fleming
- ▶ *Building a House* by Byron Barton

Shared Reading: Say a word in segmented form and have children locate the whole word. Alternate with pointing to a word and having children say it in segmented form.

Guided Reading: When children have difficulty figuring out a word, show them how to look at the first part and then the last part (e.g., *c-up*).

Interactive Writing: Have children say a word and think about the first and last parts as they write the word. If children know what vowels are, point out that the last part contains the vowel.

Independent Writing: Encourage children to say the words they want to write and think about the letters they need for the first part and the last part.

assess

- ▶ Notice whether children can identify and blend word parts. A quick check of just two or three examples will tell you whether they understand the concept.

- ▶ Do a quick assessment in the form of a Line-Up game. Present words in segmented form for the children to blend.

Expand the Learning

Repeat the minilesson if children are not using the concept in their own writing and reading. Explicitly show them how to think about a word they want to write, saying it and segmenting it into the first part and the last part.

Play Line-Up games, randomly switching from saying the word and having children segment it to saying the onset and rime and having children blend it.

Create another deck of cards for the Go Fish game using other pictures.

Repeat the minilesson adding the printed word to each card. Though the children may not be able to read the words on the card, they will be exposed to the print along with the picture.

Connect with Home

Send the directions for the oral game described in steps 2 and 3 home to family members. They can play the game with their children in the supermarket or in the car. Emphasize that the activity should be quick and fun and that the idea is to make children curious about words.

Hearing and Substituting Sounds
Picture Cards

Consider Your Children

This activity will be helpful to children if they have had experience saying and hearing sounds in words, matching initial sounds of words, and associating letters and sounds. You may have noticed children spontaneously making connections between words or using words or parts of words they know to make new words. This lesson sets up a routine for word play that can be used at any time during the school day.

Working with English Language Learners

It is important for English language learners to hear sounds and connect words that sound alike. Learning to play a phoneme manipulation game like this one will help them make connections and develop tools for spelling words. They may learn the concept of substituting a different phoneme for the first sound but have trouble recognizing whether they are making actual English words or not (since many English words are meaningless to them). Help children make this exercise concrete by providing as many comprehensible examples as possible. Play the game often, repeating the same examples over and over so that children develop a repertoire.

You Need

From *Teaching Resources:*

▶ Picture Cards (Beginning Consonants). (Enlarge some cards to use in your demonstration.)

Understand the Principle

As children become more aware of the sounds in words, they learn to isolate and identify the first sound they hear. This helps them connect initial sounds and letters, a skill that helps readers begin to decode words and monitor their reading of continuous text.

Removing one sound and replacing it with another helps learners understand how to use knowledge of one word to write or read another.

Explain the Principle

" You can change the first sound of a word to make a new word. "

plan

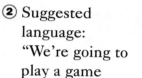

Explain the Principle

" **You can change the first sound of a word to make a new word.** "

① Tell your children they're going to play a word game.

② Suggested language: "We're going to play a game today. When you say a word, you can hear the first sound, can't you? Say *ran*. [Children respond.] What's the first sound? [Children respond.] Say the first sound by itself. [Demonstrate if needed; children respond.] Now I'm going to say the word *ran*; then I'm going to change the first sound to a /k/. Say the sound of *c* as in *cake*. [Demonstrate; children respond.] Listen while I change the first sound of *ran. Ran, can*. What did I change? [Children respond.]"

③ Suggested language: "Let's try another one. Say *land*. [Children respond.] The first sound is . . . [Children respond.] Now change the first sound to /s/ . . . *sand. Land, sand.*"

④ Continue with two or three more examples. Use the same language each time so that children know exactly what it means to change the first sound: "Say *bed*. Change the first sound to /r/. Say *red*. Change the first sound to /b/."

⑤ You may want to use some of the following words:

go—no	king—wing	pay—say	came—game
cat—hat	might—right	saw—law	can—man
pack—sack	hide—ride	late—gate	jump—bump
bank—sank	mice—rice	day—way	sale—tale
to—do	best—nest	sat—mat	mail—sail
my—by	sell—well	sock—rock	rain—pain
tap—cap	bed—red	hip—lip	bake—make
pink—link	heat—seat	bit—fit	ball—fall

⑥ Ask the children to offer examples. Explain that sometimes when you change the first sound, you don't get a real word.

⑦ Show the children how to play this word game by holding up picture cards.

take
say
change

► In pairs, children use the picture cards to play the game. They choose a picture (e.g., a dog), say the word the picture represents, and give another word that starts with a different letter *(fog, log, sog, zog)*. Nonsense words are acceptable. You can informally help children think about whether their attempts represent real words, but at this time the manipulation of sounds is the primary goal.

Have the children share their own examples and demonstrate changing the first sound.

Link

Interactive Read-Aloud: Read aloud books that include rhymes, such as:

- ▸ *Let's Go Visiting* by Sue Williams
- ▸ *A Was Once an Apple Pie* by Edward Lear

Shared Reading: Use poems and nursery rhymes, such as "Make a Pancake," "My Dog Rags," or "I'm Dusty Bill" with rhyming words showing you can change the first sound of a word to make a new word (see *Sing a Song of Poetry*).

Guided Reading: During word work, use magnetic letters to make a simple word such as *to.* Change the first letter to create the word *do.* Repeat with a few other examples (e.g., *no, go; he, we; man, can*).

Interactive Writing: If an appropriate example arises, use the whiteboard to demonstrate making new words by changing the beginning sound. In this case, children will be changing the first sound and seeing the letter change at the same time.

Independent Writing: Encourage children to use known words to spell words they want to write by changing one of the sounds.

Expand the Learning

For a funny variation, take some of the names of children in your class and change the first sound. Invite them to give names of family members and do the same.

Connect with Home

At a meeting or in a newsletter for parents or caregivers, teach them to play a game with their children in which they change the initial sound of one-syllable words. They can say a word and ask the child to change the first sound—*mop/hop, rake/bake.* Emphasize that the activity should be enjoyable and create curiosity about and power over words.

assess

- ▸ Observe whether the children can create words by replacing the initial sound with a different sound. A quick check of just two or three examples will tell you whether they understand the concept.

- ▸ Notice whether the children contribute appropriate examples during the game.

Hearing Middle Sounds
Two-Way Sort

Consider Your Children

Choose common words for this lesson, which works best when children have had experience in both independent and interactive writing. They should be able to hear consonants at the beginning and end of words. In this lesson, children will learn to match middle (vowel) sounds; you can expect some variation in the way they pronounce vowel sounds because of dialect differences and individual differences. When matching pictures, all children may not have the same label in mind, but their own labels will work. The point is for them to say the words and think about the sounds. Use only one-syllable words for this lesson.

Working with English Language Learners

Children will be categorizing picture cards by saying the label and listening for the vowel sound in the middle. These sounds may be difficult for some of your English language learners to hear. Provide more opportunities for these children to practice saying the words and hearing the middle sounds of short *a* and *o*. Be sure that children understand what you mean by *beginning, middle,* and *end;* it may take many demonstrations to get these definitions across. Also, make sure they understand what you mean by *sort;* again, demonstrating the entire application activity and supporting them while they do it will be beneficial. Point out the "take, say, put" tag and demonstrate the actions.

You Need

▶ Pocket chart.

From *Teaching Resources:*

▶ Selected picture cards representing words with similar /ă/ vowel sounds in the middle (Picture Cards, Short Vowels or Consonant-Vowel-Consonant).

▶ Additional Picture Cards, Short Vowels.

▶ Two-Way Sort Sheets.

Understand the Principle

Children need to say and hear medial sounds in words to begin to understand the structure of words.

Sometimes the vowel sounds within words are difficult to hear. Early practice attending to them in the absence of letters helps children listen more carefully to all parts of words, forming a foundation for comparing words and connecting letters and letter clusters.

Explain the Principle

❝ You can hear and say the sound in the middle of a word. ❞

❝ Some words sound the same in the middle. ❞

❝ You can match words that sound the same in the middle. ❞

PHONOLOGICAL AWARENESS — HEARING SIMILAR MIDDLE PHONEMES IN WORDS

teach

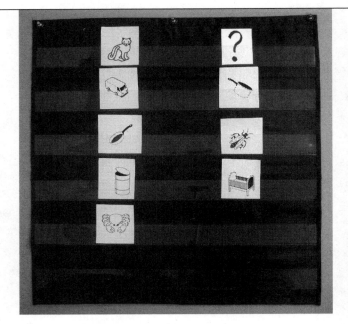

Explain the Principle

❝ You can hear and say the sound in the middle of a word. ❞

❝ Some words sound the same in the middle. ❞

❝ You can match words that sound the same in the middle. ❞

① Explain to the children that they are going to learn more about the sounds they hear in words.

② Have children say the word *cat* slowly and think about the sound in the middle of the word.

③ Suggested language: "You have been thinking hard about the beginning and ending sounds of words. Today we are going to think about some of the sounds in the middle of words. This is a word you know. Say *cat*. [Children respond.] What do you hear at the beginning? [Children respond.] What do you hear at the end of *cat?* [Children respond.]"

④ Suggested language: "Now say the word *cat* and think about the sound in the middle." After children give the /ă/ sound, you may want to write the word *cat* to confirm their understanding, but just work with pictures for the comparisons.

⑤ Suggested language: "*Cat* has an *a* in the middle. I've got some pictures here. Let's say the names of the things in these pictures and see if they sound like *cat* in the middle. *Cat, van*—they sound the same in the middle. Say them with me." Say the words with the children, *slightly* exaggerating the middle sound but keeping the words smooth rather than segmenting them.

⑥ Suggested language: "We are going to play a sorting game to decide which pictures sound like *cat* in the middle and which do not. First say *cat* and then say the name of the picture, like this [demonstrate]. If they have the same middle sound, put the picture under the cat. [Demonstrate with the stack of pictures, inviting children to join in.] By saying both words, you can tell whether the sound is the same in the middle. If it does not match, put it on the right side under the question mark."

⑦ Demonstrate with a few picture cards. Sample pictures might be *pan, can, crab, van, fan, bug, crib, mop, pot, bat.* These comparisons provide some good contrasts, so that children can just listen for the /ă/ sound.

⑧ Reiterate the routine of saying the two words and placing the picture card either under the picture of the cat or in the right column under the question mark.

take
say
put

▸ Have the children play the Two-Way Sort game with a partner. For key words, they have a cat and a question mark. They take out and mix up all the pictures. They take turns drawing a card, saying the word slowly, deciding whether the picture belongs under the cat because it has the same sound in the middle. If it does, they place it under the cat. If it doesn't, they place it in the right-hand column under the question mark. When they finish the sort, they take turns saying all the words under the cat.

▸ Children can extend this activity by drawing one object that has the /ă/ sound in the middle and writing the word.

Have children tell one word they put under the cat. Invite them to give other words that also fit the category.

Link

Interactive Read-Aloud: Read aloud books that invite play with the sounds in words, such as the following:

- ▶ *Ho for a Hat!* by William Jay Smith
- ▶ *Pigs in the Mud in the Middle of the Rud* by Lynn Plourde

Shared Reading: With a masking card or flag (*Teaching Resources,* Materials & Routines), call attention to words in the text that have the same sound in the middle—*cat, hat,* for example.

Guided Reading: During word work, create simple pairs of words that sound the same in the middle *(hot, top; cut, sun)* and point out that they also look the same.

Interactive Writing: Have children say a word slowly and think how to write the letter for the sound in the middle of the word.

Independent Writing: Encourage children to say the words they want to write and think how to write the vowel in the middle. Do not expect conventional spelling of vowel sounds, but encourage children to make attempts.

Expand the Learning

Repeat the lesson with other vowels (/ĕ/, /ĭ/, /ŏ/, /ŭ/) as medial sounds. (See *Teaching Resources* for picture cards.) Example key words are *net, pig, dog,* and *sun.*

Connect with Home

Give children a photocopy of a Two-Way Sort Sheet with a key picture (for example, a cat) and a question mark already in place. Send along a sheet of picture cards (selected from Picture Cards, Short Vowels or Consonant-Vowel-Consonant). Children can cut and sort the pictures with family members.

assess

- ▶ Check whether the children can identify the cards that represent words with /ă/ in the middle.
- ▶ Notice whether the children make good attempts to write vowels during interactive writing.

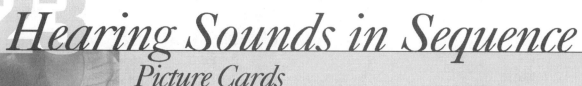

Generative
Lesson

early
mid
late

PA 23
PHONOLOGICAL AWARENESS

(PHONEMIC AWARENESS)

Hearing Sounds in Sequence
Picture Cards

Consider Your Children

Most of the work on this principle takes place during interactive writing as you help children spell the words they want to write. A lesson like this one, which makes this knowledge more explicit, is most successful if children have had a great deal of experience saying words slowly during writing. Also, they should know most letters and be able to hear some of the dominant consonants and easy-to-hear vowels in words. If children already know how to write a simple word, guide them to write it quickly rather than saying it slowly. This technique is unnecessarily tedious when it's not needed.

Working with English Language Learners

This lesson will help English language learners attend to the sequence of sounds in English words. They will hear words slowly and clearly articulated in contrast to encountering them within rapid speech. Seeing the letters written to represent the sounds in sequence will help them to map English words onto written language and make more complete attempts in their own writing. You may need to include more demonstrations and to complete the application task with children to be sure that they understand it and are using words that they know and understand. Observing them will give you an idea of their growing control of English.

You Need

▶ Chart paper.

▶ Collection of words to write.

▶ Drawing supplies.

▶ Glue sticks.

From *Teaching Resources:*

▶ Four-Box Sheet.

▶ Picture Cards (Consonant-Vowel-Consonant).

Understand the Principle

Being able to isolate and identify a large number of sounds in words helps them understand the alphabetic principle—that twenty-six letters in a variety of combinations represent all the sounds in the English language.

Hearing the component sounds in sequence makes it possible for children to think analytically about words and lays a foundation for writing more of the letters in words and digging deeper into print to decode words.

This lesson goes beyond phonological awareness to demonstrate the connections to print.

Explain the Principle

❝ You can say a word slowly to hear all the sounds from first to last. ❞

❝ You can write the letter or letters for each sound. ❞

plan

little   sleep
game   dream
slide   like
chair   fl
best

Explain the Principle

" You can say a word slowly to hear all the sounds from first to last. "

" You can write the letter or letters for each sound. "

① Explain to the children that they are going to listen to the order of sounds in words.

② From the interactive writing you have done, select nine or ten challenging words made up of three or four clear sounds. Alternatively, collect some words from the children's own writing. Examples of appropriate words are *little, flag, game, slide, chair, happy, best, sleep, like, dream.*

③ Suggested language: "If you say a word slowly, you can hear some of the sounds in it. You are getting really good at doing that. Today we are going to think hard about the sounds in some of the words you've been using during the last few weeks and then try to write those words." Do not expect children to be able to generate all the sounds in these words. The goal is for them to listen and generate some consonant and vowel sounds; you will fill in the rest of the word.

④ Suggested language: "Let's start with the word *flag.* Say it slowly. What can you hear?" Children respond by saying it slowly and offering the sounds they hear. Accept their responses and comment on them.

⑤ If a child says *g* or makes the /g/ sound, you can say, "Yes, that is at the end of the word. Keep that in mind and let's say it again and think about the beginning of the word."

⑥ Work until children have generated what they can, including the vowel sound, and then fill in the missing letters yourself. If children offer vowels other than *a*, recognize that they are thinking about vowels. Demonstrate running your finger under the word and saying it slowly. Show children how checking like this will help you know if you have connected all of the sounds you can.

⑦ Repeat the process with *game*. Here you might want to comment that there is an *e* on the end of the word that is *silent*. There is no sound connected with it, but you add it to the end of the word to make it "look right."

⑧ Repeat the process with four or five other words. Notice how many of the sounds children can produce. Children may produce the correct sound but suggest the wrong letter—*k* for *coat*. Recognize their thinking and say it could start that way, but this time the letter is *c*.

⑨ Suggested language: "You can hear lots of the sounds in words. Today you are going to write some words. Choose any words you want to learn to write and say them slowly. Challenge yourself to write some words that are new to you. Draw a picture in each box on this paper [hold up a Four-Box Sheet]. Under each picture you draw, write the letters for the sounds you hear. [Demonstrate by drawing a tree and writing *tree*.] Write as many of the letters as you can."

draw
say
write

▶ Have children draw four pictures or use picture cards and say as many sounds as they can hear in the words the pictures represent. They say words slowly to hear sounds in sequence and attempt to write the letters. Notice whether they represent each sound with at least one letter.

Have children read their words to a partner.

Link

Interactive Read-Aloud: Read aloud books such as the following:

- *Tick-Tock* by Lena Anderson
- *The Old Woman Who Named Things* by Cynthia Rylant to foster children's attention to sounds in words.

Shared Reading: Cover some words in a text that children have read several times. (Small stick-on notes work well for this.) When you approach the covered word, have children say it and predict what the first letter and some subsequent letters will be. Then gradually remove the paper to check their predictions.

Guided Reading: When a child encounters an unknown word, instead of telling her what it is, ask, "Could it be [word]?" Ask the child to say it slowly and then show her how to check the letters.

Interactive Writing: When solving a word, ask children to say it slowly and think about the letters. They can suggest many of the letters while you fill in the rest.

Independent Writing: When children are attempting to spell a new word, encourage them to say the word slowly and then represent as many letters as they can.

assess

- ▶ Check the extent to which children are able to represent sounds in words accurately in their writing.
- ▶ Notice whether children are using letter/sound cues to check on their reading and to solve new words in reading.
- ▶ Give children four or five words to write, and observe their attempts to write letters for the sounds they hear.

- ▶ Examine the completed Four-Box Sheets to see whether children are representing all easy-to-hear sounds in words. Notice which sounds are hard for the children to hear and identify.

Expand the Learning

After a few weeks, repeat the lesson with more words children have been attempting to spell. This lesson can be very quick.

Have children say words several times to identify more sounds.

Connect with Home

Have children take home the words they wrote with a brief note from you asking caregivers to notice the sounds children have represented.

Encourage family members to have their children write simple, short sentences by saying the words slowly and thinking about the sounds they hear. Explain that this helps children learn more about writing words and that the children will eventually learn conventional spellings.

Blending Sounds in Words

Lotto Game

Consider Your Children

Blending phonemes is a complex task. Use this lesson after children have worked with the name puzzles, have experienced interactive writing, and know the concept of a word. They should be able to say words slowly and to hear and identify beginning, end, and middle sounds. They should also have experience hearing and blending syllables as well as onsets and rimes. In this lesson you demonstrate close attention to sounds in words by pausing after each. This means a slight *schwa* or "uh" sound after some consonants, which distorts the word as a whole. For most children, this segmentation accelerates learning because it makes individual sounds so explicit. If children seem confused, go back to *slightly* blending the sounds so children clearly understand the word and the task.

Working with English Language Learners

Involve English language learners in this activity only after they have considerable experience hearing and manipulating sounds in words. Be sure that the examples you select are words that students know, understand, can say, and can identify the first and last sounds of. Use picture cards for which students know the labels in English. Play the game with students the first time so that you can be sure they are articulating the words correctly.

You Need

From *Teaching Resources:*

▶ Lotto Game Cards.

▶ Directions for Lotto.

▶ Selected Picture Cards (Short Vowels or Consonant-Vowel-Consonant).

Understand the Principle

Blending individual sounds to form a word requires children to articulate the individual sounds in words and then put them together to say the word smoothly. Blending sounds acquaints children with the structure of words and forms the basis for decoding and spelling words.

Identifying the individual sounds in words and blending them together can be very difficult for young children; attempts to teach this technique should be short and gamelike.

Explain the Principle

" You can blend sounds together to say a word. "

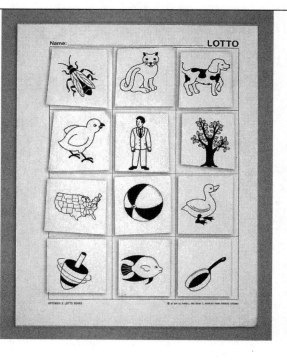

Explain the Principle

" **You can blend sounds together to say a word.** "

① Tell your children they are going to play a listening game.

② Suggested language: "Today we're going to play a game in which we put words together. You have learned a lot about hearing sounds in words. I'm going to say a word very slowly so you can hear the sounds. As I say the sounds, think about the words but don't say it out loud. [Say *t-o-p* slowly without distorting the sounds but enunciating each phoneme or sound clearly.] Are any of you thinking what the word could be? The word is *top*. Were you right? Let's try another word."

③ In the same way, say *ch-i-ck, J-o-n, g-o, b-a-ll, s-t-o-p, m-a-n, m-a-p,* and other words. Have children say the whole word.

④ If the students seem to have the idea, try asking them to say these same words slowly while they listen for the sounds. Otherwise, do this in another lesson.

⑤ Suggested language: "Now that you can make words by hearing or saying the separate sounds in them, you can play Lotto with pictures. When you draw a picture card, first say the name of the item in the picture very slowly so you can hear the sounds in it. Then look for that picture on your Lotto Game Card. If you have a match, say the word and place the picture card in the square that has the matching picture. If you have no match, place the picture card face down next to the deck." Demonstrate with two or three examples.

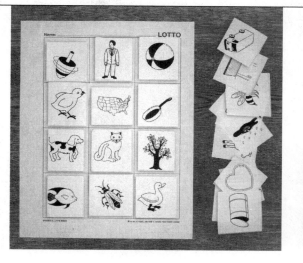

take
say
match

▸ Have children play the game in groups of three or four. Start with Lotto Game Cards and picture cards that have very regular words—no more than three sounds. Remember, each member of the group will have a different-color Lotto card with a different layout of pictures.

▸ You can gradually increase the complexity of the words as you notice children are able to say these words slowly and identify the sounds.

Invite each child to share one word from his or her Lotto card. The child says the word slowly and other children raise their hands to say the word quickly.

Link

Interactive Read-Aloud: Read aloud books that emphasize the sounds in words, such as the following:

- ▸ *Mice Squeak, We Speak* by Arnold L. Shapiro and Tomie dePaola
- ▸ *Camel Caravan* by Bethany Roberts and Patricia Hubbell

Shared Reading: After reading and enjoying a poem or chant such as "There Was An Old Woman" or "To Market, To Market" (see *Sing a Song of Poetry*), have children say a few words slowly and locate them in the text using a masking card or flag.

Guided Reading: Draw children's attention to the individual sounds of an unfamiliar word. During word work, make some words with magnetic letters and have children practice saying them slowly.

Interactive Writing: Have children say a word slowly and think about how to write the letters for all the sounds.

Independent Writing: Encourage children to say the words they want to write and think how to write the sounds. Praise children for the sounds they can represent.

assess

- ▸ Notice whether children can say individual sounds in words without distorting the pronunciation.
- ▸ Say five words very slowly and ask children to say them smoothly.
- ▸ Check whether children make good attempts at writing the letters for sounds during interactive writing.

Expand the Learning

Repeat the lesson with picture cards that have more than three sounds in the label.

Repeat the lesson with picture cards that illustrate long vowel sounds (*Teaching Resources,* Picture Cards, Long Vowels).

Connect with Home

Let children take home small picture cards and show family members how they can say the sounds slowly and then say the whole word.

Hearing, Saying, and Deleting Beginning Sounds
Picture Cards

Generative Lesson

early
mid
late

PA 25
PHONOLOGICAL AWARENESS (PHONEMIC AWARENESS)

Consider Your Children

Deleting phonemes requires children to have a strong sense of the sequence of sounds in words. Children should be able to identify and isolate beginning, middle, and ending sounds before being asked to manipulate sounds in this way. If they can delete a sound mentally, that is evidence that children can hold up words for manipulation, a foundation for taking words apart. Making phoneme deletion into a routine game that you can play for a few minutes during line-up or other times will give children power over letters and sounds in words. If children clearly understand the principle, you will not want to spend much time on it.

Working with English Language Learners

For children who are just learning the English sound system and words, deleting sounds will be quite difficult. You may want to delay using this lesson until your English language learners are very comfortable using English orally. Say words very clearly and listen carefully as they attempt to pronounce them. Accept their approximations and discard words that seem too difficult. You will want to start with only a few very simple examples and make the activity quick and lively.

You Need

From *Teaching Resources:*

▶ Selected Picture Cards (Consonant-Vowel-Consonant and Rhymes).

▶ Copies of the Alphabet Linking Chart.

Understand the Principle

As children become more aware of the sounds in words, they learn to say, recognize, and identify sounds they hear and become able to identify sounds in sequence.

Deleting sounds indicates a great deal of control of the phonology of English.

Explain the Principle

“ You can say a word without the first sound. ”

plan

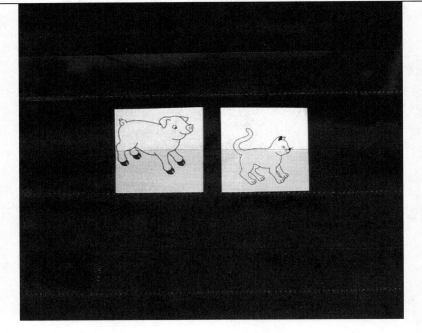

Explain the Principle

" **You can say a word without the first sound.** "

① Tell the children they are going to learn to say words without some of the sounds.

② Suggested language: "When you say a word, you can hear the first sound, can't you? Say *pig*. [Children respond.] What's the first sound? [Children respond.] Say the first sound by itself. [Demonstrate.]"

③ Suggested language: "Now I'm going to say the word *pig* without the /p/. [Demonstrate: *pig, -ig*.] Let's try another one. Say *cat*. [Children respond.] The first sound is. . . . [Children respond.] Now say *cat* without the /k/. [Isolate the sound *-at*.]"

④ Demonstrate the game using two or three more examples offered by children.

⑤ To vary the game, take some of the names of children in your class and say them without the first sound *(Mike, -ike; Jan, -an)*.

⑥ When children in the group can easily say words without the first sound, it will not be necessary to play this game anymore.

apply

▸ Have children read the consonant boxes on the Alphabet Linking Chart to a partner and then delete the first sound: *bear, -ear; cat, -at; dog, -og.*

▸ Provide a pile of selected picture cards and ask children, working with a partner, to take ten cards, saying each word represented by the pictures and then deleting the first sound.

share

Encourage children to come up with their own examples and to demonstrate deleting sounds.

Link

Interactive Read-Aloud: Read aloud books that contain words that start alike, such as the two below. See *Teaching Resources, Alliteration Bibliography,* for more examples.

- ▶ *The Wacky Wedding* by Pamela Duncan Edwards
- ▶ *Safe, Warm and Snug* by Stephen R. Swinburne

Shared Reading: Read poems and nursery rhymes (such as *Hickory, Dickory, Dock*) that feature play with words. Delete some word beginnings and read for fun: *Ickory, ickory, ock. The ouse an up the ock.* Select a variety from *Sing a Song of Poetry.*

Guided Reading: When children come to a new word, prompt them to give the sound of the first letter and then to go beyond the first letter as appropriate.

Interactive Writing: Have the children say a word slowly and think how to start it. While you don't need to delete the first sound, the activity in this minilesson will have made them more aware of the sequence of phonemes in words, and sounds will be easier to isolate and hear.

Independent Writing: Encourage the children to say the words they want to write and think how to start them; then show them how to say them again to identify more letters.

assess

- ▶ Notice whether the children can say, hear, and delete the first sounds of words. A quick check of just two or three examples will tell you whether they understand it.
- ▶ Check whether the children can generate appropriate examples for the game.

Expand the Learning

Repeat the lesson with different words/pictures if children have not gained full control of the principles.

Connect with Home

In a newsletter or meeting, teach family members to make a game of saying a word and then taking away the first sound (for example, *cat, -at*). Emphasize that the activity should be quick and fun and that the idea is to make children curious about words and get them to enjoy manipulating sounds.

Suggest that while driving in the car or going for a walk they play "I see. . . ." The adult says "I see a *h-ouse.*" The child says *house.*

26 Hearing and Deleting Sounds
Picture Cards

Consider Your Children

Use this lesson after children have had a great deal of experience saying and hearing sounds in words, matching the initial sounds of words, and associating letters and sounds. When children grasp the concept of a word and are noticing and identifying sequences of sounds, it will be easier for them to take on a complex task such as deleting sounds. This operation is also an outcome of much experience in writing, in which children take words apart to spell them. If children can easily perform the task, you do not need to spend much time on these kinds of activities.

Working with English Language Learners

Phoneme manipulation may be especially difficult for English language learners and could confuse them. You may elect not to use this activity if children are very inexperienced in English and have not worked a great deal with letters and sounds. Use only the easiest examples that focus on words children know, understand, and can say. Say words clearly yourself when you demonstrate. Accept variations in pronunciation. Make taking away sounds into a game rather than a test, and value approximation.

You Need

From *Teaching Resources:*

▶ Picture Cards (Consonant-Vowel-Consonant, Long Vowels, and Rhymes).

Understand the Principle

As children become more aware of the sounds in words, they learn to isolate and identify the first sound they hear. This helps readers connect initial sounds and letters, which in turn helps them begin to decode words and monitor their reading of continuous text.

Manipulating words by removing one of the sounds helps make the knowledge of phonemes more explicit and the application of that knowledge more flexible.

Explain the Principle

" You can say words without some of the sounds. "

" You can say a word without the first sound. "

plan

Explain the Principle

❝ You can say words without some of the sounds. ❞

❝ You can say a word without the first sound. ❞

① Tell your children they are going to play a word game.

② Suggested language: "We're going to play a word game today. When you say a word, you can hear the first sound, can't you? Say *horse*. [Children respond.] What's the first sound? [Children respond.] Say the first sound by itself. [Demonstrate if needed; children respond.] Now I'm going to say the word *horse* without the /h/. [Demonstrate.] Let's try another one. Say *cat*. [Children respond.] The first sound is. . . . [Children respond.] Now say *cat* without the /k/. [Isolate the /k/ sound.]"

③ Continue with the following words:

shy—eye	tall—all	make—ache
shout—out	mice—ice	fold—old
neat—eat	sink—ink	mat—at
hill—ill	rice—ice	farm—arm
cold—old	hair—air	feel—eel
cow—ow	pat—at	heart—art
bus—us	bend—end	

④ Use picture cards to prompt children to practice more examples.

⑤ Continue to play the game using two or three more examples offered by children.

⑥ When children in the group can easily say words without the first sound, it's no longer necessary to play this game.

take
say

▶ Have children use a selection of picture cards to play the game with a partner. They take turns drawing a card, saying the whole word, and then saying it without the first sound.

Have children share some of their own examples and demonstrate deleting sounds.

Link

Interactive-Read Aloud: Read aloud books that play with words, such as:

▶ *Small Green Snake* by Libba Moore Gray

▶ *Beach Play* by Marsha Hayles

Shared Reading: Use shared reading of poems and nursery rhymes, such as "Hickory, Dickory, Dore," and ""Higglety Pigglety, Pop!" that play with words. (See *Sing a Song of Poetry*.)

Guided Reading: During word work, write some simple words such as *cat* on the whiteboard. Tell the children the word. Wipe off the first letter and have them say what is left (*-at*).

Interactive Writing: Have the children say a word slowly and think how to start it. After generating the sound, write the first letter. (You don't need to delete the first sound in this instance.)

Independent Writing: Encourage the children to say the words they want to write and think how to start them; then show them how to say the words again to represent more letters.

assess

▶ Notice whether the children can hear the first letter in a word and then say the word without the first letter. A quick check of just two or three examples will tell you whether they understand the concept.

▶ Observe whether the children can generate appropriate examples for the game.

Expand the Learning

Repeat the process, having the children delete the last sound. For a variation, use some of the names of children in your class and say them without the first sound.

Connect with Home

At a meeting or in a newsletter, teach family members to play this game. Suggest that they try words in a category, such as animals or food *(dog–og, cow–ow,* or *banana–anana, lemon–emon)*. Emphasize that the activity should be quick and fun and that the idea is to make the children curious about words and get them to enjoy manipulating sounds.

Letter Knowledge

Letter knowledge refers to what children need to learn about the graphic characters that correspond with the sounds of language. A finite set of twenty-six letters, two forms of each, is related to all of the sounds of the English language (approximately forty-four phonemes). The sounds in the language change as dialect, articulation, and other speech factors vary. Children will also encounter alternative forms of some letters—for example, g, g; a, a; y, y—and will eventually learn to recognize letters in cursive writing. Children need to learn the names and purposes of letters, as well as the particular features of each. When children can identify letters by noticing the very small differences that make them unique, they can then associate letters and letter clusters with phonemes and parts of words. Knowing the letter names is useful information that helps children talk about letters and understand what others say about them. As writers, children need to be able to use efficient directional movements when making letters.

Connect to Assessment

See related LK Assessment Tasks in the Assessment Guide in *Teaching Resources*:

▶ Reading the Alphabet

▶ Writing the Alphabet

▶ Connecting Uppercase and Lowercase Letter Forms

Develop Your Professional Understanding

See *Word Matters: Teaching Phonics and Spelling in the Reading/Writing Classroom* by G.S. Pinnell and I.C. Fountas. 1998. Portsmouth, New Hampshire: Heinemann.

Related pages: 7–8, 46–47, 47–48, 69–72, 87–88, 90–93, 123, 138–139, 141–142, 143–147, 252–254.

1 *Exploring Letters*

Letter Play

Consider Your Children

This will be a very early lesson. Notice how many letters of the alphabet children can name and locate quickly on a chart and in a text that has continuous print. Children who are unfamiliar with letters in general will need a great deal of letter exploration such as the activity in this lesson. This lesson will help very inexperienced children learn to look for the very basic features of letters. It will also help children understand the purposes of print.

Working with English Language Learners

Exploration is a way for you to discover the thinking that English language learners are bringing to their work with the alphabet letters. Even though you will be guiding them to notice features of letters, it will be helpful to know the connections they are making on their own. For example, they may be thinking that a letter looks like something they know that is culturally related. Encourage them to talk about the letters that they are noticing.

You Need

► Tub or basket of assorted magnetic letters.
► Magnetic surface.

Understand the Principle

Young children need to know how to recognize the characteristics that make a letter different from every other letter—the *distinctive features.* These differences are often quite small. For example, the length of the "stick" distinguishes *n* from *h.* Children must be able to make these distinctions before they can match letters with the sounds they represent.

By handling letters and using them for different purposes, children learn to "look at print."

Explain the Principle

" Letters are different from each other. "

" You can notice the parts of letters. "

plan

teach

Explain the Principle

66 Letters are different from each other. 99

66 You can notice the parts of letters. 99

① Explain to the children that they are going to be using colored plastic letters to learn a lot about letters.

② Place a variety of letters on a magnetic board or magnetic cookie sheet and ask the children what they notice about them. They will offer comments such as:

"They are all different colors."

"Some letters look the same."

"Some are big and some are little."

③ Show the children that they can put letters together to make words.

④ Make some of the children's names and some simple words.

⑤ Explain to children that today they are going to have time to play with letters.

⑥ They can sort them, make words, match letters, or use them however they want.

⑦ They need to keep them on the table and put them all back in the tub when finished.

Amy	Jaquie	Pat
Alissa		Prenetta
Alex	Kara	Parker
Billy	Lisa	Rosa
		Reika
Carlton	Michael M.	
Chamique	Michael G.	Sarah
Douglas	Nora	Tanya
Denine	Nadia	Tanisha
Erin		
Elizabeth		

Denine   Reika

Erin

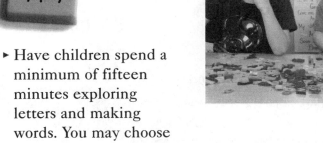

play
sort
make
match

► Have children spend a minimum of fifteen minutes exploring letters and making words. You may choose to have a few word cards that they can use as models.

In the group meeting, invite the children to talk about what they've discovered.

If they haven't noticed, explain that the twenty-six letters have uppercase and lowercase forms and that some lowercase letters look like their uppercase forms.

Link

Interactive Read-Aloud: Read aloud a variety of alphabet books about letters. (Also see the Alphabet Books Bibliography in *Teaching Resources*.) Examples are:

▶ *Animal ABC* by David Wojtowycz

▶ *Pierrot's ABC Garden* by Anita Lobel

Shared Reading: Using poems or songs about the alphabet such as the Alphabet Song, invite children to locate letters using a masking card or highlighter tape.

Guided Reading: During word work, have children find letters that have particular features, for example, "circles" or "long sticks."

Interactive Writing: Guide a child's hand as he contributes letters to the writing, or hold up a model magnetic letter for the child to copy. Use the Verbal Path description of the letter as the child writes (see *Teaching Resources*).

Independent Writing: Reinforce children's correct letter formation as they write stories. Remind them about long "sticks," etc., as needed.

Expand the Learning

Repeat the lesson, each time helping the children notice more about letters.

Connect with Home

If children do not have a set of magnetic letters at home, send letter cards (in *Teaching Resources*) home with them. See 25 Ways to Use Magnetic Letters at Home (also in *Teaching Resources*) for a variety of activities family members can do at home using letters.

assess

▶ Observe the children working with letters. Be aware of how they are using them and what they notice about them.

▶ Ask children to find specific letters or to make their names.

Recognizing Letters
Magnetic Letters

Consider Your Children

This lesson establishes the routine for sorting letters and will be helpful to children who have not noticed the details or shapes of letters and who do not know many letter names. We suggest this sequence: *(b, m, r, s) (t, g, n, p) (c, h, f, d) (l, k, j, w) (y, z, v, x, q).* Work with two or three letters at a time; select pairs that are dissimilar in shape and in the sounds related to them. Don't give this level of attention to letters children have already learned.

Working with English Language Learners

It will be important for English language learners to learn the names of the letters so that they can understand classroom instruction. They may need several demonstrations of letters and names, and you may want to work with a small set of letters at the beginning (for example, find all the *b*'s in a set of four different letters). Begin with letters that are very different from each other and have children say the name of the letter each time they find it.

You Need

▶ Class name chart (see Lesson ELC 1).

▶ MagnaDoodle® or whiteboard.

▶ Vertical surface on which magnetic letters will stick.

▶ Magnetic letters in a basket, tub, or pot.

From *Teaching Resources:*

▶ Two-Way Sort Cards or Sheets.

Understand the Principle

Recognizing and naming letters is an important tool for beginning readers and writers. Although the names of letters do not necessarily match the sound they represent, they are part of the language of the classroom.

Knowing the names of letters and connecting them to their shapes give children a way to talk about these tools.

The ability to recognize letters should become quick and automatic.

Explain the Principle

" A letter has a name and a shape. "

" You can look at the shape of a letter and say its name. "

plan

Explain the Principle

66 **A letter has a name and a shape.** 99

66 **You can look at the shape of a letter and say its name.** 99

① Tell the children they are going to learn more about the names and shapes of letters.

② Be sure that all children can see the MagnaDoodle® or whiteboard and the magnetic letter surface clearly. Begin with some *b*'s and *r*'s on the magnetic letter surface, along with several other letters. For very inexperienced children, limit the selection. First, they need to get the idea of discriminating between letters.

③ Suggested language: "I'm going to make a letter. [Make a *b*, being sure that the line is thick and black.] This is a *b*. Say *b*. [Children respond.] Whisper *b*. [Children respond.] To make *b*, pull down, half up, and around. [Repeat the motions.] This is a lowercase *b*. Who can find a *b* on the alphabet chart? Who can find a *b* on the name chart?"

④ Suggested language: "Now I'm going to find a *b* among the magnetic letters you see up here." Demonstrate finding a *b* among the letters on the magnetic surface. Place the *b* clearly away from the others.

⑤ Ask several children to come up and find additional *b*'s and group them with the first one. Help as needed so that the process moves quickly.

⑥ Say the name of the letter each time it is placed with the group. Also, show children how to "check" the group by pointing to each *b*, looking closely, and saying its name.

⑦ Repeat using the letter *m* or *r*.

⑧ Demonstrate the letter activity. Show the children that they will look at the pile of letters and find all the *b*'s first and then the *r*'s. Teach them how to place the *b*'s on the left side of the Two-Way Sort Card and the *r*'s on the right side.

apply

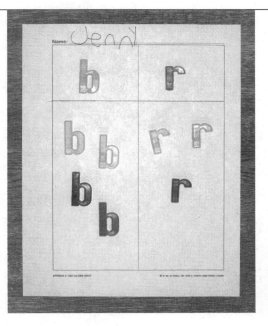

find
sort

▶ Give each child a Two-Way Sort Card and provide a tub of *b*'s, *r*'s, and other letters for children to use. You may want to post simple directions, or write a *b* and an *r* at the top of the card. Children find *b*'s and place them on the left and find *r*'s and place them on the right. Other letters are not used.

▶ Encourage children to say the letter names and look closely at the letters as they sort them.

share

Have children discuss what they noticed about *b* and *r*. Demonstrate and encourage comments like these:

"*b* is a tall letter."

"*r* has a little curl on it."

"I have a *b* in my name."

"*r* is shorter."

Link

Interactive Read-Aloud: Read aloud alphabet books (see the extensive Alphabet Books Bibliography in *Teaching Resources*), such as:

- ▸ *Action Alphabet* by Shelly Rotner
- ▸ *Away from Home* by Anita Lobel

Shared Reading: Name letters and have children locate them in poems such as "Time to Pick Up," "Tommy Snooks," or other texts (see *Sing a Song of Poetry*) using a masking card (see the *Teaching Resources*) or highlighter tape.

Guided Reading: During word work, place an array of magnetic letters on the easel. Have children sort all the examples of a particular letter and say their names.

Interactive Writing: Use the names of letters to help children locate the letter needed in a piece of writing. Make connections with the Alphabet Linking Chart and the name chart.

Independent Writing: Point out letters by name when conferring with children about their writing.

assess

- ▸ Observe whether the children can find letters quickly and match and check them.

- ▸ Observe whether the children can produce the name of the letter quickly.

- ▸ Give a quick test using cards (or a chart) of letters that are not in alphabetical order. Ask children to quickly say the name of the letter.

Expand the Learning

Repeat this lesson with different letters, two or three at a time. We have suggested a sequence for lowercase letters, which are more useful to children. (See Consider Your Children section.)

If children have very little letter knowledge, you may want to repeat these lessons for some uppercase letters.

After children understand the routines for finding and grouping specific letters, you can increase the challenge by providing a larger group of distracting letters. Prompt children to work quickly and to check their groupings.

Connect with Home

Encourage family members to purchase a set of magnetic letters for the child's use at home. If they cannot, send home letter cards (see *Teaching Resources*) as a workable substitute.

Send home a list of ways family members can have children sort letters (*Teaching Resources*, 25 Ways to Use Magnetic Letters at Home).

Ask children to search the large-print headlines and labels in magazines for several examples of a particular letter you've worked with in class, cut them out, and glue them on a sheet.

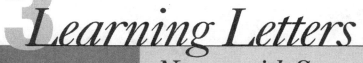

3 Learning Letters
Names with Stars

Consider Your Children

Use this lesson with children who are just beginning to learn to write and read their names. If they are able to recognize some letters in their names but do not have full control of the specific features of individual letters, this lesson will be helpful. If all children can quickly, accurately, and automatically write their first names and say the letters in them, you may want to include surnames or not use this lesson.

Working with English Language Learners

Children enjoy working with their names, and every time you recognize a child's name, his or her presence in your class will be affirmed. Noticing the features of their names will be a first step for them in distinguishing the letters from each other. Be sure that you know how to pronounce their names as they do and help them say their own names clearly along with the names of their classmates.

You Need

▸ Your name written in black on tag board.

▸ Children's names written in black on the bottom half of tag board with blank space at the top for a drawing.

▸ Boxes of gummed stars.

▸ Markers.

From *Teaching Resources:*

▸ Verbal Path for the Formation of Letters.

▸ Letter Formation Charts.

Understand the Principle

Children's names are a valuable learning resource. By examining their names, they learn to notice specific features of letters and they learn about the consistency of letter order in words. They realize that directionality in making letters and putting them together to make words is important. They also learn important ways of working with words, such as noticing first and last letters, letter clusters, and word length.

Explain the Principle

" You can notice the parts of letters. "

---

plan

Explain the Principle

" You can notice the parts of letters. "

① Tell the children you are going to show them how to notice the parts of letters in their name.

② Write your name or a child's name in large letters on a MagnaDoodle® or whiteboard.

③ As you do so, use language describing letter formation. Point out features such as circles, slants, tunnels, long sticks, and short sticks. (Refer to the Verbal Path for the Formation of Letters.)

④ Show children how to use their name cards, and, with a finger, trace over the letters in their names.

⑤ Suggested language: "After you have traced your name and noticed all the letters, take your name card and put stars on all the lines that make the letters."

stick
glue
draw

▶ Have children outline their names with stars on the name card and then glue it on the bottom half of a larger sheet of paper. They then draw their self-portraits on the top half of their papers.

Display the class "stars" on the bulletin board.

Ask children to tell about anything they noticed about the letters in their names.

Read the names in a shared way.

Point to a "star" name and ask children to quickly locate with their eyes the same name on the name chart.

Link

Interactive Read-Aloud: Read aloud alphabet books or books featuring names. Ask the children what they notice about some of the letters. Examples are:

- ► *Miss Bindergarten Stays Home from Kindergarten* by Joseph Slate
- ► *A My Name Is Alice* by Jane Bayer

Shared Reading: After enjoying a poem or song such as "Two Little Houses" or "Window Watching" (see *Sing a Song of Poetry*), ask children to notice a letter-formation feature and find a letter with that feature using a masking card (in *Teaching Resources*) or highlighter tape.

Guided Reading: During word work, place a variety of letters on the magnetic board, or give children small containers of letters. Ask them to sort the letters according to different features (circles, tunnels, long sticks, etc.).

Interactive Writing: As children form letters, guide them with the language that supports the correct formation (see *Teaching Resources*, Verbal Path for the Formation of Letters).

Independent Writing: Prompt children to use correct, efficient letter formation when writing. Post an enlarged version of the Letter Formation Charts (in *Teaching Resources*) for the children's reference.

assess

- ► Have each child write his name independently and observe how many letters he can represent.
- ► Have each child locate her name several times within continuous text as well as on the name chart. Notice how quickly children find their names.

- ► Give children copies of their names written in large print. Tell them: *Put a circle around the first letter of your name. Put a line under the last letter of your name.* Notice whether the children are able to perform the task.

Expand the Learning

Repeat the lesson with last names and the appropriate honorific: *Mr. Sonora, Miss Rivera.*

Connect with Home

Encourage family members to have children make their name several times with magnetic letters or letter cards (see *Teaching Resources*).

Generative Lesson

early
mid
late

LK 4
LETTER KNOWLEDGE

4 Learning Letters
Name Puzzle

Consider Your Children

This lesson is appropriate very early in kindergarten. It will help children begin to learn about letters using as examples those that are likely to be the most familiar to them and have the greatest meaning. You can begin working with the name puzzle once you have introduced the name chart (see Lesson ELC 1) and children have had some experience locating their names and noticing the letters in their names.

Working with English Language Learners

This generative lesson will help your English language learners make personal connections to written language and will also be a way of helping them understand the terms *name, word,* and *letter.* Be sure each child can say his or her name clearly. Demonstrate the task several times, and work with a small group if necessary so that learners understand how to look closely at the model and to build the name in exactly the same way. Use the term *letter* while pointing to the individual graphic signs. Say the letters of each child's name and have the child repeat the letter names. Work with the letter puzzle each day (in a small group if needed) until English language learners can put their names together easily and say the letters.

You Need

► File crate or basket in which to store the name puzzle folders.

► Chopsticks or other small pointers.

Prepare using directions in *Teaching Resources,* Materials & Routines:

► Name puzzles for each child.

► Name puzzle folder.

Understand the Principle

By putting together their names, children learn how to look at letters and notice their distinguishing features and orientation. They learn that words are made up of letters and that the order of letters is always the same.

These concepts are important in recognizing words on sight (by letter patterns) and also in beginning to recognize spelling patterns.

Explain the Principle

❝ Words have letters in them. ❞

❝ Your name has letters in it. ❞

❝ You can say the first letter of your name. ❞

CONTINUUM: LETTER KNOWLEDGE — UNDERSTANDING THAT WORDS ARE MADE UP OF LETTERS

plan

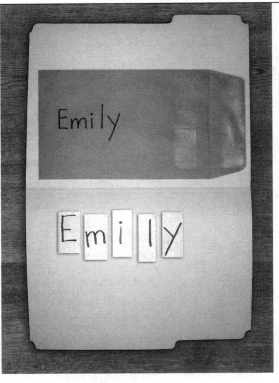

Explain the Principle

" Words have letters in them. "

" Your name has letters in it. "

" You can say the first letter of your name. "

① Tell the children that today they are going to put together their name puzzles. Arrange children in a circle so they can place their folders open flat on the floor in front of them, where you will be able to observe their work.

② Suggested language: "I'm going to show you how to put together your name puzzle. Take out the letters that are in the envelope glued in your folder. Open your folder and lay it flat in front of you. Be sure you can see your name. Use the letter pieces to make your name. Put down the first letter first; then put down the next letter. Be sure the letters match exactly."

③ Demonstrate using one child's folder and puzzle pieces. Emphasize that each letter has to look the same as the letters written on the folder and face the way those letters do.

④ Using a pointer, point to each letter, demonstrating how to check letter by letter. Say the letters as you go: "*E–E, m–m, i–i, l–l, y–y.*"

⑤ Show how to mix up the letters so they can form the name again.

⑥ Be sure all the children have formed their names at least once.

⑦ Demonstrate how to put the name puzzle away: put all the pieces back in the envelope and put the folder in a box or tub with the name on the folder facing up.

mix
fix
check

▶ Children put together their names, mix up
the letters, and make the names again
three times.

Have the children seated in a circle with their name puzzles in front of
them. Ask them to take turns saying the letters of their names while they
point to each letter with a chopstick or other small pointer. Say the letters
for or with any child who cannot yet do so independently. Be sure each
child gets a turn.

Have children talk about what they notice about their names. Model the
process first:

"I have a *b* in my name."

"I have four letters in my name."

"My name starts with a capital *B*."

If children perform this task easily, ask them to work with a partner.
Partners tell what they have noticed about the letters in each other's names.

Link

Interactive Read-Aloud: Read aloud books that have characters' names in the titles (see the bibliographies in *Teaching Resources*), such as:

- ▶ *Mary Wore Her Red Dress, and Henry Wore His Green Sneakers* by Merle Peek
- ▶ *What's Your Name? From Ariel to Zoe* by Eve Sanders and Marilyn Sanders

Shared Reading: Read poems that contain names, such as "Lucy Locket" or "Tommy Snooks." (See *Sing a Song of Poetry*.) Invite children to identify some of the names with a masking card or flag (see *Teaching Resources*).

Guided Reading: During word work, display the letters of one or two children's names. Invite the children to take their magnetic letters and make the name or names they see on the easel.

Interactive Writing: Write sentences with children's names in them: "Emily likes red. Justin likes blue." "Emily wore her blue sweater."

Independent Writing: Encourage the children to use their names as resources when writing words. Encourage them to write their names on their papers.

assess

- ▶ Notice whether the children are able to put together their names, letter by letter, from left to right.
- ▶ Check whether the children are able to say the letters of their names accurately.

Expand the Learning

When the children are able to put the letters of their names together while checking against the model, have them put the letters together, left to right, without using the model, and then check against the model.

Have children cut up a set of letter cards (see *Teaching Resources*) and use the letters to form their names. Ask them to glue the names on a piece of paper and draw a self-portrait.

When children make their names easily, ask them to make a partner's name and check it.

When children can put together and say the letters in their first names easily, add their surnames to the puzzle.

When all the children can say all the letters in their names, invite them to say the consonants or the vowels or to clap the syllables.

Have children make their names using various types of letters (letter tiles, magnetic letters, foam letters, plastic letters, or sandpaper letters).

Connect with Home

When children know the routines for putting together the name puzzle, let them take it home to show family members.

Ask family members to help children form their names using magnetic letters or letter cards that you have provided (see *Teaching Resources*).

5 Recognizing and Naming Letters

Alphabet Linking Chart

Consider Your Children

This early lesson establishes routines for "reading" the Alphabet Linking Chart and using it as a tool and is especially helpful to children who have not noticed the details or shapes of letters and who do not know many letter names. It will help all children learn how to use the chart as a tool in their own writing.

Working with English Language Learners

The Alphabet Linking Chart is a tool that will be very helpful to your English language learners. Many repetitions of "reading" this chart will help children internalize the names of the letters of the alphabet and connect them with the graphic figures. Varying the task will help English language learners become automatic with the names of the letters, knowledge that will help them understand and respond to classroom instruction.

You Need

▶ Pointer.

▶ Chopsticks (optional).

▶ MagnaDoodle®.

From *Teaching Resources:*

▶ Alphabet Linking Chart for each student. (Enlarge the small version for purposes of demonstration.)

Understand the Principle

Knowing the names of letters and connecting them to their shapes help children understand the language of the classroom.

Being able to recognize letters rapidly and automatically helps children check on their reading and solve words using letters and sounds.

Explain the Principle

❝ A letter has a name and a shape. ❞

❝ You can look at the shape of a letter and say its name. ❞

plan

Explain the Principle

" A letter has a name and a shape. "

" You can look at the shape of a letter and say its name. "

① Explain to the children that you will work together to learn more about the names of letters.

② Suggested language: "Today we are going to learn some ways to read the Alphabet Linking Chart. This chart is important because it helps you remember the names of the letters and how they look. When you have time, you can practice reading the Alphabet Linking Chart to help you remember the letter names and shapes."

③ Read the chart letter by letter, using a thin pointer. Be sure that the pointer (or your arm) does not obscure children's view of the letters; it's very important that they see them clearly. Say the letters out loud: "A–a, B–b, C–c, D–d," etc. "That's one way to read the chart. Let's do it together." Repeat with the children.

④ Suggested language: "Now let's read it another way. This time I am going to skip every other letter." Demonstrate: "A–a, C–c, E–e, G–g," etc. Have children join you. This task will be much more difficult for them, so you may need to move more slowly. They will have to look at the letters rather than just remembering the ABCs. *If children are very inexperienced and find this task challenging, repeat reading every other letter a couple of times. Save steps 5 and 6 for another lesson.*

⑤ "Now I'm going to show you another way. This time I am going to read the uppercase and lowercase letters and say the names of the pictures: *A–a–apple, B–b–bear,*" etc. Have the children join you.

6 Suggested language: "Let's try one more way. This time I am going to read just the words under the pictures: apple, bear, cat, dog, egg," etc. Have the children join you.

7 "We'll be learning lots of ways to read this chart. Today, each of you will be getting a small copy of this chart. Take your pointing finger or a chopstick and read the chart two different ways. Then bring your chart to sharing time." Demonstrate the process with a partner.

read
color

▶ Children work with a partner. They take turns reading the chart in different ways. A variation is to have the first child read the chart one way. The second child reads it in the *same* way and then in a different way, which the first child repeats. Then they color their charts.

Have children demonstrate different ways of reading the chart.

Link

Interactive Read-Aloud: Read aloud a variety of alphabet books. (See an extensive list in the Alphabet Books Bibliography, *Teaching Resources*.) Examples are:

▶ *Animal Parade* by Jakki Wood

▶ *ABC Discovery* by Izhar Cohen

Shared Reading: Name a letter or hold up a magnetic letter and have children, using a masking card (in *Teaching Resources*) or highlighter tape, locate it in poems or other texts.

Guided Reading: Give the children a bag of magnetic letters. Have them place the letters on a table one at a time, saying the name as they do so.

Interactive Writing: Use names of letters to help children locate a letter needed in a piece of writing. Make connections with the Alphabet Linking Chart and with the name chart.

Independent Writing: Point out letters by name when conferring with children about their writing.

assess

▶ Notice whether the children can find letters quickly on the Alphabet Linking Chart.

▶ Check whether the children can say the names of letters quickly.

▶ Observe whether the children use the Alphabet Linking Chart as a resource during interactive or independent writing.

▶ Point randomly to letters on the chart and ask children to read the letters and say the names of the pictures.

▶ Using a shuffled pile of letter cards, individually test children, noting the uppercase and lowercase letter names they know and need to learn.

Expand the Learning

As children learn more about letters, teach them different ways to read the Alphabet Linking Chart:

Read every other box, starting sometimes with *a* and sometimes with *b*.

Start in the middle of the chart and read back to the beginning.

Read only the letters.

Say the names of the pictures.

Read only the words under the pictures.

Read only the consonants.

Read only the vowels.

Read down the columns.

Read the chart backward.

Have half the class read the chart one way, the other half another way.

Connect with Home

Give children small versions of the Alphabet Linking Chart to read at home. Suggest that family members sing it as an alphabet song, read the uppercase or lowercase letters, read the words *(apple–bear–cat–dog),* start with the last box, read only the vowels or consonants, or use some other variation.

6 *Making Letters*

Art Materials

Consider Your Children

The procedures described here may be used many times for different lowercase and uppercase letters. Lowercase letters are more useful for children as they encounter them more frequently, so begin with them. Work on letters that most children know or nearly know. Once children grasp the principle, the lessons will be quite short; the children will have developed a system for learning the verbal path and physical movements to make a letter. It may not be necessary to go over every letter in detail. Children should have good control of efficient movements before they are asked to attend to variables such as size, lines, etc. Kindergartners attending to and gaining control of the motions needed to make letters require plenty of room on the paper. Unlined paper allows them free motion.

Working with English Language Learners

This lesson will be helpful to English language learners even if they know only a few letters. Be sure that children actually say the verbal description of the letter as they write it or trace it in sand or other material. You may want to start with a common letter for the whole group or bring them together in a small group to work with the letters they know. They can also look through magazines, newspapers, or any other collections of large print to find examples of the same letter.

You Need

► MagnaDoodle®.

► Easel and paper with thick marker.

► Name chart (see Lesson ELC 1).

► Sand/salt in tray or box.

► Tissue paper cut into small squares or circles.

► Glue.

► Large *g*'s (or another selected letter) on paper.

From *Teaching Resources*:

► Alphabet Linking Chart.

► Verbal Path for the Formation of Letters.

Understand the Principle

Learning efficient movements for making letters helps children fix the features of each letter in visual memory and associate that letter with its name.

Explain the Principle

" Letters are different from each other. "

" You can notice the parts of letters. "

plan

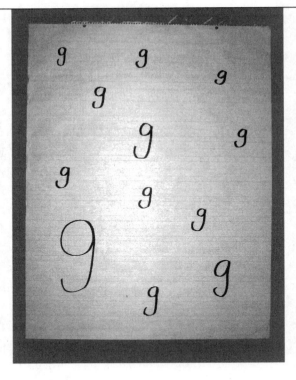

Explain the Principle

" Letters are different from each other. "

" You can notice the parts of letters. "

① Start by making a letter on the MagnaDoodle® (or other display medium). Say the name of the letter and then demonstrate how it is formed, using the simple, clear language provided in the Verbal Path for the Formation of Letters *(Teaching Resources)*. Suggested language: "I'm going to make a *g*. To make a lowercase *g*, you pull back, around, up, down, and curve back." Make the letter slowly as you describe the movement.

② Erase the letter (or use a new sheet of chart paper) and make the letter again, inviting the children to describe the verbal path with you as you write.

③ Make the letter using several other writing media (crayons, colored markers, MagnaDoodle®), each time describing the verbal path. Move along quickly. Suggested language: "I am going to make a *g* on the chart. [Demonstrate and have children describe the movements with you.] I'm going to make a big *g*. [Demonstrate, making a large version of the lowercase letter.] I'm going to make a smaller *g*. [Demonstrate.] Who can find *g* on the alphabet chart? [Children respond.] Who can find *g* on the name chart? [Children respond.] Now I'll make *g* in the salt tray. [Place the tray on the floor and let children stand to look at it.]"

④ Demonstrate *g* one more time on the MagnaDoodle®.

⑤ Suggested language: "Today, you get to make *g* with tissue paper." Show children the finished *g* and then demonstrate how to crumple small squares of tissue paper around the bottom of a pencil, dip it in glue, and arrange the paper in the form of the letter *g*.

fold
glue
put

► In pencil, write a large *g* on an 8½" × 11" piece of paper. Reproduce as many copies as you will need. Have children make a three-dimensional letter by folding and gluing tissue paper to the penciled outline. They can use several colors of tissue if you like.

Have children hold up the letter *g*, say the letter name, and describe the verbal path of the letter. Ask them what they want to remember about the letter *g*.

Look for comments like these:

"Lowercase *g* has a tail."

"Lowercase *g* looks different from uppercase *G.*"

"Lowercase *g* looks kind of like lowercase *q.*"

"I have a *g* in my name."

These comments tell you what the children are noticing about the distinctive features of letters.

Link

Interactive Read-Aloud: Read aloud alphabet books such as the following. See the Alphabet Books Bibliography in *Teaching Resources* for more examples.

▶ *The Awful Aardvarks Go to School* by Reeve Lindbergh

▶ *K Is for Kiss Goodnight* by Jill Sardegna

Shared Reading: After reading a very familiar poem or piece of interactive writing, point to a letter and ask children to name it. Ask them to mask, flag, or highlight a particular letter several times in the text.

Guided Reading: During word work, give each child a plastic bag of magnetic letters. Have them lay the letters out on the table. Call out letters for them to find quickly. If there are more than one of some letters, ask the children to find them all.

Interactive Writing: Describe the motions (the verbal path) while forming a difficult letter on the small whiteboard so the child will have a model. When a child is forming a letter at the easel, use language to describe her motions.

Independent Writing: Encourage children to use efficient motions when forming letters and to describe the motions as they make them.

assess

▶ Select a piece of familiar text (see *Sing a Song of Poetry*) that has many letters in it. Have children individually locate specific letters, or ask them to circle letters. Limit the "test" to about five letters so you can judge accuracy.

▶ Note on a class list letters you want to revisit with individual students or with the whole group.

Expand the Learning

Repeat the lesson with other letters, varying the media: for example, making the letter out of play clay (see the recipe in *Teaching Resources*) or modeling clay; gluing together beans, macaroni, or buttons in the shape of the letter; writing the letter on a piece of paper in different sizes and colors; using a letter stamp to make the letter; drawing three things whose labels begin with that letter.

Repeat the lesson with uppercase letters that children are making in an inefficient way or find difficult.

Have children make their first names by gluing tissue paper or buttons together in the shapes of the letters.

Have children "paint" (with water) letters on schoolyard cement or write the letters on the cement with chalk.

Connect with Home

Have children take home the letters they make. Give families and caregivers copies of the chart indicating the directional movements for forming letters (see *Teaching Resources*, Verbal Path for the Formation of Letters) and ask them to have children tell how to make the letters.

Invite caregivers to have children look through magazines or catalogs, cut out many different examples of the same letters in different fonts and sizes, and glue them on a sheet of paper.

Learning Letter Forms and Names

Letter Match

Consider Your Children

Use this lesson after children have learned a few letters. This lesson will not be necessary for children who already know and can identify uppercase and lowercase letters, but you may want to use the poem for enjoyment or to develop other strategies, such as word-by-word matching. You may also want to use it with a small group of children who know very few letters.

Working with English Language Learners

This lesson brings the alphabet together for English language learners and helps them understand it as a finite set of letters. You may want to work with the poem over several days in an enjoyable way, being sure children understand the meaning, before you ask them to name and locate letters. Once they have learned the poem, it will become an important resource for noticing, locating, and naming letters. Help English language learners to make connections between this poem and the Alphabet Linking Chart that is in the room. Provide opportunities for them as individuals or in small groups to "read" all of the alphabet charts in the room, as well as the poem. All of the names of letters in English may be unfamiliar to children who have talked about letters in another language. Play some extra games with English language learners to help them quickly locate letters in the poem or on the chart as you say the name of the letter.

You Need

► Chart ("The Place to Be" poem) and pointer for shared reading.

► Letter tiles or magnetic letters.

► Cups for letters.

From *Teaching Resources:*

► Laminated Alphabet Strips.

Understand the Principle

Children need to know how to look at letters and notice the small differences that make each character unique. Then they can learn to attach a name to the letter. Letter names are not necessarily a guide to the sound, and teachers should take care to distinguish between the *name* and the *sound*. Knowing the names, however, is useful for clear communication about the alphabet in the classroom.

Knowing how to look at print is basic to making connections between letters and sounds.

Explain the Principle

❝ You can look at the shape of a letter and say its name. ❞

CONTINUUM: LETTER KNOWLEDGE — PRODUCING LETTER NAMES

plan

Explain the Principle

66 **You can look at the shape of a letter and say its name.** 99

① Tell the children you are going to teach them more about letters. Display the poem you have written on chart paper.

② Read the title and read the poem.

③ Ask children what they notice (letters, alphabet, letters they know) in the poem.

④ Guide children to notice lots of different letters. Point out that each has a name.

⑤ Point and reread the poem.

⑥ Reread with children joining in.

Room 4
A B C D E
Room 4 is the place to be.
F G H I J
We will work and we will play.
K L M N O
Together we will learn and grow.
P Q R S T
I'll help you and you'll help me.
U V W X Y
So give a wave and just say "Hi."
Z Z Z Z Z
Room 4 is the place to be!

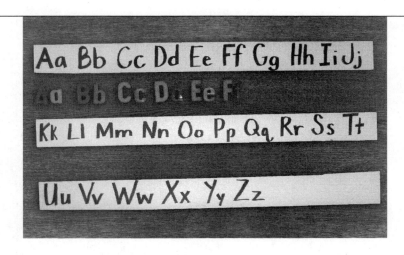

apply

take
match
check

► Have the children work in pairs on a tabletop. They take letter tiles or magnetic letters from a cup and place them under the Alphabet Strip to match each letter, saying the name of the letter. After their partner checks their work, they reverse roles.

share

Read the poem again.

Ask children to locate capital letters that match the letters that begin their names.

Link

Interactive Read-Aloud: Read aloud alphabet books that reinforce the names of letters. (Emerging readers and writers should hear a lot of alphabet books.) Examples are:

▶ *Chicka Chicka Boom Boom* by Bill Martin, Jr., and John Archambault

▶ *Alphabet Out Loud* by Ruth Gembicki Bragg

Shared Reading: Have children sing "The Alphabet Song" (see *Sing a Song of Poetry*) or chant the Alphabet Linking Chart (see *Teaching Resources*) while you point to the text.

Guided Reading: After the lesson, have children find uppercase or lowercase letters in the text. During word work, place magnetic letters on the easel. Have children take turns moving a letter to the right and saying the name until all letters have been moved.

Interactive Writing: Display the class list and read the names, pointing out the first capital letter of each. Place bright highlighter tape on the first letter of each name.

Independent Writing: When children are attempting to write a letter and need support, pull out a magnetic letter as an example.

assess

▶ Note how quickly children are able to match letters. Note the letters for which most children know the names.

▶ Give quick letter-recognition tests (uppercase, lowercase, or both) to inventory children's letter/name knowledge at different times during the year. By the end of the year, all children should be able to name all the letters in their uppercase and lowercase forms.

Expand the Learning

Use lowercase letters in the poem and have children match the letters.

Have children match lowercase magnetic letters to an uppercase Alphabet Strip.

Have children match uppercase magnetic letters to a lowercase Alphabet Strip.

Connect with Home

Invite caregivers to help children notice the capital letters on boxes in the supermarket and on street signs.

Invite caregivers to make the letters of the child's name in uppercase letters (*Teaching Resources,* Letter Cards) and place them on the table. Then have them give the child a set of lowercase letter cards (see *Teaching Resources*) and ask the child to place the corresponding lowercase letter below each uppercase letter in his name.

Encourage caregivers to sing "The Alphabet Song" with their children and read alphabet books.

8 Learning Letters

Alphabet Soup Game

Consider Your Kids

Use this lesson sometime after the children have worked with their name puzzles (Lesson LK 4) and when they are very familiar with the letters in their own names, as well as with the order of the letters. The task in this lesson requires children to hold this knowledge in their heads as they consider one letter after another, so the task is challenging.

Working with English Language Learners

English language learners may need to work in small groups with you as they attempt Alphabet Soup for the first time. Provide many opportunities for them to repeat the language they need to use. If the syntax is difficult, change it so that it is easier for children to say.

You Need

▸ Name puzzles (see Lesson LK 4).

▸ Small paper or plastic bowls.

▸ Stirring utensils.

▸ *Alphabet Soup,* by Kate Banks.

Understand the Principle

The letters of the alphabet are critically important tools for young readers. Children need to learn to distinguish the particular and specific shapes of a letter so that they can connect a name to it. Letter names provide an entry into understanding the alphabetic principle (that letters and sounds are related) because they help children understand the language of the classroom. In this lesson, children give close attention to letter features and letter names as they work with their own names. They also explore the idea that in a word (in this case, a name) the letters are always in the same order.

Explain the Principle

" You can look at the shape of a letter and say its name. "

plan

Explain the Principle

" **You can look at the shape of a letter and say its name.** "

① Read the book *Alphabet Soup*, by Kate Banks, and invite children to share whether they have ever eaten alphabet soup. Explain that the boy in this story has some very strange things happen with his alphabet soup. As an alternative you may choose to tell a short story about a little boy or girl who doesn't want to eat the soup but when he or she does, adventures happen. The purpose of the story is to get children interested in letters and their associations.

② Suggested language: "You know that we have letters in our names, and there are letters in alphabet soup, too. Today we are going to make alphabet soup with our names." Ask for a pair of volunteers to come up to the front of the group with their name puzzles.

③ Ask for two volunteers. Have a small bowl. Ask the two children to dump their names into the bowl. Then stir the letters and invite both children to help.

④ Suggested language: "Jamal is going to go first. Jamal, take one letter out of our bowl of alphabet soup." Child demonstrates. "Jamal, does that letter belong in your name?" Jamal responds, "Yes."

⑤ "Jamal is going to tell a food that begins with this letter, which is in his name. Jamal, say this: 'I have a lowercase *a* and it goes in my name, Jamal. *A* is for *apple*.'" Child demonstrates.

⑥ "This letter is in Jamal's name, so he gets to keep it. If it doesn't belong in his name—for example, if it is a *y*—he'll put it back in the soup bowl."

⑦ Continue demonstrating until the bowl is empty and the children have all the letters in their names. Suggested language: "So Jamal and Tony have all the letters in their names. They are going to put their names together, read them, and then check each other's names." Children can check the names with the model.

⑧ Suggested language: "Today we learned that we can recognize the letters in our names even if they are mixed into our alphabet soup, and we also can think of food that begins like the letters of our names." Explain that the children will play the Alphabet Soup game.

mix letters
take letter
say letter name
say food
make puzzle

▶ Get plastic or paper bowls and utensils for stirring. Children pair up and play the Alphabet Soup game. They mix the letters, take one letter, say its name, and give a food that starts with the letter. At the end of the game, they make their name puzzles and check each other.

Have children talk about what they learned about their names. Demonstrate and look for comments such as these:

    "My name has two *s*'s."

    "My name starts with uppercase *M*."

Have them share some of the foods they thought of in connection with their names.

Link

Interactive Read-Aloud: Read aloud books that connect children's names with sounds of letters, such as:

- ► *Martha Speaks* by Susan Meddaugh
- ► *Imogene's Antlers* by David Small

Shared Reading: Use a variety of ABC songs such as "Bingo" or "The Alphabet Song" (see *Sing a Song of Poetry*) to learn and reinforce letter-name knowledge.

Guided Reading: During word work, do some quick letter sorting on the magnetic easel, asking the children to name each letter as they move it from the left side of the board to the right.

Interactive Writing: Take the opportunity to have children name letters within the context of creating a text. Consider making an Alphabet Soup book or mural, with each child drawing a picture of a food that begins like his or her name and the group creating the label with a shared pen.

Independent Writing: Children have a template of a bowl. They draw food items that start like each of the letters in their names and label the foods. They can use approximated spelling.

assess

- ► Notice whether the children can recognize the letters of their names and put them together.
- ► Observe whether letter recognition is becoming quick and automatic.
- ► During writing time, conduct a quick check by asking children to name the letters in their names.

Expand the Learning

To make the task easier, children tell the letter, but not a food that begins with it.

Children can play the game again with a different partner.

Children can play the game with their last-name puzzles.

Children can make the soup with four players, increasing the challenge. Also, they can make one another's name puzzles.

Connect with Home

Have children take home their name puzzles and some letter cards (in *Teaching Resources*) with which to make names of their family members. Have them teach a family member how to play the Alphabet Soup game and play it several times with different family members.

9 Learning Letter Names
Letter Minibooks

Consider Your Children

This lesson establishes a routine for working with letter minibooks. Teach it after children have become accustomed to using pencils and paper and can follow a few simple directions. Children do not have to know any alphabet letters before beginning the letter books, but they should have worked with the name chart (Lesson ELC 1), name puzzle (Lesson LK 4), and Alphabet Linking Chart (Lesson LK 5) and have a beginning understanding of how to use these tools. Also, they should have had some practice writing their names. Working with these books is not a long, drawn-out process. Plan to introduce two or three books a week over a period of eight to twelve weeks. Suggested sequence: *(b, m, r, s); (t, g, n, p); (c, h, f, d); (l, k, j, w); (y, z, v, x, q)*. With some groups of children, you can introduce more than one book in a lesson.

Working with English Language Learners

Your English language learners will be taking home an important tool—letter minibooks. Have children use the minibooks at school until you are sure they know how to use them, store them, and care for them. These books will have pictures of objects with labels, so they will help children acquire a repertoire of nouns that they know. For each minibook, go through the pictures carefully; have children say them and then read the book several times. Have them locate the first letter for each word, say the letter, and read the word.

You Need

► *Mm* book.

► Small storage boxes with children's names on them. (A good storage box is a small tissue box with the top cut completely open. Cereal boxes cut in half are also good.) Each child will need to store twenty-six small books.

► Writing materials and crayons.

► Name chart (for making connections; Lesson ELC 1).

► Alphabet Linking Chart (for making connections; Lesson LK 5).

From *Teaching Resources:*

► Picture Cards, Beginning Consonant, to glue in the minibooks.

► Assembled *Mm* books for children (see the Letter Book Template).

Understand the Principle

Knowing the names of letters and connecting them with letter shapes allow children to identify letters as important tools. These skills help them understand teachers' and caregivers' language as they talk about letters.

Using the letter minibooks lets children practice the names of the letters and helps them build a repertoire of words they are able to connect with the letters that form them.

Explain the Principle

❝ You can look at the shape of a letter and say its name. ❞

plan

Explain the Principle

❝ **You can look at the shape of a letter and say its name.** ❞

① Show the children a boxed set of letter books and tell them they will each be getting their own box and set of books. "Today you are going to get a letter book, and I am going to show you what to do with it. [Show the *Mm* book.] This book is about the letter. . . . [Children respond.]"

② Suggested language: "That's right. It has two *m*'s on the front. This is the uppercase *M* and this is the lowercase *m*. [Point to the letters.] On this line, I am going to write my name. [Demonstrate.]"

③ Show the second page of the book and point to the letter. "On this page, it says *m* at the top, and here is a picture of a mouse. Here is the word *mouse*, which has an *m* at the beginning."

④ Suggested language: "On this page, I read the letter *m*, at the top. Then I say the name of the picture, *mouse*. Then I read the word *mouse*, and the first time I read the book, I'm going to trace over the letter *m*." Next, demonstrate the same process on the page with the mop.

⑤ "On the last page, I see the *m* at the top and I get to choose (or draw) a picture to go with *m*." Children can use picture cards, or you may guide them to draw something. Demonstrate gluing in a picture. Don't write the label, as children will perform this task independently.

⑥ "Now I'm going to show you how to read your book." Go through the book reading the letter, saying the name of the picture, and reading the label.

⑦ "Today you are going to have your own *Mm* book. You are going to write your name on the line on the first page. On the next page, read the letter *m*, say the name of the picture, and trace the *m* on the name of the picture. Do the same on page 3. On the last page, trace the *m*, glue or draw a picture that begins with *m*, and write the word below the picture. Then point to the letters as you reread your whole letter book."

write name
read
trace
glue (or draw)
read
color

▸ Have children make and read *Mm* books simultaneously at the table. You can circulate and help them perform the routines. After making the books, children can color the pictures. After children have learned this routine, they can perform it on their own with other letters.

Have each child tell another student the label of the picture glued in or drawn. Show them how to read their books to a partner, taking turns pointing and reading.

Have children make connections to the name chart by noticing names with *m*. Also, make connections to the Alphabet Linking Chart.

Link

Interactive Read-Aloud: Read aloud alphabet books (see the Alphabet Books Bibliography in *Teaching Resources*). Examples are:

- *Aster Aardvark's Alphabet Adventures* by Steven Kellogg
- *L Is for Loving: An ABC for the Way You Feel* by Ken Wilson-Max

Shared Reading: After enjoying a poem, song, or chant such as "Bouncing Ball" or "Cackle, Cackle, Mother Goose" (see *Sing a Song of Poetry*), name letters and have children find them in the text using a masking card or highlighter tape.

Guided Reading: Have children who need more letter/sound work read several of their letter minibooks quickly at the end of a group lesson.

Interactive Writing: Use letter names to help children identify the letter needed in a piece of writing. Make connections with the Alphabet Linking Chart *(Teaching Resources)* and the name chart (Lesson ELC 1).

Independent Writing: Pull out a particular letter minibook to help a child associate a sound he wants to write with the letter he is learning.

assess

- ▶ Observe whether the children can locate letters by name.
- ▶ Observe whether the children can give the correct name of a letter.
- ▶ Give a quick naming test with letter cards or a letter chart (or use the letter minibooks); don't present the letters in alphabetical order.

Expand the Learning

Repeat this lesson with different letter books (maybe two or three letters at a time).

Repeat instructions on the routine until children understand and can perform the steps independently. (You might also post simple directions with pictures.) Then work quickly on each successive letter, saying its name and linking it to the Alphabet Linking Chart, the name chart, and any other print in the room. Children can then get their letter minibooks from a tray and work with them independently.

Have children read all the books in their letter boxes, or have a small group read their books to partners.

Connect with Home

In a meeting, show family members the letter minibooks and the storage boxes. After children have practiced the routines for eleven or twelve books, you can send the boxes home, and children can then take the books home as they make them. Encourage family members to keep the box in a special place and make sure the books are always stored there. Have children read each book to a family member.

Encourage caregivers to get a set of lowercase magnetic letters for the refrigerator. Children can make their names, the names of family members, and other easy words they know. Each time the children open the refrigerator, they can say the name of one or two letters.

See *Teaching Resources* for other suggestions for using magnetic letters at home.

10 Learning Letters in Names
Name Graph

Consider Your Children

This lesson works best when a number of children can read their own names and some of the names of other children. Think about whether children are beginning to understand the concept of "first" as it applies to the letters in words and whether they have familiarity with the letters in their names. This lesson will help them begin to generalize their knowledge about names and notice letters in names. It will also help them to connect first letters and sounds.

Working with English Language Learners

Help English language learners say the names of all the children in the classroom. Provide as many repetitions as needed, but accept approximations in phonology. This lesson will provide personal connections and examples that will help them connect letters and sounds. It is very important for you to pronounce the children's names the way the children expect to hear them.

You Need

▸ Pocket chart, with the appropriate first letters of all children's names at the bottom of each column.

From *Teaching Resources:*

▸ Name card for each child (Pocket Chart Card Template).

▸ Sheet of class names for each child to cut out (Word Card Template).

▸ Laminated Alphabet Strip for each child.

Understand the Principle

By studying their own and their classmates' names, children learn that it is important to notice the beginning letter and think about its name and sound. They learn how to make connections between names and begin to generalize knowledge of first letters. They also learn aspects of word structure such as number of letters and ending letters.

All this makes children more aware of the features of words.

Explain the Principle

" Words have letters in them. "

" Your name has letters in it. "

" You can say the first letter of your name. "

plan

Explain the Principle

66 **Words have letters in them.** 99

66 **Your name has letters in it.** 99

66 **You can say the first letter of your name.** 99

① Tell the children that they can learn a lot about letters from their names.

② Show children the name cards one at a time. Ask them to read the name of the person on the card and to identify the first letter.

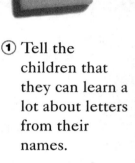

③ Suggested language: "Today we are going to see how many of us have the same first letter in our names. Whose name is this? [Hold up the card for Ariel.] What is the first letter? [Children respond.] That's right, an *A*. I'm going to put it right above the *A* on our pocket chart. Whose name is this? [Hold up a name that begins with another letter.]"

④ Continue showing the names and asking children to categorize them on the pocket chart. Place them above the previous cards, building a graph.

⑤ Then count the number of children in each letter category. Place the number above the column for each letter.

cut
say
sort

apply

► Reproduce a sheet of name cards for every student in the class. Have children cut out the names. They say each name and place it under the appropriate first letter along a laminated Alphabet Strip. Place the strip above the chalk tray or along a tabletop. After sorting their names, they put them in an envelope and take them home to sort.

Aa Bb Cc Dd Ee Ff Gg Hh Ii Jj
Alex   Douglas Erin   Jaquie
Amy

Kk Ll Mm Nn Oo Pp Qq Rr Ss Tt
Kara Lisa   Nadia   Parker   Rosa Sarah Tanisha

Uu Vv Ww Xx Yy Zz
Victor

share

Invite children to discuss what they have noticed about their own names and the names of their classmates. Elicit comments such as these:

"Ariel and Alan start with the same letter."

"Two people have names that start with *R*."

"Four people have names that start with *M*."

"Jody and James start with the same letter."

Link

Interactive Read-Aloud: Read aloud books that contain alliteration (see the Alliteration Bibliography in *Teaching Resources*). Point out that the words sound the same because they start with the same letter—like *Jody, James,* and *John.* Examples are:

▶ ***Four Famished Foxes and Fosdyke*** by Pamela Duncan Edwards

▶ ***Watch William Walk*** by Ann Jonas

Shared Reading: After enjoying a poem, chant, or song such as "Puppies and Kittens" or "Peas" (see *Sing a Song of Poetry*), play a guessing game: "I'm thinking of a word in the text that begins like Peter [or some other name]." Have children use a masking card (see *Teaching Resources*) to highlight their prediction.

Guided Reading: During word work, have children use magnetic letters to make the names of two or three classmates. They can refer to the class name chart to check.

Interactive Writing: Make connections to first letters of names on the name chart (see Lesson ELC 1) when writing words.

Independent Writing: Encourage children to use the name chart as a resource for their writing (for example, how to start a word).

Expand the Learning

Repeat the lesson with the children's last names.

Repeat the lesson, this time counting the *number of letters* in names and categorizing them that way.

Connect with Home

Have children sort the names of their classmates at home.

Encourage family members to cut up children's names into letter squares to make puzzles they can put together. Suggest that they count and say the letter names when they are finished.

Add family members' names to the list of class names for sorting.

assess

▶ Observe children's ability to remember the first letters of their names and the names of others.

▶ Notice children's use of their own names and the names of classmates as resources for writing words.

▶ Observe children's ability to make connections to names during interactive writing.

Learning Letters in Names

Marching Game

Consider Your Children

This lesson will be effective for children who know the first letters of their names but do not have automatic recall and recognition. Using letter/sound information efficiently in reading and writing requires rapid automatic processing of print. This lesson will provide the necessary practice.

Working with English Language Learners

Go over the marching song as many times as necessary to help your English language learners remember it and enjoy it. Children will like working with their own names and those of classmates. If you have a widely diverse group, go over names several times to be sure that everyone can easily say everyone else's names. Names will be an important resource for English language learners. Point out to all class members that it is important to try to pronounce everyone's name just like they do. Emphasize that everyone is learning, so we may not say names "just right" at first. Children will enjoy saying a large variety of names. Remember that a name such as *Roger* might be easy for English speakers but difficult for others.

You Need

► Chart displaying the words to the "Friends' March" song.

► Pocket chart.

From *Teaching Resources:*

► Letter Cards.

► Name cards for the pocket chart (Pocket Chart Card Template).

► Sheet of class names for each child (Word Card Template).

► Three-Way Sort Sheets.

Understand the Principle

By studying their own names, children can learn that it is important to notice the beginning letter and think about its name and sound. They will also be able to use the letters and sounds of their names to make connections to more words.

Explain the Principle

" You can look at the shape of a letter and say its name. "

plan

> Friends' March
> My friends are marching
> Round and round,
> Hurrah, hurrah.
> My friends are marching
> Round and round,
> Hurrah, hurrah.
> My friends are marching
> Round and round,
> Names beginning with C
> Sit down.
> And we'll march around
> Until we all sit down.

Explain the Principle

" **You can look at the shape of a letter and say its name.** "

① Explain to the children that they are going to sing a song that will help them learn names of letters.

② Have children practice sitting down in response according to the first letters of their names. Suggested language: "Today we are going to learn a song and a game that are about the first letter of your name. [Refer to the name chart.] Let's practice. Everyone stand up. Now, if your name begins with *C*, sit down."

③ Quickly go through all the appropriate letters to refresh children's memory of the first letters of their names. Emphasize that it is important to sit down immediately when they hear their first letter.

④ Teach children to sing "Friends' March" (sung to the tune of "When Johnny Comes Marching Home"). Don't worry about shared reading from the chart yet. At this point, make this an oral activity only. After they learn the song, you can also use the chart for shared reading, inserting self-adhesive letters (attached with Velcro® or double-sided tape). Children can also use this chart for independent reading later.

⑤ Have children march around in a circle and sing. Each time you change letters, hold up a card with the letter on it so they will know what is coming next. A child hears the first letter of his name and quickly sits down in the middle of the circle but keeps singing. (Don't let the circle get smaller; children should keep marching around the perimeter until everyone is sitting down.)

⑥ Place a letter card for each letter used in the song at the top of a pocket chart, and provide one name card for each child in the class. (For a large class, you may need two pocket charts.)

⑦ Have children read and sort the names under the appropriate first letter.

cut
sort
glue

▶ Give children a sheet of class names. Give each child a Three-Way Sort Sheet on which you have written three key letters, one at the top of each column. Have children cut apart the names and glue them under the appropriate letter. (Have children save the extra names in an envelope, and repeat the activity later using other key letters.)

Have children say their own names and identify the first letter.

Ask children to point to someone whose name begins with *C*, *M*, etc.

Link

Interactive Read-Aloud: Read aloud books that have a character's name in the title. Discuss where that name would go on the chart if that character were in your class. Examples are:

▶ *Chrysanthemum* by Kevin Henkes

▶ *Alison's Zinnia* by Anita Lobel

Shared Reading: Point and read the "Friends' March" several more times until the children can recognize the letters quickly.

Guided Reading: During word work, place an array of magnetic letters on the easel. In turn, have children point to their names on the name chart, say their names aloud, say the first letter of their names, and go to the easel and find that letter.

Interactive Writing: Use children's names and first letters as connections to words you are writing. Children can offer names of family members as examples of names that start with certain letters if there is not an example on the class name chart (see Lesson ELC 1).

Independent Writing: Encourage children to use the name chart (see Lesson ELC 1) as a resource for their writing (how to start a word, for example).

assess

▶ Observe the children's ability to quickly remember the first letter of their name.

▶ Notice the children's use of their names and the names of classmates as resources for writing words.

▶ Observe the children's ability to make connections to names during independent and interactive writing.

Expand the Learning

Repeat the lesson with children's last names.

Sing the song and change the verse to names *ending* with particular letters.

Connect with Home

Have children collect names of family members in a simple "family name book" (one name per sheet) that is stapled together. Children can draw pictures of family members.

Give caregivers the words to the alphabet song and have them sing it with their child.

Encourage children to teach the "Friends' March" song to their family members and perhaps use it as an activity at a family event (a birthday party, for example).

12

Learning to Write Your Name
Name Card Trace

Consider Your Children

This lesson, in which children learn how to form the letters in their names efficiently, is best used after children have worked with the name chart and the name puzzle. They should also be able to recognize and locate their names. Through writing their names, they will learn to attend more closely to detail. Punch a hole in the corner of their name cards and keep them on a ring for easy reference.

Working with English Language Learners

Writing their names is highly motivating for children, and it is a good place to start when teaching them to say the motions and make letters. Don't assume that English language learners will understand your directions for making letters. You may want to work with students in small groups so that you can demonstrate the task several times and then observe them to be sure they are using the tracing card, saying the directions, and making the letters correctly.

You Need

▶ Magnetic letters.

▶ Dry-erase markers.

From *Teaching Resources:*

▶ Laminated name cards for you and each of the children (Pocket Chart Card Template). Write the name carefully on one side; place dotted outlines of the letters in the name on the other side.

▶ Verbal Path for the Formation of Letters.

▶ Letter Formation Charts.

Understand the Principle

Young children must learn to form letters with efficient and consistent motions.

These consistent motions help them remember letters and words better and develop writing fluency.

Explain the Principle

❝ You can make the shape of a letter. ❞

❝ You can check to see if your letter looks right. ❞

CONTINUUM: LETTER KNOWLEDGE — USING EFFICIENT AND CONSISTENT MOTIONS TO FORM LETTERS

teach

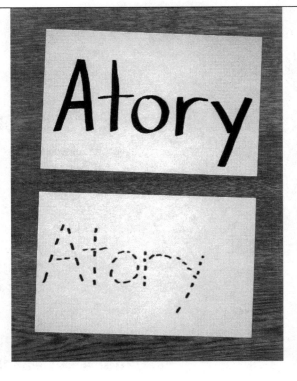

Explain the Principle

" You can make the shape of a letter. "

" You can check to see if your letter looks right. "

① Tell the children they are going to learn more about writing the letters in their names. Post the Letter Formation Charts for reference.

② Suggested language: "You are going to make your name with magnetic letters, left to right." It is important to make each letter correctly and to get the letters in the right order.

③ Show the side of a name card that has one child's name written clearly. "Here is Atory's name." Emphasize the tall letters and how the letters are placed right next to each other in an exact order.

④ Show the other side of the card, and, first with your finger and then with a dry-erase marker, trace each letter, using the arrows as a guide. As you write, use language to describe the motions. (See Verbal Path and Letter Formation Charts.)

⑤ Suggested language: "Your name is always written the same way, and you can write the letters in your name. You can say words that help you learn how to make a letter."

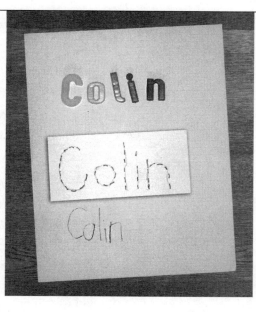

make
trace (with finger)
trace (with marker)
write

▶ Have children use magnetic letters to make their names, using the fully written side of the name card as a model.

▶ Then have them trace the dotted outlines of the letters on the other side of the card, first with a finger and then with a marker, referring to the chart with arrows as a guide.

▶ Finally, have them use lined paper to write their names.

share

Invite the children to bring their name cards to show at the group meeting.

Link

Interactive Read-Aloud: Read aloud books about letters and/or names, such as:

- ▶ *Mary Wore Her Red Dress, and Henry Wore His Green Sneakers* by Merle Peek
- ▶ *ABC Kids* by Laura Ellen Williams (illustrator)

Shared Reading: Use poems and songs into which you can incorporate the children's names such as "Johnny Taps with One Hammer" or "Rain, Rain Go Away" (see *Sing a Song of Poetry*).

Guided Reading: During word work, have children make their names two or three times with magnetic letters.

Interactive Writing: As children contribute letters, guide their formation using the Letter Formation Charts *(Teaching Resources)*.

Independent Writing: As children write, reinforce correct letter formation. Tape the Letter Formation Charts *(Teaching Resources)* in clear view.

assess

- ▶ Observe whether children are forming letters efficiently and correctly.
- ▶ Have the children write the alphabet so you have evidence of their letter formation.

Expand the Learning

Repeat the lesson for more practice.

Have children write the names of their peers.

Repeat the lesson with last names.

Repeat the lesson and have the children write their names with other media—markers, paintbrushes, crayons.

Connect with Home

Photocopy the children's dotted-outline names for them to take home and trace with their family members.

Learning to Look at Letter Features 1

Letter Sort

Consider Your Children

This lesson helps children learn how to sort letters, a useful routine during the first part of the year. The kind of sorting will depend somewhat on the particular style of letter formation you use.

When children have developed some idea of the purposes of print (through shared reading and interactive writing) and they have worked with their names enough to notice visual details, you will want them to notice the finer details of letters. Sorting will require them to look closely at the features of letters. After children can understand how to look for certain features (such as tall sticks or circles) and put letters together that have these features, they will start to notice more differences.

Working with English Language Learners

This lesson will help English language learners notice the distinctive features of letters and learn a way to talk about them. You want them to internalize language that will help them notice and locate letters. Repeat this lesson as many times as necessary for children to perform the sorting task easily. Be sure that the letters you use are consistent in form without a great deal of variation. You may need to work with a small group and take it slow, not looking at more than two features at a time. This is a generative lesson, so it will benefit all children to repeat it as needed.

You Need

► Magnetic easel (or cookie sheet placed on an ordinary easel). Alternatively, tape letter cards onto chart paper or write letters clearly on stick-on notes (be sure they do not curl up).

► Selected magnetic letters or letter cards (*l, d, h, a, m, n, k, b, r, i, u, p, q*) mixed together in a container.

From *Teaching Resources:*

► Two-Way Sort Sheets.

► Letter cards, if used instead of magnetic letters.

Understand the Principle

Children need to learn how to look at print. That means noticing the distinctive features of a letter—what makes a letter different from every other letter.

These differences are very small, but a child must learn to detect these distinctive features before a sound can be attached to a given letter.

This lesson will help children pick up on print formation more quickly when they read.

Explain the Principle

❝ You can find parts of letters that look the same. ❞

❝ You can find the letters that have long sticks and short sticks. ❞

CONTINUUM: LETTER KNOWLEDGE — CATEGORIZING LETTERS BY FEATURES

plan

Explain the Principle

" You can find parts of letters that look the same. "

" You can find the letters that have long sticks and short sticks. "

① Explain to the children that they are going to learn about letters by looking closely at them.

② Using a magnetic board, easel, or baking sheet, show children the magnetic letters.

③ Suggested language: "Every letter looks different from every other letter. One of the ways that letters are different is that some of them have long sticks and some of them have short sticks. Here is a letter with a long stick [show *h*]. Here is a letter with a short stick [show *n*]. What is different? [Children talk about the letters.]"

④ Introduce the rest of the letters: *l, d, h, a, m, l, k, b, r, i, u, p, q*. Ask children where each letter should go—with the long-stick letters or the short-stick letters.

⑤ You may want to draw a circle around each category if you are using a white magnetic easel.

⑥ Show children how to sort letters into two categories, those with long sticks and those with short sticks, using the Two-Way Sort Sheet. Model the sort using an enlarged version of the Two-Way Sort Sheet drawn on the board or on chart paper.

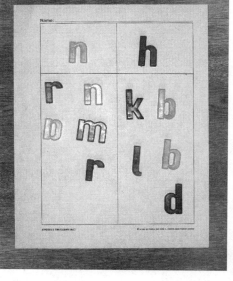

take
sort
check

▶ Have the children place a key letter
with a short stick *(n)* at the top of the
left-hand column and a key letter with
a long stick *(h)* at the top of the right-
hand column of a Two-Way Sort Sheet.
Demonstrate sorting two letters.
Working in pairs, have children sort
the letters *l, d, h, a, m, n, k, b, r, i, u, p,*
and *q* into two categories, long stick
and short stick, using the Two-Way Sort Sheet.
Partners can check each other's work.

share

Invite the children to discuss what they noticed about the letters they have
sorted. They may mention tall and short sticks along with things such as
circles, humps, tunnels, and dots.

Link

Interactive Read-Aloud: Read aloud alphabet books (see the Alphabet Books and Alliteration Bibliographies in *Teaching Resources*) that not only single out letters but use alliteration to tell an amusing story. Two examples are:

▶ *Pignic: An Alphabet Book in Rhyme* by Anne Miranda

▶ *The Absolutely Awful Alphabet* by Mordicai Gerstein

Shared Reading: Using a masking card or highlighter tape, ask children to locate letters within words that have long and short sticks and to name the letters. You might hold up a magnetic letter and invite children to find a letter that looks like it in the text or poem.

Guided Reading: During word work, conduct quick letter sorts with groups of children who need to pay more attention to print features.

Interactive Writing: When children are making letters, help them notice other distinguishing features.

Independent Writing: When holding conferences with children in independent writing, guide them to say "long stick" or "short stick" when making letters until they make them correctly without thinking.

assess

▶ Notice children's ability to sort letters by whether they have long or short sticks or by other features.

▶ Examine children's writing to note the letter features that appear in their handwriting.

Expand the Learning

Have children sort letter cards (see *Teaching Resources*) into those with long sticks and those with short sticks and glue them on a Two-Way Sort Sheet. (See *Teaching Resources*, Ways to Sort Letters.)

Have children sort letters in a variety of other ways:

Letters with circles and letters with tunnels: *a, d, b, u, n, m, o, q, h, g.*

Letters with tails and letters without tails: *a, b, c, d, e, f, g, h, i, j, k, l, m, n, o, p, q, r, s, t, u, v, w, x, y, z.*

Letters with crosses and letters without crosses: *t, f, v, a, m, o, c, l, r, s.*

Letters with dots and letters without dots: *i, j, f, t, g, x, p, s, m.*

Letters with straight lines and letters with curves: *c, o, k, s, t, w, x, y, z, i.*

Letters with straight lines, letters with curves, and letters with *both* straight lines and curves: *a, b, c, d, e, f, g, h, i, j, k, l, m, n, o, p, q, r, s, t, u, v, w, x, y, z.* (This will require a Three-Way Sort Sheet.)

Connect with Home

Send home a set of letter cards (see *Teaching Resources*) and ask children to sort them by long sticks and short sticks, circles and tails, etc.

Learning to Look at Letter Features 2

14

Letter Sort

Consider Your Children

This lesson works best when children are somewhat familiar with the features of letters (see Lesson LK 2) and understand the concept of sorting. They need many opportunities to distinguish letter features in order to be able to recognize letters in context. Once children are able to pick up on print information quickly, letter sorting should be phased out.

Working with English Language Learners

In this lesson, you will be using key letters and asking students to find letters that have similar features. Encourage your English language learners to explore letters and find relationships. Observe or work with three students at a time so that you get information about what they are attending to and can encourage them when they make connections. Use and ask children to repeat the specific terms that describe the features of letters.

You Need

► Magnetic letters.

► Magnetic easel or large magnetic baking sheet.

From *Teaching Resources:*

► Letter cards (if used instead of magnetic letters).

► Two- or Three-Way Sort Sheets (sets of three sheets with a key letter at the top for each pair of children).

Understand the Principle

Children need to be able to recognize the distinctive features of print—what makes a letter different from every other letter—before they can attach a sound to a letter.

Children need to be able to recognize the features of a letter in the context of other letters.

Explain the Principle

" You can find parts of letters that look the same. "

plan

Explain the Principle

" **You can find parts of letters that look the same.** "

① Explain to the children that they are going to learn more about how letters look.

② Place one letter to the right side of the easel.

③ Ask children to tell you what they notice about the letter you've moved. For example, if you place the *p* to the right, children may say it has a circle or a tail or a long stick.

④ Invite children to find another letter that has the same feature—for example, have them find other letters with circles or other letters with tails or other letters with a long stick. (Deal with only one feature at a time.)

⑤ Have children take turns coming up to the easel to find a letter that fits the feature category and move it to the right side—for example, if the category is letters with circles, students may move *p, g, o, b,* and *a* to the right side.

⑥ Move all the letters back to the left and repeat the process using another feature—letters with tails, for example. Suggested language: "Right now we're finding letters with tails [or whichever feature you're concentrating on]."

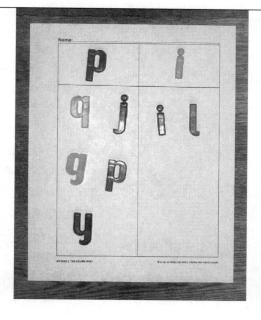

look
find
put

▶ Give containers of mixed magnetic letters to small groups or pairs of children. Have each child place a key letter at the top of a Two-Way Sort Sheet and then find other letters that have a similar feature. Each child should repeat the process with three key letters, using a Three-Way Sort Sheet. Observe children's sorting so you can reinforce and guide what they are noticing. A key element of this lesson is getting children to pay attention to and explore the features of letters—for example, what makes an *a* an *a* or a *g* a *g*.

Put a group of letters on the easel and invite children to tell what is the same about them.

Have each child come to the circle with a magnetic letter. Draw a circle on the magnetic chalkboard or whiteboard. Place a *d* in the circle. Explain that *d* has a long stick. Ask each child to take a turn placing her letter inside the circle if it has a long stick and outside if it does not. (Children may attend to a different feature—an *a* is also similar to the *d* in that it has a circle. Tell them they are correct in that it is similar, but get them to focus on the category under discussion.) Continue until all children have placed their letters inside or outside the circle.

Link

Interactive Read-Aloud: Read aloud a variety of alphabet books (see the Alphabet Books Bibliography in *Teaching Resources*). Examples are:

▶ *The Alligator Arrived with Apples: A Potluck Alphabet* by Crescent Dragonwagon

▶ *Harold's ABC* by Crockett Johnson

Shared Reading: Have children locate pairs of different letters (*o* and *d,* for example) and say why they are alike. Invite children to locate letters with a particular feature (letters with circles, for example).

Guided Reading: During word work, spend a minute or two sorting letters by various features. Emphasize speed.

Interactive Writing: When helping children make letters, use terms like *long stick, short stick,* and *circle* to help children notice the distinctive features of each letter.

Independent Writing: In conferences, use terms like *long stick, short stick, circle,* and *tail* to remind children of the distinctive features of each letter.

Expand the Learning

Select other letters as key letters for sorting into categories: *x, s, i, m, o.*

Conduct sorting exercises with different letters and distinctive features.

Connect with Home

Encourage family members to purchase a set of magnetic letters for children to play with at home, or ask your school to provide some "lending sets." At a meeting or in a newsletter, explain how valuable it is for children to handle letters as they learn about letters and words. (See *Teaching Resources,* 25 Ways to Use Magnetic Letters at Home.)

assess

▶ Notice children's growing ability to attach names to letters according to their distinctive features.

▶ Observe the speed with which children sort letters because it is an indication of their ability to pick up on print information. If they are sorting slowly, seeing the differences is probably hard work.

Identifying Letters in Words
"Bingo" Song

Consider Your Children

Use this lesson after children have worked with their own names and are beginning to realize that it is important to place the letters in the same order every time they build or write a word. You may want to shorten this lesson or use the parts over several days.

Working with English Language Learners

Be sure that your English language learners have plenty of experience learning the song "Bingo" before they do the Bingo puzzle. Be sure that they understand that Bingo is a dog and this song is all about his name. Once they have a visual frame for the word *Bingo*, you may want to have them work on it in a small group and ask children to take turns pointing to the letters as they sing the part of the song that spells the name. Then work several times with them so that they understand taking away the letters. Using the key name card, demonstrate to children how they are to put together their own names three times.

You Need

► Chart with the words to "Bingo."

► Envelope for each child.

► Sheets with the words to "There is a child . . ." (an adaptation of "Bingo").

From *Teaching Resources* (prepare using Pocket Chart and Name Card Templates):

► Individual cards with the letters B-i-n-g-o, each with double-sided tape on the back (or Velcro® on cards and chart).

► Each child's name on a card that has double-sided tape or Velcro® on the back.

► Four more name cards for each child, one to remain whole and three to cut up.

Understand the Principle

Children need to learn that words are made up of letters and that an individual word is constant—that is, always spelled the same way, with letters in the same order.

Explain the Principle

" Letters in a word are always in the same order. "

plan

Explain the Principle

" Letters in a word are always in the same order. "

1. Show the chart with the song "Bingo."

2. Introduce the song and enjoy singing it. Point to each word. Choose volunteers to point to the letters as you sing *B-i-n-g-o.*

3. Ask: "What is the name of this dog? How do you know? Show me his name. How does it start? How does it end? Can you hear *B . . . o?* Let's spell his name, *B-i-n-g-o.*"

> BINGO
> There was a farmer
> Had a dog
> And Bingo
> Was his name-o
> B-i-n-g-o
> B-i-n-g-o
> B-i-n-g-o
> And Bingo
> Was his name-o

4. Sing the complete song the traditional way. Then continue singing the song, but substitute claps for the letters, beginning with *B* and dropping each additional letter until you are clapping for all the letters.

5. Introduce the Bingo puzzle. Write the correct letters in boxes superimposed on a drawing of a dog in order to spell his name.

6. Sing the song again and use a slight pause (rather than a clap) to replace each letter of the dog's name. As you drop the letter, have volunteers remove the letter from the puzzle.

7. Put the dog puzzle back together with the letters jumbled and have children fix it and spell it. Sing the song one more time.

8. Introduce "There is a child . . .":

   There is a child in kindergarten,

   And [insert name] is the name-o.

9. Hold up a child's name card and have the child put it on the third line of the chart in place of the name Bingo. Everyone sings the song using that child's name. Repeat for a few more children.

apply

cut
match
write

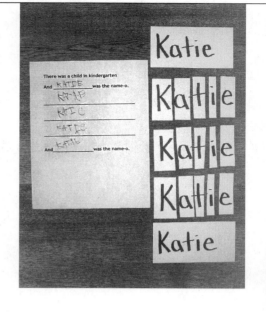

► Give each child an envelope with his name spelled four times on cards. Make one of the cards a different color: this is the model and remains in one piece. Have children cut apart the other three cards by letter. Each child puts together his name three times, matching the letters with the letters on the whole card.

► Then have children write their names in the five blank spaces on the "There is a child . . ." sheet.

share

Sing the song a final time with a surprise name (e.g., a character from a storybook: Clifford, Goldilocks, Arthur).

Link

Interactive Read-Aloud: Read aloud books about names. Invite children to think about the first and last letters of each name. Examples are:

- *From Anne to Zach* by Mary Jane Martin
- *A My Name Is Alice* by Jane Bayer

Shared Reading: After enjoying a poem, song, or chant such as "Mary Ann, Mary Ann" or "Elizabeth, Elspeth, Betsey and Bess" (see *Sing a Song of Poetry*), ask children to find the names used in it. Let them insert their own names into one rendition of the song.

Guided Reading: During word work, have children make the names of classmates with magnetic letters. Have them mix up the letters, fix the letters, and mix them up again until they have made the name three times.

Interactive Writing: Relate words you are trying to write to names. Also note that words are always spelled the same. Connect words you are trying to write to the names of the children on the name chart.

Independent Writing: When children are trying to write new words, suggest that they refer to words they know, such as the names on the name chart.

assess

- ► Notice how children begin to put together the letters in their names.
- ► Observe whether they are learning the names of other children in the class and can recognize them by the first letter.
- ► Notice whether children are writing their names with the letters in the right order.

Expand the Learning

Repeat the lesson with names of friends or family or with names of characters children have met in books: Hansel, Gretel, Jack, Jill.

Have each child find someone else whose name has the same first letter.

Make a class big book with one page for each child. Have children draw a picture of themselves and then glue the letters of their names beneath the drawings. Use the class big book for shared reading.

Connect with Home

Have children take home the envelope with their name cards so that they can do the lesson at home.

Give them a copy of the "Bingo" song and invite them to sing it with family members at home.

Give caregivers the directions for playing Alphabet Concentration (see *Teaching Resources*). They can use two sets of the uppercase or lowercase letter cards (see *Teaching Resources*) to play the game. A variation is to match uppercase letters with lowercase letters.

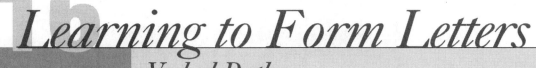

16
Learning to Form Letters
Verbal Path

Consider Your Children

The procedures described in this lesson may be used many times for different lowercase and uppercase letters. The lowercase letters are more useful for children, and they also encounter them more frequently in the texts they read, so begin with them. Work on letters that most children know or nearly know. Use children's names as a resource and to make connections. Children should have achieved good control of efficient movements before they are asked to attend to variables such as size and lines, so start with unlined paper. Once children have developed systems for learning a verbal path, lessons can be quite short, and you will not need to go over every letter in this detail.

Working with English Language Learners

Be sure that English language learners hear and say the verbal directions enough times to know what they mean. As they do more handwriting and think about and say the motions, they will take on new letters faster. At a meeting for caregivers, demonstrate efficient ways for helping children so that caregivers know the reason children are using the verbal path and what it means.

You Need

► Tool for showing children how to make letters: MagnaDoodle®, dry-erase marker and whiteboard, chart paper on easel, or chalkboard.

► Sand/salt in a box or tray.

► Sandpaper letters.

► Newsprint.

► Crayons.

From *Teaching Resources:*

► Laminated Letter Formation Cards (copy the Letter Formation Chart onto cards, including the arrows to show direction and sequence; laminate the cards so children can trace them with dry-erase markers).

► Letters Made in Similar Ways.

► Verbal Path for the Formation of Letters.

Understand the Principle

Learning efficient movements for forming letters helps children fix the features of the letters in their visual memory.

An additional benefit is the growing legibility of their handwriting.

Explain the Principle

❝ You can make the shape of a letter. ❞

❝ You can say words that help you learn how to make letters. ❞

❝ You can check to see if your letter looks right. ❞

plan

Explain the Principle

" **You can make the shape of a letter.** "

" **You can say words that help you learn how to make letters.** "

" **You can check to see if your letter looks right.** "

① Explain to the children that they are going to learn how to make good letters.

② Say the name of a letter, and then, using a MagnaDoodle® or chart paper, demonstrate how it is formed using the simple, clear language in the Verbal Path for the Formation of Letters (in *Teaching Resources*). Suggested language: "I'm going to make an *h*. To make a lowercase *h*, you pull down, up, curve, and down." Make the letter slowly as you describe the movement.

③ Make the letter again and invite the children to say the verbal path with you as you write.

④ Invite the children to talk through the movements and make the letter in the air a few times and then on the carpet in front of them. ("Writing" on the back of another child is generally not a good idea. It has no benefit and can be distracting.)

⑤ Over time, work with a group of letters that start in the same place—*h, l,* and *b*, for example. Use Letters Made in Similar Ways from *Teaching Resources*.

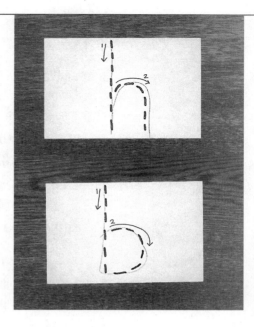

apply

trace
write

▸ Have children make today's letters, talking through the motions as they do so.

▸ Demonstrate ways you want children to make letters. Examples: Trace sandpaper letters; trace letters on laminated letter cards with a dry-erase marker; write the letter in salt or sand in a flat tray or box; write the letter on paper with a crayon.

▸ On a large piece of newsprint, make "rainbow letters." Write a letter in pencil yourself and place dots and arrows on it with black marker. Then each child, in turn, while saying the motions, traces the letter on the newsprint using a different-color crayon. At the end, you will have a large letter written in about twenty different colors. One child can take it home—perhaps someone whose name contains the letter. Ask what children noticed about today's letters.

share

Look for comments such as these:

"They are all tall letters."

"You pull down to make them all."

"The *b* is different because it has a circle."

"The *h* is different because it has a tunnel."

These comments will tell you what the children are noticing about the distinctive features of letters.

Link

Interactive Read-Aloud: Read aloud alphabet books that emphasize sounds as well as names, such as:

- ▶ *ABC Discovery* by Izhar Cohen
- ▶ *Goblins in Green* by Nicholas Heller

Shared Reading: When reading a very familiar poem or piece of interactive writing, play a game by making a letter in the air while saying the motions (see the Verbal Path for the Formation of Letters in *Teaching Resources*) and then asking children to find this letter in the text and mark it with highlighter tape.

Guided Reading: During word work, arrange magnetic letters on a cookie sheet in alphabetical order. Make a few letters in the air or on a whiteboard and have children find them on the tray.

Interactive Writing: Say the motions while writing a difficult letter on the whiteboard. When a child is writing a letter at the easel, say the motions as the child writes.

Independent Writing: Encourage children to use efficient motions when writing and to say the motions (the verbal path) if that helps them.

assess

- ▶ Observe the children as they write to see whether their handwriting is getting more efficient.
- ▶ Evaluate the children's written products to determine whether their handwriting is becoming more legible.
- ▶ Make an inventory of children's ability to write letters by asking them to write a series of letters that you dictate. This task will tell you which letters need continued detailed attention.

Expand the Learning

Repeat the lesson with other lowercase letters:

c, o, a, d, g, q

b, h, t, i, j, k, l, p

n, r, m, u

v, x, w, y

f, s

e, z

Repeat the lesson with uppercase letters that children are making in an inefficient way or finding difficult.

Connect with Home

At a meeting, explain to caregivers your reasons for using words to describe the motions for forming letters. Give them a copy of the uppercase and lowercase alphabet with the numbers and arrows (*Teaching Resources, Letter Formation Charts*) so that they can use it at home.

Also give caregivers whose children need this extra support a copy of the Verbal Path (in *Teaching Resources*).

Caution caregivers not to expect perfect handwriting right away, and say that you do not correct handwriting when students are concentrating on what they want to write (independent writing). Mention that you teach handwriting in special lessons.

Have children take home their practice handwriting.

Suggest that caregivers ask their children to "paint" (with water) large letters on the driveway or sidewalk, using the verbal path to help them form letters correctly.

Recognizing Uppercase and Lowercase Letters

Two-Way Sort

Consider Your Children

This lesson is best used after you have worked with children on handwriting and they are accustomed to noticing features of letters as well as thinking about the directional movements it takes to make letters. You want them to be able to recognize letters fluently and automatically.

Working with English Language Learners

In this lesson your English language learners will be using the terms *uppercase* and *lowercase* to describe letters. It will take many experiences working with letters to help children sort out the two categories as well as the way uppercase and lowercase letters are matched. Provide as many demonstrations as necessary to help them look closely to notice the differences and similarities between uppercase and lowercase letters. Be sure that they understand the sorting process; you may want to work with them in a small group.

You Need

► Large-print alphabet book that shows both uppercase and lowercase letters. An example is *Chicka Chicka Boom Boom,* by Bill Martin, Jr., and John Archambault (also see the Alphabet Books Bibliography in *Teaching Resources*).

► Large chart of lowercase letters.

From *Teaching Resources:*

► Alphabet Linking Chart.

► Selected letter cards (matching uppercase and lowercase letters) or magnetic letters.

► Two-Way Sort Cards and Sheets.

Understand the Principle

Becoming familiar with the alphabet is an important step for emergent readers. Children need to learn that every letter looks different and that every letter has a name. This information helps them connect sounds to letters as they begin to decode words.

Children need a sense of the entire alphabet, both uppercase and lowercase letters. Some uppercase and lowercase letters are similar in shape; other pairs look quite different. Lowercase letters are generally more difficult to learn. Connecting the lowercase letters with uppercase ones will help children learn to recognize and name the lowercase letters.

Explain the Principle

" A letter has two forms. One form is uppercase (or capital), and the other is lowercase (or small). "

plan

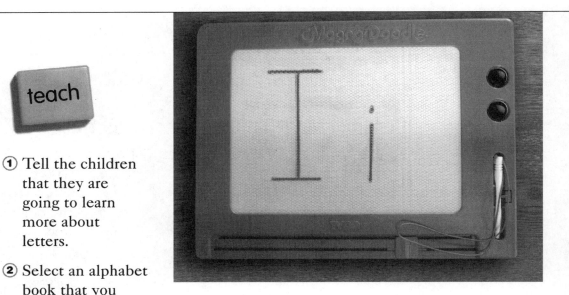

Explain the Principle

" A letter has two forms. One form is uppercase (or capital), and the other is lowercase (or small). "

① Tell the children that they are going to learn more about letters.

② Select an alphabet book that you have read with children enough times to create familiarity. Books like *Chicka Chicka Boom Boom* are very appealing because they incorporate rhyme and rhythm.

③ Suggested language: "Today we'll read one of our favorite alphabet books." Discuss the uppercase and lowercase letters. If you are using *Chicka Chicka Boom Boom*, you can talk about how the Mamas and Papas (uppercase letters) are helping their kids (lowercase letters). Have some fun with the page where the capital letters are hugging the lowercase letters. Read the book with the children joining in.

④ After the first reading, ask one child to point to a lowercase letter on a page and another child to find the same lowercase letter on the Alphabet Linking Chart. Suggested language: "In this book we see uppercase letters. Sometimes these are called 'capital' letters. [Show one.] And we also see lowercase, or small, letters. [Show one.]"

⑤ Choose a letter and write the uppercase and lowercase forms on a MagnaDoodle® or whiteboard so the children can see them clearly.

⑥ Suggested language: "This is uppercase *I*, and this is lowercase *i*. They have the same name. They're both named *I*, but one is uppercase and one is lowercase. What do you notice about the uppercase *I* and lowercase *i*?" Children may offer answers like "One is taller" or "One has a dot." Ask them to be specific and to name them as uppercase (or capital) *I* and lowercase (or small) *i*.

⑦ Repeat this action with several more letters.

⑧ Finally, have the children read the lowercase letters on the Alphabet Linking Chart: (1) read every other line; (2) read every other letter; (3) read down the columns; (4) read the letters with circles; (5) read the letters with long sticks; (6) read the letters with no curves; (7) read the letters with tails; (8) read the letters with tunnels.

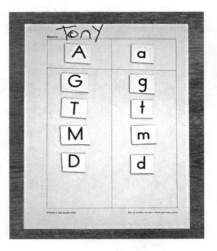

take
put
match
write

▸ Give each child a bag or tub (margarine containers work well) of selected pairs of uppercase and lowercase magnetic letters or letter cards. On a Two-Way Sort Card, have children put an uppercase letter on the left and match the lowercase letter on the right. They continue until they have sorted all the letters in their bag. They can then write the letter pairs on a Two-Way Sort Sheet. Have children swap bags/tubs and repeat.

Have an Alphabet Linking Chart (with both uppercase and lowercase letters) handy. Ask children what they noticed about how uppercase and lowercase letters are alike or different. Have them point to and talk about specific examples.

Link

Interactive Read-Aloud: Read aloud alphabet books. Point out uppercase and lowercase letters. Examples are:

- ▶ *26 Letters and 99 Cents* by Tana Hoban
- ▶ *L Is for Loving: An ABC for the Way You Feel* by Ken Wilson-Max

Shared Reading: Read alphabet charts in various ways. Put letters in the pocket chart out of order and have children read them as fast as possible.

Guided Reading: Draw children's attention to the first letter of a word at the beginning of a sentence and the first letter of a word within the sentence. Help them notice that one word starts with an uppercase or capital letter and the other starts with a lowercase or small letter.

Interactive Writing: When you are writing a word, ask children whether to use an uppercase or lowercase letter.

Independent Writing: Compliment children when they use lowercase letters in their writing. Encourage them to use a capital letter at the beginning of a name and lowercase letters for the rest of the name.

assess

- ▶ Notice the children's ability to recognize high frequency words, whether they start with an uppercase or a lowercase letter.
- ▶ Observe the children's use of lowercase letters in their writing.
- ▶ Use lowercase letter cards to check individual knowledge.

Expand the Learning

Go back to *Chicka Chicka Boom Boom* if you have it. Read the book again and look at the endpapers, which show both letter forms. Using the whiteboard or chart paper, write a lowercase letter and ask a volunteer to come up and write the corresponding uppercase letter (or vice versa). Check it with the alphabet book.

Make an audiotape of an alphabet book. Give each child a "personal" lowercase Letter Formation Chart (*Teaching Resources,* Letter Formation Charts). Have children listen to the tape while following along in the book. Then have them listen to the tape again, this time pointing to the letters on the letter chart as they are mentioned.

Connect with Home

Children can take home a personal Alphabet Linking Chart (see *Teaching Resources*) to "read" to their families.

Give children reproduced sets of alphabet letter cards, both uppercase and lowercase (see *Teaching Resources,* Letter Cards), to cut apart and match at home.

Have caregivers write the alphabet, in two or three rows, across a large sheet of paper and ask their children to find alphabet-cereal letters that match, saying each letter and gluing it below the written letter on the sheet.

Recognizing Uppercase and Lowercase Letters

Alphabet Lotto

Consider Your Children

Use this lesson after children have had some experience matching pictures for beginning sounds. They will be using the same procedure to match uppercase and lowercase letters. Lotto is similar to Bingo except that players cover every square, so there is more work to do. Children who already have rapid automatic recognition of all forms of letters will not need this lesson.

Working with English Language Learners

By the time you use this lesson, your English language learners will be familiar with the Alphabet Linking Chart, the concept of letters, and the names of many of the letters that make up the alphabet. They will have noticed that there are two forms for each letter but may not have systematized their knowledge. Provide clear demonstrations of how to match letters, calling them uppercase and lowercase letters. Have children say the words that you are using, and provide explanations that will help them understand the thinking behind the label. (Children may not understand the meaning of the words *upper* and *lower* as a foundation for looking at letters, especially as these terms refer to placement on the space of a page.) You can also use the words *big* and *little* if it helps to get the concept across.

You Need

▸ Pocket chart.

From *Teaching Resources:*

▸ Uppercase and lowercase Letter Cards.
▸ Lotto Game Cards.
▸ Directions for Lotto.

Understand the Principle

Children need to be able to discern the distinctive features that make one letter different from every other letter. The names of the letters are "labels" that we can use to talk about them, which is a big advantage when connecting letters and sounds.

Being able to connect uppercase and lowercase letters helps children understand the organization of this fixed set of graphic symbols.

Explain the Principle

" A letter has two forms. One form is uppercase and the other is lowercase. "

" Some lowercase forms look like the uppercase form and some look different. "

plan

Explain the Principle

" A letter has two forms. One form is uppercase and the other is lowercase. "

" Some lowercase forms look like the uppercase form and some look different. "

① Explain to the children that they are going to learn more about letters.

② Suggested language: "Each of the twenty-six letters of the alphabet has two forms. One is called uppercase, or capital [show an example], and the other is called lowercase, or small [show an example]."

③ Show the children the Alphabet Linking Chart and point out the pairs of letters in each box.

④ Point out the initial uppercase letter in each child's name on the name chart.

⑤ On the pocket chart, place twelve uppercase letter cards, three in each row. Suggested language: "Today we are going to learn to play a game called Alphabet Lotto. In this game you get to match letters. Let's try it with the letters I have in the pocket chart. These are uppercase letters, aren't they? Let's read them." Read through the letters on the chart.

⑥ Suggested language: "Now, on these cards, I have some lowercase letters. I'll mix them all up and then draw one. [Hold up the card.] I'm going to see if it goes with one of the letters on my card. Does it? [Children respond.]"

⑦ Model checking the lowercase letter with the uppercase one on the card. Say both letters: *A–a*. If children are very inexperienced, display the Alphabet Linking Chart right next to the easel.

⑧ Continue to draw cards one at a time, modeling how to check each one against the letters in the pocket chart and saying the names of the letters. Place matching cards with the corresponding letters. (Place cards that don't match letters on the chart to the side, face down.)

⑨ Continue until all spaces are covered. Suggested language: "I've covered all the spaces on my square. That's what you do to win the Alphabet Lotto game. Remember to say the name of the uppercase and lowercase letters as you check your matches."

⑩ Mention that some uppercase and lowercase letters look a lot alike but others look different. Ask children to look at the ones that look different and say what is different.

⑪ Demonstrate the game with three children in a circle on the floor. Show them how to take turns drawing cards and matching them to the letters on their cards. The first to fill the card wins.

take
match
cover
check

▶ Have children play the Alphabet Lotto game. If you have enough letter and game cards, several games can be played at once.

Give each child a letter. Have each, in turn, say the letter name and tell whether it is lowercase or uppercase.

Link

Interactive Read-Aloud: Read aloud alphabet books. Examples are:

- *A Is for Amos* by Deborah Chandra
- *B Is for Baby: An Alphabet of Verses* by Myra Cohn Livingston

Shared Reading: Read the Alphabet Linking Chart. Try reading every other letter, reading the uppercase letters, reading the lowercase letters, reading down the columns.

Guided Reading: During word work, give each child a bag of three letters. Have children tell the name of each letter.

Interactive Writing: When the class is thinking how to write a word, have children say it slowly and connect it to a name or another word that starts with the same letter.

Independent Writing: Encourage children to say words slowly when they are writing and to connect them to names or other words that start with the same letter. Use magnetic letters as examples when children are trying to think of the correct form.

assess

- Notice whether the children are able to identify letters by name.

- Point to a capital letter and ask the child to find the corresponding lowercase letter, or vice versa. Select letters that you think are more difficult rather than using the entire alphabet.

Expand the Learning

If children know very few letters, make a Lotto game that requires exact matching of letters (e.g., lowercase *a* to lowercase *a*). In the beginning, use a limited set, including letters that are not similar. Concentrate on either uppercase or lowercase letters. As part of the game, ask children to say the names and trace the letters.

Repeat the lesson. Have the children use uppercase letters and match them to lowercase letters on the Lotto Game Card.

Have children match magnetic or foam letters to letters on the game cards.

Play Alphabet Concentration (see *Teaching Resources,* Directions for Concentration), making pairs of cards with the same lowercase form. Alternatively, have players make pairs of one uppercase letter card with one lowercase letter card.

Connect with Home

Have children take home letter cards (one set of uppercase, one set of lowercase) reproduced on heavy paper so they can cut them apart and match them.

Give them paper copies of the Lotto Game Cards and letters so they can play the game with family members.

19 Forming Letters
Handwriting Books

Consider Your Children

This lesson establishes the procedures for using a handwriting book. The routine is best used after children are accustomed to using writing materials (paper, markers, pencils), can work independently and follow simple directions for five or more minutes, and are using mostly conventional letters in their approximated writing. Don't wait too long to show children how to write letters because you don't want them to establish inefficient habits. You will want to work with one or more letters at a time, choosing letters that begin the same way. (See Letters Made in Similar Ways in *Teaching Resources*.)

Working with English Language Learners

Be sure to demonstrate the task as many times as necessary to be certain children know how to use efficient motions to make letters and say the words that will help them. Focus on only one or two letters at the beginning. If you are storing handwriting books in colored boxes, be sure that English language learners know their colors. Demonstrate and practice having children take out the books, get writing materials, write a page of letters, and put books away in the right place. These procedures will be used over and over, so time is well spent learning routines.

You Need

- ► Handwriting book for each child. Standard composition books cut in half across the width make good small handwriting books.
- ► Large handwriting book for demonstration.
- ► Baskets or boxes for storing handwriting books.
- ► Newsprint and crayons.

Understand the Principle

Learning efficient movements for making letters helps children remember the features of the letters. Handwriting lessons take only a few minutes a day, are easy to manage, and are a way to help children practice regularly.

Frequent practice until the movements are established will help children become more efficient and fluent at handwriting.

Explain the Principle

❝ You can make the shape of a letter. ❞

❝ You can say words that help you learn how to make a letter. ❞

❝ You can check to see if your letter looks right. ❞

CONTINUUM: LETTER KNOWLEDGE — USING EFFICIENT AND CONSISTENT MOTIONS TO FORM LETTERS

plan

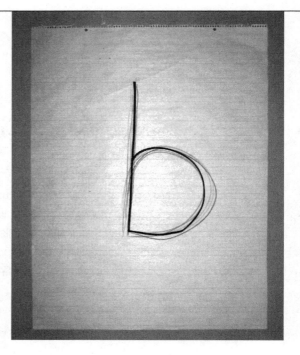

Explain the Principle

" You can make the shape of a letter. "

" You can say words that help you learn how to make a letter. "

" You can check to see if your letter looks right. "

① Tell the children today they are going to learn more about writing letters.

② Suggested language: "Today we're going to practice forming *b* by making a 'rainbow' letter. Watch while I make a big one with a pencil. Pull down, half up, and around." Make the *b*—on newsprint—about twenty-four inches tall. Have children practice making the *b* in the air and remind them of the routine. Then have them take colored crayons or markers and trace over the *b* while describing the motions. At the end of the day, let one child take the "rainbow" *b* home. (If you used Lesson LK 16, they will already know how to make rainbow letters.)

③ Show children a handwriting book. Suggested language: "Today we are going to start our handwriting books. You will each have your own book. On the front it says 'My Handwriting Book.' This is my handwriting book that I will use to show you what to write. On the front, it says 'My Handwriting Book,' and here is my name. [Demonstrate.]"

④ "We'll keep our handwriting books in these boxes. [Point out the boxes of handwriting books.] I'm going to give each of you a book with your name carefully written on the cover. It also has a colored dot that matches the color of your box. When you put your book back, you need to remember the color of your box. This colored dot will help you remember. Each time when you finish your book, you will need to put it back in the right box. How many of you remember your color? Look at the dot if you forget."

⑤ Show children the handwriting book. Suggested language: "I'm going to be showing you how to write letters on each page of this book. Every time you use your handwriting book, you will be writing a page of letters or words. This book is going to help you practice good writing."

⑥ Show the children what you want them to do in their handwriting books. Explain that they will see a letter at the beginning of the line and they will make the letter carefully several times to fill the row.

write
check

▶ Children take their handwriting books and practice lines of the letter or letters you modeled, creating a page of letters like the one you started.

Have children demonstrate saying the motions to make *b*.

Have them show a partner the best letter they made in each line.

Have several children demonstrate finding their handwriting books in the colored boxes and putting them away.

Link

Interactive Read-Aloud: Read aloud alphabet books that emphasize noticing letters, such as:

- ▸ *Old Black Fly* by Jim Aylesworth
- ▸ *Alphabet Soup: A Feast of Letters* by Scott Gustafson

Shared Reading: Have the children use masking cards or flags to locate letters they practiced writing in poems or other familiar texts such as "Make a Pancake" or "Jumping Joan" (see *Sing a Song of Poetry*).

Guided Reading: During word work, have children find the particular letter they learned. Model the formation on the whiteboard.

Interactive Writing: Describe the motions (see the Verbal Path for the Formation of Letters in *Teaching Resources*) when you are modeling a letter on the whiteboard or when a child is writing a letter at the easel. Have children "check" the letter and its formation after it is written. Have children locate a "really good" *b* (or any letter) after a piece is written.

Independent Writing: Encourage children to say the motions while writing letters that are hard for them. Encourage them by pointing to really good examples of letters that they write.

Expand the Learning

Repeat the lesson later if children are not getting and putting away handwriting books properly. It is very important for this routine to become automatic.

Repeat the lesson with groups of letters (two or three at a time) until children can form letters efficiently and correctly.

Connect with Home

Give family members a copy of the uppercase and lowercase alphabet with the dots and arrows indicating the required motions (see *Teaching Resources,* Letter Formation Charts) so that they can use them at home.

Encourage caregivers to have their children form the letters using finger paint, watercolors and a brush, a brush in water on the sidewalk, or their finger or a stick in a sandbox.

At a meeting, show caregivers the handwriting books and tell them that children will be bringing them home when they are filled up.

assess

- ▸ Evaluate the children's writing to determine other handwriting lessons they need.

- ▸ Observe the children while they are writing to determine whether they are using efficient movements to write letters and to decide which letters to focus on in handwriting lessons.

20 *Learning to Form Letters*

Handwriting Books

Consider Your Children

This lesson is best used after children have worked with the name chart (Lesson ELC 1) and have sorted letters. Each child should be able to write his or her name accurately. Select a routine way to show children the movements for writing the selected letter. (See *Teaching Resources,* Verbal Path, for simple language to describe letter formation.) Children will have begun to learn routines for using the handwriting books. At first, have them all write at the same time. After the routine has been established, they can practice in the book independently. In this lesson, you show children how to evaluate their own handwriting. The chart Letters Made in Similar Ways (in *Teaching Resources*) depicts an order in which to teach letters that begin the same way. You can teach two or three letters at a time. (See *Teaching Resources,* Letter Formation Charts, for specific directions for forming lowercase and uppercase letters.)

Working with English Language Learners

If children have not learned the routines well enough to follow them automatically, provide more demonstrations. The Verbal Path will be helpful to English language learners, but they need to understand what the words mean and how to use them. Have them say the words in unison as they make letters. You may want to use unlined newsprint at first so they can concentrate on movement. Show them what "best" means in terms of self-evaluating their handwriting.

You Need

► Tool for demonstrating letter formation: MagnaDoodle®, dry-erase marker and whiteboard, chart paper on the easel, or chalkboard.

► Individual handwriting books featuring a letter or letters to be practiced. Standard composition books cut in half across the width make good small handwriting books. Write the letter at the beginning of a line on a page.

► Large version of a handwriting book.

From *Teaching Resources:*

► Letter Formation Charts.

► Verbal Path for the Formation of Letters.

Understand the Principle

Learning efficient movements for forming letters helps children remember the features of the letters. Using simple language to describe the movements (providing a verbal path) helps children learn the most efficient movements. (Once they have internalized this language, however, it is no longer necessary and may even get in the way.)

Explain the Principle

" You can make the shape of a letter. "

" You can say words that help you learn how to make a letter. "

" You can check to see if your letter looks right. "

CONTINUUM: LETTER KNOWLEDGE — USING EFFICIENT AND CONSISTENT MOTIONS TO FORM LETTERS

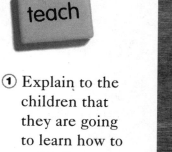

Explain the Principle

" You can make the shape of a letter. "

" You can say words that help you learn how to make a letter. "

" You can check to see if your letter looks right. "

① Explain to the children that they are going to learn how to make letters to check their writing.

② Select an easy letter that most children know and can make. Suggested language: "I'm going to make *c*. To make a lowercase *c*, pull back and around." Make the letter slowly as you describe the movement. At first, make a large letter so children see the large motor movements. Use whiteboard, chart paper, or a MagnaDoodle® (the thick writing instrument is most effective).

③ Make the letter again and invite the children to say the Verbal Path (see *Teaching Resources*) aloud with you as you write.

④ Have children make the letter in the air and on the rug or floor as they softly repeat the Verbal Path.

⑤ Show the children your large handwriting book. Open it and demonstrate writing the letter *c* several times next to the model while you say the motions. Note that the letter is formed within a set of lines. Show the children your line of *c*'s. Suggested language: "Now I'm going to choose the best *c* that I have made. I'm going to circle it with a colored marker." Then close the book.

⑥ "On the left you will see the letter I want you to practice today at the beginning of each line. Trace over it and say the name of the letter as you write it. [Demonstrate.] Then write it several more times until you fill the line. Be sure to leave spaces between the letters you practice. When you bring your handwriting book to me, I'll help you choose your best *c*."

⑦ Help the children choose their best letter and tell them why the letter is "best." This will gradually become a routine as children learn to evaluate their handwriting.

⑧ Have the children who finish first go to a table or the rug to look at books (or do some other activity) while you deal with the children who need more time.

say
write
circle

▸ Have the children use their handwriting books to practice writing the letter on each line.

▸ Help them circle their best letter with a colored marker before they return their handwriting books to the colored boxes.

Ask several children to share their handwriting. Have them put a finger under the best letter.

Bring the children together in a circle again and invite one or two children to the board (or chart or easel) to make a "beautiful *c*."

Link

Interactive Read-Aloud: Read aloud alphabet books (see the Alphabet Books Bibliography in *Teaching Resources* for additional examples) that draw attention to the shapes of letters, such as:

- ▸ *Alphabet Soup* by Kate Banks
- ▸ *The Butterfly Alphabet* by Kjell B. Sandved

Shared Reading: Make a letter and have children find it several times in a shared reading text using a masking card. Using highlighter tape, have children mark all the examples of a particular letter.

Guided Reading: After reading and discussing the story, have children find a letter two or three times in a text.

Interactive Writing: After a piece of writing is finished, ask children to locate a "really good *c*" or other letter.

Independent Writing: Encourage children to check their writing and point out letters that they have made well. If children are having difficulty with formation, support them with a Verbal Path.

assess

- ▸ Observe the children as they write to determine their ability to use efficient directional movements.
- ▸ Dictate letters to children and then look at the products. Check off the letters they are representing well. Eventually you will want to evaluate their formation of all letters.

Expand the Learning

Individualize the handwriting books by giving children different letters to practice.

Design lessons focusing on particular letters that children need to practice.

After children are able to make letters easily, have them write high frequency words or simple sentences in the books.

Connect with Home

Send home handwriting books that are filled and give the children new ones. At a meeting or in a brief note, explain that the circled letters are the child's best effort.

Let children take home pieces of lined paper to practice writing letters at home.

The development of fine motor coordination contributes to a child's ability to use small hand movements to form letters. In a newsletter, explain activities that can be done at home that help children develop fine motor skills: working with clay, Wikki Stix, or pipe cleaners; finger painting; tracing (dot to dot); building with Lego® bricks or Tinkertoys®; stringing macaroni, beads, popcorn, or cranberries.

21 Labeling Consonants and Vowels
Letter Sort

Consider Your Children

This lesson is best used after children know most of the letters and can recognize and name them quickly in words. They should also know the terms *first, middle,* and *last* as applied to letters in words and know simple high frequency words as well as some words that have regular spellings. As children notice consonants and vowels in words, the words *my* and *why* may come up. Simply explain that in some words, *y* is a vowel.

Working with English Language Learners

You may need many demonstrations and repetitions to help English language learners learn the labels *consonants* and *vowels*. Once these are learned, you will find them useful in talking about letters with children. Have them work not only with magnetic letters but with letter cards, letter tiles, link letters, and other manipulable literacy materials. Practice having children say and locate the vowels *a, e, i, o, u.* Once they can find them quickly and identify them as vowels, they can notice that the rest of the letters are consonants. Be sure to demonstrate the sorting task.

You Need

► Magnetic letters (one of each of the lowercase letters) and a surface to which they will adhere.

► Cookie sheets or plastic trays for individual work space.

► Letter strip with the vowels *a, e, i, o,* and *u* listed for reference.

► Class name chart (see Lesson ELC 1).

From *Teaching Resources:*

► Letter cards (if you do not use magnetic letters).

► Name card for each child (Word Card Template) or name puzzles (see Lesson LK 4).

Understand the Principle

The words *consonants* and *vowels* are useful labels that will allow children to talk about the principles related to how words work. If they can learn these two broad categories early, these words will be in their vocabularies when they explore more complex principles.

Later, they will learn that *y* sometimes functions as a vowel (as in *my*).

Explain the Principle

" Some letters are consonants. "

" Some letters are vowels. "

" Every word has a vowel. "

plan

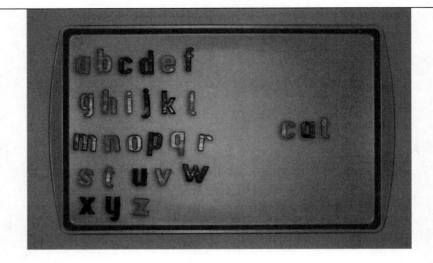

Explain the Principle

" Some letters are consonants. "

" Some letters are vowels. "

" Every word has a vowel. "

① Tell the children that they are going to learn something new about letters.

② Suggested language: "Today we are going to learn which letters are consonants and which letters are vowels. Say those words." Have children repeat the words *consonants* and *vowels*. "Knowing which letters are the consonants and which are the vowels will help you spell words better."

③ Make the word *cat* with magnetic letters. "Look at this word that you know. What is it? [Children respond.] In this word the first letter, *c*, is a consonant. The middle letter, *a*, is a vowel, and the last letter, *t*, is another consonant."

④ Suggested language: "Now I am going to show the letters that are vowels. They are *a, e, i, o,* and *u*." Place additional magnetic letters of the vowels on the blank half of the surface. "We're going to hunt for the vowels as we say the alphabet. The first one we'll look for is *a*. Who can find it?" Have a child find the *a* and place it on the blank side.

⑤ Repeat for each additional vowel, each time telling children what to look for and asking them to clap when you come to it. Then have them say the vowels as a group: *a, e, i, o, u*.

⑥ Place the vowels back in the alphabet, but leave the other set of vowels as a model. Go through the process again more quickly, this time without telling them what vowel to look for.

⑦ Use the magnetic letters to make several simple words consisting of consonant-vowel-consonant *(dog, cat)* and vowel-consonant *(at, in)* combinations. In each, have children find the vowel and ask them what they notice about the words.

⑧ Children may say vowels are "in the middle." Suggested language: "Yes, the vowels are mostly in the middle of these words, but they can be any place in the word. Every word has a vowel."

⑨ Turn to your class name chart and have children decide whose names begin with a consonant and whose begin with a vowel.

⑩ Tell children they are going to sort letters into consonants and vowels. Quickly show them how to do this and then how to check each letter in the vowel column with the list of vowels on the letter strip to be sure they are the same.

find
sort
check

► Have children place their collection of magnetic letters or letter cards on a flat or vertical surface. Individual cookie sheets or plastic trays work well because they define each child's work space. Have children place all the consonants on the left and vowels on the right. Have a sign with *a, e, i, o, u* handy so children can check their work. Provide more than one of each letter to make the task more complex.

Have children take their name cards (or name puzzles) and count the number of vowels in the name. Then have each child name the vowels.

Link

Interactive Read-Aloud: Read aloud an alphabet book (for more suggestions, see the Alphabet Books Bibliography in *Teaching Resources*). Have children clap when you come to a vowel. Two examples are:

- ▸ *A Prairie Alphabet* by Yvette Moore and Jo Bannatyne-Cugnet
- ▸ *Black and White Rabbit's ABC* by Alan Baker

Shared Reading: Read the Alphabet Linking Chart twice, first reading just the consonants and then reading just the vowels. Ask children to point out the vowels and/or consonants in a word that they locate in a familiar text.

Guided Reading: During word work, have children take turns finding the vowels in a group of letters placed on the magnetic easel.

Interactive Writing: When a word is written, have children check to see whether it has a vowel and name it. Tell what position the vowel has in the word—first, middle, last.

Independent Writing: Encourage children to check words they have written to be sure that they have vowels.

assess

- ▸ Notice whether the children are able to identify vowels quickly.
- ▸ Observe whether the children are able to locate the vowels in words.

Expand the Learning

Play Follow the Path with a game board containing a consonant or a vowel in each space. Have children throw the die, land on a letter, say the name of the letter, and tell whether it is a consonant or a vowel. (See the Directions for Follow the Path in *Teaching Resources*.)

Connect with Home

Have children take home letter cards (see *Teaching Resources*) to sort by consonant and vowel.

Have caregivers help children find uppercase and lowercase letters in their home and environment: on signs, shops, the stove or the refrigerator, food boxes, cans.

Suggest that caregivers ask children to sort consonants from vowels using magnetic letters on the refrigerator (see *Teaching Resources, 25 Ways to Use Magnetic Letters at Home* and *Ways to Sort Letters*).

Understanding Alphabetical Order

Magnetic Letters

Consider Your Children

Once children have learned letter names and can locate them easily, it is useful for them to understand the alphabet as a tool. They may be able to say or sing the alphabet, but that does not mean they understand alphabetical order. This lesson will help them use the alphabet as a tool to guide them to information.

Working with English Language Learners

This lesson will give English language learners more experience in connecting letter shapes and names. Learning alphabetical order will give them an additional tool for understanding the way written language is organized. Provide as many repetitions as necessary to help children understand the order of the alphabet. Work with a small group to help them use the Alphabet Linking Chart (in *Teaching Resources*) to put their magnetic letters in order. Then show them how to check the order by saying the alphabet or checking letter by letter with the chart.

You Need

▶ Magnetic letters.

▶ Lined sheets of paper.

From *Teaching Resources:*

▶ Alphabet Order Sheet.

Understand the Principle

Children need to develop a working knowledge of letter names and their order so they will be able to talk about letters.

Knowing letter order also gives them a tool for referring to the word wall.

Explain the Principle

❝ The letters in the alphabet are in a special order. ❞

plan

Explain the Principle

" The letters in the alphabet are in a special order. "

① Explain to the children that they are going to learn how to put letters into alphabetical order.

② Show the series of lowercase magnetic letters arranged in order on a magnetic board.

③ Mix them up.

④ Explain that you are going to put them in order. Invite individual children to place two or three letters at a time in alphabetical order.

⑤ After two or three children take their turns, have a child come up to point at each letter while the other children read the sequence of letters.

⑥ Continue until the whole alphabet is in order.

⑦ Show the children the Alphabet Order Sheet and explain how to complete the alphabetical order task.

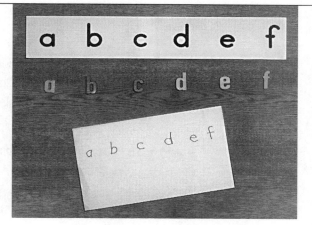

apply

mix
match
write

► Have children put the matching magnetic letter, starting with *a,* under each letter on the Alphabet Order Sheet.

► On a lined sheet of paper, have children write the alphabet in order.

share

Give each child a letter as she or he comes to the group meeting.

Play a quick alphabet game. One child says the letter he is holding and the next child tells the letter that comes after. That child then names the letter she is holding and the process is repeated.

Link

Interactive Read-Aloud: Read aloud alphabet books. Have the children predict each upcoming letter. Examples are:

- ▶ *On Market Street* by Arnold and Anita Lobel
- ▶ *The Absolutely Awful Alphabet* by Mordicai Gerstein

Shared Reading: After enjoying a poem or song such as "Teeter-Totter" or "Mix a Pancake" (see *Sing a Song of Poetry*), invite the children to give a clue about a word in the poem or song. For example, "I'm thinking of a word that starts with the letter that comes after *b*." Another child finds a word that fits the clue and isolates it with a masking card or flag.

Guided Reading: During word work, give the children a small container with nine or ten letters to put in order.

Interactive Writing: After a text has been written, have children find particular letters.

Independent Writing: Invite children to refer to the word wall (which is displayed in alphabetical order) to find a word they want to write.

Expand the Learning

Repeat the lesson with uppercase letters.

Have children place the lowercase letter on the model of the Alphabet Order Sheet and match the corresponding uppercase letter below it.

Using the Alphabet Order Sheet *(Teaching Resources),* block out some of the letters with white paper and tape (or white correction tape). Invite children to place all the magnetic letters in order, those that go on top of letters visible on the model and those that belong in spaces where the letters aren't visible.

Connect with Home

Encourage family members to obtain a set of magnetic letters. If you know homes where magnetic letters are not available, send home letter cards (in *Teaching Resources*). Have caregivers ask their children to mix up the letters (uppercase or lowercase) and put them in alphabetical order.

assess

- ▶ Notice the children's ability to navigate the word wall using alphabetical order.
- ▶ Observe the children cutting apart alphabet letters (*Teaching Resources,* Letter Cards) and gluing them in alphabetical order on a long paper strip.

23 Learning Alphabetical Order

Follow the Path

Consider Your Children

This lesson is best used after children can recognize and name most of the letters and can read and write their names. This lesson helps "tidy up" their knowledge and gives them a sense of alphabetical order. Once children learn the routine for this game, you can vary the task.

Working with English Language Learners

This lesson will help your English language learners understand the alphabet as a tool and also give them a good idea of the entire set of letters. Be sure that English language learners have plenty of opportunities to say the alphabet while pointing to each letter in turn. Also be sure that children know how to play Follow the Path. Play the game with a small group the first time they use this exercise.

You Need

► Die with 1, 2, or 3 on each side (some numbers are repeated). (You may also use cards with 1, 2, or 3 on them.)

► Game markers for players (buttons work well, but any small objects will do).

From *Teaching Resources:*

► Alphabet Linking Chart.

► Follow the Path Game Board using letters of the alphabet (see Directions for Follow the Path).

► Large version of a Follow the Path game for demonstration.

► Copies of Alphabet Linking Chart for partners.

Understand the Principle

The alphabet is a very important tool for emergent and early readers. They need to understand the concept of a fixed set of letters.

Knowing the order of letters is a helpful organizational tool.

Explain the Principle

❝ The letters in the alphabet are in a special order. ❞

plan

Explain the Principle

" **The letters in the alphabet are in a special order.** "

① Explain to the children that they are going to learn more about the alphabet.

② Using the Alphabet Linking Chart as a reference, invite children to sing the alphabet song: *A, B, C, D, E, F, G, H, I, J, K, L, M, N, O, P, Q, R, S, and T, U, V, W, X, Y, Z. Now I've said my ABCs. Tell me what you think of me.*

③ Suggested language: "You know lots of the letters on our chart. Today we're going to learn how to play the game of alphabetical order. Let's name some of these letters on the Alphabet Linking Chart." Point quickly to different letters and have children name them.

④ Show the class a Follow the Path Game Board that has the lowercase letters of the alphabet in the spaces in random order. Have children read the letters on the game board while you point to them. Suggested language: "The letters on our game are not in alphabetical order like the letters on our chart. When you have the whole alphabet, it is almost always in this order. It's called *alphabetical order.* You say that. [Children respond.] When you say the alphabet, you always say it in the same order. We're going to play this game to help us remember the letters in order."

⑤ Ask a volunteer to come up and play the game with you as your partner. Demonstrate how to throw the die (or draw a card) and advance the marker the appropriate number of spaces. Demonstrate saying the letter you land on. Suggested language: "When you land on a letter, say the name of the letter and tell the next two letters in the alphabet. Where could you look if you can't remember them? [Children suggest the Alphabet Linking Chart.] Your partner will have a small copy of the Alphabet Linking Chart. Your partner's job is to check to see whether you said the right letters."

6 Take a few turns until the children understand how to play. Explain that the person who reaches the end is the winner of the game.

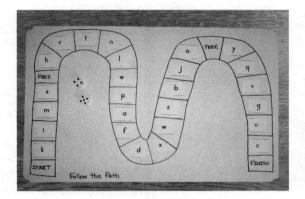

toss (or take)
move
say

► Working in partners, children play the Follow the Path game two times.

Suggest letters to children and have them say the next two letters without looking at the chart.

Link

Interactive Read-Aloud: Read aloud alphabet books (see the Alphabet Books Bibliography in *Teaching Resources*). Pause and ask children to predict the next letter. Examples are:

- ▸ *Tomorrow's Alphabet* by George Shannon
- ▸ *Animal Action ABC* by Karen Pandell

Shared Reading: Have children read the Alphabet Linking Chart in different ways: read consonants, read vowels, read pictures, read words in every other box, sing it, read the first box and clap or snap the next box, read it in reverse order (starting at the end), read letters with circles.

Guided Reading: During word work, place a magnetic letter on the whiteboard and ask children to tell what letter comes before or after it.

Interactive Writing: Use the Alphabet Linking Chart to locate and connect letters in the words children are writing.

Independent Writing: Encourage children to check the letters they write against the Alphabet Linking Chart.

assess

- ▸ Check children's knowledge by giving them a set of alphabet cards (*Teaching Resources,* Letter Cards) and asking them to put the letters in order.

Expand the Learning

Have children name the two letters that come *before* the one they land on.

Have children name the letter *before* and the letter *after* the one they land on.

If using cards to direct movement on the board, add directions like *Back Up, Extra Turn, Lose a Turn.* (You may need to include visual clues or first teach children what these cards mean.)

Use cards that say *Go to F* and so forth. Children have to find the letter, move to that space, and then tell the next letter in alphabetical order.

Make new game boards with different letter arrangements.

Use uppercase and lowercase letters on the board.

Connect with Home

Reproduce a Follow the Path game on heavy paper and send a copy of the game home with each child. Give each child a small numbered die made from a block or simple pieces of paper with the numbers 1, 2, 3, or directions *(Extra Turn, Miss a Turn)* written on them. Be sure children have played the game several times and know how to do it, but also give simple directions so that family members can read them.

24 Learning the Initials for Names

Name Chart

Consider Your Children

This lesson is best used after children have worked with the name chart (Lesson ELC 1) and name puzzles (Lesson LK 4) and can read and write their first and last names. They should also know most of the uppercase letters. This lesson will help them learn a new way letters are used and introduce them to the idea that letters followed by periods can represent larger units (as in abbreviations).

Working with English Language Learners

Like other children, English language learners will enjoy working with their initials as a unique way of expressing their names. This lesson will give them more practice saying the names of letters and noticing uppercase letters. As they locate their own initials by thinking about the first letter, they will be encouraged to think about the letter/sound connections. Give English language learners more practice locating their own and others' names using the initials (first letters).

You Need

► Name chart with children's names in one or two columns. Leave space to the right to match initials and names and/or to write initials.

► Cards containing children's initials, a separate card for each set of initials. (You can use the Word Card Template in *Teaching Resources*.)

► Writing materials.

Understand the Principle

Children need to learn that there are special conventions in written language.

Names can be represented by initials.

Explain the Principle

❝ Your initials are the first letters of your first name and your last name. ❞

❝ You use capital letters to write your initials. ❞

plan

teach

Our Names	Our Initials
Andy Harper	A.H.
Cecilia Steranga	C.S.
Charley Myers	C.M.
Clifford Johnson	C.J.
David Carter	D.C.
Douglas Heath	D.H.
Faeria Brooks	F.B.
Forest MacIntire	F.M.
Janet Gaffney	J.G.
Javon McKenzie	J.M.
Julia Shannon	J.S.
Mary Dunn	M.D.
Mary O'Donnell	M.O.
Nora Robert	N.R.
Olie Polanski	O.P.
Quanisha Banks	Q.B.
Ron Melhado	R.M.
Sandy Wallach	S.W.
William Banks	W.B.
Zoe Williamson	Z.W.

Explain the Principle

❝ Your initials are the first letters of your first name and your last name. ❞

❝ You use capital letters to write your initials. ❞

① Explain to the children that today they are going to learn something special about using letters.

② Show children the name chart with their first and last names. Suggested language: "You can read and write your names. Today you are going to do something special with your names—writing your initials. Does anyone know what initials are?"

③ Some children will know their initials, but they may not be able to describe exactly what initials are. Suggested language: "Initials are a short form of your name. Instead of writing your whole name, you just write the first letter of your first name and the first letter of your last name. Watch while I write Andy's initials. [Use a whiteboard to demonstrate.] What else do you notice? [Children may say or you can point out that there is a period after each letter.] Yes! We can use periods to show that initials stand for a whole name."

④ Suggested language: "Andy's first name starts with . . . ? [Children respond.] An *A*. So I'm going to write an uppercase *A* here. [Write a capital letter large enough for all children to see.] His last name is Harper, which begins with . . . ? [Children respond.] An *H*. So I'm going to write an uppercase *H* here. [Show the children the initials.] These are Andy's initials—*A. H.* What do you notice?"

⑤ Model and encourage comments like these:

"They are the same letters as at the beginning of his name."

"They are *A* and *H*."

"They are uppercase letters."

"They have periods after them."

⑥ Demonstrate with one or two more sets of initials so that children get the idea.

⑦ Invite each child to come up and find the initials that match his or her name. (The initials are on cards, which may be placed on the chart using Velcro® or double-sided tape. Or you can do this activity using the pocket chart.)

⑧ Tell the children to look for the first letter and then for the next letter. Each time, you can ask children in the class to think of what letter the individual is looking for. The activity will become easier and faster as more initials are eliminated.

write
draw
write

▸ Have the children take a blank piece of paper, write their whole name, draw a picture of themselves, and write their initials.

▸ Then have the children draw pictures of several of their friends, writing the appropriate initials under each.

Have children share their illustrations and initials.

Alternatively, play a mystery game: "I'm thinking of someone whose initials are J. G. Who is it?" Encourage children to find the name quickly.

Link

Interactive Read-Aloud: Read aloud books that have children's names in them, such as:

▶ *Miss Bindergarten Celebrates the 100th Day of Kindergarten* by Joseph Slate

▶ *My Son John* by Jim Aylesworth

Shared Reading: Read the class name chart and initials—top to bottom, bottom to top, every other name.

Guided Reading: Notice any initials that appear in the stories children read, such as D. W. in the Arthur series by Marc Brown.

Interactive Writing: When writing a story with the class, try using someone's initials instead of the name and having children guess who the person is.

Independent Writing: Let children put their initials instead of their name on a paper. During sharing time, hold up the paper and ask the class who wrote it.

assess

▶ Check the children's writing to be sure they understand the concept of initials, using uppercase letters with periods to represent people's names.

Expand the Learning

Have all the initials on cards. Then have children, working alone or with partners, match all the initials with the names on the pocket chart, saying the letter names as they put the initial card over the appropriate name.

Connect with Home

Have children identify and write the initials of their family members and friends and bring them back to school to share.

Have children draw pictures of their family members and glue each person's initials (using alphabet pasta or alphabet cereal) above or below his or her picture.

Letter/Sound Relationships

The sounds of oral language are related in both simple and complex ways to the twenty-six letters of the alphabet. Learning the connections between letters and sounds is basic to understanding written language. Children first learn simple relationships that are regular in that one phoneme is connected to one grapheme, or letter. But sounds are also connected to letter clusters, which are groups of letters that appear often together (for example, *cr, str, ch, st, bl, fr*) and in which you hear each of the associated sounds of the letters; and to consonant digraphs *(sh, ch)*, in which you hear only one sound. Vowels may also appear in combinations *(ea, oa)*, in which you usually hear the first vowel *(ai)* or you hear a completely different sound *(ou)*. Children learn to look for and recognize these letter combinations as units, which makes their word solving more efficient. It is important to remember that children will be able to hear and connect the easy-to-identify consonants and vowels early and progress to the harder-to-hear and more difficult letter/sound relationships—for example, letter clusters with two and three letters and those with more than one sound. You will want to connect initial letter sounds to the Alphabet Linking Chart (see *Teaching Resources*). It is not necessary to teach every letter as a separate lesson. When using the children's names to teach about words, substitute *name* for *word* when explaining the principle.

Connect to Assessment

See related LS Assessment Tasks in the Assessment Guide in *Teaching Resources:*

- ► Matching Consonant Letters and Sounds at the Beginning of Words

- ► Matching Consonant Letters and Sounds at the End of Words

- ► Hearing Sounds in Words and Writing Letters

Develop Your Professional Understanding

See *Word Matters: Teaching Phonics and Spelling in the Reading/Writing Classroom* by G.S. Pinnell and I.C. Fountas. 1998. Portsmouth, New Hampshire: Heinemann.

Related pages: 46–48, 71–72, 72–73, 90–93, 123, 141.

Beginning Consonant Letters and Sounds

Pocket Chart Match

Consider Your Children

This lesson is best used after children can name most letters of the alphabet and have demonstrated that they are able to hear sounds in words, match pictures by sounds, and understand the concept of matching letters and sounds. You can use any of the picture cards for beginning consonant sounds. Select first consonants that you think most children know or "nearly know."

Working with English Language Learners

Be sure that children say and understand the name for each picture. Have them say the words rather than just listening to your pronunciation. Demonstrate saying the names of the letters and matching letters with the picture cards. Begin with a small set of letters that are easy to hear and then repeat the lesson, gradually increasing the number of sounds and letters children will match. Demonstrate the application task using the Two-Way Sort Sheet; you may want to work with a small group to be sure they understand the task.

You Need

► Pocket chart.

From *Teaching Resources:*

► Picture Cards, Beginning Consonants. Some examples of picture cards to start with are *ball, banana, candle, football, girl, helicopter, log, muffin, quilt, tiger,* and *zebra.* Enlarge some cards to use in your demonstration.

► Letter cards for the entire alphabet, several of each letter. You can use cards with uppercase letters, both uppercase and lowercase letters, or lowercase letters.

► Two-Way Sort Sheets.

Understand the Principle

Connecting the initial sound of a word with a letter helps children begin to use the alphabet to solve words while reading.

Once children can identify initial sounds and connect letters to them, they can use this information to monitor their reading and distinguish between words.

Children can check letter/sound information with their sense of meaning and language structure as they read.

Explain the Principle

" You can hear the sound at the beginning of a word. "

" You can match letters and sounds at the beginning of a word. "

CONTINUUM: LETTER/SOUND RELATIONSHIPS — RECOGNIZING AND USING BEGINNING CONSONANT SOUNDS AND THE LETTERS THAT REPRESENT THEM

plan

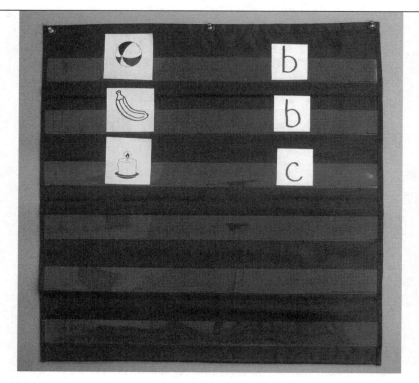

Explain the Principle

" **You can hear the sound at the beginning of a word.** "

" **You can match letters and sounds at the beginning of a word.** "

① Explain to the children that they are going to learn more about letters and their sounds.

② Suggested language: "Today we are going to match sounds and the first letters of words. Let's say the names of the pictures in the pocket chart and listen for the first sound of the word." Invite children to say the name of each picture.

③ Suggested language: "I'm going to take a Letter Card from this stack and see if I can match it to the pictures on my chart."

④ Hold up the first letter card. Suggested language: "I can see that this is *b*. Now I'm going to see if there is a picture in the chart that has the sound of /b/ at the beginning. Can anyone see something that starts with a *b*?" Provide an example of a *b* word if necessary; wait for children to respond.

⑤ Match *b* with *ball* and place the *b* next to the picture.

⑥ Draw cards one at a time, saying the letter and matching it with a picture each time. (If a letter doesn't match anything on the chart, return it to the bottom of the pile.) Continue until all pictures have a matching letter.

⑦ Show the children a Two-Way Sort Sheet with a key picture on the left and a letter card that matches the initial letter of the picture's name on the right.

LS 1
LETTER/SOUND RELATIONSHIPS

cut
glue
find
match

▶ Give the children (1) a group of selected picture cards whose names have different beginning consonants and (2) a Two-Way Sort Sheet with a key picture and a letter as an example at the top.

▶ Have the children cut apart the sheets of pictures and letters. They glue a picture on the left of the Two-Way Sort Sheet, find the corresponding initial letter for the picture's name, and glue it on the right.

Ask the children to tell about some of the first letters and names they matched.

Link

Interactive Read-Aloud: Read aloud stories that emphasize words that begin with the same sound. (See the Alliteration Bibliography in *Teaching Resources* for suggestions.) Two additional examples are:

- ► *In the Small, Small Pond* by Denise Fleming
- ► *A Summery Saturday Morning* by Margaret Mahy

Shared Reading: When rereading familiar texts such as "Three Blind Mice" or "Snail, Snail" (see *Sing a Song of Poetry*), mask the first letter of a word. Ask children to read up to the word and predict the first letter by thinking about the sound.

Guided Reading: Teach children to say the first sound when they come to an unknown word. This will help them think of a word that starts with that letter and makes sense in the story.

Interactive Writing: Before writing a word, have children say it slowly and think about what the first letter is likely to be.

Independent Writing: When they are writing, encourage children to say words slowly and to write the first letter. Accept approximations that represent good sound analysis (for example, *cit* for *kite*).

assess

- ► Observe whether the children are able to generate the first letters of words during writing.
- ► Notice whether the children can say the first sound of a word while reading.
- ► Check whether the children can use the first letter/sound of a word to monitor and check their reading.

- ► Place picture cards in the pocket chart and ask individual children to match letters.

Expand the Learning

Repeat the lesson with other pictures and letters.

Repeat the lesson with more difficult consonant sounds (for example, *w, y,* or *q*).

Connect with Home

Make reproducible pictures and letters that children can take home, cut apart, and match.

Have family members play "I Say, You Say." The caregiver says a word that begins with a certain letter (for example, "I say dish") and then the child says one that begins with the same letter ("I say dog"). They do this with several letters.

Connecting Beginning Sounds and Letters

Picture-Word Match

Consider Your Children

You will want to use this lesson with just two or three consonants at first: *s, m, t,* and *b* are the easiest to distinguish. Then continue with three or four other consonants at a time *(f, r, n, p, d, h, c, g, j, l, k, v, w, z, q, y)*.

Working with English Language Learners

By the time you use this lesson with English language learners, they should be familiar with a large group of picture cards. Use only those for which they know and understand the labels. Avoid concepts that are too far beyond their experience. They should also be able to say the words, identify the initial sound, and recognize the corresponding letter. Work with a small group as needed to be sure that they understand the task and are checking their work by saying the words.

You Need

▸ Pocket chart or easel.

From *Teaching Resources:*

▸ Picture Cards, Beginning Consonants.

▸ Word cards (use the Word Card Template for the items in the selected picture cards).

▸ Enlarged pictures from the Alphabet Linking Chart.

▸ Three-Way Sort Cards.

▸ Three-Way Sort Sheets.

Understand the Principle

Connecting individual letters with the sounds they represent allows children to begin to take words apart.

While there is not a one-to-one relationship between the letters and sounds in English, there are many words with regular letter/sound relationships. Exploring simple letter/sound matches will help children begin to search for them in all words.

Explain the Principle

❝ You can hear the sound at the beginning of a word. ❞

❝ You can match letters and sounds at the beginning of a word. ❞

❝ You can find a word by saying it and thinking about the first sound. ❞

CONTINUUM: LETTER/SOUND RELATIONSHIPS — RECOGNIZING AND USING BEGINNING CONSONANT SOUNDS AND THE LETTERS THAT REPRESENT THEM

313

plan

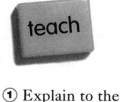

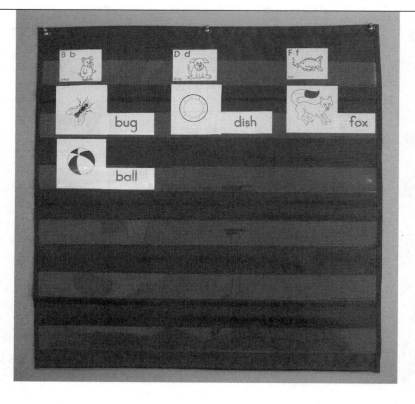

Explain the Principle

" You can hear the sound at the beginning of a word. "

" You can match letters and sounds at the beginning of a word. "

" You can find a word by saying it and thinking about the first sound. "

① Explain to the children that they are going to learn more about letters and their sounds at the beginning of words.

② Place key picture cards cut from the Alphabet Linking Chart at the top of three or four columns (in a pocket chart or on an easel or whiteboard).

③ Ask children to say the word (for example, *bear*) and think about the first sound.

④ Then ask them to tell the letter that would come first *(b)*.

⑤ Ask children to think of another word beginning with that letter (e.g., *bug*). Have children place the picture of a bug under the *Bb Bear* heading and place the word *bug* next to it.

⑥ Repeat with other words beginning with consonants that correspond to the key picture cards.

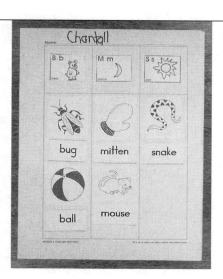

take
sort
read
write

▶ Have children sort pictures and words using a Three-Way Sort Card, placing each picture and word under the appropriate key picture.

▶ Then have them read each column with a partner.

▶ Finally, have them copy the words on a Three-Way Sort Sheet.

Have children read their Three-Way Sort Sheets to a new partner.

Have two or three children share with the group what they have noticed about letters and sounds.

Link

Interactive Read-Aloud: Read aloud books that emphasize the beginning sounds in words. (See the Alliteration Bibliography in *Teaching Resources* for additional suggestions.) Examples are:

▶ *Six Sandy Sheep* by Judith Ross Enderle and Stephanie Gordon Tessler

▶ *The Worryworts* by Pamela Duncan Edwards

Shared Reading: On the first reading of a text, cover the last part of some words, leaving only the first letter in view. Invite the children to predict the word using the first letter. Uncover the whole word to confirm their prediction.

Guided Reading: When children come to an unknown word, prompt them to say the sound of the first letter and think what word would make sense.

Interactive Writing: When children want to write the next word in a sentence, ask them to say the word and think about the first sound.

Independent Writing: Remind children to say a word and write the letter associated with the first sound.

Expand the Learning

Repeat the lesson with other groups of consonants and other pictures and words. (Select pictures from Picture Cards, Beginning Consonants, in *Teaching Resources*.)

Connect with Home

Send home sheets of pictures and words for children to cut out and match.

assess

▶ Observe the children to determine how well they are connecting initial letters and sounds. Have children who seem confused match the pictures and letters individually as you observe which ones cause them confusion.

▶ Give the children a sheet with pictures and letters and have them draw lines to match them.

Beginning Consonant Letters and Sounds

Picture Sort

Consider Your Children

This lesson is best used after children can name most letters of the alphabet and have demonstrated that they are able to hear sounds in words, match pictures by sounds, and understand the concept of matching letters and sounds. Learning letters and sounds together will accelerate learning letter/sound relationships and allow children to apply that knowledge to solving words. Children who are very proficient at identifying first letters and sounds will not need this lesson.

Working with English Language Learners

For this lesson, children will need to identify the objects in pictures and associate them with letters representing first letters. It will help your English language learners if you select pictures that they have worked with before and for which they know the names. Be sure that they understand the procedures for the Three-Way Sort Sheet. You may need to do an extra demonstration for a small group to be sure that they can perform the application task independently. Recognize and accept answers that show they are using names in their own language and categorizing them, for example, *luna* (moon) under *L*.

You Need

► Pocket charts with a row of letter cards (large and small). Select letters that children know or "nearly know." Start with three or four letters: *Bb, Mm, Pp,* for example.

From *Teaching Resources:*

► Picture Cards, Beginning Consonants, whose names have initial sounds that match the letters on the chart: *book, bear, bed; mouse, mask, mitten, moon, motorcycle; pizza, pumpkin, piano, pig, pillow.* Mix in a few that do not match the letters in the chart: *rake, watch, zipper, ladder.*

► Letter Cards.

► Three-Way Sort Sheets.

Understand the Principle

Connecting an initial letter with its sound helps children begin to decode words in reading.

Once children can identify first letters and generate the sounds associated with them, they can use this information to monitor their reading and to distinguish between words.

Children can check letter/sound information with their sense of meaning and language structure as they read.

Explain the Principle

❝ You can hear the sound at the beginning of a word. ❞

❝ You can match letters and sounds at the beginning of a word. ❞

CONTINUUM: LETTER/SOUND RELATIONSHIPS — RECOGNIZING AND USING BEGINNING CONSONANT SOUNDS AND THE LETTERS THAT REPRESENT THEM

317

plan

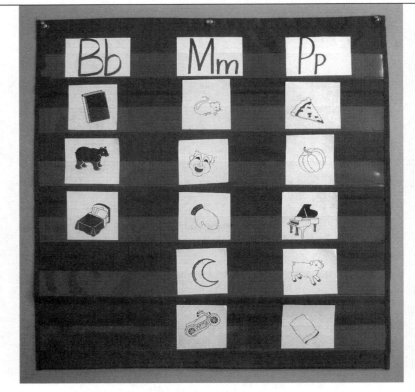

Explain the Principle

66 **You can hear the sound at the beginning of a word.** 99

66 **You can match letters and sounds at the beginning of a word.** 99

① Explain to the children that they're going to learn more about letters and sounds.

② Suggested language: "Today we are going to work with letters and pictures of things that have names that start with the same sound. Let's say the names of the letters in the pocket chart."

③ Ask children to think of a word, perhaps from the word wall, the Alphabet Linking Chart, or the name chart, that starts with that letter.

④ Suggested language: "I'm going to take a picture card from this stack and see if I can match it to any of the letters."

⑤ Hold up the first picture card. Suggested language: "This is a pizza. Say *pizza*. [Children respond.] Say the first sound of *pizza*. [Children respond.] What is the first sound of *pizza?* [Children respond.]"

⑥ Model checking /p/, *pizza, p*.

⑦ Take picture cards one at a time, showing how to say the sound, the word, and the letter. Some picture names will not match a letter on the chart and will be placed face down at the bottom of the pile. Continue until all pictures with names that match letters have been placed on the chart.

apply

take
sort
read
check

▶ Give the children a Three-Way Sort Sheet with key letters in the top spots. They will also need selected picture cards, including some with names that match the key letters and some that don't. One child takes the cards, sorts them, and then reads them while her partner watches and checks the completed sort. Then they mix the cards up and switch roles.

share

Ask children what pictures they have matched with letters. Invite them to give one more word for each letter in the chart.

Link

Interactive Read-Aloud: Read aloud stories that emphasize beginning sounds. (See the Alliteration Bibliography in *Teaching Resources* for suggestions.) Examples are:

▶ ***The Accidental Zucchini: An Unexpected Alphabet*** by Max Grover

▶ ***The Wacky Wedding*** by Pamela Duncan Edwards

Shared Reading: When rereading familiar texts, such as "This Is the Way We Wash Our Face" (see *Sing a Song of Poetry*), cover the first letter of a word. Ask children to read up to the word and predict the first letter by thinking about the sound.

Guided Reading: Encourage children to try unfamiliar words by reading up to the new word and saying the sound of the first letter: "I like to eat /p/ancakes."

Interactive Writing: When thinking how to write a word, have children say it slowly and decide what the first letter is likely to be.

Independent Writing: Encourage children to say words slowly when they are writing and to write the first letter.

assess

▶ Notice whether the children are able to write the first letters of words.

▶ Observe whether the children say the first sound of a word while reading.

▶ Notice whether the children use the first letter/sound of a word to monitor and check on their reading.

▶ Place letter cards in the pocket chart and ask individual children to match a limited set of pictures quickly.

Expand the Learning

Extend the activity by increasing the number and variety of letters.

Mix children's names and high frequency word cards (*Teaching Resources,* High Frequency Words) into the picture card set so that they are matching both pictures and words with the letters.

Connect with Home

Reproduce picture cards and letters (*Teaching Resources,* Picture Cards, Beginning Consonants, and Letter Cards) that children can take home, cut apart, and match.

Have family members make letter posters with the children. They write a letter at the top of a sheet and draw (or cut out from a magazine) pictures of objects whose names start with that letter. Have them check the beginning sound of the name with the first letter.

Beginning Consonant Letters and Sounds

Picture Lotto

Consider Your Children

Use this lesson after children can name most letters of the alphabet and have demonstrated that they are able to hear sounds in words, match pictures by sounds, and understand the concept of matching letters and sounds. The directions below assume that children already know how to play Lotto (see the directions in *Teaching Resources*). To play, you need to place one card in each square until all the squares are filled.

Working with English Language Learners

The children may be only beginning to notice letters and sounds, and they may be doing so in both their own languages and English. If you can, provide some examples of words that begin the same in their languages. Repeat the English words many times, using pictures and explanations, so that the words become meaningful to them. Eliminate words that are meaningless. Even though the children will be matching sounds, their learning will be limited if they are not working with words they understand. Do a quick check to be sure that children know all the names for the pictures in the Picture Lotto game.

You Need

▸ Pocket chart.

From *Teaching Resources:*

▸ Letter cards. You can use cards with uppercase letters, both uppercase and lowercase letters, or lowercase letters.

▸ Lotto Game Cards in four different colors.

▸ Picture Cards, Beginning Consonants.

Understand the Principle

Children do not need to know all letters of the alphabet before reading stories, but knowing letters and their relationship to sounds in words is valuable information as they read their first storybooks.

Once children can identify first sounds and connect letters to them, they can use this information to connect letters and sounds and distinguish between words.

Explain the Principle

" You can match letters and sounds at the beginning of a word. "

" When you see a letter at the beginning of a word, you can make its sound. "

" When you know the sound, you can find the letter. "

CONTINUUM: LETTER/SOUND RELATIONSHIPS — RECOGNIZING AND USING BEGINNING CONSONANT SOUNDS AND THE LETTERS THAT REPRESENT THEM

plan

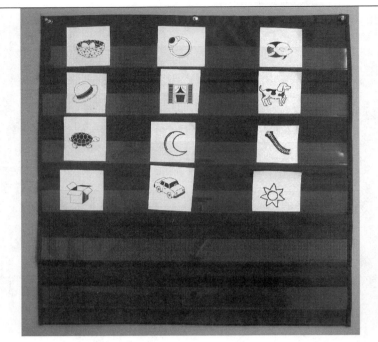

Explain the Principle

" You can match letters and sounds at the beginning of a word. "

" When you see a letter at the beginning of a word, you can make its sound. "

" When you know the sound, you can find the letter. "

① Tell the children they are going to learn more about letters and sounds.

② Using the pocket chart, place picture cards in a rectangular pattern.

③ Suggested language: "Today we are going to play Picture Lotto. Remember that you take turns drawing a card and matching it to the pictures on your game card. This time we are going to use cards that have letters on them. Let's say the names of each of the pictures and listen for the first sound of the word." Have children say the names of each picture.

④ "I'm going to take a letter card from this stack and see if I can match it to the pictures on my game card."

⑤ Hold up the first letter card. Suggested language: "I can see that this is *t*. Now I'm going to see if there is a picture on my game card that has the sound of /t/ at the beginning. Can anyone see something that starts with a /t/?" Provide an example of a *t* word if necessary; children respond.

⑥ Model checking *t, turtle* and place the *t* card on the picture of the turtle.

⑦ Take cards one at a time, showing how to say the letter and the label of the picture. Some letters will not match anything on the card and will be placed face down again.

⑧ Suggested language: "I've covered all the spaces on my game card. That's what you do to win the Picture Lotto game. Remember to say the letter and the name of the picture to check your matches. If you are not sure, you can look at the Alphabet Linking Chart."

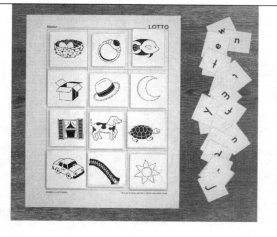

take
say
match

► Have children play the Picture Lotto game in groups of three or four at a time, each with a different-color card. They take turns taking a letter card and saying the name of the picture that matches it. If there is a match, they place the letter card on the picture in the square. If there is no match, the card is returned to the bottom of the card pile. The game continues until one child fills her card.

Ask children to share some of the first letters and pictures they matched while playing the Picture Lotto game.

Link

Interactive Read-Aloud: Read aloud stories that draw attention to beginning letters and sounds. Examples are:

► *Watch William Walk* by Ann Jonas

► *Some Smug Slug* by Pamela Duncan Edwards

Shared Reading: When rereading familiar texts, such as "Two Little Blackbirds" (see *Sing a Song of Poetry*), cover the first letter of a word with a stick-on note. Ask children to read up to the word and predict the first letter by thinking about the sound.

Guided Reading: When children are trying to figure out new words, prompt them to go back to the beginning of the sentence, read up to the word, and get their mouths ready to say the first sound.

Interactive Writing: When thinking how to write a word, have children say it slowly and think about what the first letter is likely to be.

Independent Writing: Encourage children to say words slowly when they are writing and to write the first letter.

assess

► Observe whether the children are able to generate beginning letters of words when they are writing.

► Notice whether the children can say the first sound of a word while reading.

► Notice whether the children can use the first letter/sound of a word to monitor and check their reading.

► Place picture cards in the pocket chart and ask children to match letters.

Expand the Learning

Extend the Picture Lotto game by varying the pictures. Start with pictures that represent simple initial sounds, such as those suggested in this minilesson, but gradually increase the complexity of the game and/or eliminate the easy-to-match sounds.

Connect with Home

Have family members make an alphabet book of objects from their home. Send home twenty-six plain pieces of paper stapled together. Caregivers write one uppercase and the matching lowercase letter at the bottom of each page—*Aa, Bb,* etc. (You can also duplicate letters and assemble these books yourself.) With the child, they identify an object in the home for each letter. The child draws the object on the appropriate page and the family member writes the word (for example, *table* for *t, lamp* for *l, pillow* for *p,* and *refrigerator* for *r*).

Beginning Consonant Letters and Sounds

Finding Words in Print

Consider Your Children

Use this lesson after children can recognize some beginning sounds in words and connect them to letters of the alphabet. They should have had some experience writing words in interactive writing and should also understand the concept of "first" as it applies to words. The overall expectation is that children will be able to notice and locate words and first letters that are embedded in text.

Working with English Language Learners

Go over the poem in an enjoyable way many times until English language learners know it and can say it with little support. Point to the words as you have them read it; if they know the poem well, you may want to support individual children in pointing to the words. Talk about the meaning of the words in the poem— for example, *jelly* and *plate*—so that you are sure students know the individual words and what they mean. Invite them to share their own experiences and make connections to the poem. Once the poem is well known, the words will be more available to students and you can have them locate words, match letters, and so on.

You Need

▶ Chart with an alliterative poem, rhyme, song, or chant, such as "Jelly on the Plate."

▶ Duplicated versions of the poem, rhyme, song, or chant.

▶ Highlighter tape.

▶ Highlighter pen.

▶ Clipboards and paper.

Understand the Principle

Connecting the first sound of a word with a letter helps children begin to use the alphabetic system to solve words in reading.

Once children can identify first sounds and connect letters to them, they can use this information to monitor their reading and to distinguish between words.

Children can cross-check letter/sound information with their sense of meaning and language structure as they read.

Explain the Principle

" You can match letters and sounds at the beginning of a word. "

" When you see a letter at the beginning of a word, you can make its sound. "

" When you know the sound, you can find the letter. "

" You can find a word by saying it and thinking about the first sound. "

CONTINUUM: LETTER/SOUND RELATIONSHIPS — RECOGNIZING AND USING BEGINNING CONSONANT SOUNDS AND THE LETTERS THAT REPRESENT THEM

325

plan

teach

Explain the Principle

" You can match letters and sounds at the beginning of a word. "

" When you see a letter at the beginning of a word, you can make its sound. "

" When you know the sound, you can find the letter. "

" You can find a word by saying it and thinking about the first sound. "

① Explain to the children that they are going to learn about letters and their sounds.

② Have the children read the rhyme or song several times and enjoy it.

③ Suggested language: "I see a word in this rhyme that starts with *p*. Can you find it?" [Children will come up with *plate*, *pudding*, *pan*, and *pot*.]

④ Write and say the *p* words on another piece of paper or a whiteboard. Suggested language: "Let's read the words: *plate*, *pudding*, *pan*, *pot*. These are all words that start with *p*."

⑤ Have several children, using a masking card or highlighter tape, locate the words in the text that start with *p*. Read the text again to discover what they are. At this point, children probably will not know how to discriminate between *pan* and *pot* and that is not important. They will be able to read the words because they're learning them in the rhyme. In later readings, you can draw their attention to the last sound and letter as a way of distinguishing the two words.

⑥ Suggested language: "Can you think of any other words that start with *p*?" Children can draw from their experience, from the class name chart, or from the word wall. Add the words to the list. Display the list beside the rhyme.

⑦ Help children notice the *p* at the beginning of each word.

⑧ Review the directional movements needed to make a *p*.

Jelly on the Plate

Jelly on the plate.
Jelly on the plate.
Wibble wobble,
Wibble, wobble,
Jelly on the plate.

Pudding in the pan.
Pudding in the pan.
Ooey, gooey,
Ooey, gooey,
Pudding in the pan.

Soup in the pot.
Soup in the pot.
Bubble, bubble,
Bubble, bubble,
Soup in the pot.

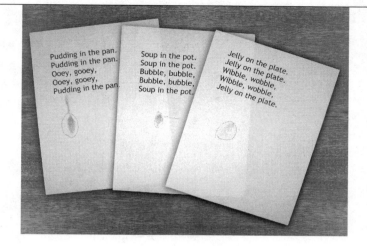

apply

▶ Give the children duplicated versions of the poem or rhyme. Consider separate pages for each verse. (*Sing a Song of Poetry* contains many appropriate rhymes, such as "Pease Porridge," "Peter Piper," and "The Pumpkin Eater.") The children can read it, illustrate it, and highlight or circle the *p*'s at the beginning of words.

share

Have the children read the rhyme together again as a group, and ask individuals to come up and identify words that start with *p*.

Link

Interactive Read-Aloud: Read aloud stories that feature words that have the same first letters and sounds. Point out that *k* and *c* often have the same sound, as in *kangaroo* and *cricket*. Examples are:

- ▸ **Kangaroo and Cricket** by Lorianne Siomades
- ▸ **Goblins in Green** by Nicholas Heller

Shared Reading: When rereading familiar texts, ask the children to locate words in the text by saying the words and thinking about the first sound and first letter.

Guided Reading: After enjoying and discussing a story, tell the children to turn to a particular page. Tell them to find and put their finger under a particular word. Choose words that start with a letter children need work on.

Interactive Writing: When they are thinking how to write a word, have the children say it slowly and think about what the first letter is likely to be. Connect it with other words that start the same and locate those words on the word wall.

Independent Writing: When children want to write a word, encourage them to say it slowly and write the first letter. Make connections to other words they know that start the same.

assess

- ▸ Notice whether the children are able to categorize words by beginning sound and letter.
- ▸ Observe whether the children can locate words in the text by saying the word and predicting the first letter.
- ▸ Notice whether the children are representing first letters in words they try to write in stories.

Expand the Learning

Repeat the activity with other rhymes or songs (see *Sing a Song of Poetry*), locating other words that begin with the same letter and sound.

Have children take a clipboard, go around the room looking for words that start with a particular letter, and copy the words on a piece of paper.

Connect with Home

Send home copies of simple poems or songs. (See *Sing a Song of Poetry* for poems in the public domain.) Explain to family members how to point under each word with a pencil or chopstick as they read the text so children will be looking in the right place. Then caregivers can have children point under words that begin with a particular letter.

Learning Letters and Beginning Sounds

Class Alphabet Book

Consider Your Children

Before you select this lesson, be sure children know what letters are, know the names of some letters and some associated sounds, and have worked with letters in simple ways. This lesson will be effective in helping children bring together their growing knowledge of letters and sounds so that they have a concept of the entire set of the twenty-six letters that make up the alphabet.

Working with English Language Learners

This lesson will help children systematize their knowledge of letters and associated key words that represent sounds. It is especially important for English language learners to acquire these key words that they can use as resources when they are working with new words. Be sure that the children understand the names for the pictures you are using for the class alphabet books. Have them talk about and use the names of the familiar objects that will be represented on the pages. Reread the book several times so that they can say the names of the objects on each page, noticing the first sounds and saying the name of each letter.

You Need

▶ Twenty-seven large pieces of folded craft paper or large pieces of tag stapled as a book or held together by rings (the first page is the cover).

▶ Disposable or other kind of camera (optional).

▶ Small alphabet books for every student (twenty-seven stapled blank book pages—the first page is the cover) with a picture from the Alphabet Linking Chart in the corner of each page.

From *Teaching Resources:*

▶ Alphabet Linking Chart, enlarged and cut up into squares.

▶ Blank Book Page Template (to make the student alphabet books).

Understand the Principle

Beginning readers need to recognize that the first letter of a word is on the left and is connected to a sound that they can say.

Once this concept is established, children notice the first letter and start to say the word, which is the beginning of learning to decode.

Explain the Principle

❝ You can match letters and sounds at the beginning of a word. ❞

CONTINUUM: LETTER/SOUND RELATIONSHIPS — RECOGNIZING AND USING BEGINNING CONSONANT AND VOWEL SOUNDS AND THE LETTERS THAT REPRESENT THEM

329

plan

Explain the Principle

❝ You can match letters and sounds at the beginning of a word. ❞

① Tell the children they are going to learn more about letters and sounds and will make a class alphabet book together.

② Read the Alphabet Linking Chart with the children several different ways: point and read *A–a–apple, B–b–bear*, etc.; read the lowercase letters only; read the uppercase letters only; read the consonants; read the vowels; read the pictures only.

③ Explain that they will spend a few days making a class alphabet book to show letters and their sounds. Begin with *a*. Staple the *a* square from the enlarged chart to the corner of the first page in your large model book. Read *A–a–apple*. Continue with the other letters.

④ Over a period of several days, with children's input, come up with names of objects in the school that you can photograph (or draw) that begin with the sound of each alphabet letter—an ant, a ball, a cap, etc.

⑤ Take a walk and photograph the objects, or have the children help draw them. As an alternative, you could use enlarged picture cards.

⑥ Glue the developed photos (or the drawings or cards) on the appropriate pages of your large class alphabet book.

⑦ Each day, read together the pages completed so far to review words with the same beginning sound.

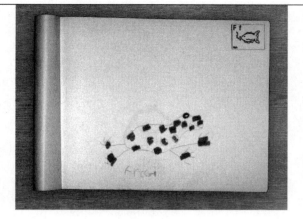

make
draw
write

▶ Have the children make their own alphabet books, drawing a minimum of three pictures for each page (or gluing picture cards and coloring them). Then they can write any letters for sounds that they know. It will take them several days.

Read the class alphabet book together.

Have the children read their completed alphabet book to a partner.

Link

Interactive Read-Aloud: Read aloud a variety of alphabet books (see the Alphabet Books Bibliography in *Teaching Resources*). Particularly good ones are:

- ▸ *Occupational Alphabet* by fifth graders at Holly Spring Elementary School
- ▸ *Ogres, Ogres, Ogres* by Nicholas Heller

Shared Reading: Read an alphabet poem together. Read big book versions of alphabet books.

Guided Reading: During word work, have children sort one particular letter from a set of magnetic letters. Then have them tell a word that begins with the letter.

Interactive Writing: When you write a word on the chart, encourage the children to say the word slowly and tell the sound and name of the first letter.

Independent Writing: Model how to say a word and write the first letter. Encourage the children to do this for themselves as they write words.

assess

- ▸ Observe the children's ability to write the first letter of words in independent writing.
- ▸ Ask particular students to give a word that starts with each letter of the alphabet.

Expand the Learning

Create other class alphabet books based on a theme: foods, animals, clothing, etc.

Connect with Home

Have children take home blank stapled books (twenty-seven sheets) and copies of the Alphabet Linking Chart to cut up. Have them make alphabet books with family members.

Learning Letter Names and Sounds

ABC Board

Consider Your Children

Use this lesson after children have learned to distinguish letters by their features, can recognize and name most letters, and can match words by beginning sounds. This lesson will help them systematize and summarize their knowledge because it includes the full set of letters and sounds. For some groups of children, you may want to show all the objects and review their names to build vocabulary prior to the lesson.

Working with English Language Learners

You may want to center this lesson on a "theme"—for example, using food words for every letter of the alphabet. This approach will help children widen their English vocabularies and learn words that are related to one another by meaning. In addition, it will give them experience relating letters and sounds, and it focuses on concrete objects. Be sure that you introduce the objects in the bags to children so that they know the English labels for them before they begin the activity. Alternatively, work with a small group so that when they encounter an object, you can give them the label and have them repeat it.

You Need

▶ Bulletin board with an area for each letter of the alphabet.

▶ Grab bags for every letter of the alphabet filled with small objects (or pictures of objects) that begin with that letter.

▶ An 8½" × 11" sheet of heavy paper for each letter of the alphabet; the letter should be lightly drawn and cover the full sheet.

Understand the Principle

Words are made up of sequences of letters, and all letters have names.

The beginning letter of a word can be connected to a sound and has a name.

Explain the Principle

" You can match letters and sounds at the beginning of a word. "

CONTINUUM: LETTER/SOUND RELATIONSHIPS — RECOGNIZING AND USING BEGINNING CONSONANT AND VOWEL SOUNDS AND THE LETTERS THAT REPRESENT THEM

333

plan

teach

Explain the Principle

" You can match letters and sounds at the beginning of a word. "

① Explain to the children that they are going to learn more about letters and sounds at the beginning of words.

② Some teachers like to use a theme, such as food, for the pictures related to the letters of the alphabet. In this lesson, "inventions" are used: *animal crackers, buttons, cups, dice, envelopes, fans, glitter, hats, ice cream, jelly beans, Kleenex®, letters, markers, numbers, Oreos®, pencils, Q-tips®, rubber bands, stamps, toothbrush, Unifix cubes, valentines, whistles, x-ray, yarn, zippers.* Facsimiles (or picture cards) are used for many items—cutouts of jelly beans, ice cream cones, etc.

③ Show children the bulletin board with letters only. Suggested language: "We've been learning about [theme]. Today we will make an alphabet board to go with our work on [theme]." Or: "We've been learning about letters and their sounds. Today we are going to make an alphabet that will help us learn more."

④ Hand each child a sheet of heavy paper stock with a letter lightly drawn on it as a guide.

⑤ Ahead of time, prepare grab bags containing pictures or small objects whose names begin with each letter/sound. Suggested language: "I have one of these bags for every letter of the alphabet. How many do I have? [Children think about the number twenty-six.] I'm going to take one of these grab bags and open it. Watch what I do so that you will know what to do with your grab bag."

⑥ Demonstrate opening the bag and looking at the contents.

⑦ Take each object or picture and say the word associated with it. Have the children repeat the name.

⑧ Help the children think about the sound they hear at the beginning of each word and name the letter that represents the sound.

⑨ Show the children how to make a large letter the size of a piece of paper. They can use the letter you've already drawn lightly as a guide. Then show them how to trace the letter with glue and then how to stick on the objects or pictures in the shape of the letter.

⑩ When the project is dry, have each child hang his letter on the ABC wall in the area for the particular letter.

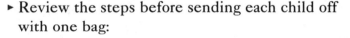

say
write
glue

▶ Review the steps before sending each child off with one bag:

Open the bag.

Say the name and first letter for each object or picture inside the bag.

Write the capital letter on your paper. (Fill the paper to make a big letter.)

Glue your objects on the line to make the shape of the letter.

Have each child share his letter, name the objects glued to it, and put the letter on the wall.

Link

Interactive Read-Aloud: Read aloud alphabet books (see the Alphabet Books Bibliography in *Teaching Resources*). Examples are:

- ▶ *Word Play ABC* by Heather Cahoon
- ▶ *Q Is for Duck* by Mary Elting and Michael Folsom

Shared Reading: Read or sing the alphabet linking chart to the tune of "A, You're Adorable."

Guided Reading: Prompt children to solve unfamiliar words by looking at the first letter, making its sound, and thinking what would make sense in the sentence.

Interactive Writing: Create labels for objects in the classroom, emphasizing saying the word and listening for the first sound.

Independent Writing: Encourage the children to record at least the first letter for every word they want to write. If appropriate, invite the children to write the first letter for objects in their pictures.

assess

- ▶ Notice whether the children are linking the first sounds of words to their names and other words.
- ▶ Show the children three to five pictures and have them tell the letter for the first sound.

Expand the Learning

Repeat the lesson with each child getting another grab bag so they work with different letters over time.

Increase the number of pictures/objects in the bags by asking children to bring in objects and pictures from home.

Connect with Home

Send the children home with a paper bag that has an initial consonant written on it, and have them work with family members to put in objects or pictures of objects whose names begin with the letter; have them bring the bag back to school.

Have the children find an object or a picture of an object at home for each letter of the alphabet.

Have the children find several objects or pictures of objects whose names start like their names.

Recognizing Beginning and Ending Consonant Sounds

Making Words

Consider Your Children

Use this lesson when children are able to identify and connect words by beginning sounds and letters. To make children more flexible in using their knowledge, focus on hearing dominant consonant sounds at both the beginning and the end of words and connecting them with letters. Children may also begin to notice the vowels. Select picture cards that represent easy three-letter words with easy-to-hear consonants.

Working with English Language Learners

This lesson will help English language learners become more flexible as they think about the sounds in words and look at words. Be sure that the pictures and words you use in this lesson are those that children have seen before and/or know the English labels for. Work with a small group if necessary to be sure that they understand the task of taking picture cards, saying the word matching the word and picture, and writing the word.

You Need

From *Teaching Resources:*

► Picture Cards, Beginning Consonants.

► Word cards (Word Card Template).

► List Sheets.

Understand the Principle

Recognizing and knowing the letter/sound relationships for beginning and ending consonants gives children strong visual information with which to check the accuracy of their reading as well as solve new words.

Becoming familiar with words that have regular letter/sound correspondence will help children learn this word-solving process.

Explain the Principle

" You can match letters and sounds at the beginning of a word. "

" You can find a word by saying it and thinking about the first sound. "

" You can find a word by saying it and thinking about the ending sound. "

CONTINUUM: LETTER/SOUND RELATIONSHIPS — RECOGNIZING AND USING BEGINNING AND ENDING CONSONANT SOUNDS
AND THE LETTERS THAT REPRESENT THEM

337

plan

Explain the Principle

" You can match letters and sounds at the beginning of a word. "

" You can find a word by saying it and thinking about the first sound. "

" You can find a word by saying it and thinking about the ending sound. "

① Tell the children they are going to learn more about sounds in words.

② Place three magnetic consonant letters (*b, s, m*, for example) at the top of a magnetic easel or whiteboard.

③ From a selected pile of picture cards (*bat, bike, sun, six, bus, mouse, mop*, for example), pick an object whose name begins with one of the selected consonant letters.

④ Ask the children to say the word, listen for the first sound, and tell the first letter.

⑤ Have a child place the picture under the correct letter.

⑥ Continue with the rest of the cards.

⑦ When all the cards have been placed, write the whole word each picture represents on a card and place it next to the appropriate picture. Have the children read the words with you. Have them check to be sure that the letter matches at the beginning of the word.

⑧ Repeat using different letters and pictures, and focus on ending sounds.

take
say
write

▸ Have the children take ten picture cards, one at a time.

▸ Each time they take a card, have them say the word and write the first consonant they hear on the list sheet. Notice the children's ability to give the correct first sound. The rest of the word may not be written conventionally.

Have the children tell where to place a few more picture cards on the easel or whiteboard used in the Teach section.

Link

Interactive Read-Aloud: Read aloud books that emphasize consonant sounds in words. Examples are:

- ▶ *Run, Jump, Whiz, Splash* by Vera Rosenberry
- ▶ *Bear's Busy Family* by Stella Blackstone

Shared Reading: After reading and enjoying a text such as "Papa's Glasses" or "My Little Sister" (see *Sing a Song of Poetry*), ask the children to say a word, tell the first letter, and highlight the word in the text. Repeat for ending sounds.

Guided Reading: During word work, make a few easy three-letter words on the easel and have children read them.

Interactive Writing: Invite the children to say words slowly and contribute first and last sounds in words you write together.

Independent Writing: Model saying words slowly and listening for the first and last sounds. Encourage the children to write first and last sounds in words they are trying to write.

assess

- ▶ Observe the children's growing ease with hearing first and last sounds. When they are building words fluently and easily, they are beginning to internalize the principle.
- ▶ Have the children quickly locate words in a shared reading text by noticing the beginning and ending sounds.

Expand the Learning

Repeat the lesson with other letters and pictures.

Increase the difficulty by using beginning consonant clusters (*spit,* for example) and introducing words with easy-to-hear long vowel sounds (*make,* for example). (See *Teaching Resources,* Picture Cards, Beginning Consonant Clusters and Digraphs and Long Vowels.)

Connect with Home

Send home sheets of picture cards and letter cards (see *Teaching Resources*). Have the children build each picture name using the letter cards or magnetic letters.

Spelling Patterns

Phonograms are spelling patterns that represent the sounds of *rimes* (last parts of words). They are sometimes called *word families.* You will not need to teach children the technical word *phonogram,* although you may want to use *pattern* or *word part.* A phonogram is the same as a rime, or ending of a word or syllable. We have included a large list of phonograms that will be useful to primary-age children in reading or writing, but you will not need to teach every phonogram separately. Once children understand that there are patterns and learn how to look for patterns, they will quickly discover more for themselves.

Another way to look at phonograms is to examine the way simple words and syllables are put together. Here we include the consonant-vowel-consonant (CVC) pattern in which the vowel often has a short, or terse, sound; the consonant-vowel-consonant-silent *e* (CVC*e*) pattern in which the vowel usually has a long, or lax, sound; and the consonant-vowel-vowel-consonant (CVVC) pattern in which the vowel combination may have either one or two sounds.

Knowing spelling patterns helps children notice and use larger parts of words, thus making word solving faster and more efficient. Patterns are also helpful to children in writing words because they will quickly write down the patterns rather than laboriously work with individual sounds and letters. Finally, knowing to look for patterns and remember them helps children make the connections between words that make word solving easier. The thirty-seven most common phonograms are marked with an asterisk in the Continuum.

Connect to Assessment

See related SP Assessment Tasks in the Assessment Guide in *Teaching Resources:*

▶ Reading Words with Phonogram Patterns

▶ Writing Words with Phonogram Patterns

▶ Reading Unfamiliar Words with Patterns in Texts

▶ Matching Pictures Whose Labels Contain the Same Phonogram Pattern

▶ Matching Words That Contain the Same Phonogram Pattern

▶ Matching Pictures with the Words That Contain the Appropriate Phonogram Pattern

Develop Your Professional Understanding

See *Word Matters: Teaching Phonics and Spelling in the Reading/Writing Classroom* by G.S. Pinnell and I.C. Fountas. 1998. Portsmouth, New Hampshire: Heinemann.

Related pages: 65, 82, 95, 236.

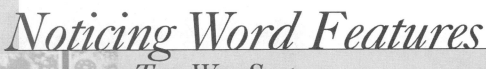

Noticing Word Features
Two-Way Sort

Consider Your Children

In this lesson, children take a closer look at known or "almost known" words and make connections between them. Knowing common patterns will make reading and writing more efficient. Use words from the word wall (which are arranged alphabetically by beginning letter), so that children will have already encountered them in interactive writing, shared reading, or a word study minilesson. There should be about twenty words on the word wall before you teach this lesson.

Working with English Language Learners

Looking at visual features of words will help children connect words and build networks of understanding that will accelerate learning. Be sure that all of the words you use for this comparison are within children's oral vocabularies and that most are recognizable high frequency words.

You Need

► Pocket chart.

From *Teaching Resources:*

► Word Cards for word wall words (Pocket Chart Card Template).

► Two-Column Sheet.

► Word cards (Word Card Template).

Understand the Principle

As children become familiar with letters and words, they begin to notice visual patterns, which is an important step in understanding how words work.

Children are able to use the patterns they know to figure out new words.

Explain the Principle

" Some words have parts (patterns) that are the same. "

" You can find patterns (parts) that are the same in many words. "

SP 1
SPELLING PATTERNS

CONTINUUM: SPELLING PATTERNS — Recognizing That Words Have Letter Patterns That Are Connected to Sounds

plan

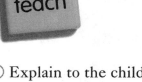

Explain the Principle

❝ Some words have parts (patterns) that are the same. ❞

❝ You can find patterns (parts) that are the same in many words. ❞

① Explain to the children that they are going to learn how words are alike.

② Give each child one of the word wall words on an index card as a "ticket" to the group meeting. Ask children to say the word and then place it on the left side of the pocket chart. (You can have duplicates of some words.)

③ Select particular word cards (ones with the letter *i* in them, for example) and hold up one card after another, asking the group to read them. Place them on the right side of the pocket chart. Ask, "What do you notice about the words?"

④ Guide children to discover that every word has an *i* in it.

⑤ Repeat the process with other letters or letter patterns. Select words by first letter, last letter, middle vowel. Vary the patterns so that children will develop flexibility.

⑥ Demonstrate the activity until children know what you mean by selecting words that are alike in some way.

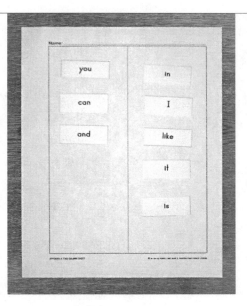

look
sort
tell

▸ Give the children selected word cards (the words can be the same ones you used in the lesson) and a Two-Column Sheet. Have children work with a partner.

▸ The first child looks at all the words and chooses one criterion for each column: for example, words with *o* (or any other letter), words with two letters, words with three letters. The child places the word cards in the two columns. After the words are sorted, the partner reads the lists and tells how the words are alike (categorized).

▸ Then the partners reverse roles.

Ask the children to talk about the ways in which they sorted words.

Ask one or two children to do a "mystery sort" for the whole group and have children guess the way the words are alike.

Link

Interactive Read-Aloud: Read aloud books that emphasize connections between words, such as:

- *Bearobics* by Vic Parker and Emily Bolam
- *Pets in Trumpets* by Bernard Most

Shared Reading: Look for similarities and differences in words. Use a masking card or highlighter tape to call attention to words that are alike or have particular letters (all words ending in *e*, for example).

Guided Reading: Encourage the children to make connections between the words they know and new words they encounter in texts. During word work, make two or three words and have the children read them and tell how they are alike.

Interactive Writing: Make explicit connections between words on the word wall and words children are writing. After writing a piece, make connections among words in the text.

Independent Writing: Encourage the children to use words on the word wall as resources for their spelling.

Expand the Learning

Introduce the idea that a word may fit into more than one group—for example, words that have three letters and words that end in *e*.

Connect with Home

Send home word wall words on cards for children to read to their families and caregivers. Encourage family members to have children use a word card as a model to build the words with magnetic letters or letter cards.

assess

- ▸ Notice whether the children are representing word patterns in their writing.
- ▸ Notice whether the children are connecting words in shared or guided reading.

Making Words with -at
Magnetic Letters

Consider Your Children

This lesson and the next five introduce simple common spelling patterns. It is best used after children have had extensive experience hearing and recognizing rhymes, can distinguish most letters, and know many consonant sounds. They should also understand what words are and have grasped the idea of "first" and "last" as it applies to the component parts of words. Knowing some high frequency words or easy words from the word wall also helps. The goal of this lesson is to draw children's attention to word parts so that they will begin to look for and recognize patterns *(at, bat, cat, fat, hat, mat, pat, rat, sat, brat, chat, flat, that).* In this lesson the children learn a vowel and consonant (VC) pattern.

Working with English Language Learners

English language learners' previous work with rhymes will form a foundation for learning about word patterns. Articulate the words clearly for children, and also make sure that they understand the words and can pronounce them clearly, although there may be some approximation. You may need to use the words in sentences or use pictures and concrete objects where appropriate. Work with a small group and help them practice making words. Observe them writing words with *-at*.

You Need

► Chart paper and markers.

► Magnetic letters *a, b, c, f, h, m, p, r, s,* and *t*.

From *Teaching Resources:*

► List Sheets.

Understand the Principle

Learning common word patterns provides very useful information about written language.

A phonogram, or *rime*, is a cluster of letters that forms a word part or a spelling pattern. It usually comprises a vowel sound and a consonant sound.

Children easily hear the break between the first part of the word and the rest of the word *(h–op, br–own);* they can use these parts as they write and read other words.

Explain the Principle

" Some words have patterns (parts) that are the same. "

" You can look at the pattern (part) you know to help you read a word. "

" You can use the pattern (part) you know to help you write a word. "

CONTINUUM: SPELLING PATTERNS — Recognizing and Using Simple Phonograms with a **VC** Pattern

plan

Explain the Principle

" Some words have patterns (parts) that are the same. "

" You can look at the pattern (part) you know to help you read a word. "

" You can use the pattern (part) you know to help you write a word. "

① Explain to the children that they are going to learn to think about word parts.

② Select a word children know as the first example. Suggested language: "You know this word. [Write *cat*. Children read the word.] Today we're going to look at some other words that are like *cat*. All of these words have *-at* as the ending part of the word. Say *cat*. [Children respond.] The last part of the word is *-at*: *cat, at*.

③ Children may say that *at* is a word by itself. "That's right, *at* is a word, but you also see it as part of other words." Write *-at* on the chart.

④ Suggested language: "I can think of another word that has *-at* for the last part. It's *hat*." Write *hat* on the chart and read: "*Cat, at, hat*. What do you notice?" Children will notice that they rhyme or sound the same at the end.

⑤ Ask the children to give more examples that have the *–at* pattern. Three or four are enough. You want children to discover more on their own. Leave room on the chart to add more children's examples later. Children don't need to learn the label *phonogram*. It's more useful to call it a "word part" or "spelling pattern."

⑥ Suggested language: "Now we're going to make some *-at* words with magnetic letters. You can make words by taking different letters and putting *at* after them. You have to say the word you have made to be sure it's really a word. I'm going to take a *b* and then put *at* after it. [Demonstrate with magnetic letters on a cookie sheet or other magnetic surface.] What word did I make? [Children respond.]"

⑦ Demonstrate building *-at* words with magnetic letters.

—at

cat
at
hat
bat
sat
Pat
Matt

cat
at
hat
bat
sat
Pat
Matt

⑧ When the chart is finished, hang it on the wall to support children when they are building words.

⑨ If any of the children's names include the pattern *-at*, draw the class's attention to them and include them on the chart.

**make
write
read**

▶ Have the children use magnetic letters, letter tiles, or letter cards to make words with consonants and *-at*. Provide only letters that will make real words.

▶ Include some letters that make words that are not on the chart you have just finished making with the children. (For this phonogram, include *a, b, c, f, h, m, p, r, s, t*.)

▶ Have children write the words they make on a List Sheet. They can read the list to a partner and bring it to sharing time.

Go around the circle and have the children share one *-at* word they wrote.

Go back to the *-at* chart and add any new *-at* words children have discovered.

Link

Interactive Read-Aloud: Read aloud rhyming books, drawing children's attention to the rhyming words. (See *Teaching Resources,* Rhyme Books Bibliography.) Good resources are:

- ▶ *Here Comes Mother Goose,* edited by Iona Opie and illustrated by Rosemary Wells
- ▶ *The Cat in the Hat* by Dr. Seuss

Shared Reading: After reading and enjoying a poem (such as "Make a Pancake" or "The Cat" in *Sing a Song of Poetry*), have children use a masking card or highlighter tape to point out words that contain spelling patterns the class has learned.

Guided Reading: Before or after reading, have children locate words containing the phonograms they have learned. Remind them of the minilesson and show how the chart helps them connect words. During word work, give the children a bunch of letters to make several *-at* words. Then have them read the words to a partner.

Interactive Writing: Draw children's attention to phonograms they have learned, or have them use a known word that contains the phonogram to write a new word.

Independent Writing: Encourage the children to use their knowledge of phonograms as a resource to write words.

assess

- ▶ Ask individual students to read the *-at* phonogram chart or make the *-at* phonogram with magnetic letters.
- ▶ Observe the children as they read to determine whether they are noticing and using the *-at* pattern to solve new words.

Expand the Learning

Use other rhyme books (*Teaching Resources,* Rhyme Books Bibliography) to help children hear and notice other rhyme patterns. If the text includes *-at* words, call children's attention to them and build some after the reading.

Connect with Home

Reproduce letter cards and the pattern chart for *-at* (see *Teaching Resources* Templates) for children to take home, cut apart, and use to build and read words.

Send home copies of nursery rhymes such as "Jack Sprat" or "Pat-a-Cake" (see *Sing a Song of Poetry*) after children have read them in shared reading.

3 *Making Words with* -an

Magnetic Letters

Consider Your Children

This lesson builds on the previous phonogram lesson. If you have selected it as the first lesson on phonograms, you'll want to present more explicit demonstrations (as in the lesson on -*at*). It is best used after children have had extensive experience hearing and recognizing rhymes, can distinguish most letters, and know many consonant sounds. They should also understand what words are and have grasped the idea of "first" and "last" as it applies to the component parts of words. Knowing some high frequency words or easy words from the word wall also helps. The goal of this lesson is to draw children's attention to word parts so that they will begin to look for and recognize patterns (*an, can, fan, man, pan, ran, tan, van, plan, than*). The part -*an* is a vowel and consonant (VC) pattern.

Working with English Language Learners

Be sure that you begin with some -*an* words that English language learners already know and can read and/or write. Use them in sentences and invite children to repeat your sentences, or make sentences of their own. Be sure to articulate consonant clusters (as in *plan*) slowly and carefully and have children repeat the words themselves.

You Need

► Chart paper and markers.

► Magnetic letters *a, c, f, h, l, m, n, p, r, t,* and *v*.

From *Teaching Resources:*

► List Sheets.

Understand the Principle

Learning common word patterns provides very useful information about written language.

A phonogram, or *rime*, is a cluster of letters that forms a word part or a spelling pattern. It usually comprises a vowel sound and a consonant sound.

Children easily hear the break between the first part of the word and the rest of the word (*m–an, pl–an*); they can use these parts as they write and read other words.

When children have learned simple word patterns, or phonograms, they can then use these parts as they write and read other words.

Explain the Principle

" Some words have patterns (parts) that are the same. "

" You can look at the pattern (part) you know to help you read a word. "

" You can use the pattern (part) you know to help you write a word. "

CONTINUUM: SPELLING PATTERNS — Recognizing and Using Simple Phonograms with a VC Pattern

plan

Explain the Principle

" Some words have patterns (parts) that are the same. "

" You can look at the pattern (part) you know to help you read a word. "

" You can use the pattern (part) you know to help you write a word. "

① Tell the children they are going to learn a new pattern they will see in many words.

② Suggested language: "Remember when we looked at this word part? [Write -*at* and then have children read the -*at* chart.] Today we are going to look at another part that you see in lots of words. [Write -*an* on the chart.]"

③ Children may say that *an* is a word by itself. "Yes, *an* is a word all by itself, but we also see *an* in other words." Write -*an* on the chart. Don't tell children to look for the "little word inside the big word"; that strategy works sometimes but can be quite misleading (for example, noticing *me* in *come* will not help them).

④ Suggested language: "A word that has -*an* for the last part of the word is *man*."

⑤ Ask the children to give three or four more examples that have the -*an* pattern. Leave room on the chart for the children to add more examples later.

⑥ You don't have to teach children to call this word part a *phonogram*. The concept of "word part" or "spelling pattern" is more useful.

⑦ Suggested language: "Let's make some -*an* words with magnetic letters. [Demonstrate with magnetic letters on a cookie sheet or other magnetic surface.] What word did I make? [Children respond.]"

⑧ If any of the children's names include -*an*, draw the class's attention to them and put them on the chart. (If you encounter one that is not a phonetically regular example, say so and place it to the side rather than in the row of names.)

⑨ Display the -*an* chart on the wall.

apply

make
write
read

▸ Have the children use magnetic letters, letter tiles, or letter cards to make words with consonants and *-an*. Provide only the letters that will make real words.

▸ Include some letters that make words that are not on the chart you have just finished making with the children. (For this phonogram, include *a, c, f, h, l, m, n, p, r, t,* and *v.*)

▸ Have children write the words they make on a List Sheet. They can read the list to a partner and bring it to sharing time.

share

Go around the circle and have the children share one *-an* word they wrote.

Go back to the *-an* chart and add any new *-an* words children have discovered.

Link

Interactive Read-Aloud: Read aloud rhyming stories that emphasize words whose ending parts sound alike (see *Teaching Resources,* Rhyme Books Bibliography, for ideas). Examples are:

▸ *Pass the Fritters, Critters* by Cheryl Chapman

▸ *Play Day* by Bruce McMillan

Shared Reading: Read nursery rhymes and songs, such as "This Old Man, "We Can," and "The Muffin Man" (see *Sing a Song of Poetry*). Using a masking card or highlighter tape, point out words that contain spelling patterns the children have learned. Invite children to find a word that rhymes with a word you give them.

Guided Reading: Before or after reading, have children locate words containing the phonograms they have learned. Remind them of the minilesson and show how the chart helps them connect words. During word work, have the children use magnetic letters to make two or three words with the *-an* pattern.

Interactive Writing: Draw the children's attention to phonograms they have learned, or have them use a known word that contains the phonogram to write a new word.

Independent Writing: Encourage the children to use their knowledge of phonograms as a resource to write words.

Expand the Learning

Use other rhyme books (see *Teaching Resources,* Rhyme Books Bibliography) to help children hear and notice other rhyme patterns. If the text includes *-an* words, call children's attention to them and build some after the reading.

Connect with Home

Reproduce letter cards and the pattern chart for *-an* (see *Teaching Resources* Templates) for children to take home, cut apart, and use to build and read words.

Send home copies of nursery rhymes such as "This Old Man" (see *Sing a Song of Poetry*) after children have read them in shared reading.

assess

▸ Ask individual students to read the *-an* phonogram chart or make the *-an* phonogram with magnetic letters.

▸ Observe the children as they read to determine whether they are noticing and using the *-an* pattern to solve words.

Making Words with -ay
Magnetic Letters

Consider Your Children

This lesson builds on previous phonogram lessons. It is best used after children have had extensive experience hearing and recognizing rhymes, can distinguish most letters, and know many consonant sounds. They should also understand what words are and have grasped the idea of "first" and "last" as it applies to the component parts of words. The goal of this lesson is to draw children's attention to word parts so that they will begin to look for and recognize patterns *(bay, day, hay, jay, lay, may, pay, ray, say, way, clay, gray, play, pray, spray, stay, tray)*. The part *-ay* is a vowel and consonant (VC) pattern.

Working with English Language Learners

Begin with words that English language learners have in their speaking vocabularies and also have encountered as high frequency words or in shared reading. You may want to refer to the word wall or to the calendar. Be sure they know the meaning of the words that you create. Remember that they will not necessarily know that substitutions they suggest do not create real words (for example, *tay*). Recognize their efforts and give them feedback as to which words are real by using them in a sentence.

You Need

▶ Chart paper and markers.

▶ Magnetic letters *a, b, c, d, g, h, j, l, m, p, r, s, t, w,* and *y*.

From *Teaching Resources:*

▶ List Sheets.

Understand the Principle

Learning common word patterns provides very useful information about written language.

A phonogram, or *rime*, is a cluster of letters that forms a word part or a spelling pattern. It usually comprises a vowel sound and a consonant sound.

Children easily hear the break between the first part of the word and the rest of the word *(h–ay, pl–ay);* they can use these parts as they write and read other words.

When children have learned simple word patterns, or phonograms, they can then use these parts as they write and read other words.

Explain the Principle

❝ Some words have patterns (parts) that are the same. ❞

❝ You can look at the pattern (part) you know to help you read a word. ❞

❝ You can use the pattern (part) you know to help you write a word. ❞

CONTINUUM: SPELLING PATTERNS — RECOGNIZING AND USING SIMPLE PHONOGRAMS WITH A VC PATTERN

plan

Explain the Principle

" **Some words have patterns (parts) that are the same.** "

" **You can look at the pattern (part) you know to help you read a word.** "

" **You can use the pattern (part) you know to help you write a word.** "

① Tell the children they are going to learn a new word part they will see in many words.

② Suggested language: "We've been looking at the ending parts of words. Here is one you see in a lot of words." Write -*ay* on the chart.

③ Children may say that -*ay* is not a word. "You're right: *ay* isn't a word by itself, but it is a part of some words you know. A word that has -*ay* for the last part of the word is *day*." Write *day* on the chart.

④ Ask the children to give three or four more examples that have the -*ay* pattern, or phonogram. Leave room on the chart to add more examples later.

⑤ You don't have to teach children to call this word part a *phonogram*. The concept of "word part" or "spelling pattern" is more useful.

⑥ Suggested language: "Let's make some -*ay* words with magnetic letters. [Demonstrate with magnetic letters on a cookie sheet or other magnetic surface.] What word did I make? [Children respond.]"

⑦ If any of the children's names include -*ay*, draw the children's attention to them and put them on the chart. (If you encounter one that is not a phonetically regular example, say so and place it to the side rather than in the row of names.)

⑧ Display the -*ay* chart on the wall.

make
write
read

▶ Have the children use magnetic letters, letter tiles, or letter cards to make words with consonants and -*ay*. Provide only the letters that will make real words.

▶ Include some letters that make words that are not on the chart you have just finished making with the children. (For this phonogram, include *a, b, c, d, g, h, j, l, m, p, r, s, t, w,* and *y*.)

▶ Have children write the words they make on a List Sheet. They can read the list to a partner and bring it to sharing time.

Go around the circle and have the children share one -*ay* word they wrote.

Go back to the -*ay* chart and add any new -*ay* words children have discovered. (If children know the word *today,* you may want to bring it to their attention and add it to the chart.)

Link

Interactive Read-Aloud: Read aloud rhyming stories that emphasize words whose ending parts sound alike. Examples are:

► *One Monkey Too Many* by Jackie French Koller

► *Ants in My Pants* by Wendy Mould

Shared Reading: Read nursery rhymes and songs such as "Rain, Rain, Go Away," "Five Little Snowmen," or "How Many Days?" (see *Sing a Song of Poetry*). Using a masking card or highlighter tape, point out words that contain phonograms children have learned.

Guided Reading: Before or after reading, have children locate words that contain the phonograms they have learned. Remind them of the minilesson and show how the chart helps them connect words.

Interactive Writing: Draw the children's attention to spelling patterns they have learned, or have them use a known word that contains the phonogram to write a new word.

Independent Writing: Encourage the children to use their knowledge of phonograms as a resource to write words.

assess

► Ask individual students to read the *–ay* phonogram chart or make two or three words with the *–ay* phonogram with magnetic letters.

► Observe children as they read to determine whether they are noticing and using the *–ay* pattern to solve new words.

Expand the Learning

Use other rhyme books (see *Teaching Resources,* Rhyme Books Bibliography) to help children hear and notice other rhyme patterns. If the text includes *-ay* words, call the children's attention to them and build some after the reading.

Connect with Home

Reproduce letter cards and the pattern chart for *-ay* (see *Teaching Resources* Templates) for children to take home, cut apart, and use to build and read words.

Send home copies of nursery rhymes such as "Rain, Rain, Go Away" or "London Bridge" (see *Sing a Song of Poetry*) after children have read them in shared reading.

Making Words with -and
Magnetic Letters

Consider Your Children

This lesson builds on previous phonogram lessons, helping children understand the relationship between letters and sounds. *And* should be a known word, so children are learning how to use a part they already know. Children should have had experience hearing and recognizing rhymes and working with letters and consonant sounds. They should also have grasped the idea of "first" and "last" as it applies to the component parts of words and know some high frequency words. The goal of this lesson is to draw children's attention to word parts so that they will begin to look for and recognize patterns *(and, band, hand, land, sand, bland, brand, grand, strand)* in many words.

Working with English Language Learners

And is a real word that children will probably recognize, so it is appropriate to talk about how sometimes letters can be added to the beginning of words to make other words. Be sure that English language learners understand the meaning of the new words they make with *-and* (for example, *sand*). Use words in sentences, or describe and show pictures of concepts as necessary.

You Need

▶ Chart paper and markers.

▶ Magnetic letters *a, b, d, g, h, l, n, r, s,* and *t.*

From *Teaching Resources:*

▶ List Sheets.

Understand the Principle

Learning common word patterns provides very useful information about written language.

A phonogram, or *rime*, is a cluster of letters that forms a word part or a spelling pattern. It usually comprises a vowel sound and a consonant sound.

Children easily hear the break between the first part of the word and the rest of the word *(b–and, h–and);* they can use these parts as they write and read other words.

When children have learned simple word patterns, or phonograms, they can then use these parts as they write and read other words.

Explain the Principle

❝ Some words have patterns (parts) that are the same. ❞

❝ You can find patterns (parts) that are the same in many words. ❞

CONTINUUM: SPELLING PATTERNS — RECOGNIZING THAT WORDS HAVE LETTER PATTERNS THAT ARE CONNECTED TO SOUNDS

plan

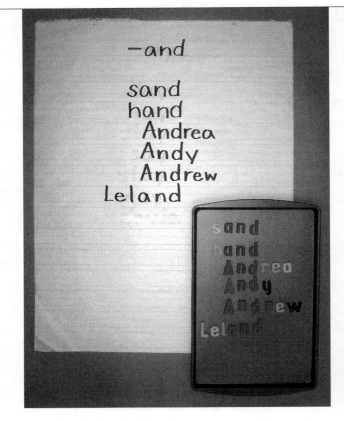

Explain the Principle

" Some words have patterns (parts) that are the same. "

" You can find patterns (parts) that are the same in many words. "

① Explain to the children they are going to learn a new word part they will see in many words.

② Suggested language: "We've been looking at the ending parts of words. Here is one you see a lot." Write -*and* on the chart.

③ Explain that *and* is a word they know. The letters can appear by themselves but also can be part of other words.

④ Suggested language: "A word that has -*and* for the last part of the word is *sand*." Write it on the chart.

⑤ Ask children to give another example of a word with -*and* at the end. Leave room on the chart for more.

⑥ You don't have to teach children to call this word part a *phonogram*. The concept of "word part" or "spelling pattern" is easier to understand.

⑦ Suggested language: "Let's make -*and* words with magnetic letters. [Demonstrate with magnetic letters on a cookie sheet or other magnetic surface.] What word did I make? [Children respond.]"

⑧ If any of the children's names include the -*and* pattern, draw the class's attention to them and put them on the chart. (If you encounter one that is not a phonetically regular example, say so and place it to the side rather than in the row of names.)

⑨ Display the -*and* chart on the wall.

apply

say
make
write
read

▸ Have the children use magnetic letters, letter tiles, or letter cards to make words with consonants and *-and*. Provide only the letters that will make real words. (For this phonogram, include *a, b, d, g, h, l, n, r, s,* and *t*. After they have built all the words on the chart, they will have the letters to discover two more: *land* and *band*.) The word *candy* may come up.

▸ Have the children write the words they make on a List Sheet. They can read their list to a partner and bring it to sharing time.

▸ More proficient children may make words using letters you have not provided (*stand* and *grand*, for example).

share

Go around the circle and have the children share the *-and* words they wrote.

Go back to the *-and* chart and add any new *-and* words children have discovered.

Link

Interactive Read-Aloud: Read aloud rhyming stories that emphasize words whose ending parts sound alike. For example:

- ► *Jesse Bear, What Will You Wear?* by Nancy White Carlstrom
- ► *Better Not Get Wet, Jesse Bear* by Nancy White Carlstrom

Shared Reading: Read nursery rhymes and songs, such as "If You're Happy and You Know It" or "The Beach" (see *Sing a Song of Poetry*). Using masking cards and flags, point out words that contain phonograms the class has learned.

Guided Reading: Before or after reading, have children locate words containing the phonograms the class learned. Remind them of the minilesson and show how the chart helps them connect words. During word work, have children make and mix a word several times. Then have them make two other words with the same pattern.

Interactive Writing: Draw the children's attention to phonograms they have learned, or have them use a known word that contains the phonogram to write a new word.

Independent Writing: Encourage the children to use their knowledge of phonograms as a resource to write words.

assess

- ► Ask individual students to read the *-and* phonogram chart or make an *-and* word with magnetic letters.
- ► Observe the children as they read to determine whether they are noticing and using the *-and* pattern to solve new words.

Expand the Learning

Use other rhyme books (see *Teaching Resources,* Rhyme Books Bibliography) to help children hear and notice other rhyme patterns. If the text includes *-and* words, call the children's attention to them and build some words after the reading.

Connect with Home

Reproduce letter cards and the pattern chart for *-and* (see *Teaching Resources* Templates) for children to take home, cut apart, and use to build and read words.

Send home copies of nursery rhymes such as "If You're Happy and You Know It" (see *Sing a Song of Poetry*) after children have read them in shared reading.

6 *Making Words with* -ake

Magnetic Letters

Consider Your Children

This lesson builds on previous phonogram lessons. By the time you use this lesson, children will know how to recognize and use patterns in words. This sequence of lessons will help them develop systems for noticing and learning patterns. The goal of this lesson is to draw children's attention to word parts so that they will begin to look for and recognize patterns *(cake, lake, make, quake, rake, take, brake, flake, shake, snake).* In this lesson, children learn the vowel-consonant-silent *e* (VC*e*) pattern.

Working with English Language Learners

If you have some English language learners who are having difficulty using spelling patterns, work with them in a small group and focus on easier phonograms. Be sure they understand and can pronounce the words. Use the words in context, and use pictures and real objects when possible. Appreciate their efforts to use patterns even when their constructions are invented rather than actual English words.

You Need

► Chart paper and markers.

► Magnetic letters *a, b, c, e, f, h, k, l, m, q, r, s, t, u,* and *w.*

From *Teaching Resources:*

► List Sheets.

Understand the Principle

Learning common word patterns provides very useful information about written language.

A phonogram, or *rime*, is a cluster of letters that forms a word part or a spelling pattern. It usually comprises a vowel sound and a consonant sound.

Children easily hear the break between the first part of the word and the rest of the word *(b–ake, t–ake);* they can use these parts as they write and read other words.

When children have learned simple word patterns, or phonograms, they can then use these parts as they write and read other words.

Explain the Principle

❝ Some words have a vowel, a consonant, and a silent *e.* The vowel sound is usually the name of the vowel. ❞

CONTINUUM: SPELLING PATTERNS — Recognizing and Using Phonograms with a Vowel-Consonant-Silent *e* (VC*e*) Pattern

plan

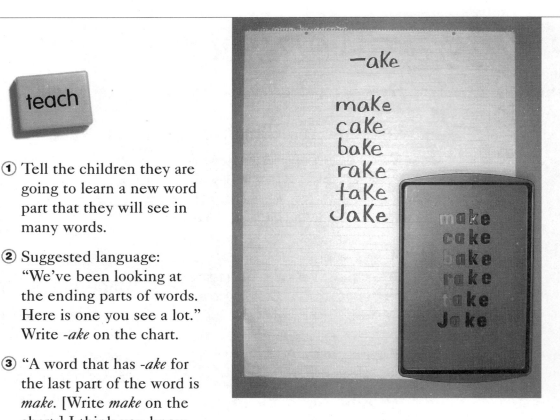

Explain the Principle

" **Some words have a vowel, a consonant, and a silent *e*. The vowel sound is usually the name of the vowel.** "

① Tell the children they are going to learn a new word part that they will see in many words.

② Suggested language: "We've been looking at the ending parts of words. Here is one you see a lot." Write *-ake* on the chart.

③ "A word that has *-ake* for the last part of the word is *make*. [Write *make* on the chart.] I think you know this word because it is on our word wall." Have a child locate *make* on the word wall, or have everyone find it visually.

④ Ask children to give another example of a word with the *-ake* phonogram. Accept the words they offer, add them to the chart, and leave room to add more later.

⑤ Suggested language: "Let's make *-ake* words with magnetic letters. [Demonstrate with magnetic letters on a cookie sheet or other magnetic surface.] What word did I make? [Children respond.]"

⑥ If any of the children's names include the *-ake* pattern, draw the class's attention to them and put them on the chart. (If you encounter one that is not a phonetically regular example, you can say so and place it to the side rather than in the row of names.)

⑦ Display the *-ake* chart on the wall.

apply

make
write
read

▶ Have the children use magnetic letters, letter tiles, or letter cards to make words with consonants and *-ake*. Provide only the letters that make real words. (For this phonogram, include *a, b, c, e, f, h, k, l, m, q, r, s, t, u,* and *w.*)

▶ Have the children write the words they make on a List Sheet. They can read the lists to a partner and bring it to sharing time.

share

Go around the circle and have children share the *-ake* words they wrote.

Go back to the *-ake* chart and add any new *-ake* words children have discovered.

Link

Interactive Read-Aloud: Read aloud rhyming stories that emphasize words with ending parts that sound alike. Examples are:

- ► *Tracy's Mess* by Elise Petersen
- ► *Hippos Go Berserk!* by Sandra Boynton

Shared Reading: Read nursery rhymes and songs, such as "As I Was Walking," "Hiccup, Hiccup," or "Pat-a-Cake" (see *Sing a Song of Poetry*). Point out words that contain phonograms the class has learned.

Guided Reading: Before or after reading, have children locate words containing the phonograms they have learned. Remind them of the minilesson and show how the chart helps them connect words.

Interactive Writing: Draw the children's attention to phonograms they have learned, or have them use a known word that contains the phonogram to write a new word.

Independent Writing: Encourage children to use their knowledge of phonograms as a resource to write words.

assess

- ► Ask individual students to read the *-ake* phonogram chart or make an *-ake* word with magnetic letters.

- ► Observe children as they read to determine whether they are noticing and using the *-ake* pattern to solve words.

Expand the Learning

Use other rhyme books (*Teaching Resources, Rhyme Books Bibliography*) to help children hear and notice other rhyme patterns. If the text includes *-ake* words, call children's attention to them and build some after the reading.

Connect with Home

Reproduce letter cards and the pattern chart for *-ake* (see *Teaching Resources* Templates) for children to take home, cut apart, and use to build and read words.

Send home copies of nursery rhymes such as "Pat-a-Cake" or "Three Men in a Tub" (see *Sing a Song of Poetry*) after children have read them in shared reading.

Making Words with -ike
Magnetic Letters

Consider Your Children

This lesson builds on previous phonogram lessons and helps children not only to expand the repertoire of patterns they know but also to develop systems for learning patterns. As these systems develop, learning will accelerate. The goal of this lesson is to draw children's attention to word parts so that they will begin to look for and recognize patterns *(bike, hike, like, Mike, spike, strike)*. In this lesson, they learn a VC*e* pattern similar to the part in the word *like,* which they already know.

Working with English Language Learners

As your English language learners take on new phonograms, you may want to have them go back and review others in random order so that they grasp the larger principle of words that are the same at the end. This process will give them generative power over words. Understanding these word patterns will greatly expand their ability to spell. Help children pronounce the words with the long *i* sound /ī/.

You Need

▶ Chart paper and markers.

▶ Magnetic letters *b, e, h, i, k, l, m, p, r, s,* and *t.*
From *Teaching Resources:*

▶ List Sheets.

Understand the Principle

Learning common word patterns provides very useful information about written language.

A phonogram, or *rime,* is a cluster of letters that forms a word part or a spelling pattern. It usually comprises a vowel sound and a consonant sound.

Children easily recognize the break between the first part of the word and the rest of the word *(b–ike, h–ike);* they can use these parts as they write and read other words.

When children have learned simple word patterns, or phonograms, they can then use these parts as they write and read other words.

Explain the Principle

❝ Some words have a vowel, a consonant, and a silent *e.* The vowel sound is usually the name of the vowel. ❞

CONTINUUM: SPELLING PATTERNS — RECOGNIZING AND USING PHONOGRAMS WITH A VOWEL-CONSONANT-SILENT *E* (VC*E*) PATTERN

plan

Explain the Principle

" Some words have a vowel, a consonant, and a silent *e*. The vowel sound is usually the name of the vowel. "

—iKe

liKe
biKe
MiKe

like
bike
Mike

① Explain to the children that they are going to learn a new word part they will see in many words.

② Suggested language: "We've been looking at the ending parts of words. Here is one you see a lot. [Write *-ike* on the chart.] What's a word that has *-ike* for the last part? [Children respond.]"

③ "You're right. *Like* has *-ike* for the last part. I think you know that word, and it is on our word wall." Write *like* on the chart. Have a child locate *like* on the word wall, or have everyone find it visually.

④ Ask the children to give another example of a word with *-ike*. Add the word to the chart and leave room for students to add more later.

⑤ Suggested language: "Let's make words with *-ike* using the magnetic letters. [Demonstrate with magnetic letters on a cookie sheet or other magnetic surface.] What word did I make? [Children respond.]"

⑥ If any of the children's names include the *-ike* pattern, draw the class's attention to them and put them on the chart. (If you encounter one that is not a phonetically regular example, say so and place it to the side rather than in the row of names.) If you don't have a Mike in your class, children might know the abbreviation of *microphone*, so you can still use it, with a lowercase letter.

⑦ Display the *-ike* chart on the wall.

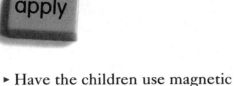

make
write
read

apply

► Have the children use magnetic letters, letter tiles, or letter cards to make words with consonants and *-ike*. Provide only the letters that will make real words. (For this phonogram, include *b, e, h, i, k, l, m, p, r, s,* and *t*. After they have built all the words on the chart, they will have the letters to discover *likes, strike,* and *spike*.)

► Have the children write the words they make on a List Sheet. They can teach the list to a partner and bring it to sharing time.

share

Go around the circle and have children share the *-ike* words they wrote.

Go back to the *-ike* chart and add any new *-ike* words children have discovered.

Link

Interactive Read-Aloud: Read aloud rhyming stories that emphasize words whose ending parts sound alike. (See the Rhyming Books Bibliography in *Teaching Resources.*) Examples are:

▸ *Miss Mary Mack* by Mary Ann Hoberman

▸ *Hush! A Thai Lullaby* by Minfong Ho

Shared Reading: Read nursery rhymes and songs, such as "The Elephant Goes Like This" or "Pease Porridge Hot" (see *Sing a Song of Poetry*). Using a masking card or highlighter tape, point out words that contain phonograms the class has learned.

Guided Reading: Before or after reading, have children locate words containing the phonograms they have learned. Remind them of the minilesson and show how the chart helps them connect words. During word work, have children make the word *like* three times or make two other *-ike* words.

Interactive Writing: Draw the children's attention to phonograms they have learned, or have them use a known word that contains the phonogram to write a new word.

Independent Writing: Encourage the children to use their knowledge of phonograms as a resource to write words.

assess

▸ Ask individual students to read the *-ike* phonogram chart or make an *-ike* word with magnetic letters.

▸ Observe children as they read to determine whether they are noticing and using the *-ike* pattern to solve words.

Expand the Learning

Use other rhyme books (*Teaching Resources, Rhyme Books Bibliography*) to help children hear and notice other rhyme patterns. If the text includes *-ike* words, call children's attention to them and build some after the reading.

Connect with Home

Reproduce letter cards and the pattern chart for *-ike* (see *Teaching Resources* Templates) for children to take home, cut apart, and use to build and read words.

Send home copies of nursery rhymes such as "The Elephant Goes Like This" or "Pease Porridge Hot" (see *Sing a Song of Poetry*) after children have read them in shared reading. They can read them with a family member.

High Frequency Words

A core of known high frequency words is a valuable resource as children build their reading and writing processes. Young children notice words that appear frequently in the simple texts they read; eventually, their recognition of these words becomes automatic. In this way, their reading becomes more efficient, enabling them to decode words using phonics as well as attend to comprehension. These words are powerful examples that help them grasp that a word is always written the same way. They can use known high frequency words to check on the accuracy of their reading and as resources for solving other words (for example, *this* starts like *the*). In general, children learn the simpler words earlier and in the process develop efficient systems for learning words. They continuously add to the core of high frequency words they know. Lessons on high frequency words help them look more carefully at words and develop more efficient systems for word recognition.

Connect to Assessment

See related HFW Assessment Tasks in the Assessment Guide in *Teaching Resources:*

► Reading Words

► Writing Words

Develop Your Professional Understanding

See *Word Matters: Teaching Phonics and Spelling in the Reading/Writing Classroom* by G.S. Pinnell and I.C. Fountas. 1998. Portsmouth, New Hampshire: Heinemann.

Related pages: 35–41, 44–46, 71–72, 88–90, 237–238.

Building and Writing High Frequency Words 1
Making Words

Consider Your Children

Use this lesson after children know the concept of "word" and are familiar with a few high frequency words. This is the first lesson for teaching twenty-five easy high frequency words. Children will already have encountered these words many times in shared reading, interactive writing, and guided reading. You will have placed at least some of them on the word wall. In this lesson and the next four, you will make sure that children know these words in detail and teach them a system for learning and remembering words.

Working with English Language Learners

Building and writing high frequency words will help English language learners attend to the details that they will need to remember when reading or writing the words. Knowing some English words in detail will help them make connections between their own pronunciation and grasp of the sound system and the letters and letter combinations that they see. Be sure that children can say (in approximated form) the words they are building and writing.

You Need

▶ Chart, magnetic whiteboard, chalkboard, or easel displaying high frequency words down the left column (similar to the reproducible Three-Column Sheet in *Teaching Resources*).

▶ Magnetic letters or letter tiles.

▶ Dry-erase markers or chalk.

From *Teaching Resources:*

▶ Letter cards (if used instead of magnetic letters or letter tiles).

▶ Word cards (High Frequency Words) for *to, a, it, me,* and *I.* (Enlarge them for demonstration purposes.)

▶ Making Words Sheets (two per child).

Understand the Principle

Children use a core of known high frequency words as anchors to monitor and check their reading. These known words help them read simple texts and engage in the behavior of reading, such as moving from left to right across the page and matching word by word.

Known words are powerful exemplars because children connect new words to these familiar words by beginning letters or sounds.

Explain the Principle

" You see some words many times when you read. "

" Some have only one letter. Some have two letters. "

" Words you see a lot are important because they help you read and write. "

CONTINUUM: HIGH FREQUENCY WORDS — RECOGNIZING AND USING HIGH FREQUENCY WORDS WITH ONE OR TWO LETTERS

plan

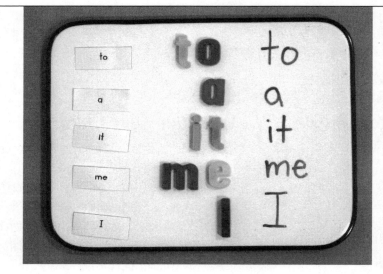

Explain the Principle

" You see some words many times when you read. "

" Some have only one letter. Some have two letters. "

" Words you see a lot are important because they help you read and write. "

① Explain to the children that when they read and write, there are some words that they will see and use a lot. Today they will learn some of these words.

② Place the words for this lesson in the left column. Be sure most of the children know or "nearly know" these words. (Vary the words according to the children. If they are inexperienced, use fewer words so that it is easier for them to learn the routine.)

③ Suggested language: "We're going to make some more words today. You know most of these words because you've been reading them. Let's read the words on the chart." Children respond.

④ "The first word is *to*. You read it. [Children respond.] Get a good look at the word *to*. Now watch while I find the magnetic letters to make *to*. I'm looking for a *t*." Continue looking for *o*.

⑤ Suggested language: "Now watch while I check to be sure I have every letter in the right order." Check by pointing to each letter in both words, in order, and checking: *t–t, o–o, to*.

⑥ "Now I'm going to write the word with a marker: *t, o;* I'll check it letter by letter. [Demonstrate.] Let's make the next word."

⑦ Demonstrate reading the second word, building it with magnetic letters, checking it, and finally writing the whole word. Continue with the remaining words.

⑧ Place the words on the word wall for reference if they aren't already there.

⑨ Explain to the children that they will repeat the same process with word cards today.

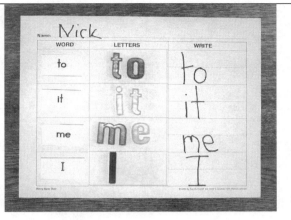

read
make
write

▶ Give the children a Making Words Sheet, a set of word cards for the words used in this lesson, and magnetic letters. Have the children place each word card in the first column of the sheet, read it, make it, and write it.

▶ Children can work on the words independently. Partners can check each other's completed list.

Ask children to show on the word wall some of the words they have learned to make and write.

Show the high frequency word cards one at a time for a quick review.

Have children read their list of words to a different partner.

Link

Interactive Read-Aloud: Read aloud books that have enlarged print. (See *Teaching Resources,* Large Print Books Bibliography.) Examples are:

- ▸ *We're Going on a Bear Hunt* by Michael Rosen and Helen Oxenbury
- ▸ *The Big Fat Worm* by Nancy Van Laan

Shared Reading: When reading poems and stories, draw children's attention to high frequency words and have them locate them with a masking card, flag, or highlighter tape. See *Sing a Song of Poetry* for examples: "As I Was Going Along" *(I),* "I Had a Loose Tooth" *(a),* "To Market, to Market" *(to),* "I Have a Little Wagon" *(it),* "Great A" *(me).*

Guided Reading: After enjoying a story, have children turn to particular pages and put a finger under selected high frequency words: "Turn to page four and put your finger under the word *to."*

Interactive Writing: Have a child write a high frequency word quickly while others locate it on the word wall. If all children can write the word, write it yourself to save time, but have children check it with their eyes.

Independent Writing: Encourage the children to recognize that they know some words really well. They should write them quickly without having to say them slowly. In conferences, point out words that children have written quickly because they know them.

assess

- ▸ Notice whether the children are able to recognize high frequency words when reading.

- ▸ Notice whether the children can write high frequency words quickly and accurately.

Expand the Learning

Have children match pairs of word tiles or word cards with high frequency words.

Each time children learn a new high frequency word, give them a card to add to their collection of words in a box or on rings. Have them practice reading all the words in the box or on the ring.

Connect with Home

Send home two sets of high frequency words on cards and encourage children to play High Frequency Concentration (see *Teaching Resources* for cards and directions). Be sure to include a set of directions, even though the children will have learned to play at school.

Send home copies of rhymes containing high frequency words (see *Sing a Song of Poetry*).

Building and Writing High Frequency Words 2

Making Words

Consider Your Children

Use this lesson after children know what words are and are familiar with a few high frequency words. It is the second lesson in becoming familiar with twenty-five easy high frequency words. Children will already have encountered these words many times in shared reading, interactive writing, and guided reading. Here you draw their attention to ways of learning words.

Working with English Language Learners

Be sure to use high frequency words in sentences that children can understand and repeat. Help them articulate the words and locate them in print. Work with them in a small group to be sure that they are building words left to right; have them say the words several times and "read" them left to right—word card, word built in magnetic letters, word written by the child.

You Need

► Chart, magnetic whiteboard, chalkboard, or easel displaying high frequency words down the left column (similar to the reproducible Three-Column Sheet in *Teaching Resources*).

► Magnetic letters or letter tiles.

► Dry-erase markers or chalk.

From *Teaching Resources:*

► Letter cards (if used instead of magnetic letters or letter tiles).

► Word cards (High Frequency Words) for *the, and, is, in,* and *can.* (Enlarge them for demonstration purposes.)

► Making Words Sheets (two per child).

Understand the Principle

Children use a core of known high frequency words as anchors to monitor and check their reading. These known words help them read simple texts and engage in the behaviors of reading, such as moving from left to right across the page and matching word by word.

Known words are powerful exemplars because children can connect new words to these familiar words by beginning letters or sounds.

Explain the Principle

" You see some words many times when you read. "

" Some have only one letter. Some have two letters. Some have three or four letters. "

" Words you see a lot are important because they help you read and write. "

HF 2
HIGH FREQUENCY WORDS

plan

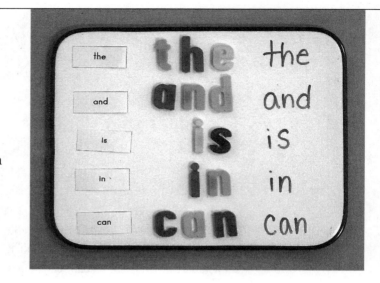

Explain the Principle

" You see some words many times when you read. "

" Some have only one letter. Some have two letters. Some have three or four letters. "

" Words you see a lot are important because they help you read and write. "

① Explain to the children that when they read and write, there are some words that they see and use a lot. Today they will learn more of these words.

② Place the words for this lesson in the left column. Be sure most of the children know or "nearly know" these words. (Vary the words according to the children. If they are inexperienced, use fewer words so that it is easier for them to learn the routine.)

③ Suggested language: "Today we are going to make more words in several different ways. Here are some words. You know most of these words because you've been reading them. Let's read the words on the chart." Children respond.

④ "Now look at the first word and read it. [Children respond.] Get a good look at the word *the*. Now watch while I find the magnetic letters to make *the*. I'm looking for a *t*." Continue looking for *h* and *e*.

⑤ Suggested language: "Now watch while I check to be sure I have every letter in the right order." Check by pointing to each letter in both words, in order, and checking: *t–t, h–h, e–e, the.*

⑥ "Now I'm going to write the word with a marker—*t, h, e*—and I'll check it letter by letter. [Demonstrate.] Let's do the next word."

⑦ Demonstrate reading the second word, building it with magnetic letters, checking it, and finally writing the whole word. Continue with the remaining words.

⑧ Place the words on the word wall for reference if they aren't already there.

⑨ Explain to the children that they will repeat the same process with word cards today.

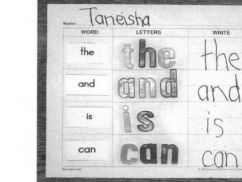

read
make
write

▶ Give the children a Making Words Sheet, a set of word cards for the words used in this lesson, and magnetic letters. Have the children place each word in the first column of the sheet, read it, make it, and write it.

▶ Children can work on the words independently. Partners can check each other's completed list.

share

Ask the children to show on the word wall some of the words they have learned to make and write.

Show the high frequency word cards one at a time for a quick review.

Have the children read their list of words to a different partner.

Link

Interactive Read-Aloud: Read aloud books that have enlarged print. (See the Large Print Books Bibliography in *Teaching Resources*.) Examples are:

- *Little White Dog* by Laura Godwin
- *Ten Cats Have Hats* by Jean Marzollo

Shared Reading: When reading poems and stories, draw the children's attention to high frequency words and have them locate them with a masking card or flag (in *Teaching Resources*) or highlighter tape. See *Sing a Song of Poetry* for examples: "Fiddle-de-dee" *(the)*, "Did You Ever See a Lassie" *(and)*, "I'm a Little Teapot" *(is)*, "Jack in the Box" *(in)*, "My Eyes Can See" *(can)*.

Guided Reading: After enjoying a story, have the children turn to particular pages and put a finger under selected high frequency words: "Turn to page four and put your finger under the word *the*."

Interactive Writing: Have a child write a high frequency word quickly while others locate it on the word wall. If all children can write the word, write it yourself to save time, but have children check it with their eyes.

Independent Writing: Encourage the children to recognize that when they know a word well, they can write it quickly. In conferences, point out words that children have written quickly because they know them.

assess

- Notice whether the children are able to recognize high frequency words when reading.
- Notice whether the children can write high frequency words quickly and accurately.

Expand the Learning

Have the children match pairs of word tiles or word cards with high frequency words.

Each time the children learn a new high frequency word, give them a card to add to their collection of words in a box or on rings. (Punch holes in the cards for the rings.) Have them practice reading all the words in the box or on the ring.

Connect with Home

Send home two sets of high frequency word cards and encourage children to play High Frequency Word Concentration (see *Teaching Resources* for cards and directions). Be sure to include a set of directions, even though the children will have learned to play the game at school.

Recognizing High Frequency Words

Word Lotto

Consider Your Children

Use this lesson after children understand that it will help them to know some words so well that they can read and write them quickly. Word Lotto is similar to Bingo except that players cover every space, so there is more work to do. In this game, children will be matching words simply by looking at their visual features, although they will also be saying the words. They can help one another in this activity, so every player does not have to know every word in isolation to play the game.

Working with English Language Learners

Working with high frequency words will help your English language learners monitor their own reading of beginning texts. It will also make words more available to them phonologically. Provide many repetitions, and be sure that children know how to use high frequency words in comprehensible sentences. Create some simple sentences that children can repeat. For example, "It is time to play" and "I can jump."

You Need

▶ Pocket chart with word cards arranged in rows to represent a Lotto Game Card.

From *Teaching Resources:*

▶ Selected High Frequency Word Cards—two sets. (Enlarge some of them for demonstration purposes.)

▶ Lotto Game Cards.

▶ Directions for Lotto.

Understand the Principle

Known high frequency words are important as children begin to explore words and how they work. A core of known words helps children monitor and check their reading.

High frequency words are anchors in word-by-word matching.

High frequency words are powerful exemplars because children can connect new words to these familiar words by beginning letters or sounds.

Explain the Principle

" You see some words many times when you read. "

" Some have only one letter. Some have two letters. Some have three or four letters. "

" Words you see a lot are important. They help you read and write. "

CONTINUUM: HIGH FREQUENCY WORDS — RECOGNIZING AND USING HIGH FREQUENCY WORDS WITH ONE TO FOUR LETTERS

plan

Explain the Principle

" You see some words many times when you read. "

" Some have only one letter. Some have two letters. Some have three or four letters. "

" Words you see a lot are important. They help you read and write. "

① Tell the children they are going to play a word game.

② Using the pocket chart, arrange the high frequency word cards in rows.

③ Suggested language: "Today we are going to play a game called Word Lotto. In this game you get to match words. Let's try it with the words I have in the pocket chart."

④ "I'm going to take a word card from this stack and see if I can match it to a word on my chart."

⑤ Hold up the first word card. Suggested language: "This word is *a*. [Let children say the name of the word if they can.] Now I'm going to see if there is a word on my chart that looks just like the word *a*. Can anyone see *a* on my chart?"

⑥ Model checking the *a* on the card with the *a* on the chart by pointing to each and saying *a*. Then place the card you drew over the word on the chart.

⑦ Draw one card at a time, showing how to say and check the words until all words on the chart are covered. (Words that don't match any on the chart are put at the bottom of the stack.)

⑧ Suggested language: "I've covered all the spaces on my chart. That's what you do to win the Word Lotto game. Remember to say both words to check your matches."

⑨ Demonstrate the game with three children in a circle on the floor.

⑩ One child can show and read the word cards aloud. Players who have that word can cover it (as in Bingo), but all spaces must be covered to win.

⑪ One player takes a turn drawing a card and covering the word if he has it. Then the next child takes a card and covers the word if she has it.

take
read
match

▶ Have children play Word Lotto in groups of three or four.

Ask the children to show on the word wall some of the words they have learned.

Ask the children to talk about how they "know" (recognize) a word. This elicitation will give you information about their thinking processes.

Link

Interactive Read-Aloud: Read aloud large-print books so children can notice high frequency words in the text. (See *Teaching Resources,* Large Print Books Bibliography.) Examples are:

▸ *Animals Should Definitely Not Wear Clothing* by Judi Barrett

▸ *Runaway Bunny* by Margaret Wise Brown

Shared Reading: When reading poems and rhymes, such as "Baby Mice" or "I Have a Little Wagon" (see *Sing a Song of Poetry*), draw the children's attention to high frequency words and have them locate them.

Guided Reading: Note the high frequency words children do not read quickly. Keep a list, and at the end of the lesson, have children make these words quickly several times with magnetic letters.

Interactive Writing: Have a child write a high frequency word quickly while others locate it on the word wall.

Independent Writing: Encourage children to recognize that they know some words in detail. They don't have to construct them by hearing and representing the sounds. They can write them quickly because they know them. In conferences, point out words that children have written quickly because they know them.

assess

▸ Notice whether the children are able to recognize high frequency words in reading.

▸ Notice whether the children can write high frequency words quickly.

▸ Show cards one at a time to individual children and notice their ability to recognize them.

Expand the Learning

Expand the Word Lotto game to include all twenty-five high frequency words (see *Teaching Resources*).

Write some high frequency words on a whiteboard and ask children to quickly recognize them.

Connect with Home

Give each child a small collection of cards containing the most useful high frequency words (see *Teaching Resources*). Explain to family members that these are words that appear often in books, so children need to learn to read them quickly. (*I, the,* and *and* make up 10 percent of all printed text. "Bouncing Ball" or "Billy, Billy" in *Sing a Song of Poetry* can be used to practice all three in one rhyme.) Explain that children's ability to recognize these words easily will help them in many ways. They will be able to read more smoothly and use parts of these words to figure out other words.

Send home the list of twenty-five high frequency words. Have family members and children make two or three of these words using letter cards or magnetic letters.

Building and Writing High Frequency Words 3

Making Words

Consider Your Children

Use this lesson to continue expanding children's knowledge of easy high frequency words. Children will already have encountered these words many times in shared reading, interactive writing, and guided reading. They will also be learning how to check the spelling of the words they write. If your assessment indicates children already know these words, select others and/or move on to Lesson HF 5.

Working with English Language Learners

As English language learners say, build, and write high frequency words, they will also be acquiring a system for learning new words and noticing how letters work together to make words. Be sure that children say the words while building them and read each row after they complete the task—word card, word built in magnetic letters, and word written by the child.

You Need

▶ Chart, magnetic whiteboard, chalkboard, or easel displaying high frequency words down the left column (similar to the reproducible Three-Column Sheet in *Teaching Resources*).

▶ Magnetic letters or letter tiles.

▶ Dry-erase markers or chalk.

From *Teaching Resources:*

▶ Letter cards (if used instead of magnetic letters or letter tiles).

▶ Word cards (High Frequency Words) for *at, am, he, my,* and *like*. (Enlarge them for demonstration purposes.)

▶ Making Words Sheets (two per child).

Understand the Principle

Children use a core of known high frequency words as anchors to monitor and check their reading. These known words help them read simple texts and engage in the behaviors of reading, such as moving from left to right across the page and matching word by word.

Known words are powerful exemplars because children connect new words to these familiar words by beginning letters or sounds.

Explain the Principle

" You see some words many times when you read. "

" Some have only one letter. Some have two letters. Some have three or four letters. "

" Words you see a lot are important because they help you read and write. "

CONTINUUM: HIGH FREQUENCY WORDS — RECOGNIZING AND USING HIGH FREQUENCY WORDS WITH TWO, THREE, OR FOUR LETTERS

plan

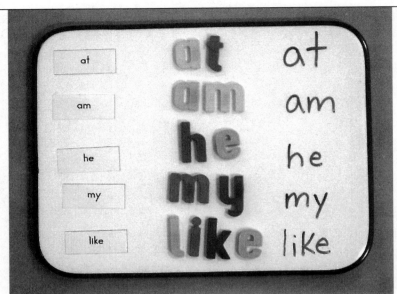

Explain the Principle

" You see some words many times when you read. "

" Some have only one letter. Some have two letters. Some have three or four letters. "

" Words you see a lot are important because they help you read and write. "

① Remind the children that they know how to read and write some words and tell them that today they will be learning more.

② Place the words for this lesson in the left column. Be sure most of the children know or "nearly know" these words.

③ Suggested language: "You know most of these words because you've been reading them. Let's read the words on the chart." Children respond.

④ "The first word is *at*. You read it. [Children respond.] Get a good look at the word *at*. Now watch while I find the magnetic letters to make *at*. I'm looking for an *a*." Continue looking for *t*.

⑤ Suggested language: "Now watch while I check to be sure I have every letter in the right order." Check by pointing to each letter in both words, in order, and checking: *a–a, t–t, at*.

⑥ "Now I'm going to write the word with a marker—*a, t*—and I'll check it letter by letter. [Demonstrate.] Let's make the next word."

⑦ Demonstrate reading the second word, building it with magnetic letters, checking it, and finally writing the whole word. Continue with the remaining words.

⑧ Place words on the word wall for reference if they aren't already there.

⑨ Explain to the children that they will repeat the same process with word cards today.

apply

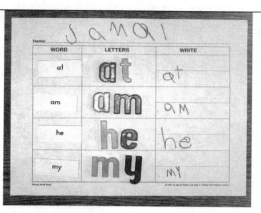

▶ Give children a Making Words Sheet, a set of word cards for the words used in the lesson, and magnetic letters. Have children place each word in the first column of the sheet, read it, make it, and write it.

▶ Children can work on the words independently. Partners can check each other's completed list.

share

Ask the children to show on the word wall some of the words they have learned to make and write.

Show high frequency word cards one at a time for a quick review.

Have the children read their list of words to a different partner.

Link

Interactive Read-Aloud: Read aloud books that have large print. (See *Teaching Resources, Large Print Books Bibliography.*) Examples are:

▶ *Lucky Song* by Vera B. Williams

▶ *Everything Has a Place* by Patricia Lillie

Shared Reading: When reading poems and stories, draw children's attention to the high frequency words and have them locate them with a masking card, flag, or highlighter tape. *Sing a Song of Poetry* contains numerous examples: "Wee Willie Winkie" *(at),* "Sometimes" *(am),* "Little Jack Horner" *(he),* "Milkman, Milkman" *(my),* "Pease Porridge Hot" *(like).*

Guided Reading: After enjoying a story, have children turn to particular pages and put a finger under selected high frequency words: "Turn to page six and put your finger under the word *at.*"

Interactive Writing: If all children can write the word, write it yourself to save time, but have children check it with their eyes.

Independent Writing: Encourage the children to recognize that they know some words really well. They can write them quickly without having to think about the individual letters and sounds. They can use their knowledge of letters and sounds to quickly check spelling.

Expand the Learning

Have children match pairs of word tiles or word cards of high frequency words (see *Teaching Resources*).

Each time children learn a new high frequency word, give them a card to add to their collection of words in a box or on rings. Have them practice reading all the words in the box or on the ring.

Connect with Home

Send home two sets of selected high frequency words on cards and encourage children to play High Frequency Word Concentration (see *Teaching Resources* for cards and directions). Be sure to include a set of directions, even though the children will have learned to play at school.

assess

▶ Notice whether the children are able to recognize high frequency words when reading.

▶ Notice whether the children can write high frequency words quickly and accurately.

Building and Writing High Frequency Words 4

Making Words

Consider Your Children

This lesson is the fourth in expanding children's knowledge of high frequency words. It is designed to establish flexible familiarity with twenty-five easy high frequency words. Children will already have encountered these words many times in shared reading, interactive writing, and guided reading. Emphasize learning how to make, write, and check words. You may want to assess children's knowledge to determine whether more lessons on high frequency words will be needed.

Working with English Language Learners

By the time you use this lesson, your English language learners will know a small core of high frequency words that they can say, build, and write. Encourage them to look carefully at words in order to learn more words. Use the words in very simple, repetitive sentences to help children understand them. Be sure that you check their ability to recognize and say the words before they take home word cards. If there are no English speakers in the home, show them how to use the cards at home and have them practice independently.

You Need

► Chart, magnetic whiteboard, chalkboard, or easel displaying high frequency words down the left column (similar to the reproducible Three-Column Sheet in *Teaching Resources*).

► Magnetic letters or letter tiles.

► Dry-erase markers or chalk.

From *Teaching Resources:*

► Letter cards (if used instead of magnetic letters or letter tiles).

► Word cards (High Frequency Words) for *an, go, do, no,* and *come.* (Enlarge them for demonstration purposes.)

► Making Words Sheets (two per child).

Understand the Principle

Children use a core of known high frequency words as anchors to monitor and check their reading. These known words help them read simple texts and practice important behaviors, like moving from left to right across the page and matching word by word.

Known words are powerful exemplars because children connect new words to these familiar words by beginning letters or sounds.

Explain the Principle

❝ You see some words many times when you read. ❞

❝ Some have only one letter. Some have two letters. Some have three or four letters. ❞

❝ Words you see a lot are important because they help you read and write. ❞

CONTINUUM: HIGH FREQUENCY WORDS — RECOGNIZING AND USING HIGH FREQUENCY WORDS WITH TWO, THREE, OR FOUR LETTERS

plan

Explain the Principle

❝ You see some words many times when you read. ❞

❝ Some have only one letter. Some have two letters. Some have three or four letters. ❞

❝ Words you see a lot are important because they help you read and write. ❞

① Remind the children that they are learning to read and write a lot of words.

② Place the words for this lesson in the left column.

③ Suggested language: "We're going to make some more words today. You know most of these words because you've been reading them. Let's read the words on the chart." Children respond.

④ "The first word is *an*. You read it. [Children respond.] Get a good look at the word *an*. Now watch while I find the magnetic letters to make *an*. I'm looking for an *a*." Continue looking for *n*.

⑤ "Now watch while I check to be sure I have every letter in the right order." Check by pointing to each letter in both words, in order, and checking: *a–a, n–n, an.*

⑥ "Now I'm going to write the word with a marker—*a, n*—and I'll check it letter by letter. [Demonstrate.] Let's make the next word."

⑦ Demonstrate reading the second word, building it with magnetic letters, checking it, and finally writing the whole word. Continue with the remaining words.

⑧ Place words on the word wall for reference if they aren't already there.

⑨ Explain to the children that they will repeat the same process with word cards today.

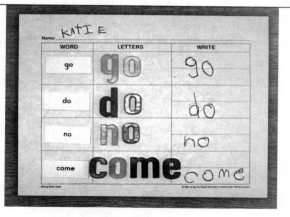

read
make
write

▸ Give the children a Making Words Sheet, a set of word cards for the words used in this lesson, and magnetic letters. Have children place each word in the first column of the sheet, read it, make it, and write it.

▸ Children can work on the words independently. Partners can check each other's completed list.

share

Ask the children to show on the word wall some of the words they have learned to make and write.

Show high frequency word cards one at a time for a quick review.

Have the children read their list of words to a different partner.

Link

Interactive Read-Aloud: Read aloud books that have large print. (See the Large Print Books Bibliography in *Teaching Resources* for examples.) Two good books are:

- ▶ *Mama Cat Has Three Kittens* by Denise Fleming
- ▶ *This Train* by Paul Collicutt

Shared Reading: When reading poems and stories, draw children's attention to high frequency words and have them locate them with a masking card, flag, or highlighter tape. *Sing a Song of Poetry* contains numerous examples: "There Was an Old Woman" *(an)*, "Wheels on the Bus" *(go)*, "Sing Sing" *(do)*, "Jack Sprat" *(no)*, "Billy, Billy" *(come)*.

Guided Reading: After enjoying a story, have children turn to particular pages and put a finger under selected high frequency words: "Turn to page three and put your finger under the word *come*."

Interactive Writing: Have a child write a high frequency word quickly while others locate it on the word wall. If all children can write the word, write it yourself to save time, but have children check it with their eyes.

Independent Writing: Encourage children to recognize that they know some words really well. They can write them quickly without having to construct them by hearing and representing the sounds. In conferences, point out words that children have written quickly because they know them.

assess

- ▶ Notice whether the children are able to recognize high frequency words when reading.

- ▶ Notice whether the children can write high frequency words quickly and accurately.
- ▶ Give a quick "test" by dictating the list of words and asking children to write them. Focus another lesson on words most of the children do not yet know.

Expand the Learning

Have children match pairs of word tiles or word cards with high frequency words (see *Teaching Resources*).

Each time children learn a new high frequency word, give them a card to add to their collection of words in a box or on rings. Have them practice reading all the words in the box or on the ring.

Connect with Home

Send home two sets of high frequency words on cards and encourage children to play High Frequency Word Concentration (see *Teaching Resources* for cards and directions). Be sure to include a set of directions, even though the children will have learned to play at school.

Building and Writing High Frequency Words 5

Making Words

Consider Your Children

Use this lesson to help children expand their knowledge of the twenty-five easy high frequency words. Emphasize working quickly and checking spelling.

Working with English Language Learners

Acquiring a core of high frequency words that they know in every detail and can automatically recognize and read will be very helpful to English language learners. Most high frequency words are abstract in that they function in sentences but are not concrete nouns. For English language learners, it will be especially important to use these words in the context of sentences so that they become familiar with hearing them and see how they are used in sentences. Construct sentences for each word that will be meaningful to students and that they can repeat—for example: "I see John." [John says, "I see Mike." Children repeat the phrase as a way of calling on others in the group.] Sentences will become more complex—for example: "Johnny can ride. So can I." Be sure the high frequency words you use are available to English language learners with your support.

You Need

▶ Chart, magnetic whiteboard, chalkboard, or easel displaying high frequency words down the left column (similar to the reproducible Three-Column Sheet in *Teaching Resources*).

▶ Magnetic letters or letter tiles.

▶ Dry-erase markers or chalk.

From *Teaching Resources*:

▶ Letter cards (if used instead of magnetic letters or letter tiles).

▶ Word cards (High Frequency Words) for *see, so, up, we,* and *you.* (Enlarge them for demonstration purposes.)

▶ Making Words Sheets (two per child).

Understand the Principle

Children use a core of known high frequency words as anchors to monitor and check their reading. These known words help them read simple texts and engage in the behaviors of reading, like moving from left to right across the page and matching word by word.

Known words are powerful exemplars because children connect new words to these familiar words by beginning letters or sounds.

Explain the Principle

" You see some words many times when you read. "

" Some have only one letter. Some have two letters. Some have three or four letters. "

" Words you see a lot are important because they help you read and write. "

plan

Explain the Principle

" You see some words many times when you read. "

" Some have only one letter. Some have two letters. Some have three or four letters. "

" Words you see a lot are important because they help you read and write. "

① Remind the children that when they read and write, they see some words many times. Today they will learn some more of these words.

② Place the words for this lesson in the left column.

③ Suggested language: "We're going to make some more words today. You know most of these words because you've been reading them. Let's read the words on the chart." Children respond.

④ "The first word is *see*. You read it. [Children respond.] Get a good look at the word *see*. Now watch while I find the magnetic letters to make *see*. I'm looking for an *s*." Continue looking for the two *e*'s.

⑤ "Now watch while I check to be sure I have every letter in the right order." Check by pointing to each letter in both words, in order, and checking: *s–s, e–e, e–e, see.*

⑥ "Now I'm going to write the word with a marker—*s, e, e*—and I'll check it letter by letter. [Demonstrate.] Let's look at the next word."

⑦ Demonstrate reading the second word, building it with magnetic letters, checking it, and finally writing the whole word. Continue with the remaining words.

⑧ Place words on the word wall for reference if they aren't already there.

⑨ Explain to the children that they will repeat the same process with word cards today.

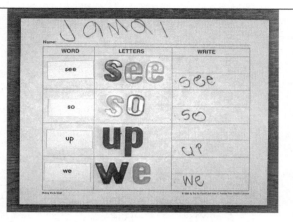

apply

read

make

write

► Give the children a Making Words Sheet, a set of word cards for the words used in this lesson, and magnetic letters. Have children place each word in the first column of the sheet, read it, make it, and write it.

► Children can work on the words independently. Partners can check each other's completed list.

share

Ask the children to show on the word wall some of the words they have learned to make and write.

Show high frequency word cards one at a time for a quick review.

Have the children read their list of words to a different partner.

395

Link

Interactive Read-Aloud: Read aloud books that have large print. (See *Teaching Resources, Large Print Books Bibliography*.) Examples are:

- *Quack, Quack* by Patricia Casey
- *What Will the Weather Be Like Today* by Paul Rogers

Shared Reading: When reading poems and stories, draw children's attention to high frequency words and have them locate them with a masking card, flag, or highlighter tape. See *Sing a Song of Poetry* for examples: "Hey Diddle Diddle" *(see)*, "Little Snail" *(so)*, "Point to the Right" *(up)*, "This Is the Way We Wash Our Face" *(we)*, "Are You Sleeping" *(you)*.

Guided Reading: After enjoying a story, have children turn to particular pages and put a finger under selected high frequency words: "Turn to page five and put your finger under the word *see*."

Interactive Writing: Have a child write a high frequency word quickly while others locate it on the word wall. If all children can write the word, write it yourself to save time, but have children check it with their eyes.

Independent Writing: Encourage the children to recognize that they know some words really well. They can write them quickly. Have them check their spelling.

assess

- Notice whether the children are able to recognize high frequency words when reading.
- Notice whether the children can write high frequency words quickly and accurately.

- Take a quick inventory by dictating a list of words for children to write. Have them practice words they do not yet know.

Expand the Learning

Have children match pairs of word tiles or word cards with high frequency words (see *Teaching Resources*).

Each time children learn a new high frequency word, give them a card to add to their collection of words in a box or on rings. Have them practice reading all the words in the box or on the ring.

Connect with Home

Send home two sets of high frequency words on cards and encourage children to play High Frequency Word Concentration (see *Teaching Resources* for cards and directions). Be sure to include a set of directions, even though the children will have learned to play at school.

Locating High Frequency Words in Text

Poems and Songs

Consider Your Children

Use this lesson after you have read a favorite poem, rhyme, song, or chant several times to the children and several more times from an enlarged text during shared reading. Any favorite song or rhyming story (or a portion of it) is suitable. Lessons like this one help children realize how they can use their knowledge of known words to check on their reading and to read quickly.

Working with English Language Learners

In this lesson, you use "Pat-a-Cake" as a known rhyme to practice finding high frequency words in text. You may select any easy rhyme for this lesson, so be sure that your choice is one that has meaning for your English language learners (see *Sing a Song of Poetry*). After selecting the rhyme, act it out with students and repeat it enough times for students to be comfortable reading it and matching word by word. This will provide a context for using the words *first* and *last*. Demonstrate the task, and have students use the words so that they understand the directions.

You Need

► Chart or pocket chart.

► Highlighter tape or strips of colored transparent plastic.

► Photocopies of poem(s).

► Magnetic letters.

Understand the Principle

Children need to learn to discriminate and identify words that are embedded in text.

The concept of "word," as defined in print, is important basic knowledge as children begin to read. Being able to locate words in text helps children monitor their reading.

Being able to identify particular high frequency words in text helps children learn how words work. This core of known words is useful for monitoring reading.

Explain the Principle

❝ When you know a word, you can read it every time you see it. ❞

❝ You can find a word by knowing how it looks. ❞

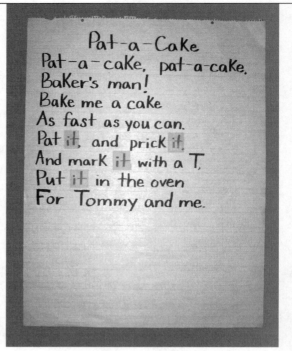

Explain
the Principle

" When you know a word, you can read it every time you see it. "

" You can find a word by knowing how it looks. "

① Tell the children they are going to practice finding easy words in a poem.

② Read the poem, rhyme, song, or chant with the children, pointing to the words. Read and enjoy the poem several times.

③ Select a few high frequency words you want to have children locate.

④ Suggested language: "You know the word *it*. This time when we read, stop when you come to the word *it*." Read the rhyme with the children, stopping at the word *it*.

⑤ Have children underline, circle, or place highlighter tape over the word on the chart. (The pocket chart has the advantage of allowing you to use colored plastic.)

⑥ Suggested language: "I'm going to highlight the word *it*. Now use your eyes to find another word *it*." Children look, and one child comes up to point to another *it*.

⑦ Repeat the process with one or two more words. Remove the highlighter tape (or plastic) from the previous word each time so that children can focus on the word they are looking for.

⑧ This game can be repeated with any text that children know and are using for shared reading.

read
circle
make

▶ Give the children a copy of the rhyme, and perhaps additional poems as well. (See *Sing a Song of Poetry*.) Display a word card where they can see it. Have them read the poem(s) and find and circle the displayed word each time it appears. Then have them make the word with magnetic letters three times.

Pat-a-cake

Pat-a-cake, pat-a-cake,
Baker's man!
Bake me a cake
As fast as you can.
Pat it, and prick it,
And mark it with a T.
Put it in the oven
For Tommy and me.

Have the children read the poem(s) to a partner, pointing out a high frequency word. Remember that the primary reasons for reading the poem are to enjoy it and learn more about language, so keep your attention to words "light."

Link

Interactive Read-Aloud: Read aloud books that include familiar rhymes and songs. (See *Teaching Resources* Bibliographies, Rhymes and Songs.) Point out easy high frequency words children are learning. Examples are:

- ▸ *Down by the Station* by Will Hillenbrand
- ▸ *Green Eggs and Ham* by Dr. Seuss

Shared Reading: Have the children locate one or two high frequency words using highlighter tape, a masking card, or a flag in poems such as "Little Red Apple" or "I Clap My Hands" (see *Sing a Song of Poetry*).

Guided Reading: During word work, have the children quickly make simple high frequency words with magnetic letters.

Interactive Writing: Draw attention to words that children can write quickly because they know them. Connect these words to the word wall and to the poems, rhymes, songs, and chants that children have encountered in shared reading.

Independent Writing: Encourage the children to use the texts they know from shared reading as resources for their writing.

assess

- ▸ Notice whether the children are able to locate high frequency words in their shared reading texts.
- ▸ Observe whether the children can read and write high frequency words.

Expand the Learning

Repeat the lesson using other poems and different words. *Locating words in shared reading should be quick and fun. Don't do too much in any single session.*

During shared reading, place a stick-on note over one or two high frequency words and have children read up to them, predicting what the word will be: what letters will they see? Then take off the stick-on note so they can check their predictions.

If children are very familiar with the text and find high frequency words easily, vary the task:

Find a word that starts with *a* (or any letter).

Find a word that ends with *e* (or any letter).

Find a word with *ing*.

Find a word with a capital ("big" or "uppercase") letter.

Find a word that is the first word in a line.

Find a word that is the last word in a line.

Find a period (or a question mark).

Connect with Home

Give each child a reproduced copy of the poem, rhyme, chant, or song used in the lesson to take home and enjoy.

Have children take home two Lotto Cards (see *Teaching Resources*) on which you've randomly written various high frequency words. Include a small set of high frequency word cards. Using pennies or buttons for markers, family members can play High Frequency Word Lotto.

Word Meaning

Children need to know the meaning of the words they are learning to read and write. It is important for them to expand their vocabulary constantly as well as develop a more complex understanding of words they already know. Word meaning is related to the development of vocabulary—labels, concept words, synonyms, antonyms, and homonyms. Concept words such as numbers and days of the week are often used in the texts they read, and they will want to use these words in their own writing. When children learn concept words (color words are another example), they can form categories that help in retrieving concept words when needed. In our complex language, meaning and spelling are intricately connected.

Often you must know the meaning of the word you want to spell or read before you can spell it accurately. In addition to lists of common concept words that children are often expected to know how to read and spell, we include synonyms, antonyms, and homonyms, which may be homographs (same spelling, different meaning, and sometimes different pronunciation) or homophones (same sound but different spelling). Knowing synonyms and antonyms will help children build more powerful systems for connecting and categorizing words; it will also help them comprehend texts better and write in a more interesting way. Being able to distinguish between homographs and homophones assists in comprehension and helps spellers to avoid mistakes.

Connect to Assessment

See related WM Assessment Tasks in the Assessment Guide in *Teaching Resources:*

▶ Understanding Concept Words—Number

▶ Understanding Concept Words—Color

Develop Your Professional Understanding

See *Word Matters: Teaching Phonics and Spelling in the Reading/Writing Classroom* by G.S. Pinnell and I.C. Fountas. 1998. Portsmouth, New Hampshire: Heinemann.

Related pages: 78–81, 88–89, 199–205.

Learning Color Words
Matching Words

Consider Your Children

Decide how many words to include in the first lesson. Children should understand what a word is and should have worked with their names. They should have had some experience reading color words in shared reading and interactive writing. They do not have to know all the letters and sounds to do this activity successfully. If they are very inexperienced, start with just three or four color words. It is a good idea to conduct an informal assessment to determine which color words children already know. Start with one that most of the children know. Color words should be written in black (not in the color) because children need to learn to attend to the features of the letters to distinguish the words.

Working with English Language Learners

Color words are helpful for English language learners to know. You'll need to consider whether they know the concept and word in their own language or whether they have not yet connected the concept/color with the label in any language. In either case, be sure that you present many different examples so that you are sure children understand about looking at a characteristic—color—and knowing that the label applies to all objects that carry that characteristic. Once children understand the concept, they will rapidly acquire the labels.

You Need

► Pocket chart.

From *Teaching Resources:*
► Color Word Cards. (Enlarge them for demonstration purposes.)
► Two-Way Sort Sheets.
► Two sheets of color words per child.

Understand the Principle

Good word solvers are able to connect words by their meanings. Knowing the meaning of words and placing them in categories provide a useful foundation for early readers and writers.

Children can use these words in writing and recognize them quickly in reading. They can make connections between these words and others that they want to read or write.

Color words are especially helpful in interactive writing, where many early stories will be about colors.

Explain the Principle

" A color has a name. "

" You can read and write the names of colors. "

WM 1
WORD MEANING

plan

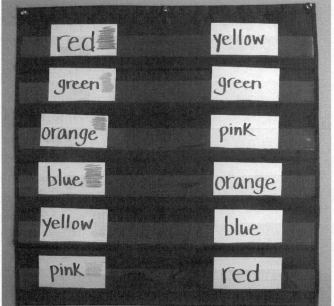

Explain the Principle

" A color has a name. "

" You can read and write the names of colors. "

① Explain to the children that they're going to learn to read color words.

② Suggested language: "We are going to read and match some color words today. What's a color word you know? [Children respond.] Can someone come up to our chart and point to the word *red?* [A volunteer comes up to point.]"

③ Have the pocket chart ready with one set of Color Word Cards on the left and another set in a different order on the right. Place a square patch of the appropriate color next to each word on the left as a visual clue.

④ Go over the words on the left of the pocket chart. If children know color labels, the color patches and pictures will help them say the words easily. (If they do not know color labels, more experience and work will be needed before you present this lesson.)

⑤ Now draw the children's attention to the words on the right side of the chart. Probably some children will already have noticed them and started to pick out the ones they know.

⑥ Suggested language: "These are all color words. We're going to play a matching game. We're going to match these words to the ones on the other side of our chart."

⑦ Select a word. "This word is. . . . [Children respond.] That's right. Malika, can you come up and match this word *red* to the word *red* on this side of the chart?" Point to color words on the right. Guide the student to put the word card from the left beside the word *red* on the right.

⑧ "Is she right? [Children respond.] Let's talk about how she can check to be sure she is right." Children may suggest looking at the first letter. Show them how to check letter by letter to be sure the words match: *r–r, e–e, d–d*. Then have the child read the two words *red*, running her finger *under* them each time.

⑨ Continue matching color words and checking until all are matched. Tell children they are going to be matching color words on a Two-Way Sort Sheet. They will see one color word at the top left and the matching color word next to it (for example, *red, red*). They will take and read a color word, glue it in the left column and glue a matching word to its right. Then they will color it with the right color. Demonstrate the steps.

read
glue
match
glue
color

▶ Have the children match words. You can place a small card with directions on the side of the chart.

▶ After they have matched them, they can use crayons or markers to color the word cards with the appropriate color.

Have children tell what they noticed about color words. (If they do not spontaneously offer observations, model by saying what you are noticing.)

Comments like these show that children are noticing features of words:

"*Purple* has more letters than *red*."

"*Black* starts like *blue* and *brown*."

"*Black* and *blue* both have *b* and *l* at the beginning."

"*Purple* has the same number of letters as *orange*."

"*Red* is the shortest."

WM 1
WORD MEANING

Link

Interactive Read-Aloud: Read aloud books that focus children's attention on colors and color words, such as:

- ▶ *Growing Colors* by Bruce McMillan
- ▶ *A Beasty Story* by Bill Martin, Jr.

Shared Reading: Read poems that feature color words, such as "Mary Wore Her Red Dress" or "Red, White, and Blue" (see *Sing a Song of Poetry*). Invite children to highlight color words with highlighter tape.

Guided Reading: There are color words in some of the first simple texts children read. Help them decode these words by using meaning in connection with the way the word looks. For example, prompt them to check the picture for the color *and* look at the letters. "Does it start with an *r* like *red?*" Prompt them to try the color word and see if it makes sense and looks right.

Interactive Writing: Innovate using texts such as *Brown Bear, Brown Bear, What Do You See?* by Bill Martin, Jr. Create a new text—*Green Frog, Green Frog, What Do You See?*—so they can learn more about color words as they construct a text.

Independent Writing: When appropriate, encourage children to use color words as they write. For example, if a child is writing a story about her house, ask what color it is.

assess

- ▶ Have individual children read a set of Color Word Cards.
- ▶ Have children match color words written on two sets of cards.

Expand the Learning

Cut up the color words into onsets and rimes (for example, *bl–ack; br–own; wh–ite*) and have children build them as they match them.

Have children make a stapled color word book that has one color word on each page. They draw a picture for each.

Connect with Home

Invite family members to make personalized color charts with their children, using a sheet of color words you send home. Children read the word, glue it in the box, write it, and draw something representative of that color.

Locating Color Words in Text

Words in Poems

Consider Your Children

Decide how many color words and sentences you will use in the lesson. Children should have worked with their names and other words and also have had some experience reading color words in shared reading and interactive writing. They do not have to know all the letters and sounds to locate color words successfully. If the children are very inexperienced, start with one or two sentences for two or three colors.

Working with English Language Learners

Be sure that English language learners have had plenty of opportunity to explore color concepts in many ways and to use the color words in oral language as well as see the words in print. The repetitive sentences in this lesson will help them gain familiarity with English syntax. Provide many opportunities for repetition, substituting different colors.

You Need

► Pocket chart.
► Sentence Strips.
► Magnetic letters.

From *Teaching Resources:*

► Color Word Cards. (Enlarge them for demonstration purposes.)

Understand the Principle

Knowing the meaning of specific words in categories and eventually being able to recognize and locate these words in text are a useful foundation for expanding children's reading vocabulary.

Early readers and writers can use color words in writing and recognize them quickly in reading. They can make connections between these words and others that they want to read or write.

Color words are especially helpful in interactive writing and early reading because many stories include simple color words.

Explain the Principle

" A color has a name. "

" You can read and write the names of colors. "

" You can find the names of colors. "

plan

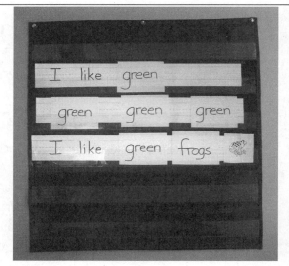

Explain the Principle

" A color has a name. "

" You can read and write the names of colors. "

" You can find the names of colors. "

① Tell the children that they are going to learn to read color words.

② Set up a color word sentence template in the pocket chart (see below). (You may want to let the children choose the object to complete the third line.) Begin with whatever color you wish—green is used in the example below.

I like green,
green, green, green.
I like green frogs.

You may want to add a small picture or a dot of color as a clue at the beginning or end of the line to support emergent readers.

③ Read the chart together several times. Point carefully under each word.

④ Ask a child to come up and point to the word *green*. Show the children that the word *green* appears five times. Help children notice that the word *green* starts with a *g*. Suggested language: "*G* can be uppercase or lowercase, and the word has five letters."

⑤ Reread the verse. Take out the five word cards that say *green*. Explain to the children that you are going to make a new verse about a new color. Hold up the color card that says *red*. Help children notice it has three letters and starts with an *r*.

⑥ Put the five cards that say *red* in the verse in the appropriate places.

⑦ Invite children to suggest a new red-color object for the third line (strawberries, for example). Write that word on a card and insert it. You may want to quickly draw strawberries next to the word as a picture clue.

⑧ Repeat the process with the other color words—yellow, white, orange, blue, purple, brown, black, pink. (This may take several days.)

early
mid
late

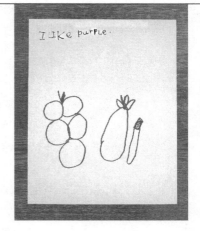

take
make
check
mix

► Give the children a set of word cards for colors used in the lesson. Have them take a card, make the color word with magnetic letters (or with letter cards), use the word card to check the word they've made, mix up the letters, and make the color word two more times.

► Have children take a blank piece of paper, choose one of the colors they worked with (blue, for example), and write *I like blue* at the top. (They will be able to copy the color word from the word card, and if they need support with *I* and *like*, they can refer to the enlarged-print verse.) Have them draw two or three objects of that color to go with their sentences.

Invite the children to talk about their individual "I like" sentences and pictures. Ask them what they noticed about color words. (If they do not spontaneously offer observations, model by saying what you are noticing.) Comments like these are evidence that children are noticing features of words:

"Color words can start with uppercase or lowercase letters."
"*Orange* is the same name for the color and the fruit."
"We could say *apples* for *red*."
"*White* and *blue* have an *e* at the end."
"*Orange* and *red* both have an *r*."
"*Orange* and *green* both have a *g*, but it sounds different."

WM 2
WORD MEANING

409

Link

Interactive Read-Aloud: Read aloud books that include color words. (See the Concept Books Bibliographies in *Teaching Resources*.) Examples are:

▶ ***Brown Bear, Brown Bear, What Do You See?*** by Bill Martin, Jr.

▶ ***Brown Cow, Green Grass, Yellow Mellow Sun*** by Ellen Jackson

Shared Reading: Read poems that feature color words, such as "Roses Are Red," Color Song," or "Who Is Wearing Red?" (see *Sing a Song of Poetry*).

Guided Reading: There are color words in some of the first simple texts children read. Ask them to locate color words in texts.

Interactive Writing: Help the children conduct a survey of favorite colors of class members. Graph the results. Use interactive writing to write a sentence or two about their conclusions.

Independent Writing: Encourage the children to use a color word chart or colors on the word wall as a resource in writing.

assess

▶ See how many color words individual children can recognize without clues.

Expand the Learning

Ask the children to build other color words with magnetic letters or other media.

Use other poems, rhymes, songs, or chants with color words, such as "Mary Had a Little Lamb" (see *Sing a Song of Poetry*).

Give children several Color Word Cards, and have them read them and choose the appropriate crayon to color over the word. Have them glue these word cards onto a blank sheet as a personal reference.

Connect with Home

Send home a sheet of color words (see *Teaching Resources,* Color Word Cards). Encourage family members to have children draw a rainbow with crayons or watercolors. They can then cut out the appropriate color words and glue them on or next to the colors of the rainbow.

Learning Number Words
Matching Words

Consider Your Children

This lesson is best used after children have read poems like "One, Two, Buckle My Shoe" (see *Sing a Song of Poetry*) and are able to count objects. Children should understand what a word is and should have worked with their names. They should have encountered numerals and number words in shared reading and interactive writing. If they are very inexperienced, start with just three number words. It is a good idea to conduct an informal assessment before this lesson to determine which numerals and number words children already know. Start the lesson with a number word that most of the children know.

Working with English Language Learners

English language learners need to understand the concept of numbers as well as the English labels. They may know number concepts and labels in their own languages, or they may still be developing number concepts and just beginning to learn labels in any language. Number concepts take some time to acquire; for example, children must be able to match one by one (count) and must understand the number word as the label for the accumulation of objects. Then the child must be able to match the number concepts and words with written symbols—both the numeral and the word. You will need to be explicit and clear in your instructions and have children count (matching one by one) and say number labels as many times as necessary.

You Need

► Pocket chart.

► Sentence Strips with number words, illustrations, and numerals.

From *Teaching Resources:*

► Numeral Cards.

► Number Word Cards.

► Four-Box Sheets.

Understand the Principle

Good word solvers are able to recognize many words that appear frequently in text and connect words by meaning.

Knowing the meaning of and eventually being able to recognize some specific words in categories is a useful foundation for early readers and writers. They can use these words when writing and recognize them quickly when reading. They can make connections between these words and others that they want to read or write.

Explain the Principle

❝ A number has a name. ❞

❝ You can read and write the names of numbers. ❞

❝ You can find the names of numbers. ❞

plan

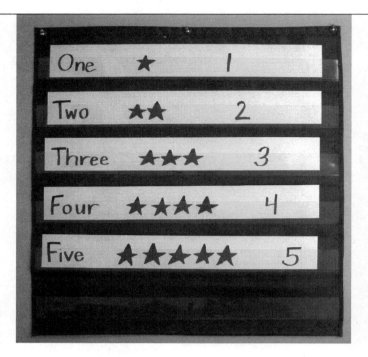

Explain the Principle

" A number has a name. "

" You can read and write the names of numbers. "

" You can find the names of numbers. "

① Explain to the children that they are going to learn how to read number words.

② Put the word and number cards that appear to the left of the chart on an easel, on a separate pocket chart, or in another area where children can see them clearly.

③ Suggested language: "We are going to read and match some numbers and number words today. Can someone come up to our chart and point to the numeral *1*?" A volunteer comes up to point. Continue with the other numerals. Use the stars to emphasize the quantity the numeral represents.

④ Now draw children's attention to the cards outside the chart. Suggested language: "These are all numbers and number words. We're going to play a matching game. We're going to match these numbers and words to the ones on our chart."

⑤ Select a number word. Suggested language: "This word is *two*. Aaron, can you come up and match this word *two* to the number *2* on the chart?" Guide the child to put the number word *two* beside the other number word *two*.

⑥ "Is he right? [Children respond.] Let's talk about ways we can check to be sure he is right." Children may suggest looking at the first letter. Show them how to check letter by letter to be sure the words match: *t–t, w–w, o–o*. Then have the child read the two words *two*, running a finger under them each time.

⑦ Then have a child find the numeral *2*, place it on the chart right next to the word *two*, and read the strip.

⑧ Suggested language: "Look at the numeral *2*. It has a curve at the top, goes down to the bottom, and then has a straight line. Who can come and point to the numeral *2*? [Volunteer does so.] Who can come up and point to the word *two*? [Volunteer does so.]"

⑨ Continue matching numerals and number words and checking until all are matched.

read
match
glue
draw
check

▶ Have children match words and numerals. (You can place a small card with directions on the side of the chart.) Give children a Four-Box Sheet. Also give them Number Word Cards and corresponding Numeral Cards. Have them match a numeral with the corresponding number word and glue them in a box. Then ask them to draw that number of objects in the box. Have them fill all the boxes in this way. After the children check their work, they can take another sheet and repeat the process.

Model and then have children tell what they noticed about number words. Comments such as these show that children are noticing features of words:

"*Two* and *three* start with the same letter—*t*."
"*Three* has more letters than *two*."
"*Four* starts with an *f*."
"*Four* and *five* both start with an *f*."
"*One* and *two* have three letters."

Link

Interactive Read-Aloud: Read aloud books that contain number words. Examples are:

- ▶ *Every Buddy Counts* by Stuart J. Murphy
- ▶ *Counting Is for the Birds* by Frank Mazzola, Jr.

Shared Reading: Read poems such as "One, Two, Buckle My Shoe," "One, Two, Three, Four," and "One Potato, Two Potato" (see *Sing a Song of Poetry*). Have children locate number words with a masking card or highlighter tape.

Guided Reading: There are number words in some of the first simple texts children read. Help children use meaning in connection with the way the word looks. For example, prompt them to check the picture for the number *and* look at the word. "Does it start with a *t* like *two?*" Prompt them to try the word and see if it makes sense and looks right.

Interactive Writing: Construct texts similar to "One, Two, Buckle My Shoe" to help children learn more about number words: *One, two, look at you; three, four, get off the floor.*

Independent Writing: Encourage the children to use the number word chart as a resource as they write. Be sure they write number words instead of numerals in their stories.

assess

- ▶ After the children have matched number words several times, mix up the number cards and notice which number words individual children can recognize quickly.

Expand the Learning

Repeat the lesson with more number words.

Cut up the Number Word Cards into onsets and rimes *(thr–ee; f–our)* and have children build them as they match them.

Connect with Home

Invite family members to make personalized number charts with their children, using Number Word Cards (from *Teaching Resources*). Children can read the word, glue it in the box, write it, and draw that many objects in the box.

Duplicate a separate set of Numeral Cards (see *Teaching Resources*) that children can cut apart, take home, and match with the number words in the boxes in their charts.

Locating Numerals and Number Words in Text

Making Words

Consider Your Children

Decide how many lines of the poem and how many numbers to include in the lesson. You can use the first two lines (with the numbers 1 through 5) or all four lines (with the numbers 1 through 10). Children should understand what words are and should have worked with their names. They should have encountered number words in shared reading and interactive writing. They do not have to know all the letters and sounds to do this activity successfully. Prepare for the lesson by reading the poem several days in shared reading.

Working with English Language Learners

Help children understand the concept of the numbers 1 through 5 by counting on fingers or counting objects. They may understand the concept but not the English word. Once they understand the concept, show them the numeral and then the word. Spend some time counting and matching. All children may need help understanding that a "hare" is really a "rabbit." If this is a difficult concept, substitute other words such as *bird, bug,* or *bee.* Act out the poem to support understanding, and provide many repetitions.

You Need

▶ Pocket chart.

▶ Sentence Strips (number poem).

▶ Magnetic letters.

From *Teaching Resources:*

▶ Numeral Cards. (Enlarge them for demonstration purposes.)

▶ Number Word Cards. (Enlarge them for demonstration purposes.)

▶ Three-Way Sort Sheets.

Understand the Principle

Knowing the meaning of and eventually being able to recognize and locate in text some specific words in categories is a useful foundation for early readers and writers.

Children can use these words when writing and recognize them quickly when reading. They can make connections between these words and others that they want to read or write.

Number words appear in many simple texts children read and are also used frequently in interactive writing.

Explain the Principle

" A number has a name. "

" You can read and write the names of numbers. "

" You can find the names of numbers. "

plan

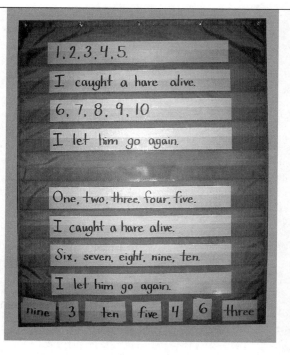

Explain the Principle

" A number has a name. "

" You can read and write the names of numbers. "

" You can find the names of numbers. "

① Tell the children they are going to find numerals and number words in text.

② When children can read the chart with you, introduce them to the Number Word Cards and this matching activity. Have the Numeral Cards and matching word cards on the left side of the pocket chart or on a separate chart or easel. Suggested language: "We are going to read and match numerals and number words today. Let's read the rhyme together." Read the numeral version and then read the version with the numbers spelled out.

③ "Now let's match the numbers with the numbers in the poem."

④ Show children the word cards outside the chart. "Can someone find the number *1* on our number cards?"

⑤ Have a volunteer find the numeral *1*, and then show children how to match it with the text by placing the card over the number on the sentence strip. Show children how to check to be sure the number matches: "The number *1* has a straight stick."

⑥ Suggested language: "Can someone find the number *2?*" Have a volunteer find the numeral *2*.

⑦ Continue matching until children have found all the numerals and placed them over the numerals in the sentence strip.

⑧ Suggested language: "Now let's match the number words. Who can find the word *one?*" Select a volunteer to find the word *one* and place it over the word *one* in the text. "How can we check to be sure the words match?" Children may suggest looking at the letters. Show them how to check letter by letter.

⑨ Continue finding words until all the words are matched.

⑩ Tell children they will be using a Three-Way Sort Sheet. Have the key number and word at the top of the first two columns. Children will match numerals with their corresponding words. Then, in the third column, they will make the number word with magnetic letters.

put
match
make

▶ Give children a set of selected Numeral and Number Word Cards and a container of magnetic letters. Have children place the numeral in the first column, place the number word in the second column, and make the word with magnetic letters in the third column of a Three-Way Sort Sheet.

share

Have children tell what they noticed when they read and matched numerals and number words. (If they do not spontaneously offer observations, model the process by saying what you are noticing.)

Comments like these show that children are noticing features of numerals and number words:

"*Two* and *three* start with *t.*"
"Numbers are just one thing, but words have letters."
"*Four* and *five* start alike."

Link

Interactive Read-Aloud: Read aloud books and point out numerals and number words. Examples are:

- ▶ *Feast for 10* by Cathryn Falwell
- ▶ *Hippos Go Berserk!* by Sandra Boynton

Shared Reading: Read poems such as "One for Sorrow" or sing songs such as "Jumping Beans" (see *Sing a Song of Poetry*).

Guided Reading: There are number words in some of the first simple texts children read. After reading the story, have them locate number words in the text. Say, "On page _____, put your finger under the word _____."

Interactive Writing: Have children conduct surveys that involve numbers (for example, "How many letters are in your name?"). Graph the class results and write about them. The sentences you write with the children will contain many number words.

Independent Writing: Encourage children to use the number chart as a resource in writing. Be sure they write words instead of numerals in their stories.

Expand the Learning

Introduce other numerals and number words and repeat the lesson.

Connect with Home

Reproduce the poem "One, Two, Three, Four" (see *Sing a Song of Poetry*) or other number poems you have taught the children and send them home. Invite family members to have their children highlight the number words with a colored highlighter.

assess

- ▶ After all children have matched numerals and number words several times, notice how many individual children can recognize them without clues.

Connecting Words That Go Together

Family Pictures

Consider Your Children

This lesson is intended to help children focus directly on related words and should be used after reading aloud many stories that include such words so that the children can experience them in context. As you use this lesson and repeat it, keep on reading stories with words that are related. The lesson deals with very simple relationships, but you can expand it to increase children's knowledge of word meanings. You can use this lesson early in kindergarten and repeat it with different sets of words as often as necessary throughout the year.

Working with English Language Learners

Knowing the meaning of words in English is an important factor in English language learners' literacy. Unless they have an understanding of the words they encounter in reading, decoding will be meaningless. Repeating this lesson will help English language learners connect words, making learning more powerful and efficient. You will want to have pictures representing the words you are using and also to be sure that children say the words themselves. It will help to have children use repetitive language. For example, "Marisa has one sister. Raquel has one brother and two sisters." Keep in mind that English language learners may have different names for family members and this will add to the interest of the lesson.

You Need

▶ Pocket chart.

▶ Pictures or drawings of families.

From *Teaching Resources:*

▶ Pocket Chart Card Template.

Understand the Principle

Words that are in children's spoken vocabulary are easier to decode; knowing the meaning of words in oral language makes it easier for children to comprehend the texts that they read.

The texts children read should include mostly words that they already know. That also means it is important that children constantly expand their speaking vocabularies.

They need to know not only words but also the important relationships among words.

When children begin to form powerful categories for connecting words, it is easier for them to add to their speaking and listening vocabulary and to consider the subtle shadings of meaning that are often involved in comprehension.

Explain the Principle

" Some words go together because of what they mean. "

CONTINUUM: WORD MEANING — RECOGNIZING AND USING WORDS THAT ARE RELATED

plan

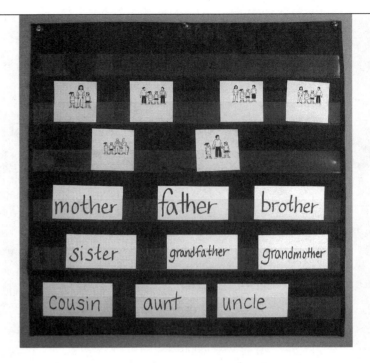

Explain the Principle

" **Some words go together because of what they mean.** "

① Explain to the children that today they will be learning about words that go together.

② Place a picture (or several different pictures) of a family on the easel. You could include your own family. Be sure you show diversity among families—for example, a grandmother and children; a father, mother, and several children; a mother, grandmother, and child; a father and child; several generations of a family.

③ Suggested language: "Here are some families. There are special names for people in our families. What do you call the people in your families?" Let children talk generally about the people in their families. Point out that families are different because people are different, but there are some words that we can all use to mean people in our families.

④ "One important family word is *mother*. Who can find someone in this family who looks like the *mother?* Do you know some other words for *mother?*" Let children talk about what they call their mothers: *mom, mommy, mama*, or words in a language other than English.

⑤ "A word that is connected to *mother* is *father*." Repeat the process with *father* and then select either *grandmother/grandfather* or *sister/brother*. Children may have special names for *grandmother*. Children may also offer words such as *aunt/uncle* or *cousins*.

⑥ Encourage children to talk about family members who are not actually related to them but are considered family or function as caregivers and have special names. Explain that special people can be part of a family even if they are not related to you.

⑦ Make a quick chart of words that go together. Read the names on the chart in a shared way.

⑧ Suggested language: "Some words go together because of what they mean. We will keep these family words on our chart. There will be other words that we can think of that go together because of what they mean."

▸ Have children draw pictures of their families (or a selected member of the family) and label the picture with words. You should expect approximated spelling.

Have children share their family pictures and locate words on the chart.

Link

Interactive Read-Aloud: Read aloud books that feature family themes. Point out words such as *parents* that can be added to the "family" category. Examples are:

- ▶ *Flower Garden* by Eve Bunting
- ▶ *Julius, the Baby of the World* by Kevin Henkes

Shared Reading: Read texts and poems that feature family themes, such as "Five Little Ducks" or "Went in for a Swim" (see *Sing a Song of Poetry*).

Guided Reading: Children may be familiar with their own names for family members and will need to learn the more formal words they will see in books. During introductions, have children say and locate family words.

Interactive Writing: Have children write sentences about their families—for example, "Javon has two brothers." You can also draw their attention to singular and plural forms of words.

Independent Writing: Have children make a "family book" that can also include friends and caregivers.

assess

- ▶ Observe the children's use of family words in their oral language.
- ▶ Perform a quick oral assessment by asking children to generate connected words when you say this list: *mother, sister, grandmother, aunt* or *father, brother, grandfather, uncle.*
- ▶ Notice whether children can accurately predict categories of words and locate them while reading simple texts.

Expand the Learning

Repeat the lesson with "clothing" words: *hat, shirt, skirt, shoes, socks, T-shirt, jacket, coat, gloves, mittens, belt, dress, sweatshirt.* Place charts of related words together in one part of the room so that children can quickly see the words and the categories.

Repeat the lesson with "weather" words: *hot, warm, cold, windy, sunny, rainy, snowy; snow, rain, sleet, drizzle, wind.* As you read aloud to children, add words to this or any other category.

Repeat the lesson with "animal" words: *cow, horse, cat, dog, sheep, elephant, gerbil, turtle, monkey.* Form subcategories for pets, animals you would see on a farm, and animals you would see at the zoo.

Repeat the lesson with "food" words: *breakfast, lunch, supper* or *dinner; juice, cereal, apples, oranges, peanut butter, chicken, steak, hamburger,* etc. Subcategorize words by what you would eat for breakfast, lunch, or dinner. Emphasize that different people often have different preferences; for example, some people might eat fish and rice for breakfast and others eat pancakes or cereal.

Connect with Home

Have children take home their "family" books with members drawn and labeled. Leave some blank pages for more drawings that they do at home. You might want to have one page that says: "I like to _____ with my family." With a family member's help, the child can fill in the blank and draw a picture. Or family members can draw or write something that they like to do with the child.

Learning the Days of the Week
Matching Words

Consider Your Children

Use this lesson after children have heard you read aloud stories such as *Cookie's Week,* by Cindy Ward, or *The Very Hungry Caterpillar,* by Eric Carle, that present the days of the week in context. Also be sure you have worked with the calendar very briefly as part of the opening meeting, so that children have heard the days of the week many times. You'll want to emphasize the consistent circular order of the days of the week. If you work with the calendar as a regular part of the day, this lesson may not be necessary. Remember that if children fully understand these words and concepts, you will no longer need to spend much time on the calendar.

Working with English Language Learners

Be sure that your students understand the concept of the calendar and days of the week. Most kindergarten students, whatever their language background, will just be beginning to understand time as measured by the calendar. You'll want to use the calendar as a visual aid and help students understand time as it goes by, marking the days and helping students say the names of the days of the week and months of the year. After students have had some experience with the calendar, you can begin to make this knowledge systematic by helping them focus on the seven days of the week.

You Need

► Pocket chart.

From *Teaching Resources:*

► Two sets of Day-of-Week Word Cards. (Enlarge them for demonstration purposes.)

► Two copies of Day-of-Week Word Cards for each child.

► Two-Way Sort Sheets.

Understand the Principle

Knowing specialized words in categories lets children use these words when writing and recognize them quickly when reading.

Texts are often organized around ordered categories of words such as the days of the week.

Explain the Principle

" Days of the week have names and are always in the same order. "

" You can read and write the names of the days of the week. "

" You can find the names of the days of the week. "

plan

Explain the Principle

❝ Days of the week have names and are always in the same order. ❞

❝ You can read and write the names of the days of the week. ❞

❝ You can find the names of the days of the week. ❞

① Tell the children that they are going to learn how to read the days of the week.

② Suggested language: "Here are some words you know—*Sunday, Monday, Tuesday, Wednesday, Thursday, Friday, Saturday.* What are those words? [Children respond.] That's right. They are the names of the days of the week that we see on our calendar. We are going to read and match the days of the week today. Can someone read the first word [point to Sunday]?" A child responds.

③ Suggested language: "Now can someone find the word *Sunday* on the right side of the chart and put it next to the word *Sunday* in the list on the left?" A child responds.

④ Continue matching and checking until all the words are matched. Point out that all the words on the list end with *day.*

⑤ Mix up the words and match and check them again, this time beginning with *Monday.* Children may observe that they have to look beyond the first letter for *Saturday, Sunday* and *Tuesday, Thursday.*

⑥ Tell children they are going to be matching days of the week on a Two-Way Sort Sheet.

cut
glue
match
glue

▶ Give children a Two-Way Sort Sheet with a key word glued at the top of both columns (for example, *Sunday, Sunday*) and two copies of the Days-of-Week Word Cards. Have children cut the word cards apart and glue a day word in the left column and then glue the matching day word next to it in the right column.

Have children tell what they noticed about the names of the days of the week. (If they do not spontaneously offer observations, model the process by saying what you are noticing.)

Comments like these show that children are noticing features of words:

"*Tuesday* and *Thursday* both start with *T.*"

"All the days start with a capital (or uppercase) letter."

"They all have *day* at the end."

"*Saturday* and *Sunday* start the same."

Link

Interactive Read-Aloud: Read aloud books that are structured around the days of the week, such as:

- *Cookie's Week* by Cindy Ward
- *Dear Daisy, Get Well Soon* by Maggie Smith

Shared Reading: Read poems and songs that feature days of the week, such as "How Many Days?" or "Tommy Snooks" (see *Sing a Song of Poetry*).

Guided Reading: The days of the week are featured in some of the first simple texts children read. Help children use meaning in connection with the way the word looks. For example, prompt them to look at the word. "Does it start with an *M,* which would make the word *Monday?*" Prompt them to try the word and see if it makes sense and looks right.

Interactive Writing: Write texts structured around the days of the week: "On Tuesday, we go to gym." These texts can later be used for shared reading.

Independent Writing: Encourage children to use the days of the week in their writing. The calendar can be a resource.

assess

- After all children have matched the days of the week several times, mix up the word cards, hold them up one at a time, and notice which words individual students know.

Expand the Learning

Cut up the days-of-the-week words into syllables *(Mon–day, Tues–day, Fri–day)* and have children build the words as they match them.

Connect with Home

Encourage family members to use a calendar with their children at home. They can point out the names of the days of the week.

Send home one set of Days-of-Week Word Cards (see *Teaching Resources*). Ask family members to staple seven sheets of paper together and have the child glue the name of a day on each sheet and draw a picture of something she did that day.

Locating Days of the Week in Text
Making Sentences

Consider Your Children

Decide how many days and variations to include in the lesson. Children should have worked with the names of the days of the week as well as with the calendar in general. Also, children should be familiar with high frequency words such as *we, like, on,* and *to.* The example in this lesson shows what the chart will look like after you have worked with it for several days. For the first day, work with two or three sentences only.

Working with English Language Learners

This lesson requires students to use their knowledge of the words representing days of the week as they read a series of sentences. For English language learners, you may want to use the sentences as a shared reading task and be sure that they understand the key words (for example, "read books"). You can act out any verbs that you think your English language learners will not understand and have them repeat the language structure. Have students locate the names of the days of the week and connect them to the calendar.

You Need

▶ Pocket chart.

▶ Sentence Strips.

From *Teaching Resources:*

▶ Day-of-Week Word Cards.

Understand the Principle

Being able to recognize words they will see and use often helps children in a variety of reading and writing contexts. These words build a foundation for learning other words.

Explain the Principle

❝ Days of the week have names and are always in the same order. ❞

❝ You can read and write the names of the days of the week. ❞

❝ You can find the names of the days of the week. ❞

plan

teach

Explain the Principle

" **Days of the week have names and are always in the same order.** "

" **You can read and write the names of the days of the week.** "

" **You can find the names of the days of the week.** "

① Explain to the children that they are going to learn how to read the days of the week.

② Start by constructing two or three sentences through shared writing. (The children and teacher compose the sentence, and the teacher writes it quickly.) Suggested language: "Let's write down some of the things we like to do during the week." Guide the children to think of something they like to do each day. Write the words on Sentence Strips. Read each one together after writing it. You can leave the strip whole, but put plenty of space between words so that you can cut the sentences up into words and phrases later.

③ Have children locate the day names on cards and match them with the day names in the sentences on the chart.

> Fun in Room 5
>
> We like to read books on Monday.
>
> We like to write stories on Tuesday.
>
> We like to play music on Wednesday.
>
> We like to play games on Thursday.
>
> We like to   on Friday.
>
> do math   go to gym   take walks
>
> listen to stories   see movies   sing songs

We like to read books on Monday.

apply

cut
fix
glue
draw

▸ Give children a sheet containing the words for the first sentence in the lesson. Have children cut out the words, arrange them to make the sentence, glue them in order on plain white paper, and illustrate the sentence.

▸ Have children match word cards with the days of the week in the sentences.

▸ Have children change the sentences by substituting other activities and days, and ask them to read their new sentences out loud.

share

With the children, read the sentences on the chart several times, each time in a different order.

Link

Interactive Read-Aloud: Read aloud books that are structured around the days of the week. Examples are:

- ▶ *One Monday Morning* by Uri Shulevitz
- ▶ *Today Is Monday* by Eric Carle

Shared Reading: Read the calendar and other texts or poems and songs that incorporate the days of the week, such as "How Many Days?" or "Today" (see *Sing a Song of Poetry*). Have children use a masking card (see *Teaching Resources*) to locate a particular day.

Guided Reading: Many books incorporate the words for the days of the week. After enjoying a story, help children locate names of days in the text.

Interactive Writing: Have children choose a "favorite" day and graph the class results. Then construct some simple sentences about their favorite day: *Jane likes to swim on Saturday. Jane likes Saturday because there is no school.* Children can illustrate their sentences. You may want to bind a class book of these sentences for children to read.

Independent Writing: Encourage children to use the calendar or charts as a resource.

assess

- ▶ Do a quick individual check, using word cards, to see how many days of the week each child can recognize.

- ▶ Using two sets, have the children match and say the words on the Days-of-Week Word Cards.

Expand the Learning

Revise the sentences you have written: "We can substitute other things you like to do. What are some more things to do that we can put into our sentences?" Write children's suggestions on Sentence Strips as phrases. Substitute these phrases for phrases in the sentences and read the new sentences together.

Introduce the idea of beginning the sentences differently: "You can start sentences differently to make them more interesting. Remember in *Cookie's Week*, the sentences started like this: 'On Monday, Cookie fell in the toilet.' Watch while I change our first sentence." Change the sentence to say, "On Monday, we like to read books." Have the children help you change the rest of the sentences to start like the first one.

Connect with Home

Put another sentence from the day's writing on word cards (for example, "We like to play games on Thursday"). Give the children a blank sheet along with the word cards so they can put the sentence back together at home and illustrate it.

Word Structure

Looking at the structure of words will help children learn how words are related to each other and how words can be changed by adding letters, letter clusters, and larger parts of words. Being able to recognize syllables, for example, helps children break down words into smaller units that are easier to analyze. In phonological awareness lessons, children learn to recognize the word breaks and to identify the number of syllables in a word. They can build on this useful information in reading and writing.

Words often have affixes, parts added before or after a word to change its meaning. An affix can be a prefix or a suffix. The word to which affixes are added can be a *base* word or a *root* word. A base word is a complete word; a root word is a part with Greek or Latin origins (such as *phon* in *telephone*). It will not be necessary for young children to make this distinction when they are beginning to learn about simple affixes, but working with suffixes and prefixes will help them read and understand words that use them as well as use them accurately in writing.

Endings or word parts that are added to base words signal meaning. For example, they may signal relationships *(prettier, prettiest)* or time *(running, planted)*. Principles related to word structure include understanding the meaning and structure of compound words, contractions, plurals, and possessives as well as knowing how to make and use them accurately. We have also included the simple abbreviations that children often see in the books they read and want to use in their writing.

Connect to Assessment

See related WS Assessment Tasks in the Assessment Guide in *Teaching Resources:*

- ▶ Repeating Sentences That Include Words with Different Endings

- ▶ Selecting Sentences with Correct and Incorrect Word Endings

Develop Your Professional Understanding

See *Word Matters: Teaching Phonics and Spelling in the Reading/Writing Classroom* by G.S. Pinnell and I.C. Fountas. 1998. Portsmouth, New Hampshire: Heinemann.

Related pages: 97–98.

Learning Words: Simple Plurals
Plural Concentration

Consider Your Children

This lesson is best used after children can count and group objects and know the concept of plural. They should also be able to identify the sounds in words. Use nouns that children know.

Working with English Language Learners

English language learners may have difficulty understanding English word structure for plurals and will need many experiences talking about concrete objects—for example: "I see one pencil. I see two pencils." They can also use singular and plural forms to talk about pictures and to talk about the stories that you read aloud to them. Be sure to articulate clearly, slightly emphasizing the final sound on plural words. Drawing attention to the *s* at the end of the plural will help children realize the sound that is added.

You Need

▶ Chart paper and markers.

▶ Whiteboard and dry-erase marker.

From *Teaching Resources:*

▶ Concentration Cards (Deck Card Template).

▶ Directions for Concentration.

Understand the Principle

Children need to attend to word endings that indicate more than one of something.

The /s/ sound at the end of a word tells you that someone is talking about more than one.

Explain the Principle

❝ Add -*s* to some words to show you mean more than one. ❞

You can add –s to a word
when you mean more than one.

dog	dogs
cat	cats
boy	boys
girl	girls
ball	balls
tree	trees
Mom	Moms
Dad	Dads
sister	sisters
brother	brothers

Explain the Principle

" Add *-s* to some words to show you mean more than one. "

① Tell the children you are going to show them something new about words.

② Begin by having children orally generate singular and plural forms of simple nouns. Suggested language: "I'll say the word for one thing, and you say the word for more than one." Demonstrate by saying *one cat* and then *two cats*. Follow with words such as *tree, can, boy,* and *girl*.

③ After the children generate plurals by adding -*s*, write some simple words on the left side of a chart, or make them with magnetic letters. Invite children to write the words with *s* on the right side. If you are using magnetic letters, you can have a child add -*s* and read the new plural form.

④ Ask the children what they have noticed about the words. Be sure to help children understand that you add -*s* for two or more things. You may demonstrate. Comments like these indicate that children are analyzing words and thinking about the principle:

"You add -*s*."
"Some sound like *z* and some sound like *s* at the end."
"Boy is one boy and boys is two boys."

⑤ With the children, formulate the principle "You can add -*s* to a word when you mean more than one" and write it at the top of the chart.

⑥ With two children, demonstrate how to play the card game Plural Concentration. The goal is to match one singular word with its plural form. The player who makes the most pairs wins the game.

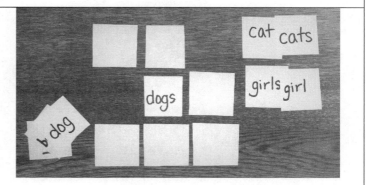

apply

turn
read
match

▶ Have children play Plural Concentration with the words from the lesson.

share

Ask the children to show one plural word. Place one or two examples on the word wall.

Link

Interactive Read-Aloud: Read aloud a story such as those below. Point out an interesting new word for children that illustrates the principle of this lesson.

- ▸ *Just One More* by Michele Koch
- ▸ *Hide and Snake* by Keith Baker

Shared Reading: After reading and enjoying a poem, such as "Hot Cross Buns" or "Here Are My Ears" (see *Sing a Song of Poetry*), ask the children to find plural nouns that are made by adding -*s*, using a masking card or highlighter tape.

Guided Reading: During word work, make the noun with magnetic letters and then make it again as a plural, showing children how to add the -*s*.

Interactive Writing: Call attention to the principle. Ask the children who are having difficulty with the principle to come up to the easel and write the plural ending for a simple noun.

Independent Writing: Draw attention to the principle while conferring with children.

assess

- ▸ Notice whether the children are using conventional spelling for simple plurals in their writing.
- ▸ Notice whether the children are using conventional plural forms for nouns that end in *y* in their writing.

Expand the Learning

When the children are familiar with all the simple plurals you have used, remove the singular forms from the matching. Then have them sort the plurals by the ending sound (*s* or *z*). This extension will help children understand that the *s* at the end can have either sound.

Connect with Home

Send home copies of word cards (see *Teaching Resources,* Word Card Template) with singular and plural forms of simple nouns so that children can cut them apart and match them.

Adding *s* to Change Word Meanings

Making Words

Consider Your Children

One of the first affixes children learn is adding *s* to change a verb. Many of the simple texts children read will have verbs that have an added *s*. Children who have developed a small core of known words will find it easy to distinguish this ending letter. Most speakers of English will have an internalized sense of how to use this inflectional ending within sentences. Build on children's sense of what "sounds right."

Working with English Language Learners

Working with English language structure is often quite difficult for English language learners because they do not have a fully developed implicit sense of the syntactic rules. After they have heard English read aloud many times, engaged in shared reading and interactive writing, and had a great deal of experience using sentences that help them learn the language structures, you can help them see that they can use their knowledge of language to help them check on their reading and figure out words. Engage in as many repetitions as necessary to help them become fluent with sentences so they can notice the differences in words. Introduce many activities in which children use repetitive language.

You Need

► Pocket chart.

► Sentence Strips.

► Magnetic letters.

From *Teaching Resources:*

► Two-Way Sort Sheets.

Understand the Principle

Many of the simple texts that children read use verbs that have an added *s* to agree with a third-person subject.

Noticing the ending *s* and at the same time paying attention to how the verb sounds in the sentence (using their knowledge of language structure) help children attend to both visual information and syntax while reading and familiarize them with subject-verb agreement.

Explain the Principle

❝ Add *s* to the end of a word to make it sound right in a sentence. ❞

plan

Explain the Principle

" Add *s* to the end of a word to make it sound right in a sentence. "

① Tell the children they are going to learn more about words.

② Read the sentence, *I walk home*. Then have the children read it with you.

③ Add an *s* to *walk* and put *He* over the word *I*. Read the sentence and have the children read it with you.

④ Repeat using two or three other sentences: *We play with the toys. I run to the store*. Each time change the subject to *she* or *he* and add an *s* to the verb.

⑤ Discuss how you have made the sentence "sound right" by adding *s*.

⑥ Show children a list of simple verbs that they will use in the application activity and read them together.

make	
add *s*	
read	
write	
add *s*	
read	

▸ Give the children a Two-Way Sort Sheet and have them use magnetic letters to make some simple verbs *(run, sit, dig, put, play)* in the left-hand column. Have them add *s* and read the word.

▸ On the right side of the sheet, have them write the word, add an *s*, and read the word again.

▸ Then have them read the pairs of words to a partner.

Ask the children to use the verbs ending with *s* in a sentence.

Link

Interactive Read-Aloud: As you read aloud stories such as the following, help children notice the *s* added to verbs.

- *Hand, Hand, Fingers, Thumb* by Al Perkins
- *Sunrise* by Helena Clare Pittman

Shared Reading: After reading and enjoying a text, such as "The Rooster" *(flaps, sings),* "Papa's Glasses" *(folds, puts),* and "Beets" *(makes, keeps)* (see *Sing a Song of Poetry*), have children use a masking card or flag to isolate verbs that have *s* added to agree with a third-person subject.

Guided Reading: During word work, have the children make some simple verbs and add *s*.

Interactive Writing: As you construct a message together, point out verbs that have *s* added to them.

Independent Writing: Point out places where students have added (or should add) *s* to a verb.

assess

- Notice whether the children add *s* to verbs when writing.
- Observe the children's handling of verbs with *s* as they read simple texts.

Expand the Learning

Repeat the lesson with other parts of speech to which *s* is added.

Connect with Home

Invite the children to make the same verbs with word cards or magnetic letters at home.

Alternatively, give them a new list of verbs to use at home.

Learning about Compound Words

Highlighting Words

Consider Your Children

If children understand what words are, can notice some letters and word parts, and know some high frequency words, they can begin to work with the easy compound words in this lesson. Start with examples that are in the children's speaking vocabulary and that they have previously seen in print.

Working with English Language Learners

For your English language learners, begin with very simple compound words made up of words that children know and can recognize (for example, *into* or *today*). It is important that they understand the principle of compound words so that they can begin to recognize them when they meet them in a text. Also be sure that children have many enjoyable experiences in shared reading of a text before they start to search for details.

You Need

► Magnetic letters.

► Poems, written on charts, that contain compound words. (For example, "Mary Had a Little Lamb" contains "everywhere.")

► Highlighter tape.

► Photocopies of two or three selected poems.

Understand the Principle

Learning to look at the structure of words will help children become more skillful at taking words apart to solve them.

One way to help children begin to look at word parts is to draw their attention to easy compound words. They see the smaller words that have been combined to make the compound word and learn that these words usually give you a clue to the meaning.

Explain the Principle

" Some words are made up of two words that are put together and are called compound words. "

" You can read compound words by looking at the two words in them. "

plan

teach

into	inside
today	myself
cannot	sunshine
maybe	goodnight
birthday	

Explain the Principle

❝ Some words are made up of two words that are put together and are called compound words. ❞

❝ You can read compound words by looking at the two words in them. ❞

① Tell the children they are going to learn something new about words.

② Put some easy compound words on a chart, or make them with magnetic letters on the easel. Choose words from familiar poems used in shared reading so they will be well known by the children.

③ Point at and read the words to the children.

④ Ask, "What do you notice about the words I read?" The children will probably say each word is made up of two smaller words.

⑤ Confirm their statement. Say each word again and have the children clap the parts they hear.

⑥ Explain that a word made of two smaller words put together is a compound word. Point out that there is no space between the words.

⑦ Reread two or three poems that have compound words, and ask the children to listen for, clap, and mark the words with a highlighter pen or with highlighter tape.

⑧ Explain that you are going to give them three poems to read. (Use poems they have read many times before.) They should read the poems to a partner, find the words that are made of two smaller words, and highlight these words with a highlighter pen.

read
mark

► Have the children read each poem and highlight the compound words.

> **I'm a Little Teapot**
>
> I'm a little teapot
> short and stout.
> Here is my handle.
> Here is my spout.
> When I get all steamed up,
> then I shout,
> "Just tip me over and
> pour me out."

Have the children bring their poems to the group meeting.

Read each poem together and have children tell the compound words they highlighted.

Link

Interactive Read-Aloud: Read aloud books that contain compound words, and help children notice them. Examples are:

- ▸ *If You Give a Pig a Pancake* by Laura Numeroff
- ▸ *Airport* by Byron Barton

Shared Reading: After reading poems such as "Milkman, Milkman," "Someone's Birthday," "Hickety Pickety," "Bouncing Ball," or "I Stand on Tiptoe" (see *Sing a Song of Poetry*), use highlighter tape to isolate compound words in texts.

Guided Reading: After reading and discussing stories, have children point to compound words. During word work, use magnetic letters to make some easy compound words.

Interactive Writing: As you construct messages together, have children clap and notice words that are made of two words put together.

Independent Writing: Point out compound words in stories children write.

assess

- ▸ Observe the ease with which children locate and identify the parts of compound words.

- ▸ Give the children a copy of a new poem. Read it with them a few times using shared reading. Then ask them to work independently, highlighting each compound word and circling the parts.

Expand the Learning

Use other poems with compound words and have children mark them.

Teach children songs or poems orally and invite them to listen for compound words.

Connect with Home

Have the children take these poems home and show family members the compound words.

Encourage family members to play compound word games in the car or while shopping. Each takes a turn telling the compound word that designates something they can see: a *policeman*, a *raindrop*, *sunshine*, a *mailman*, a *notebook*.

Recognizing Syllables

Syllable Sort

Consider Your Children

This lesson will be effective for children who understand and can name the consonants and vowels, have had some experience taking words apart, have had considerable experience saying words slowly to identify sounds or word parts, and are familiar with clapping syllables.

Working with English Language Learners

It will be very important to use words that your English language learners can pronounce and to say each syllable so that they can hear and clap them. Begin with simple words they know and remind them of how to listen for and clap the parts. You may need to perform this task individually a few times with children who have difficulty coordinating the action with words they are just beginning to learn in another language. Work with a small group to help them understand the sorting task and be sure to include only pictures that they can say and understand.

You Need

► Magnetic letters.

► Pocket chart.

From *Teaching Resources:*

► Picture Cards, Syllables.

► Three-Way Sort Sheets.

Understand the Principle

An effective way to take words apart is to recognize syllable breaks and look within the syllables to notice letters and letter clusters.

These smaller parts of words can more easily be associated with sounds.

Explain the Principle

❝ You can hear the syllables in words. ❞

❝ You can look at the syllables to read a word. ❞

❝ Every syllable of a word has a vowel. ❞

plan

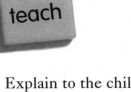

Explain the Principle

" You can hear the syllables in words. "

" You can look at the syllables to read a word. "

" Every syllable of a word has a vowel. "

① Explain to the children that they are going to learn about the parts in words.

② Using magnetic letters, place three or four one-syllable words (*hat*, for example) on an easel.

③ Read each word and ask the children to clap the parts they hear. All the words will get one clap.

④ Then make three or four words that have two syllables (*apple*, for example), read them, and have the children clap the two parts with you.

⑤ Repeat using words that have three parts (*tornado*, for example).

⑥ Explain that we can hear parts in words. Suggested language: "Some words have one part, some have two parts, and some have three parts or more."

⑦ Tell the children that the parts are called syllables, and have children say the word *syllable*.

⑧ Point out that each syllable has a vowel (*a, e, i, o, u,* or sometimes *y*) in it.

⑨ Put *1, 2, 3* at the top of a pocket chart. Take a pile of picture cards. Show each picture and have children clap the syllables in the word the picture represents.

⑩ Have the children place each picture under *1, 2,* or *3*, according to the number of syllables they can hear in the word.

⑪ Explain to the children that they are going to write *1, 2, 3* at the top of the columns of the Three-Way Sort Sheet. Then they are to take a picture, say and clap the parts of the word it represents, and glue the picture in the column under the appropriate number.

say
sort
clap
glue

▶ Have the children complete the three-way syllable sort.

Have each child choose one word and clap the syllables.

Link

Interactive Read-Aloud: Enjoy books such as the following, stopping to clap a few of the words.

- ▸ *Counting Kisses* by Karen Katz
- ▸ *A Place to Bloom* by Lorianne Siomades

Shared Reading: After enjoying a text such as "What's the Weather?," "Ladybug! Ladybug!," or "Pussycat, Pussycat" (see *Sing a Song of Poetry*), invite children to find and clap three or four words with different numbers of syllables.

Guided Reading: After reading and discussing a text, have children clap the syllables in two or three words.

Interactive Writing: Before writing a two- or three-syllable word, have children clap the parts so they can hear the sounds more clearly.

Independent Writing: Encourage children to listen for syllables in words as they try to write them.

assess

- ▸ Look at children's sort sheets to determine the extent to which children understood the task and were able to place pictures in the appropriate category.
- ▸ Have a small group of children take turns clapping syllables of new words. Observe and note their behavior.

Expand the Learning

Repeat the lesson with other syllable pictures.

Repeat the lesson and add four-syllable words.

Connect with Home

In a newsletter or note to family members, suggest that they play the Clapping Syllables game in the market or on a walk. The child picks out words and the family member says and claps the syllables. Then they reverse roles.

Word-Solving Actions

Word-solving actions are the strategic moves readers and writers make when they use their knowledge of the language system to solve words. These strategies are "in-the-head" actions that are invisible, although we can infer them from some overt behavior. The principles listed in this section represent children's ability to *use* the principles in all previous sections of the Continuum.

All lessons related to the Continuum provide opportunities for children to apply principles in active ways, for example, through sorting, building, locating, reading, or writing. Lessons related to word-solving actions demonstrate to children how they can problem-solve by working on words in isolation or while reading or writing continuous text. The more children can integrate these strategies into their reading and writing systems, the more flexible they will become in solving words. The reader/writer may use knowledge of letter/sound relationships, for example, either to solve an unfamiliar word or to check that the reading is accurate. Rapid, automatic word solving is a basic component of fluency and important for comprehension because it frees children's attention to focus on the meaning and language of the text.

Connect to Assessment

See related WSA Assessment Tasks in the Assessment Guide in *Teaching Resources:*

- ► Sorting Names

- ► Sorting Words

- ► Using Known Words to Monitor Reading

- ► Using Known Words to Solve New Words

- ► Using Letter/Sound Relationships to Solve New Words

Develop Your Professional Understanding

See *Word Matters: Teaching Phonics and Spelling in the Reading/Writing Classroom* by G.S. Pinnell and I.C. Fountas. 1998. Portsmouth, New Hampshire: Heinemann.

Related pages: 46–47, 63–64, 90–93, 95, 222–228, 237–244.

Making Connections Between Names and Other Words

Name Lotto

Consider Your Children

This lesson is best used after you have made a name chart (Lesson ELC 1) with the children and they have done a great deal of interactive writing in which you have made connections between their names and the words they want to write. Your goal is to teach children that words they know are a good resource for learning new words.

Working with English Language Learners

This lesson will help children use their names as resources for learning more about English words. It also sets up the expectation that they can actively search for connections rather than waiting to be told words. Be sure that they can pronounce (with some understandable variation) the words that they are using to make connections with their names. Limit the set at first so that they can easily find examples. Encourage them to use words from the word wall.

You Need

► Name chart (see Lesson ELC 1).

 From *Teaching Resources:*

► Lotto Game Cards.

► Name cards (Word Card Template).

► Directions for Lotto.

Understand the Principle

Making connections between how words sound, how words look, and what words mean is a powerful word-solving strategy.

Making connections helps word solvers develop categories of words and derive principles for how words work.

Explain the Principle

" You can connect your name with other words. "

Explain the Principle

" You can connect your name with other words. "

Adrian	Han	Tony B.
Alex	Hanna	Tony O.
Annesa		
Atory	Kenny	Vickie
	Kimberly	
Brett		
Brian	Marcus	
	Michael	
Charlia		
	Peter	
Esther	Pria	
Frankie	Sara	
	Suzanne	

① Explain to the children that they are going to use their names to learn about other words.

② Suggested language: "We have used our name chart a lot to help us write words. Today we are going to talk about the way the name chart helps us. We are going to make connections between our names and other words."

③ Read the name chart with the children.

④ Suggested language: "You can use what you know about the letters and sounds in your names to help you read and write other words. Let's look at an example. *Marcus* and *mom* start with the same letter, with an. . . . [Children respond.] Yes, an *m*. They are alike at the beginning of the word because they both start with an *m*. [Write the word *mom* on the whiteboard.] Do you see the *M* in *Marcus?* Do you see the *m* in *mom?* It's a lowercase *m*, isn't it? And *Marcus* has an uppercase *M*, but they both start the same—the same sound and the same letter."

⑤ The primary focus here is the sound match; however, confirming it with the letter is a way to help children begin making connections with how words look as well.

⑥ Make additional connections between children's names and other words:
"*Annesa* and *away* start the same."
"*Sara* and *sun* start the same."
"*Brett* and *box* start the same."
"*Peter* and *play* start the same."

⑦ Most kindergartners learn beginning sounds quickly, early in the year. If children are familiar with most of the beginning sounds, you can also point out final sounds:

"*Peter* and *mother* end the same."
"*Marcus* and *bus* end the same."
"*Brett* and *pot* end the same."

⑧ Tell children that they are now going to play Name Lotto with partners or in groups of three or four.

take
read
tell
cover

▶ Prepare a Name Lotto game with the names of children in the classroom in the spaces. Children can work with partners or in groups of three or four. Each child takes a name of a classmate and then tells a word that starts the same. Then, if the name card matches a name on their game card, the child covers the space with a marker (button, penny, or paper square). The first child to cover the names on his card wins the game.

Go around the group quickly and ask each child to say her or his name and a word that starts the same.

Link

Interactive Read-Aloud: Read aloud books that focus on how children's names connect to other words, such as:

- *Alison's Zinnia* by Anita Lobel
- *Away from Home* by Anita Lobel

Shared Reading: After enjoying a poem or chant, play a game: "I'm thinking of a word that starts like *Mary* [or ends like *Peter*]. Who can find it?" Have children locate the word with a masking card, flag, or highlighter tape.

Guided Reading: Help children use connections with names to solve words.

Interactive Writing: Post the name chart next to the easel where you write. Help children make connections with names to spell unknown words: "Do you know a name that starts like that?"

Independent Writing: Remind the children to use the name chart as a resource in spelling words they want to write.

assess

- Notice whether the children can connect names with other words when reading and writing.

Expand the Learning

When the children have good control of initial and final sounds, you may also connect names to consonant clusters (*Shaun* or *Shayla* with *short*), easy-to-hear vowel sounds (*a* as in *Sam*), and other word parts (*and* in *Andrew* or *us* in *Marcus*).

Connect with Home

Write the child's first name on a piece of paper and have him look for a small object or picture of something that begins like his name. Have him bring the picture or object to school to glue on a special version of the name chart.

Using Letter/Sound Analysis
Writing Words

Consider Your Children

This lesson focuses on saying words slowly and then writing them. It is best used when children have done a great deal of interactive writing and can hear some consonants at the beginning and end of words. Interactive writing is a powerful context for teaching children to say words slowly and record the sounds and is especially effective because the writing is for authentic purposes. You'll want to show explicitly how children can use this technique in their own writing.

Working with English Language Learners

Saying words slowly to hear sounds is a technique that will help English language learners make connections between letters and the sounds in words. At first, encourage them to write words that they can pronounce easily and avoid those that require sounds that are hard for them to say. You are trying to establish a principle rather than teaching a particular letter/sound relationship. Saying words slowly will help English language learners understand the pronunciation of English.

You Need

▶ Large easel with blank paper.

▶ Writing materials.

▶ Small pictures or objects.

From *Teaching Resources:*

▶ Two-Way Sort Sheets.

▶ Selected Picture Cards, Short Vowels and Long Vowels. (Enlarge them for demonstration purposes.)

Understand the Principle

Saying a word slowly helps beginning readers attend to and hear the individual sounds in the word.

Supported by teaching, saying words helps children hear more of the sounds and develop the concept that words are made up of sequences of sounds.

This concept is basic to connecting sounds to letters, letter clusters, and letter patterns.

Explain the Principle

" You can say words slowly to hear the sounds. "

" You can hear the sounds at the beginning, middle, or end of a word. "

" You can write the letters for the sounds you can hear. "

plan

teach

Explain the Principle

" You can say words slowly to hear the sounds. "

" You can hear the sounds at the beginning, middle, or end of a word. "

" You can write the letters for the sounds you can hear. "

1. Explain to the children that they are going to learn how to listen for sounds so they can write words.

2. Show the children an object or a picture of an object. Have them look at your mouth while you say the label for the object slowly (*hat*, for example).

3. Have the children say the word with you.

4. Ask children what they hear first and write it on the chart or whiteboard. Then fill in the middle letter(s). Ask them what they hear last, and as they tell you, write the letter.

5. Repeat this procedure with many easy words. For beginners, focus only on words with two or three sounds. Include easy-to-hear middle vowel sounds if the children are well in control of beginning and ending consonant sounds. Possible pictures/objects include *bat, bike, bone, box, bus, cake, can, cat, cave, dime, dog, doll, egg, fan, feet, game, gate, gum, hat, kite, leg, log, mop, net, pan, pig, pot, rope, rug, sock, sun, tent, web.*

feet	hat	pot
bat	Kite	rope
cat	cave	can
net	dime	top
ten	egg	van
rug	game	bite
web	pig	take
fan	cake	

glue
say
write
read

► Give the children a Two-Way Sort Sheet with a key picture (of a cake, for example) at the top of the left column and the sounds included in the object's label on the right (*cak* in this case). (Notice that all three sounds are represented even though the word is not spelled conventionally.) Have children glue pictures in the left column (they can use both the front and the back of the paper), say each label slowly, write the first sound, and attempt to write the middle and last sounds as well, depending on what they can control. Then ask them to read their list to a partner while they point at each word. (Some children will be able to represent only one or two sounds in the words so you should expect differences.)

Invite individual children to the chalkboard or easel to say one of their words slowly and write the sounds.

Link

Interactive Read-Aloud: Read aloud books that help the children attend to the sounds in words. Examples are:

- ► *Hide and Seek* by Brenda Shannon Yee
- ► *The Cat Barked?* by Lydia Monks

Shared Reading: Have children locate high frequency words in familiar texts such as "Who Stole the Cookies" or "Little Red Apple" (see *Sing a Song of Poetry*), first saying them slowly to think about what they hear and what letters they might see and then checking the letters to see if they are right.

Guided Reading: At an unfamiliar word, ask, "Could it be _____?" Have the child think about what letters would be in the word and check to see if your suggestion is right. During word work, show children one or two pictures and have children predict the letters while you write their predictions on a whiteboard.

Interactive Writing: Select words that will expand children's ability to hear sounds. Have children say them slowly and think what letters would be in the word—at the beginning, middle, and end. Have one child come up to the easel and write the word or parts of the word.

Independent Writing: Remind the children to say words slowly and think about what letters to write at the beginning, middle, and end.

Expand the Learning

Repeat the lesson with other pictures or objects.

Move from words with two or three sounds to words with three or four sounds.

Connect with Home

Suggest to family members that they play "Listen for the Sounds" with their children in the car or in the supermarket. They give their child a clue about a word ("I'm thinking of a fruit that is yellow," "I'm thinking of a fruit that is huge," "I'm thinking of a vegetable that is green"), and she guesses the word *(banana, watermelon, spinach)* and tells the letter it starts with *(b, w, s)*.

assess

- ► Notice whether the children are representing more sounds in the new words they attempt to spell.

- ► Notice whether the children are using letter/sound relationships to solve words.

Making New Words by Changing the First Letter 1

Magnetic Letters

Consider Your Children

This lesson helps children focus on a strategic process for reading and writing new words and is best used after children know some high frequency/high interest words and can recognize some easy word patterns. They should have some familiarity with (though not a thorough knowledge of) consonant sounds and have worked with rhymes.

Working with English Language Learners

Be sure that English language learners have worked with and can easily recognize word parts and take apart simple words. If they have difficulty with the task, go back to showing them known words and having them make connections. By the time you use this lesson, children will understand "first" and "last" and have experience in working with beginning and ending sounds and letters.

You Need

▸ Magnetic letters.

▸ Magnetic easel.

From *Teaching Resources:*

▸ Making Connections Sheets.

Understand the Principle

Competent word solvers take words they know and use them to read or spell words they don't know.

Good readers recognize the connections between words and can flexibly manipulate the parts of words to solve words.

Explain the Principle

❝ You can change the first letter or letters of a word to make a new word. ❞

plan

Explain the Principle

❝ **You can change the first letter or letters of a word to make a new word.** ❞

① Tell the children they are going to learn something new about words.

② Make the word *dog* with magnetic letters on the easel. Suggested language: "You know this word. [Children respond.] Yes, it's *dog*. Now watch while I make another word, *log*. Say those words: *log, dog*. [Children respond.] What do you notice?"

③ Children may make comments such as these:
"They rhyme."
"They sound the same at the end."
"*Dog* has *d* and *log* has *l*."

④ Suggested language: "*Log* and *dog* are the same except for the beginning letter and beginning sound. If you know *dog*, you can figure out *log*. Let's try another one. [Make the word *can*.] This word is. . . . [Children respond.] I'll make another word like *can* and you try to figure out what it is." Make *man* and invite children to say *can, man* to solve the word.

⑤ Follow the same procedure with *pet, get*. After the words are made, summarize by showing children that all the pairs of words have different first letters but the same last part.

⑥ Explain to the children that they will be making connections between words to make new words.

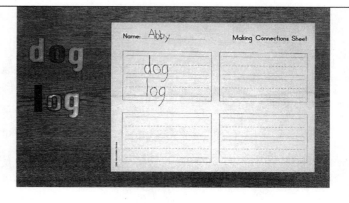

make
write
make
write
read

► Demonstrate how to use the Making Connections Sheet: "This is a piece of paper called "making connections." First, make a word you know, such as *dog*, with magnetic letters and then write it in the first box of the Making Connections Sheet. Then make another word that is like it at the end, such as *log*, and write it on the next line. Finally, read both words to check. Bring your word links to sharing."

Invite children to read examples of word links they created.

Link

Interactive Read-Aloud: Read aloud books that help children attend to words that are alike in their sound and spelling. Examples are:

- ▶ *The Hungry Thing* by Jan Slepian and Ann Seidler
- ▶ *Green Eggs and Ham* by Dr. Seuss

Shared Reading: After enjoying a poem or chant, play a game: "I'm thinking of a word that ends like *cat* [or whatever]. Can you find it?" Have children isolate the word using a masking card or highlighter tape.

Guided Reading: Help children solve words by making connections to known words. Use the whiteboard to illustrate word-solving principles with words that are new or difficult. During word work, use magnetic letters to make a few words by changing the first letter.

Interactive Writing: Help children spell words by making connections to words they know. Encourage them to think of a word that is like the word they are trying to write: "Do you know another word that begins [or ends] like that?"

Independent Writing: Encourage children to use words they know to help them write new words. Demonstrate by writing a word they know on a small piece of paper or stick-on note. Show how to change the first letter to make the word they want to write *(hot, not).*

assess

- ▶ Notice whether the children can use known words to figure out new words in reading and writing.

- ▶ Give a child three words and ask her to change the first letter of each to make a new word.

Expand the Learning

Introduce additional word patterns, such as *make, take*. Instead of making both words, simply change the letters to make the new word.

Alternate changing first letters and last letters to make new words. This will help children become more flexible in word solving.

Connect with Home

On a blank Making Connections Sheet (see *Teaching Resources*), fill in the top line of each box with a known word. Send a copy of the sheet home with letter cards (see *Teaching Resources*). Have children change the first letter of each word to create a new word, write the new word on the open line in the box, and read all the pairs of words to family members.

Making New Words by Changing the First Letter 2

Magnetic Letters

Consider Your Children

This lesson sets up a routine for work with magnetic letters and is best used after children understand the concept of words and the concept of "first" relative to the sequence of letters or sounds in a word. They should recognize letters, know most of the letter names, have worked extensively with rhymes, and have made connections between words during interactive writing. In this lesson you show the children how to change the first letter of a word by removing it and substituting a new one. If children need more support, keep the first word visible and make the new word below it.

Working with English Language Learners

You may need to start by showing them words that have the same phonogram but different first letters. Let them notice and talk about the connections. Then explicitly demonstrate how you can take one word and change the first letter to make the other word. Provide many opportunities for practice.

You Need

▶ Magnetic letters.
▶ Magnetic surface.

Understand the Principle

As children become more aware of letter/sound relationships within words, they learn that words have parts. These parts can be changed to make new words.

Taking away the first letter of a word and substituting another helps children understand a basic principle of how words work.

This understanding helps children see relationships among words and use their knowledge to take words apart while reading and to spell words while writing.

Explain the Principle

" You can change the first letter or letters of a word to make a new word. "

plan

Explain the Principle

" **You can change the first letter or letters of a word to make a new word.** "

① Explain to the children that they are going to learn something interesting about words.

② Show the children the word *cat* made with magnetic letters on the board. Suggested language: "When you say a word, you can hear the first sound, can't you? Say *cat*. [Children respond.] What's the first sound? [Children respond.] And when you look at the word *cat*, you can see the first letter. [Indicate the magnetic letters spelling *cat*; point to the *c*.] When I read the word *cat*, I can hear the first sound, /c/, and the rest of the word."

③ "Now watch what I am going to do with the word *cat*. I'm going to take away the first letter, the *c*, and put a *b* at the beginning of the word. [Demonstrate with magnetic letters.] Now the word is *bat*."

④ "Now I'll take away the *b* and put the *c* back in as the first letter. The word is. . . . [Children respond.]"

⑤ Change *cat* to *bat* and back again several times. Suggested language: "*Cat* and *bat* sound the same at the end and they look the same at the end. Changing the first letter makes another word."

⑥ "Now I'm going to change the first letter again. I'll take away the *c* and put an *m* at the beginning of the word. Now my word is. . . . [Children respond.]"

⑦ Provide one or two more examples if needed: *pat, sat, rat*. Have children come up to the easel and change the first letter. The rest of the children read the new word each time.

⑧ Suggested language: "Today you are going to make words by using the ending letters *at* and changing the first letter, just like we did on the board. Take away the first letter, put in a new letter, and read the word, running a finger under it."

make
change
read

▶ Have children make -*at* words using magnetic letters or letter cards. Ask them to make a word and change the first letter to make a new word. Then ask them to make another -*at* word and again change the first letter to make a new word. Have them do this five times, making ten different words, saying each word aloud each time: *hat–fat, rat–mat, bat–cat, sat–pat, flat–brat.*

Have children go up to the easel and demonstrate making a new word by changing the first letter of a word.

Link

Interactive Read-Aloud: Read aloud books with simple rhymes. (See the Rhyme Books Bibliography in *Teaching Resources* for suggestions.) Examples are:

- ▶ *Grandma's Cat* by Helen Ketteman
- ▶ *The Grumpy Morning* by Pamela Duncan Edwards

Shared Reading: After you read poems and rhymes such as "The Cat" or "Make a Pancake" (see *Sing a Song of Poetry*), have children locate, with a masking card or highlighter tape, words that are alike at the end but have different first letters.

Guided Reading: During word work, demonstrate three or four examples of changing the first letter to make a new word. Use simple patterns starting with a word that children know well (*dad–sad*, for example).

Interactive Writing: Within the texts children compose, look for opportunities to connect words by changing the first letter. For example, if they want to write *be* and they know *me*, show them on the whiteboard how to go from *me* to *be* (or perhaps to *see*, pointing out that you also add another *e*).

Independent Writing: Encourage the children to make connections to known words when writing new words (*like–bike*, for example).

Expand the Learning

Repeat the lesson using other predictable phonogram patterns: *-an, -ad, -in, -ot, -it*.

Connect with Home

Send home letter cards (see *Teaching Resources*) and a short list of words for children to make and then change the first letter. Have children glue their words on a sheet of paper and read them to a family member.

assess

- ▶ Observe the children's ability to use what they know to figure out new words.
- ▶ Show three words and ask each child to change the first letter of each word to make a new word.

Using Known Words in Simple Texts

Cut-Up Sentences

Consider Your Children

This lesson is best used after children know and have worked with some high frequency words. The purpose is to give children opportunities to notice how they can read many words quickly and easily because they know them. This lesson can be repeated with many other simple texts that are only a few lines long.

Working with English Language Learners

When you prepare a simple text for children to read on their own, be sure that the words are known and understood by English language learners. Also be sure that the topic is very familiar and that they have had exposure to the language structure through hearing it read aloud and in shared reading. If needed, work with a small group of children who need more repetition. Observing children perform this task will tell you a great deal about their ability to use knowledge of letters, sounds, and words while reading text. Repeat this lesson with easy sentences over several days.

You Need

▶ Chart displaying a new unfamiliar text.

▶ Pointer.

▶ Photocopies of the text.

Understand the Principle

Children use a core of known high frequency words as anchors to monitor their reading. They can use known words to check on the accuracy of their reading. Also, knowing a core of words that are rapidly recognized promotes fluency.

Explain the Principle

❝ You can read or write a word quickly when you know how it looks. ❞

❝ When you know how to read some words quickly, it helps you read fast. ❞

plan

To Room 5 Kids,

I am proud of you.

You are good readers!

I like the way you read books.

Love,
Mrs. Hawkins

Explain the Principle

❝ **You can read or write a word quickly when you know how it looks.** ❞

❝ **When you know how to read some words quickly, it helps you read fast.** ❞

① Tell the children they are going to learn more about reading words.

② Suggested language: "Today we are going to read something together. You know so much about reading that I'm not going to read it to you first. I'll tell you some of the words, but there are lots of words you already know."

③ "This is a letter to Room 5 kids. What's the first word? [Children respond.] That's right! You know the word *to*. Let's read the beginning together." Read the salutation with the children.

④ Go on to the first line. "Read the first line." Children will read *I*, *am*, and they may pause on *proud*. Join in to read *proud of* with them, but drop out again on *you*. "You read the whole first sentence. Were you right?" Children respond.

⑤ "You know some of the words, don't you? Checking on words you know helps you know that you are right."

⑥ Have a child come up and read the line, pointing underneath each word. Assist on *proud of* if necessary. Ask other children to check whether the child read accurately.

⑦ Have children locate known high frequency words or put highlighter tape over the known words.

⑧ Have children read the next line, helping if needed. Point out that they will almost always see some words they know in the stories they are reading. Knowing these words helps them read faster and also helps them check their reading as they point to these words.

⑨ Read the text together again quickly, using the pointer.

⑩ Suggested language: "You did such a great job that I am going to add two more lines to my letter! Watch me write two more lines. You can think about what I'm writing, but don't say it out loud."

⑪ Write two more lines that are easy and that have some high frequency words in them. For example: *I like the way you read books. We can read books together.*

To Room 5 Kids,

I am proud of you.

You are good readers!

I like the way you read books.

We can read books together.

Love,
Mrs. Hawkins

cut
mix
glue
read

▶ Give each child a copy of your class letter, including the one or two lines you added. Have them cut the letter into Sentence Strips. Then ask them to mix up the strips and re-create the note by gluing the strips on a blank sheet of paper. Have them point under each word as they read it to a partner.

Invite one or two children to read the letter to the class while another child points under each word.

Link

Interactive Read-Aloud: Read aloud standard-size books that have large bold print that the class can easily see. As you read aloud, invite children to read some of the words with you, particularly on second and third readings. (See *Teaching Resources,* Large Print Books Bibliography.) Examples are:

► *A Pair of Socks* by Stuart Murphy

► *Feathers for Lunch* by Lois Ehlert

Shared Reading: When reading, let children predict a word or two and check whether they were right.

Guided Reading: After reading a text, have children locate two or three high frequency words.

Interactive Writing: Remind the children of words they know how to read and write. Write them quickly yourself to demonstrate how to write them from beginning to end without stopping.

Independent Writing: Encourage the children to use conventional spelling for the words they know in detail and to reread their writing and notice these words.

assess

► Notice whether the children are able to recognize high frequency words when they read.

► Check whether the children can write high frequency words quickly.

Expand the Learning

Repeat this lesson with other simple texts that you write yourself. Include as many high frequency words as you can. (Start each sentence on a new line.)

Bring together a group of children who are waiting for help rather than actively solving words. Read new texts with them and demonstrate strategies explicitly. Stick with easy texts with only one or two words to solve.

Connect with Home

Have the children take home copies of the letter to read to family members.

Using Parts of Words to Solve New Words

Highlighting Word Parts

Consider Your Children

This lesson is best used after children realize the connections between letters and sounds in words and have learned some letter/sound relationships and a few high frequency words. They should know what you mean by parts of words. The understanding established in this minilesson will be reinforced every time children engage in shared and guided reading.

Working with English Language Learners

You will want your English language learners to be generally familiar with the text (although they should not have it memorized), and this may take a few more repetitions than for English speakers. You may want to work with children in a small group and remind them of words they know that can be connected to the new words they are trying to solve. Be sure that the piece they are reading does not have too many words that are hard for them and that it is comprehensible.

You Need

▶ Chart.

▶ Rhyme or other material for shared reading (see *Sing a Song of Poetry*).

▶ Dry-erase whiteboard or MagnaDoodle®.

Understand the Principle

Noticing word parts, such as phonograms or rimes, is useful in reading and in solving words.

Knowing about word parts can help readers check their reading for accuracy.

Explain the Principle

" You can use parts of words you know to read or write new words. "

plan

Weekend News

Today is Monday, March 3, 2002

It rained on Sunday.

Kelly went to the playground anyway.

Kayla went to church.

Explain the Principle

" You can use parts of words you know to read or write new words. "

① Tell the children they are going to read a favorite poem and learn about solving new words.

② Select a rhyme or piece of shared writing that you have read to the children and they have read with you several times. They should be generally familiar with the text but not have memorized it.

③ Read the text in a shared way.

④ Suggested language: "We've been learning about word parts. One word part you know is *-ay*. Let's read the words that have *-ay* in them."

⑤ Underline in red or highlight the *-ay* parts of words in the text: *day, play, today, Sunday, playground, anyway, Kayla.*

⑥ Suggested language: "You can look for the parts of words you know to help you read a new word."

⑦ Demonstrate for children how to use the poem "Rain, Rain, Go Away" for the day's activity.

Rain, rain, go away.

Come again some other day.

Little Taylor wants to play.

write
cut
mix
glue
circle
read

▸ Give children a copy of "Rain, Rain, Go Away." Have them write their names in the blanks. Then they cut the poem into sentence strips, mix up the strips, and glue the strips in the correct order onto another sheet of paper. Ask them to highlight or circle all the *-ay* words and then read the rhyme to a partner.

Reread the poem with the group and ask what they notice about the words in the poem. You might point out that:

"*Play* has two letters (*p* and *l*) that you often see together in words."
"*Away* has two parts. Clap it and cover first *a* and then *way*."

Link

Interactive Read-Aloud: Read aloud books that draw attention to words that end in the same phonogram. (See the Rhyme Books Bibliography, *Teaching Resources*.) Two examples are:

- ► *Let's Go Visiting* by Sue Williams
- ► *Play Day* by Bruce McMillan

Shared Reading: Show children how to figure out words they do not know and to check their reading by noticing word parts in familiar texts such as "Five Little Snowmen" or "Go to Bed Early" (see *Sing a Song of Poetry*).

Guided Reading: Prompt children to use their knowledge of word parts in connection with meaning and structure to solve words in the simple texts they are reading and to check their reading: "Does it look right? Does it sound right? Does it make sense?"

Interactive Writing: Prompt children to think about word parts in the words they are writing. Ask, "Do you see a part you know?"

Independent Writing: Prompt children to use their knowledge of word parts to spell words.

assess

- ► Observe the children's reading behavior to see if they are using what they know about words to figure out new words.

- ► Note the high frequency words and spelling patterns that individual children are beginning to read easily.

Expand the Learning

Repeat the lesson using other texts children have read during shared reading. Take words out of the text and write them on a whiteboard, showing word parts, so the children will notice them. Then read the text to be sure the words they solve make sense and sound right.

Repeat the lesson with other phonograms or spelling patterns you have taught.

Connect with Home

When you are sure that the children can read the texts you have used in the minilesson, send home copies.

Changing Last Letters to Make New Words

Magnetic Letters

Consider Your Children

Use this lesson after children can recognize some simple high frequency words, are able to relate most letters to the sounds they represent, and have had some experience constructing words in interactive writing and on their own. They should also have had experiences changing the first letter of a word to make new words (see Lessons WSA 3 and 4). This lesson helps children realize that they can make words by changing parts of words they know. It lays the foundation for a flexible range of connections that will help them solve words.

Working with English Language Learners

This lesson will help children realize that they can use what they know to figure out what they do not know. Be sure to begin with words that English language learners know very well and have used in reading and writing. Go over the words with them and help them articulate the sounds, especially the last letter, which they will be changing. When they first begin the activity, work with them to be sure they are saying and understanding the words they make. Help them to distinguish which words are real English words and to learn what they mean. It will not be helpful to have children simply changing last letters to make meaningless combinations.

You Need

► Magnetic easel.
► Magnetic letters.

From *Teaching Resources:*
► Making Connections Sheets.

Understand the Principle

Good readers and writers solve words by drawing on what they already know. They make connections not only to letters and sounds but also to words and word patterns.

Connections to known words help children form powerful strategies that will make them rapid, flexible word solvers.

Explain the Principle

" You can change the last letter or letters of a word to make a new word. "

plan

Explain the Principle

"" **You can change the last letter or letters of a word to make a new word.** ""

① Tell the children they are going to learn about changing parts of words.

② Suggested language: "You have been learning to find what is the same in certain words and you have been making new words by changing the beginning of the word. Today we are going to make new words by changing the last part of the word."

③ Make *is* with magnetic letters. Work quickly to show *it, in, if*. Move the letters with your hands. Be sure children are looking and responding.

④ Suggested language: "You know *is*, don't you? I'm going to change the last letter to *t*. Now I have. . . . [Children respond.] Yes, that's *it*. Now I'm going to change the last part again. [Make *in* and have the children read the word.] Now, what if I put an *f* at the end of the word? [Make *if* and either let children read it or tell them what it is.]"

⑤ Repeat using *as, at, am; cat, can, cap;* and *an, at,* back to *an, and*. In the last example, you will be adding a letter, but if children are with you so far, they will understand. Sometimes it is helpful to change back to the original word before making the new word. The more explicit this teaching is, the more effective it will be.

⑥ Suggested language: "When you are wondering how to write a word or read a word, the words you know can help you. Just look how many words we made by changing the letter at the end."

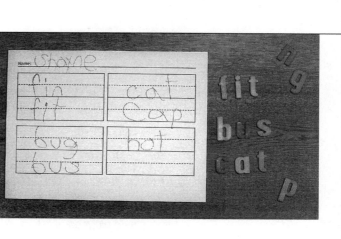

make
change
write

▸ Give children a Making
Connections Sheet. Post
a list of ten words such as
*fit, bug, cat, hot, him, pig,
dog, sit, car,* and *cup*. Have children use magnetic letters or letter cards to
make each of four words.

▸ One child makes a word. A partner changes the last letter of the word to
make a new word (possibilities for the examples above include *fin, bus,
cap, hop, his, pin, dot, sip, can,* and *cut*).

▸ The children write each word on the Making Connections Sheet as they
make each one.

Have children go up to the easel and demonstrate changing the last letter of
a word to make a new word. Call on the class to read the new word.

Link

Interactive Read-Aloud: Read aloud books that help children make connections among words. Examples are:

- ▶ *One Duck Stuck* by Phyllis Root
- ▶ *Frozen Noses* by Jan Carr

Shared Reading: After reading and enjoying a text, play a word game: "I am thinking of a word that I can make by changing the last letter of *bag*." (If children are very proficient, they can give the clues for the game.)

Guided Reading: Help children use words they know to solve new words: "What do you know about the word? Can you find a part you know? Do you know a word like that?" (Don't encourage children to "find the little word inside the big word," however. That strategy can be confusing and misleading.) Use the whiteboard to make the point explicit. During word work, make two or three words and change the last letters to make new words. Invite the children to suggest and change the letters at the easel.

Interactive Writing: When the children are writing a new word, help them connect it to a word they already know.

Independent Writing: Encourage the children to use words they know to help them spell new words.

assess

- ▶ Observe how the children use words they know to figure out new words.
- ▶ Observe as individual students make or write three words and change the last letters to make new words.

Expand the Learning

Explore simple patterns of changing last letters: *pig–pit–pin; hug–hum–hut; pet–pen–pep*.

Connect with Home

Send home letter cards (see *Teaching Resources*) and a short list of words that children can use to make and then change last letters. They can glue their words on a sheet of paper and read them to a family member.

Changing First and Last Letters to Make New Words

Magnetic Letters

Consider Your Children

Use this lesson after children have had experience constructing words in interactive and independent writing and have made words by substituting beginning sounds. This lesson helps children realize that they can make words by changing different parts of words they know. It lays the foundation for a flexible range of connections that will help them to take words apart while reading and spell words they want to write.

Working with English Language Learners

When English language learners know some basic information about letters, sounds, and spelling patterns, it is useful for them to approach words more flexibly. In this lesson they connect words by first and last letters. They need to know that learning about words is not just a matter of memorizing them but of recognizing, changing, and putting together patterns. Have them work with words that they know and have used before.

You Need

► Magnetic easel.
► Magnetic letters.

Understand the Principle

Good readers and writers solve words by drawing on what they already know. They make connections not only to letters and sounds but also to words and word patterns.

Connections to known words help children form powerful strategies that will make them rapid, flexible word solvers.

Explain the Principle

❝ You can change the first letter or last letter of a word to make a new word. ❞

plan

Explain the Principle

❝ **You can change the first letter or last letter of a word to make a new word.** ❞

① Tell the children they are going to learn more about making new words.

② Suggested language: "Today we are going to play a game by changing either the first letter or the last letter of a word."

③ Make the word *in* with magnetic letters. Work quickly to show *in, it, at, as.*

④ Suggested language: "You know *in*, don't you? I'm going to change the last letter to *t*. [Make the word *it*.] Now I have. . . . [Children respond.] Yes, that's *it*. Now I'm going to change the first letter to *a*. [Make *at* and have the children read the word.] Now I'll change the last letter to *s*. I'll change it to make. . . . [Children respond.]"

⑤ Repeat using *sat, pat, cat, can; me, my, by, be; we, me, my, by*. Sometimes it is helpful to change back to the original word before making the new word. The more explicit this teaching is, the more effective it will be.

⑥ Suggested language: "When you are thinking about how to write a word or read a word, think about how the words you know can help you. Just look how many words we made by changing letters at the beginning and at the end."

make
change
change

apply

▶ Have the children work in pairs. One partner will change the first letters, and the other partner will change the last letters. Working with magnetic letters, the children make a word from a list you provide. They take turns changing first and last letters to make new words. (Some words will lend themselves to more variations. Some good beginning words are *sad, ham, let, bed, pig,* and *bad.*)

share

Invite two or three children to make a word, change the first or last letter, and call on the class to read the new word.

Link

Interactive Read-Aloud: Read aloud books that help children make connections among words, such as:

- ▸ *There's an Ant in Anthony* by Bernard Most
- ▸ *Hippopotamus Hunt* by Bernard Most

Shared Reading: After reading and enjoying a text, play a word game: "I'm thinking of a word that I can make by changing the last letter of *it*." "I'm thinking of a word that I can make by changing the first letter of *make*."

Guided Reading: During word work, make a simple word and have children make the same word with magnetic letters on the table. Give them simple directions such as, "Make the word *dog;* now change the last letter to a *t*. What word did you make? Now change the first letter to *p*. What word do you have now?"

Interactive Writing: As children try to write new words, prompt them to think of a similar word: "Do you know another word that starts like that?" Have children write the first few letters and then help them think of the last sound.

Independent Writing: Encourage the children to use words they know to help them spell words. The word wall can be a useful reference.

assess

- ▸ Notice how flexible the children are in being able to change the first or last letter in a word.
- ▸ Give each child a word made with magnetic letters and ask him or her to change the first or last part. Look for flexibility and independence.

Expand the Learning

Place seven or eight words that children will recognize on a chart or easel. After reading the words, invite the children to cover or replace the first or last letter to make a new word. Encourage the discovery of many new options.

Connect with Home

Have the children take home the words they made. Show them how to explain them to their families. Caregivers can help them make one more word.

Send home a list of four or five words that the children can read. Ask them to make the words on the refrigerator with magnetic or taped letters (see *Teaching Resources,* Letter Cards). Have them show their families how they can change a letter (first or last) to make a new word. Send home 25 Ways to Use Magnetic Letters at Home (in *Teaching Resources*) for families to use.

Using Known Words to Solve New Words

Cut-Up Sentences

Consider Your Children

Use this lesson after children can recognize between ten and twenty high frequency words. They should also be able to change the first letter of a word to make a new word (see Lessons WSA 3 and 4). Don't work on all the words in the rhyme in any one lesson because that can decrease children's enjoyment and sense of purpose. Extend learning by making additional connections in successive readings.

Working with English Language Learners

In this lesson, children are using their knowledge of known words and parts of words to figure out a poem for themselves. You may want to work with English language learners in a small group first so that you can give them more support, but this is also a time to observe their problem solving. If they have difficulty with the four lines, try some very simple sentences that use words they know except for one new word that they know enough to figure out. This routine will set up the expectation that they need to search for what they know to solve problems in reading.

You Need

► Chart with a new unfamiliar rhyme for shared reading.
► Pointer.
► Photocopies of simple rhymes.
► Whiteboard.

Understand the Principle

Children use a core of known high frequency words as anchors to monitor their reading.

Children use known words to solve other words they are trying to read or write.

Explain the Principle

" You can use parts of words you know to read or write new words. "

plan

teach

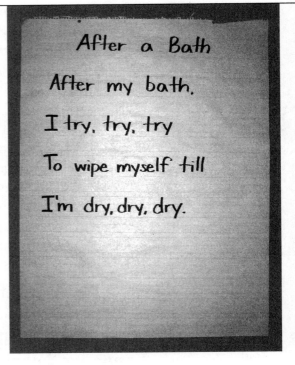

After a Bath

After my bath.

I try, try, try

To wipe myself till

I'm dry, dry, dry.

Explain the Principle

" **You can use parts of words you know to read or write new words.** "

① Tell the children they are going to read a new poem.

② Suggested language: "Today we are going to read something together. You know so much about reading that I'm not going to read it to you first this time. I'll tell you some of the words, but there are lots of words in this poem that you know. This is a new rhyme that you haven't heard before. It's a little bit funny. It's about what you do *after* a bath. You take a towel and you wipe yourself dry, don't you? The first word is *after*. Let's read the first line about after a bath."

③ Point and read *after* with the children, but drop out for the rest of the line. Children should be able to read *my* and *bath*, drawing from both the meaning and their knowledge of the words and word parts.

④ Go on to the next line. Children may be able to read *try*, but if not, say, "I'm going to show you a way to figure out *try*."

⑤ Write *my* on the whiteboard. Suggested language: "What is this word? [Children respond.] I'm going to take away the *m* and put *t* and *r* at the beginning of the word. The word is *tr–*. . . . [Children respond.] That's right, it's *try*. Let's see if it makes sense in our rhyme."

⑥ Point and read from the beginning through line 2.

⑦ Go on to the next line, helping children with *wipe myself till*.

⑧ Quickly use the whiteboard to help children see *my* in *myself*. (Remember, don't encourage them to look for the "little word inside the big word," which is not always an effective strategy.) "*Myself* has two parts. Clap it.

[Children respond.] I'll write the first part, *my*. [Write it.] You know the word *my*, which is the beginning part of *myself*. It helps when you know part of the word." Write the rest of the word *myself*, and have children read it.

⑨ Read the last line of the rhyme with the children. You may need to show them how to figure out *dry* by connecting it with *my* or *try*.

⑩ Read the text together again quickly, using the pointer.

cut
glue
draw
read

▶ Give children a photocopy of a rhyme such as "After a Bath." Have them cut apart the words and glue them onto another sheet of paper in the appropriate order.

▶ Have them illustrate the poem and read it to a partner.

Read the rhyme together again.

Have some children make words from the poem on the easel with magnetic letters.

Have a child demonstrate going from a known word to a new word.

Link

Interactive Read-Aloud: Read aloud books that encourage the manipulation of sounds, such as the two below. (See additional examples in the Language Play Bibliography in *Teaching Resources*.)

- ► *Sheep on a Ship* by Nancy Shaw
- ► *Edward the Emu* by Sheena Knowles

Shared Reading: After reading a new text, invite the children to think about how a few particular words are like other words they know. During shared reading, drop out for parts children can read for themselves.

Guided Reading: When children come to words they don't know, prompt them to use what they *do* know: "Do you know a word that starts like that? Ends like that?"

Interactive Writing: When solving new words, use high frequency words from the word wall as resources.

Independent Writing: Encourage the children to write words they know rather than consult the word wall.

Expand the Learning

Repeat the lesson with other unfamiliar rhymes or songs (see *Sing a Song of Poetry*).

Connect with Home

Send home a copy of the rhyme for children to read with family members after their bath.

assess

- ► Observe whether the children are able to recognize high frequency words when they read.

- ► Notice whether the children can write high frequency words quickly.

- ► Give the children three to five words and ask them to change the first letter to make a new word.

Glossary

Affix A part added to the beginning or ending of a base or root word to change its meaning or function (a *prefix* or *suffix*).

Alphabet book A book for helping children develop the concept and sequence of the alphabet by showing the letters and people, animals, or objects that have labels related to the letters (usually the labels begin with the letters).

Alphabetic principle The concept that there is a relationship between the spoken sounds in oral language and the graphic forms in written language.

Analogy The resemblance of a known word to an unknown word that helps you solve the unknown word.

Antonym A word that has a different sound and opposite meaning from another word (*cold* vs. *hot*).

Assessment A means for gathering information or data that reveals what learners control, partially control, or do not yet control consistently.

Automaticity Rapid, accurate, fluent word decoding without conscious effort or attention.

Base word A whole word to which you can add affixes, creating new word forms *(washing).*

Blend To combine sounds or word parts.

Buddy study A word study system for learning conventional spelling strategies.

Closed syllable A syllable that ends in one or more consonants *(lem-on).*

Comparative form A word that describes a person or thing in relation to another person or thing (for example, *more, less; taller, shorter*).

Compound word A word made up of two or more other words or morphemes *(playground).* The meaning of a compound word can be a combination of the meanings of the words it comprises or can be unrelated to the meanings of the combined units.

Concept book A book organized to develop an understanding of an abstract or generic idea or categorization.

Connecting strategies Ways of solving words that use connections or *analogies* with similar known words (knowing *she* and *out* helps with *shout*).

Consonant A speech sound made by partial or complete closure of the airflow that causes friction at one or more points in the breath channel. The consonant sounds are represented by the letters *b, c, d, f, g, h, j, k, l, m, n, p, q, r, s, t, v, w* (in most of its uses), *x, y* (in most of its uses), and *z.*

Consonant blend Two or more consonant letters that often appear together in words and represent sounds that are smoothly joined, although each of the sounds can be heard in the word *(trim).*

Consonant cluster A sequence of two or three consonant letters that appear together in words *(trim, chair).*

Consonant digraph Two consonant letters that appear together and represent a single sound that is different from the sound of either letter *(shell).*

Consonant-vowel-consonant A common sequence of sounds in a single syllable (*hat,* for example).

Contraction A shortening of a syllable, word, or word group usually by the omission of a sound or letters *(didn't).*

Decoding Using letter/sound relationships to translate a word from a series of symbols to a unit of meaning.

Dialect A regional variety of a language. In most languages, including English and Spanish, dialects are mutually intelligible; the differences are actually minor.

Directionality The orientation of print (in the English language, from left to right).

Distinctive letter features Visual features that make every letter of the alphabet different from every other letter.

Early literacy concepts Very early understandings related to how print works.

English language learners People whose native language is not English and who are acquiring English as an additional language.

Fluency Speed, accuracy, and flexibility in solving words.

Grammar Complex rules by which people can generate an unlimited number of phrases, sentences, and longer texts in that language. *Conventional grammar* refers to the accepted conventions in a society.

Grapheme A letter or cluster of letters representing a single sound, or phoneme *(a, eigh, ay)*.

Graphophonic relationship The relationship between the oral sounds of the language and the written letters or clusters of letters.

Have a try To write a word, notice that it doesn't look quite right, try it two or three other ways, and decide which construction looks right; to make an attempt and check oneself.

High frequency words Words that occur often in the spoken and written language *(the)*.

Homograph One of two or more words spelled alike but different in meaning, derivation, or pronunciation (the *bat* flew away, he swung the *bat*; take a *bow*, *bow* and arrow).

Homonym (a type of *homograph*) One of two or more words spelled *and* pronounced alike but different in meaning (we had *quail* for dinner; I would *quail* in fear).

Homophone One of two or more words pronounced alike but different in spelling and meaning (*meat* vs. *meet*, *bear* vs. *bare*).

Idiom A phrase with meaning that cannot be derived from the conjoined meanings of its elements *(raining cats and dogs)*.

Inflectional ending A suffix added to a base word to show tense, plurality, possession, or comparison *(darker)*.

Letter knowledge The ability to recognize and label the graphic symbols of language.

Letters Graphic symbols representing the sounds in a language. Each letter has particular distinctive features and may be identified by letter name or sound.

Lexicon Words in a language.

Long vowel The elongated vowel sound that is the same as the name of the vowel. It is sometimes represented by two or more letters *(cake, eight, mail)*.

Lowercase letter A small letter form that is usually different from its corresponding capital or uppercase form.

Morpheme The smallest unit of meaning in a language. Morphemes may be *free* or *bound*. For example, *run* is a unit of meaning that can stand alone. It is a *free morpheme*. In *runs* and *running*, the added *s* and *ing* are also units of meaning. They cannot stand alone but add meaning to the free morpheme. *S* and *ing* are examples of *bound morphemes*.

Morphemic strategies Ways of solving words by discovering *meaning* through the combination of significant word parts or morphemes *(happy, happiest; run, runner, running)*.

Morphological system Rules by which morphemes (building blocks of vocabulary) fit together into meaningful words, phrases, and sentences.

Morphology The combination of morphemes (building blocks of meaning) to form words; the rules by which words are formed from free and bound morphemes—for example, root words, prefixes, suffixes.

Multiple-meaning words Words that mean something different depending on the ways they are used (*run*—home run, run in your stocking, run down the street, a run of bad luck).

Onset In a syllable, the part (consonant, consonant cluster, or consonant digraph) that comes before the vowel *(cr-eam)*.

Onset-rime segmentation The identification and separation of onsets (first part) and rimes (last part, containing the vowel) in words *(dr-ip)*.

Open syllable A syllable that ends in a vowel sound *(ho-tel)*.

Orthographic awareness The knowledge of the visual features of written language, including distinctive features of letters as well as spelling patterns in words.

Orthography The representation of the sounds of a language with the proper letters according to standard usage (spelling).

Phoneme The smallest unit of sound in spoken language. There are approximately forty-four categories of speech sounds in English.

Phoneme addition Adding a beginning, middle, or ending sound to a word *(h + and, an + t)*.

Phoneme blending Identifying individual sounds and then putting them together smoothly to make a word *(c-a-t = cat)*.

Phoneme deletion Omitting a beginning, middle, or ending sound of a word *(cart − c = art)*.

Phoneme-grapheme correspondence The relationship between the sounds (phonemes) and letters (graphemes) of a language.

Phoneme isolation The identification of an individual sound—beginning, middle, or end—in a word.

Phoneme manipulation The movement of sounds from one place to another.

Phoneme reversal The exchange of the first and last sounds of a word to make a different word.

Phoneme substitution The replacement of the beginning, middle, or ending sound of a word with a new sound.

Phonemic (or *phoneme*) awareness The ability to hear individual sounds in words and to identify particular sounds.

Phonemic strategies Ways of solving words that use how words *sound* and relationships between letters and letter clusters and phonemes in those words *(cat, make)*.

Phonetics The scientific study of speech sounds—how the sounds are made vocally and the relation of speech sounds to the total language process.

Phonics The knowledge of letter/sound relationships and how they are used in reading and writing. Teaching phonics refers to helping children acquire this body of knowledge about the oral and written language systems; additionally, teaching phonics helps children use phonics knowledge as part of a reading and writing process. Phonics instruction uses a small portion of the body of knowledge that makes up *phonetics*.

Phonogram A phonetic element represented by graphic characters or symbols. In word recognition, a graphic sequence composed of a vowel grapheme and an ending consonant grapheme (such as *an* or *it*) is sometimes called a *word family*.

Phonological awareness The awareness of words, rhyming words, onsets and rimes, syllables, and individual sounds (phonemes).

Phonological system The sounds of the language and how they work together in ways that are meaningful to the speakers of the language.

Plural Of, relating to, or constituting more than one.

Prefix A group of letters that can be placed in front of a base word to change its meaning *(preplan)*.

Principle In phonics, a generalization or a sound/spelling relationship that is predictable.

R-controlled vowel sound The modified sound of a vowel when it is followed by *r* in a syllable *(hurt)*.

Rhyme The ending part (rime) of a word that sounds like the ending part (rime) of another word *(mail, tale)*.

Rime The ending part of a word containing the vowel; the letters that represent the vowel sound and the consonant letters that follow it in a syllable *(dr-eam)*.

Root The part of a word that contains the main meaning component.

Schwa The sound of the middle vowel in an unstressed syllable (for example, the *o* in *done* and the sound between the *k* and *l* in *freckle*).

Segment To divide into parts *(to-ma-to)*.

Semantic system The system by which speakers of a language communicate meaning through language.

Short vowel A brief-duration sound represented by a vowel letter *(cat)*.

Silent *e* The final *e* in a spelling pattern that usually signals a long vowel sound in the word and does not represent a sound itself *(make*, for example).

Suffix An affix or group of letters added to a base or root word to change its function or meaning *(replace, handful)*.

Syllabication The division of words into syllables *(pen-cil)*.

Syllable A minimal unit of sequential speech sounds composed of a vowel sound or a consonant-vowel combination. A syllable always contains a vowel or vowel-like speech sound *(to-ma-to)*.

Synonym One of two or more words that have different sounds but the same meaning *(chair, seat)*.

Syntactic awareness The knowledge of grammatical patterns or structures.

Syntactic system Rules that govern the ways in which morphemes and words work together in sentence patterns. Not the same as *proper grammar,* which refers to the accepted grammatical conventions.

Syntax The study of how sentences are formed and of the grammatical rules that govern their formation.

Visual strategies Ways of solving words that use knowledge of how words *look*, including the clusters and patterns of the letters in words *(bear, light)*.

Vowel A speech sound or phoneme made without stoppage of or friction in the airflow. The vowel sounds are represented by *a, e, i, o, u,* and sometimes *w* and *y*.

Vowel combinations Two vowels that appear together in words *(meat)*.

Vowel digraph Two successive vowel letters that represent a single vowel sound *(boat)*, a vowel combination.

Word A unit of meaning in language.

Word analysis The breaking apart of words into parts or individual sounds in order to parse them.

Word family A term often used to designate words that are connected by phonograms or rimes (for example, *hot, not, pot, shot*). A *word family* can also be a series of words connected by meaning (affixes added to a base word; for example: *base, baseball, basement, baseman, basal, basis, baseless, baseline, baseboard, abase, abasement, off base, home base; precise, précis, precisely, precision*).

References

Adams, J.J. (1990). *Beginning to Read: Thinking and Learning about Print.* Cambridge, MA: MIT Press.

Allington, R. (1991). Children who find learning to read difficult: School responses to diversity. In E.H. Hiebert (ed.). *Literacy for a Diverse Society.* New York: Teachers College Press.

Armbruster, B.B., Lehr, F., and Osborn, J. (2001). *Put Reading First: The Research Building Blocks for Teaching Children to Read: Kindergarten Through Grade 1.* Jessup, MD: National Institute for Literacy.

Ball, E.W., and Blachman, B.A. (1991). Does phoneme awareness training in kindergarten make a difference in early word recognition and developmental spelling? *Reading Research Quarterly* 26 (1): 49-66.

Biemiller, A. (1970). The development of the use of graphic and contextual information as children learn to read. *Reading Research Quarterly* 6: 75-96.

Blachman, B. (1984). The relationships of rapid naming ability and language analysis skills to kindergarten and first grade reading achievement. *Journal of Educational Psychology* 76: 614-622.

Blanchard, J.S. (1980). Preliminary investigation of transfer between single-word decoding ability and contextual reading comprehension of poor readers in grade six. *Perceptual and Motor Skills* 51: 1271-1281.

Bradley, L., and Bryant, P.E. (1983). Categorizing sounds and learning to read—a causal connection. *Nature* 301: 419-421.

Bryant, P.E., Bradley, L., Camlean, M., and Crossland, J. (1989). Nursery rhymes, phonological skills and reading. *Journal of Child Language* 16: 407-428.

Bryant, P.E., MacLean, M., Bradley, L.L., and Crossland, J. (1990). Rhyme and alliteration, phoneme detection, and learning to read. *Developmental Psychology* 26 (3): 429-438.

Ceprano, M.A. (1980). A review of selected research on methods of teaching sight words. *The Reading Teacher* 35: 314-322.

Chall, J.S. (1989). Learning to read: The great debate. 20 years later. *Phi Delta Kappan* 70: 521-538.

Clay, M.M. (1991). *Becoming Literate: The Construction of Inner Control.* Portsmouth, NH: Heinemann.

Clay, M.M. (1998). *By Different Paths to Common Outcomes.* York, ME: Stenhouse Publishers.

Clay, M.M. (2001). *Change over Time in Children's Literacy Development.* Portsmouth, NH: Heinemann.

Daneman, M. (1991). Individual difference in reading skills. In R. Barr, M.L. Kamil, P. Mosenthal, and P.D. Pearson (eds.). *Handbook of Reading Research* (Vol. II, pp. 512-538). New York: Longman.

Ehri, L.C. (1991). Development of the ability to read words. In R. Barr, M.L. Kamil, P. Mosenthal, and P.D. Pearson (eds.). *Handbook of Reading Research* (Vol. II, pp. 383-417). New York: Longman.

Ehri, L.C., and McCormick, S. (1998). Phases of word learning: Implications for instruction with delayed and disabled readers. *Reading and Writing Quarterly* 20: 163-179.

Fountas, I.C., and Pinnell, G.S. (1996). *Guided Reading: Good First Teaching for All Children.* Portsmouth, NH: Heinemann.

Fountas, I.C., and Pinnell, G.S. (eds.) (1999). *Voices on Word Matters: Learning about Phonics and Spelling in the Literacy Classroom.* Portsmouth, NH: Heinemann.

Fox, B., and Routh, K.D. (1984). Phonemic analysis and synthesis as word-attack skills: Revisited. *Journal of Educational Psychology* 76: 1059-1064.

Hohn, W., and Ehri, L. (1983). Do alphabet letters help prereaders acquire phonemic segmentation skill? *Journal of Educational Psychology* 75: 752-762.

Holdaway, D. (1987). *The Foundations of Literacy.* Portsmouth, NH: Heinemann.

Hundley, S., and Powell, D. (1999). In I.C. Fountas and G.S. Pinnell (eds.). *Voices on Word Matters* (pp. 159-164). Portsmouth, NH: Heinemann.

Juel, C. (1988). Learning to read and write: A longitudinal study of 54 children from first through fourth grades. *Journal of Educational Psychology* 80: 437-447.

Juel, C., Griffith, P.L., and Gough, P.B. (1986). Acquisition of literacy: A longitudinal study of children in first and second grade. *Journal of Educational Psychology* 78: 243-255.

Lesgold, A.M., Resnick, L.B., and Hammond, K. (1985). Learning to read: A longitudinal study of word skill development in two curricula. In G.E. MacKinnon and T.G. Walker (eds.). *Reading Research: Advances in Theory and Practice* (Vol. 4, pp. 107-138). New York: Academic Press.

Liberman, I., Shankweiler, D., and Liberman, A. (1985). The Alphabetic Principle and Learning to Read. U.S. Department of Health and Human Services. Reprinted with permission from The University of Michigan Press by the National Institute of Child Health and Human Development. Adapted from Phonology and the problems of learning to read and write. *Remedial and Special Education* 6: 8-17.

Liberman, I.Y., Shankweiler, D., Fischer, F.W., and Carter, B. (1974). Explicit syllable and phoneme segmentation in the young child. *Journal of Experimental Child Psychology* 18: 201-212.

Lundberg, I., Frost, J., and Petersen, O.P. (1988). Effects of an extensive program for stimulating phonological awareness in preschool children. *Reading Research Quarterly* 23: 264-284.

McCarrier, A.M., Pinnell, G.S., and Fountas, I.C. (2000). *Interactive Writing: How Language and Literacy Come Together.* Portsmouth, NH: Heinemann.

Moats, L.C. (2000). *Speech to Print: Language Essentials for Teachers.* Baltimore: Paul H. Brookes.

Nagy, W.E., Anderson, R.C., Schommer, M., Scott, J., and Stallman, A. (1989). Morphological families in the internal lexicon. *Reading Research Quarterly* 24: 262-282.

National Institute of Child Health and Human Development (2001). *Report of the National Reading Panel: Teaching Children to Read: An Evidence-Based Assessment of the Scientific Research Literature on Reading and Its Implications for Reading Instruction. Reports of the Subgroups.* Washington, DC: National Institutes of Health.

New Standards Primary Literacy Committee (1999). *Reading and Writing: Grade by Grade.* Washington, DC: National Center on Education and the Economy and the University of Pittsburgh.

Perfetti, C.A., Beck, I., Bell, L., and Hughes, C. (1987). Children's reading and the development of phonological awareness. *Merrill Palmer Quarterly* 33: 39-75.

Pinnell, G.S., and Fountas, I.C. (1998). *Word Matters: Teaching Phonics and Spelling in the Reading/Writing Classroom.* Portsmouth, NH: Heinemann.

Pinnell, G.S., and Fountas, I.C. (2004). *Sing A Song of Poetry K: A Teaching Resource for Phonemic Awareness, Phonics, and Fluency.* Portsmouth, NH: Heinemann.

Pinnell, G.S., Pikulski, J., Wixson, K.K., et al. (1995). *Listening to Children Read Aloud: Data from NAEP's Integrated Reading Performance Record (IRPR) at Grade 4.* Report No. 23-FR-04, prepared by the Educational Testing Service. Washington, DC: Office of Educational Research and Improvement, U.S. Department of Education.

Pressley, M. (1998). *Reading Instruction That Works: The Case for Balanced Teaching.* New York: The Guilford Press.

Read, C. (1971). Pre-school children's knowledge of English phonology. *Harvard Educational Review* 41: 1-34.

Snow, C.E., Burns, M.S., and Griffin, P. (eds.). *Preventing Reading Difficulties in Young Children.* Washington, DC: Committee on the Prevention of Reading Difficulties in Young Children, Commission on Behavioral and Social Sciences and Education, National Research Council.

Treiman, R. (1985). Onsets and rimes as units of spoken syllables: Evidence from children. *Journal of Experimental Child Psychology* 39: 161-181.

Vellutino, F.R., and Denckla, M.B. (1991). Cognitive and neuropsychological foundations of word identification in poor and normally developing readers. In R. Barr, M.L. Kamil, P. Mosenthal, and P.D. Pearson (eds.). *Handbook of Reading Research* (Vol. II, pp. 571-608). New York: Longman.

Vellutino, F.R., and Scanlon, D.B. (1987). Phonological coding, phonological awareness, and reading ability: Evidence from longitudinal and experimental study. *Merrill Palmer Quarterly* 33: 321-363.

Vellutino, F.R., Scanlon, D.M., Sipay, E.R., et al. (1996). Cognitive profiles of difficult-to-remediate and readily remediated poor readers: Early intervention as a vehicle for distinguishing between cognitive and experiential deficits as basic causes of specific reading disability. *Journal of Educational Psychology* 88: 601-638.